LOST PERTH

Picture credits

All images are courtesy of the State Library of Western Australia, except for the following:

WestPix (West Australian Newspapers Limited): 26, 30, 31 bottom, 34 bottom, 40, 41 bottom right, 44 bottom left, 62 left, 63, 65, 66 left, 73 top right, 75 top, 90 left, 109 left, 122, 123 top, 132, 137 bottom.

Royal Western Australian Historical Society: 16, 17.

The University of Western Australia Archives: 36, 37.

Getty Images: 102 right.

Aviation Heritage Museum of WA: 142 top.

Ken Hodge: 142 bottom.

Acknowledgements

A great many people have both wittingly and unwittingly contributed to the production of this book and I would like to particularly thank the ever friendly staff at the State Library of Western Australia and WestPix (the photographic library of the *West Australian* newspaper), who have enabled this book to contain many rarely seen photographs from Perth's history.

Thanks also go to the staff and volunteer researchers of Heritage Perth and the Museum of Perth, whose work has contributed a great deal of information incorporated into this publication. The inimitable Ivan King, Curator of the Museum of Performing Arts at His Majesty's Theatre, provided all the information on the skating barmaids and also many useful titbits on the other performance venues featured in this book. Finally, the good people of Perth who, over many years, have fed me invaluable personal recollections and information on the history of Perth, all of which have enthused and inspired me to find out more.

Richard Offen, 2018

First published in the United Kingdom in 2018 by
PAVILION BOOKS
43 Great Ormond Street
London
WC1N 3HZ
An imprint of Pavilion Books Group Limited

ISBN: 978-1-911595-60-1

A CIP catalogue record for this book is available from the British Library.

10 9 8 7 6 5 4 3 2

Repro by Rival Colour Ltd, UK
Printed by 1010 Printing International Ltd, China

www.pavilionbooks.com

LOST PERTH

RICHARD OFFEN

PAVILION

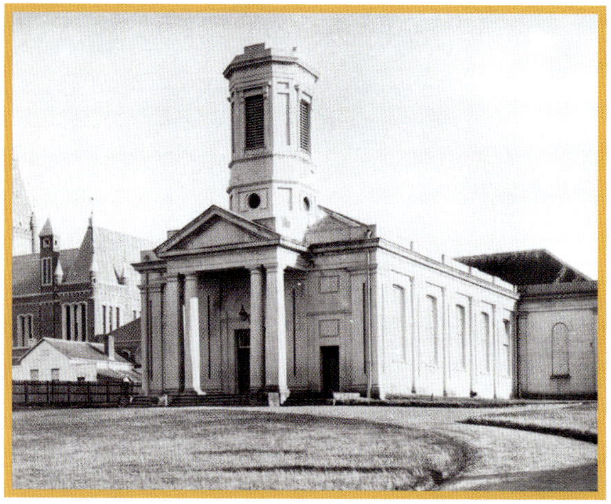

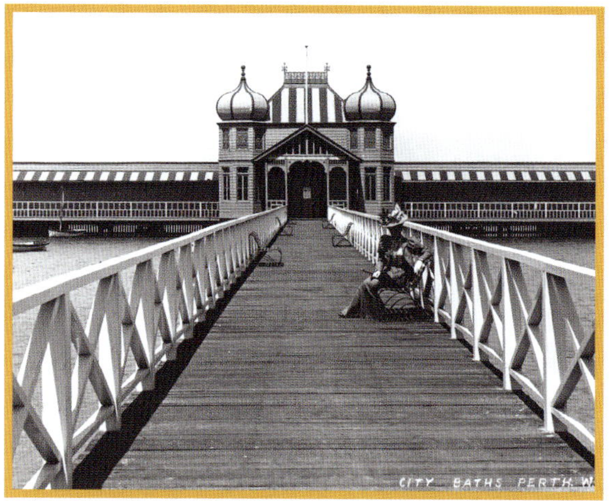
CITY BATHS PERTH W.

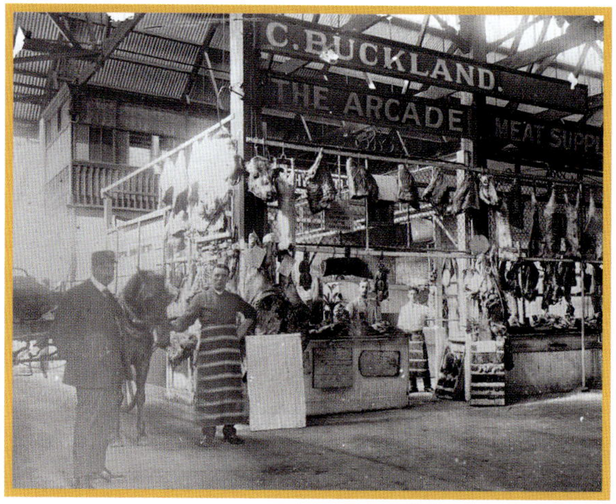
C. BUCKLAND.
THE ARCADE

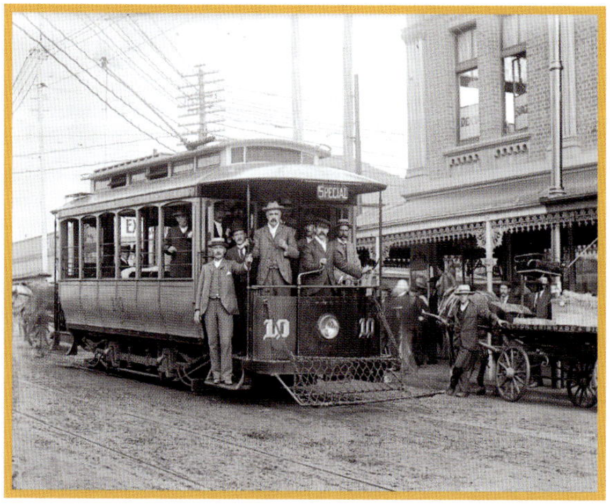
SPECIAL
10

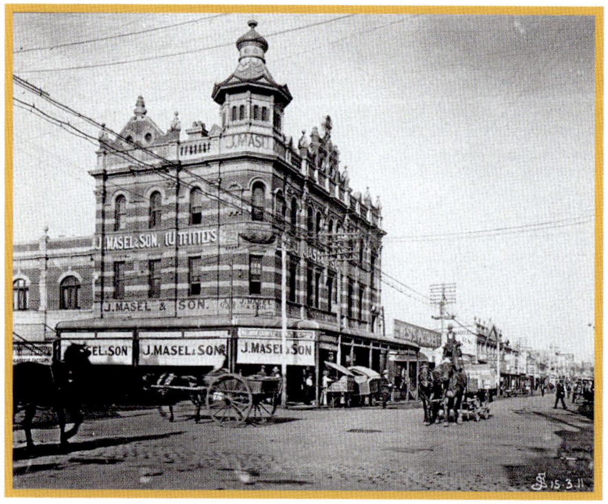
J.MASEL & SON.
J.MASEL & SON
J.MASEL & SON

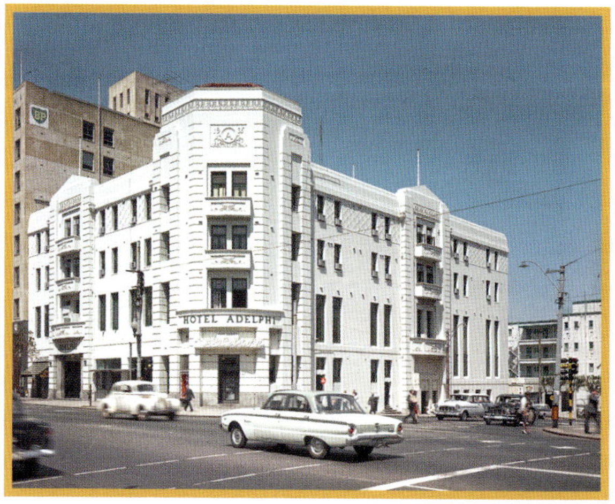
HOTEL ADELPHI

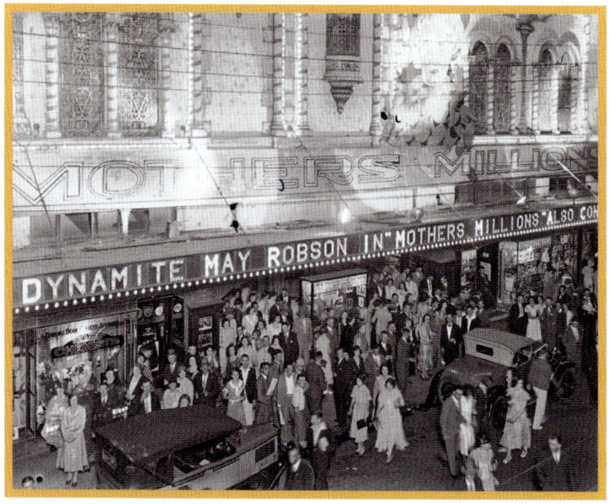
DYNAMITE
MAY ROBSON IN "MOTHERS MILLIONS"

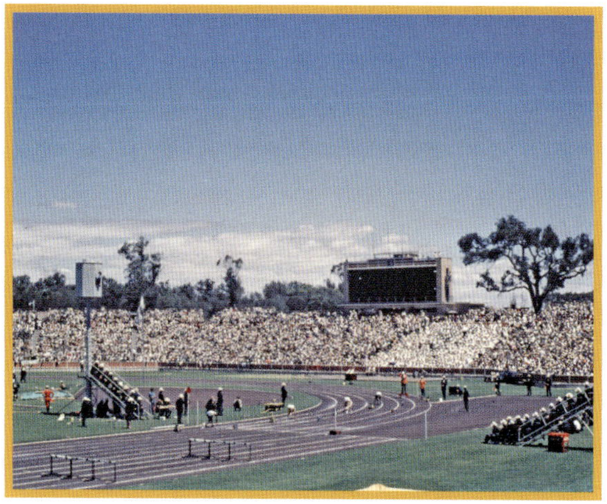

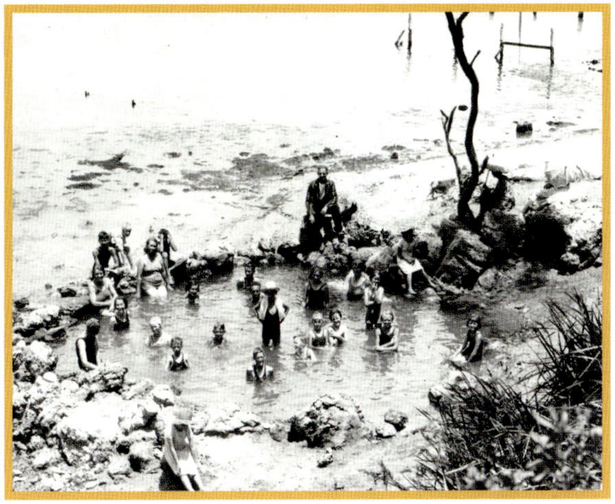

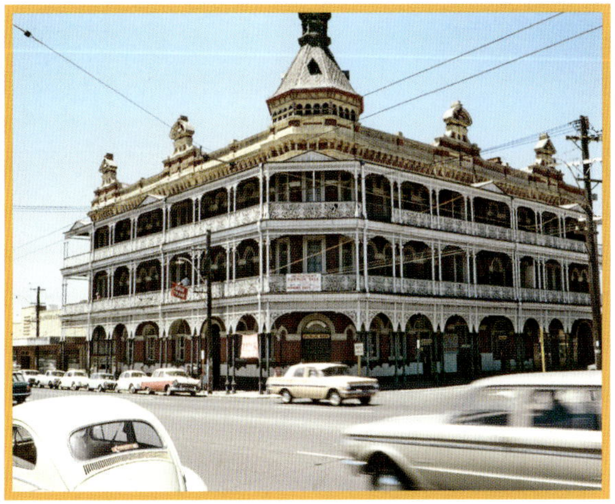

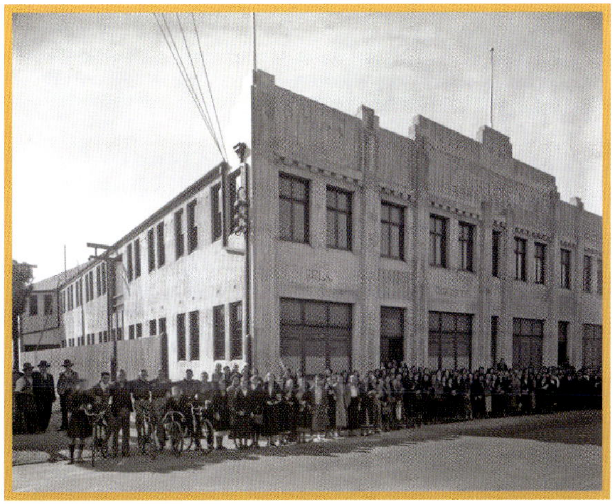

LOST IN THE...

INTRODUCTION

Archaeological evidence confirms that the Swan River area has been inhabited by human beings for at least 40 to 50,000 years. During that time the Aboriginal people have been the custodians of the land on which Perth now stands, using the Swan River and its surrounds as an important source of food. As a result, the area also became an important cultural meeting place for the Whadjuk Noongar tribe, who have gathered here for thousands of years.

The arrival of European settlers in the Swan River catchment in 1829 had a profound and devastating effect on thousands of years of land stewardship by the Whadjuk Noongar people, depriving them of their hunting grounds and places of cultural significance. Noting this change, the leader of the Swan River Colony, Captain James Stirling, observed that the Noongar people "seemed angry at the invasion of their territory".

The displacement of the Aboriginal people, who until that time had enjoyed unbroken access to the land, is perhaps the first loss that should be acknowledged in this history.

The foundation of the town of Perth was marked by the felling of a tree on King George IV's birthday, 12 August 1829. Following the ceremony, development was comparatively slow, and a year later many of the first settlers were still camping on the banks of the Swan River, or on the beach in Fremantle.

The Surveyor General, John Septimus Roe, was almost single-handedly laying out the towns of Perth, Fremantle and Guildford at the same time, leaving the majority of settlers waiting to hear where their allocation of land would be. Things were further complicated by the fact that promises of a rich and fertile flood plain were simply unfounded. In the words of Elizabeth Shaw, who arrived with her husband William in February 1830, they discovered, "Each side of the river is nothing more or less than sand – white sand – incapable of being made to produce anything for the sustenance of man!" It wasn't long before news of the parlous state of the Swan River Colony reached Britain and hopes of rapid investment in the colony evaporated.

Perth gradually took shape as a town, despite the problems of land grants, lack of fertile land and the added difficulty of finding suitable local building materials. Early drawings and paintings of Perth in the 1830s, many of them by Charles Wittenoom, show St Georges Terrace as a wide dirt-track street with modest houses and smallholdings scattered along its length, all mainly of timber or brick construction. Slowly these buildings gave way to more substantial structures and the place began to take on the air of a modest country town, which indeed was all it was.

Much of the early construction in Perth was therefore temporary in nature, built with the resources to hand and expected to last only until better materials, more funds and skilled labour were available. Replacement of these buildings was part of the natural progression of development, with upgrades wholeheartedly supported by the general public.

Sadly, but not surprisingly, only two small buildings remain in the centre of Perth from the pre-convict era of Perth's history (1829–1850): the Old Court House and St John's Pro-Cathedral. Fortunately, we have a more representative sample from later periods.

With the discovery of gold in the Murchison and Eastern Goldfields in the late 1880s and early 1890s, Perth witnessed a massive influx of population and wealth. This prosperity brought about a transformation from sleepy country town to prosperous, bustling commercial city, demonstrated by the grandeur of many of the buildings we see today, all erected to demonstrate Perth's status as a significant gold city. This time the change was more sudden, more extreme and involved the loss of buildings that were not just temporary space-fillers, but buildings that had their own history and had become an established part of Perth's streetscape. The people of Perth began to question whether change was always for the better.

Through the 20th century, communities around the world had started challenging the concept that the demolition and development of private property was at the sole discretion of the landowner, and the principles of cultural heritage became established. In the state's earliest Town Planning Act of 1928, local authorities were empowered to include in their local planning schemes provisions to ensure "the preservation of historic buildings and objects of historical or scientific interest." Acting on behalf of their communities, however, local authorities had little to say about heritage conservation until it started making headlines.

During Perth's history, other less tangible things have come and gone as cultural needs and fashions change, some of the more unusual ones are mentioned in these pages. One which has not proved possible to include for lack of suitable photographs is the Coolbaroo Club. This Aboriginal social club of the 1940s to 60s was formed at a time when there was an "exclusion zone" around Perth. Most Aboriginal activities in the city centre were banned and the movement of Aboriginal people within the zone was tightly controlled. The club organised dances and other cultural events which catered for a seriously disenfranchised section of the community. Whilst emphasising a government policy that is now viewed as totally unacceptable, the club made a small step towards significant changes in attitude and legislation for the people of the oldest surviving culture on the planet.

It is tempting to see this book as evidence that Perth has thrown away its history, but I would encourage a rather more considered approach and a nod to the positive. As in every age, attitudes to what constitutes our history and heritage change and these days we are very prone to looking at history through the wrong end of the telescope, judging decisions of the past by the criteria of today. With a few notable exceptions, the places, activities and events recorded in this book were, at the time of their disappearance, considered inconsequential by the vast majority of Perth's population.

We now have different attitudes and the evident interest in our past and our architectural history is, to me, a great encouragement that the decisions of our future will be better informed. From the demise of these iconic places we can learn; if history is for nothing else, it is for guiding our future.

RIGHT The Ambassadors Theatre orchestra, c. 1932. The Hollywood-inspired picture palace was demolished in 1972. See page 90.

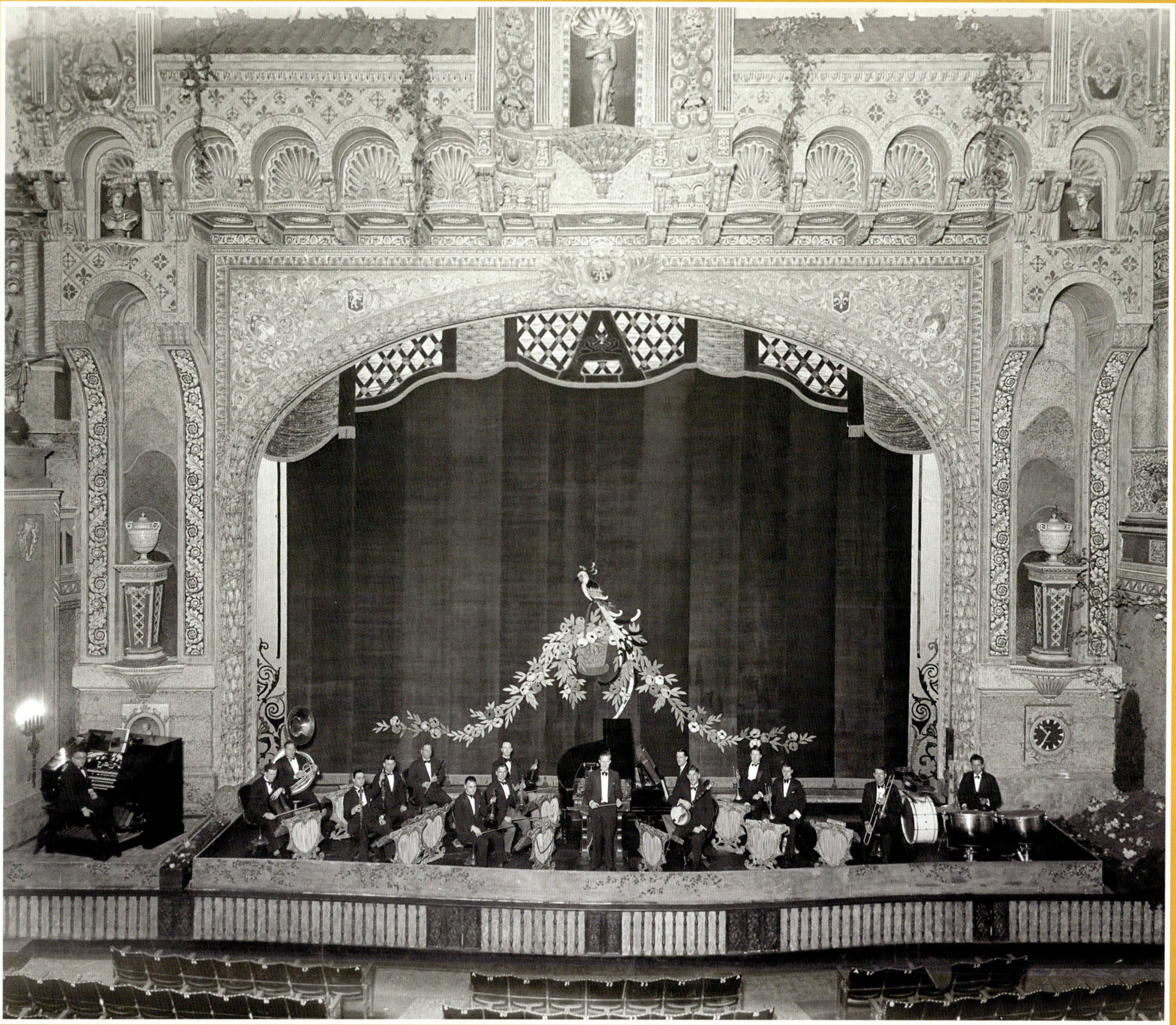

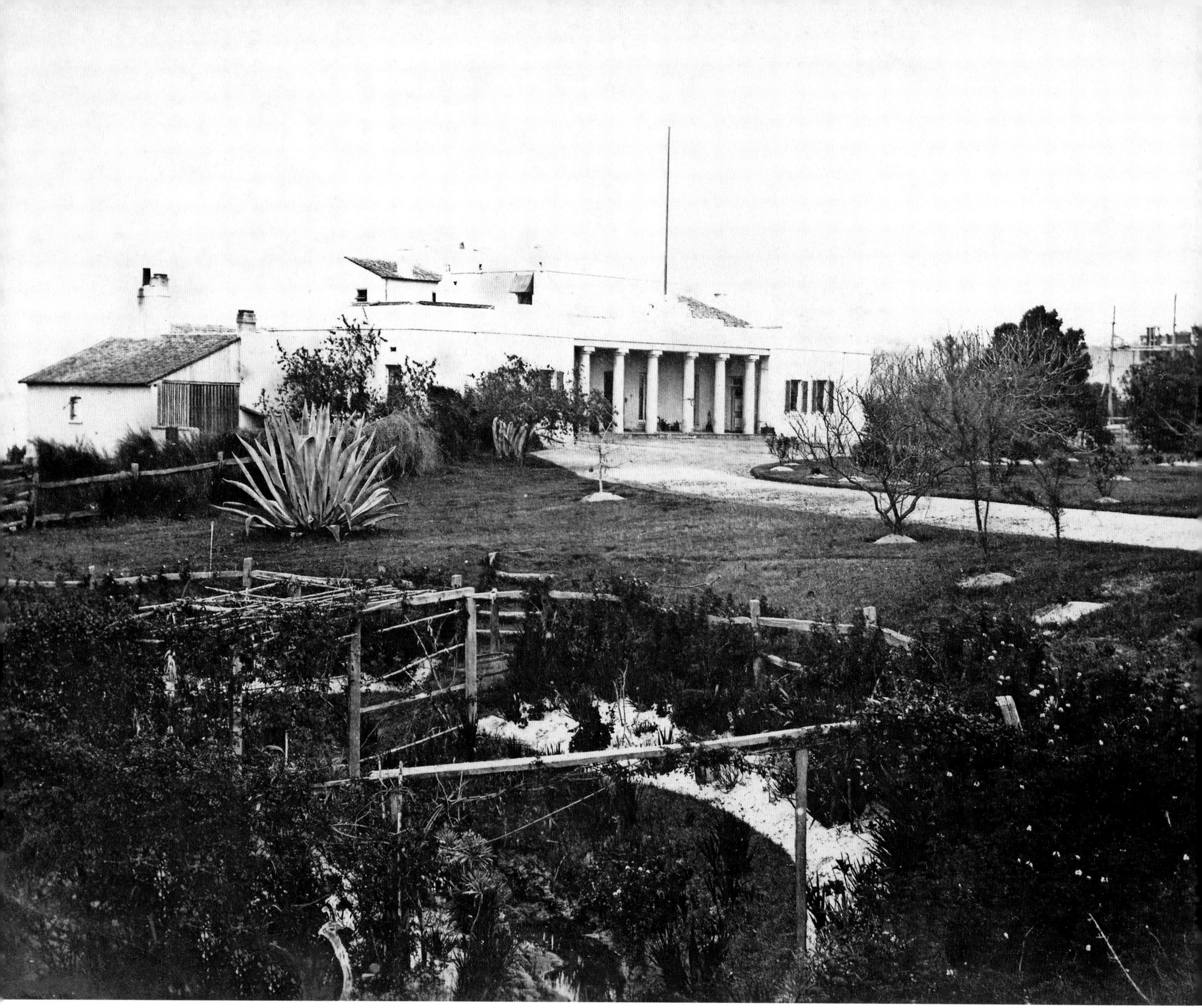

FIRST GOVERNMENT HOUSE

DEMOLISHED 1887

In December 1828, Sir George Murray, Secretary for the Colonies, signed orders giving Captain James Stirling permission to found the Swan River Colony in what was to become Western Australia. Murray also appointed Stirling Vice Regal of the fledgling colony.

Upon arrival in June 1829, Stirling proclaimed the British colony and set up the first vice-regal residence in a tent camp on Garden Island, where they had been forced to land because of inclement weather. Following the founding of Perth on 12 August 1829, Stirling and his family set up another tent on the corner of St Georges Terrace and Barrack Street. In November 1831 James Stirling's official title became Governor of the Colony and by 1832 the family were living in a temporary wooden building on the same site as their tent.

Following a visit to England in 1834 to be knighted, the governor temporarily moved into the newly completed Officers' Barracks on St Georges Terrace, whilst Henry Reveley, Perth's chief civil engineer, prepared designs for a permanent and more substantial Government House. The construction of the house was initially paid for from Stirling's own funds, as he knew the British Government were unwilling to foot the bill and it was only after a considerable amount of discussion and correspondence that he was reimbursed the £900 he had invested. Ellen Stirling laid the foundation stone in October 1834 and the Stirling family moved into the incomplete building in the following year. It was only fully completed in 1838.

In common with most of Reveley's building designs for the colony, Government House followed a well-proportioned but rather stark form of classical architecture. However, its greatest disadvantage was that it was neither big enough for the functions it had to cater for, nor built to a high standard. From the outset, the building, and its residents, suffered from leaking roofs, termites eating the floorboards and rising damp. Combined with the unbearable heat in summer and freezing cold in winter, it is apparent that the accommodation was not of the standard expected for a governor's residence.

Four successive governors resided uncomfortably in the house until 1855 when Governor Arthur Kennedy arrived to take up his post. He was singularly unimpressed with the accommodation provided, as this dispatch to the Secretary of State demonstrates: "The House was and is in such a state that I would not have occupied it had I been able to rent a suitable House. It will be scarcely habitable in winter and there will be a constant outlay for repairs and replacing decayed woodwork etc., while it is occupied."

A board of inquiry set up to investigate the condition of the building reported, "It is our opinion that the walls of the building are in so unsound a state and that the carpenter's work has been so badly executed that it would be much more advisable to erect a new building than to attempt to repair the present one, and further that any attempt to repair it, and to increase the accommodation would ultimately entail more expense upon the Government than the immediate erection of a new building."

This eventually brought about the construction of the present Government House. Despite its substantial inadequacies, the old Government House continued as a private residence until its demolition in 1887.

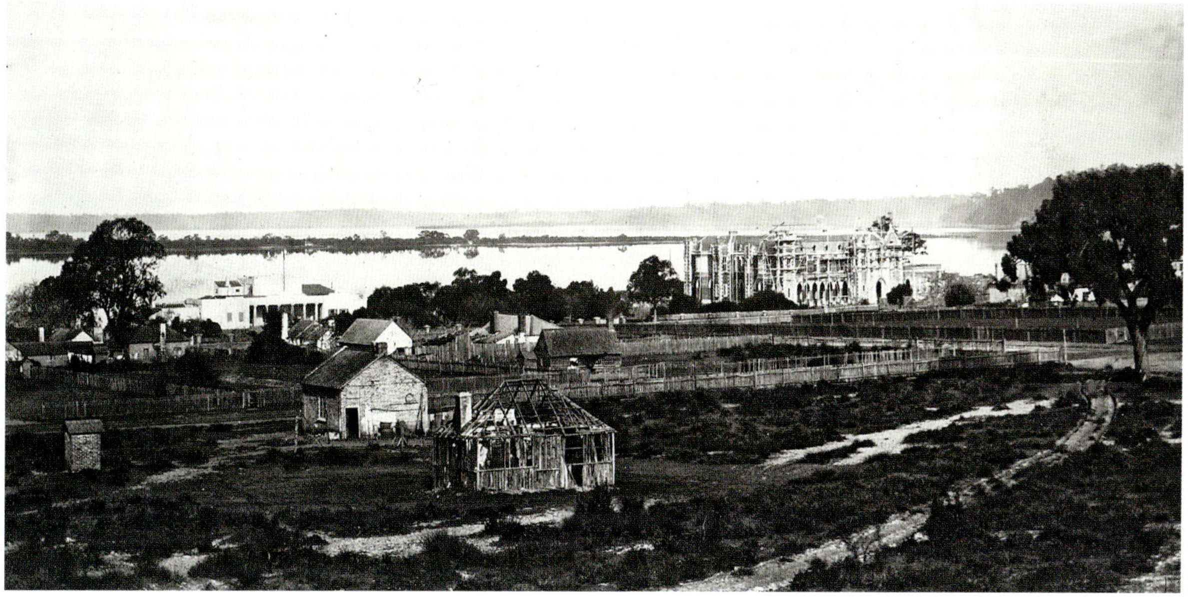

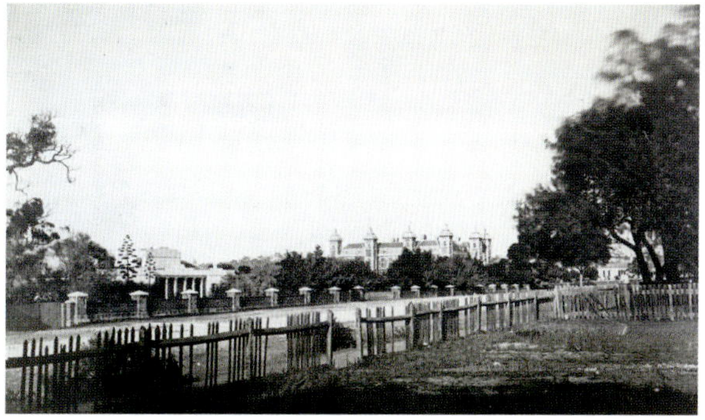

ABOVE An 1862 view from Murray Street showing the new Government House under construction on the right (built 1859–1863) and the old Government House on the left.

LEFT Old Government House from Alpha Cottage across St Georges Terrace in 1864. By this time the house was occupied by prominent local politician Sir James Lee Steere.

OPPOSITE Old Government House in 1861, two years before the new Government House was completed.

PENSIONER GUARDS

DISBANDED 1887

Pensioner Guards were former soldiers of the British Army, Royal Marines and East India Company, who had been discharged having either served a 20-year term, or been made redundant to reduce army numbers. Although termed "pensioners" they were generally fit and able young men. Many had served in the British Army, with a few from other colonial armies. They had seen action in China, the Crimea, South Africa, India, Persia or Afghanistan, and were awarded pensions for long service, good conduct, or wounds received in the line of duty.

These ex-servicemen were offered free passage for themselves and their families, six months employment as convict guards and either accommodation in the Pensioner Barracks (or specially-built cottages in various locations), or a grant of land on which to build their home. The employment offered was in the Convict Establishment as warders, but their main purpose was to act as a disciplined body of men who could be called upon by the authorities in times of civil unrest. As such, the guards engendered a sense of stability and security at a time when people felt unhappy about the influx of convicts into their community. They also helped to maintain a more comfortable balance between the number of free settlers and convicts.

In order to encourage the guards to stay in the colony once their term of service was complete, they were offered grants of 10 acres of land. Initially held on lease, after seven years the land would become their freehold property. As an added bonus, convict labour was made available to help clear their land, plus a grant of £10. Not all the men who sailed with the convicts remained as guards and many sought general employment whilst keeping themselves available to the government should trouble arise.

The scheme ended in 1864, by which time over 1,100 guards and their families had arrived in the colony. The land grants the guards received varied in size according to location; in rural areas it was between 10 to 20 acres, whilst in Perth it was one-third of an acre. The areas set aside were known as pensioner villages and the first established was in South Perth. However, this proved not to be a satisfactory location as it was very isolated and only accessible by boat. More successful villages were created at Freshwater Bay (Claremont), Perth and West Guildford.

When free passage to Western Australia ended in 1868, the role played by the Enrolled Pensioner Force decreased and six years later the Colonial Office instructed the Staff Officer of Pensioners to reduce the level of expenditure until, finally, in November 1880, the force was officially disbanded. However, guards were still required for Government House and Fremantle Gaol, so as a temporary measure an Enrolled Guard was formed under the command of the Commissioner of Police. This was a short-lived move and the force was disbanded in March 1887.

RIGHT Inspection of the Pensioner Guard Force by the Governor, Sir Frederick Broome, on 31 March 1887; probably the last inspection before the force was disbanded.

BELOW Pensioner Guard Sergeant John Scott, late of the 3rd Roxburgh Rifle Volunteers (1870).

BELOW LEFT Pensioner Guards from an album that the photographer Alfred Stone gave to his daughter Fanny in October 1868, when she and her husband left Western Australia.

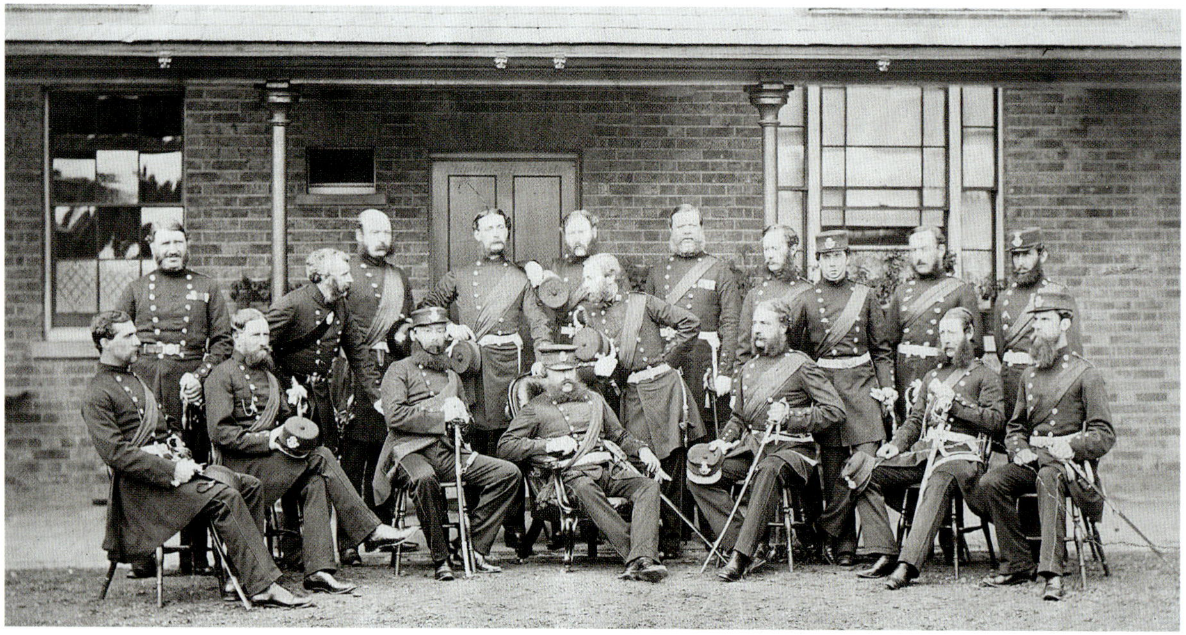

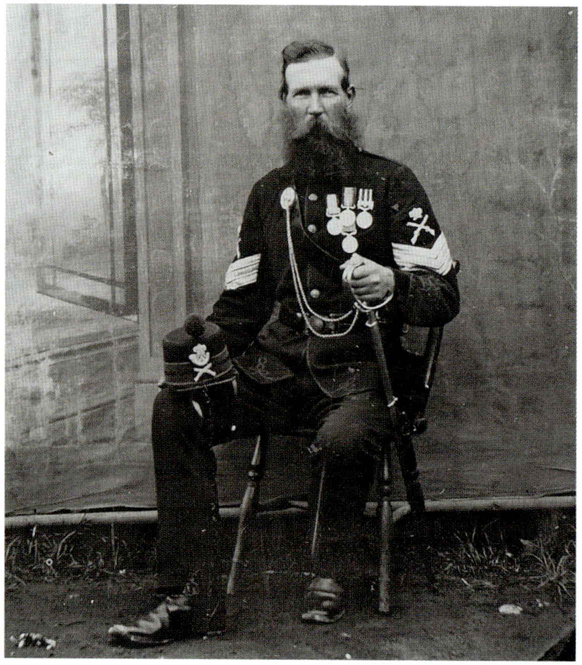

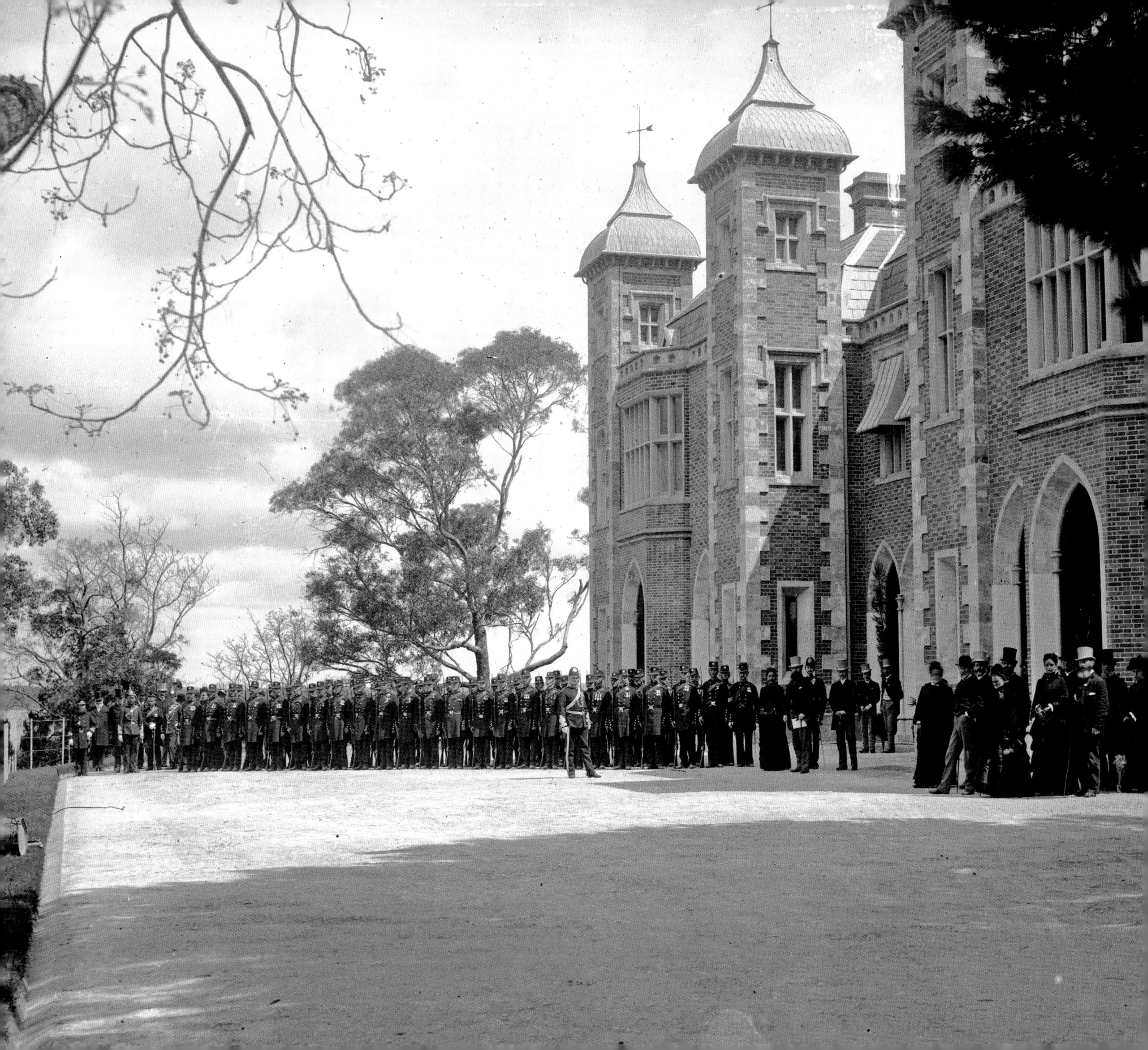

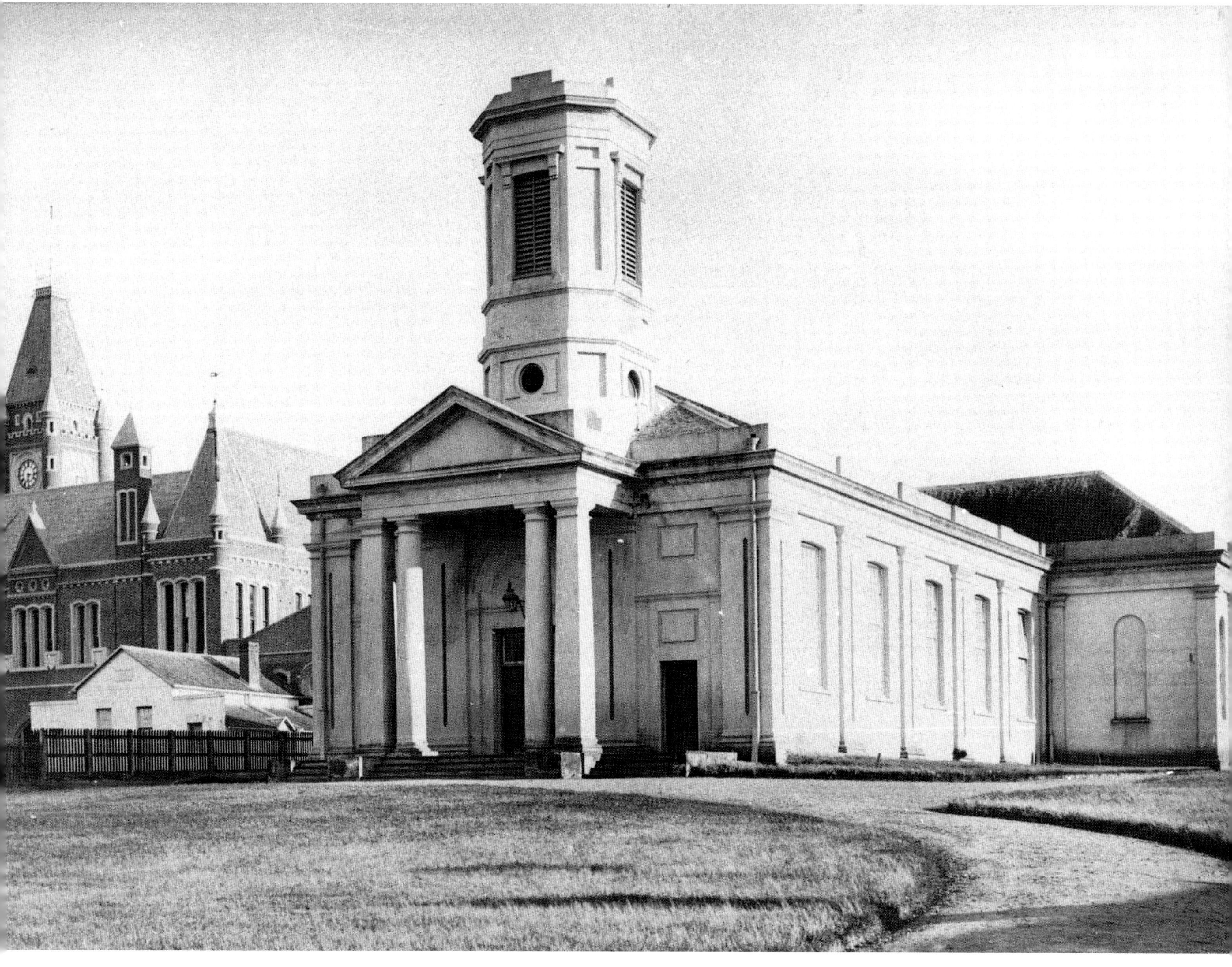

ST GEORGE'S CHURCH

DEMOLISHED 1891

There was no ordained priest amongst the first settlers of the Swan River Colony, so the settlers' first Christmas was destined to be without religious leadership. A remedy for this deficiency came from an unexpected quarter when the HMS *Success* ran aground just off Fremantle on its way to London.

It was November 1829 and the *Success* was carrying Archdeacon Thomas Scott, who found himself marooned in Perth. With Christmas only weeks away, Scott took up the pastoral role. With community help, he set to work to build a temporary church of pit-sawn timber and rushes cut from the banks of the nearby Swan River. Records show that 80 people attended the first service in the "Rush Church", as it became known, on Christmas Day.

The temporary church was to continue to serve the community for the next seven years, but it was clear that a more permanent replacement would be needed. In 1838 fundraising for a new church began and the Church Societies in England gave £800. At a thinly attended meeting a further £375 was pledged from the local community towards the estimated construction cost of £1,000, which turned out to be an underestimate.

In September 1840 the Trustees invited submissions of plans and estimates for the church. Designs for a classical style building, submitted by an amateur architect, Joseph Brown, were accepted and a tender of £1,658 from Richard Morell of Fremantle was taken up for the construction work. Unusually, the church faced north-south and stretched from approximately the west end of the present St jGeorge's Cathedral almost to Howick Street. Most Anglican and Catholic churches, for symbolic reasons, are orientated with the main axis east-west.

On New Year's Day 1841, "in the presence of a goodly assemblage of the inhabitants and several strangers", the foundation stone for the new church was laid by Governor Hutt, and about 500 people were present when the church was opened on 22 January 1845, although its consecration did not take place until 15 November 1848 for want of a bishop to conduct the service.

On 11 January 1856 the Diocese of Perth was created and simultaneously Perth was granted the status of a city. On the arrival in 1858 of Matthew Hale, Perth's first bishop, the church became St George's Cathedral. A considerable increase in the population of Perth at this time meant the cathedral soon became too small and two transepts were added in 1864. However, as the colony grew further, a much larger cathedral was felt to be necessary. The new St George's Cathedral was eventually opened on 15 November 1888 and the old church demolished in 1891.

On 7 August 1888 the *West Australian* reported on the last services to take place in the old building, which it described as being of "unpretentious appearance, both internally and externally, it fulfilled the purposes for which it was needed while the colony was yet young ... But the exigencies of the time demand something more ornate, more imposing in appearance, and this want has been met by the erection of the new edifice which in the present and probably to future generations will be known as the Cathedral of St. George." So ended the life of the old St George's Church, which, according to some reports, had got into a sorry state, the walls covered in mould and the building infested with cockroaches.

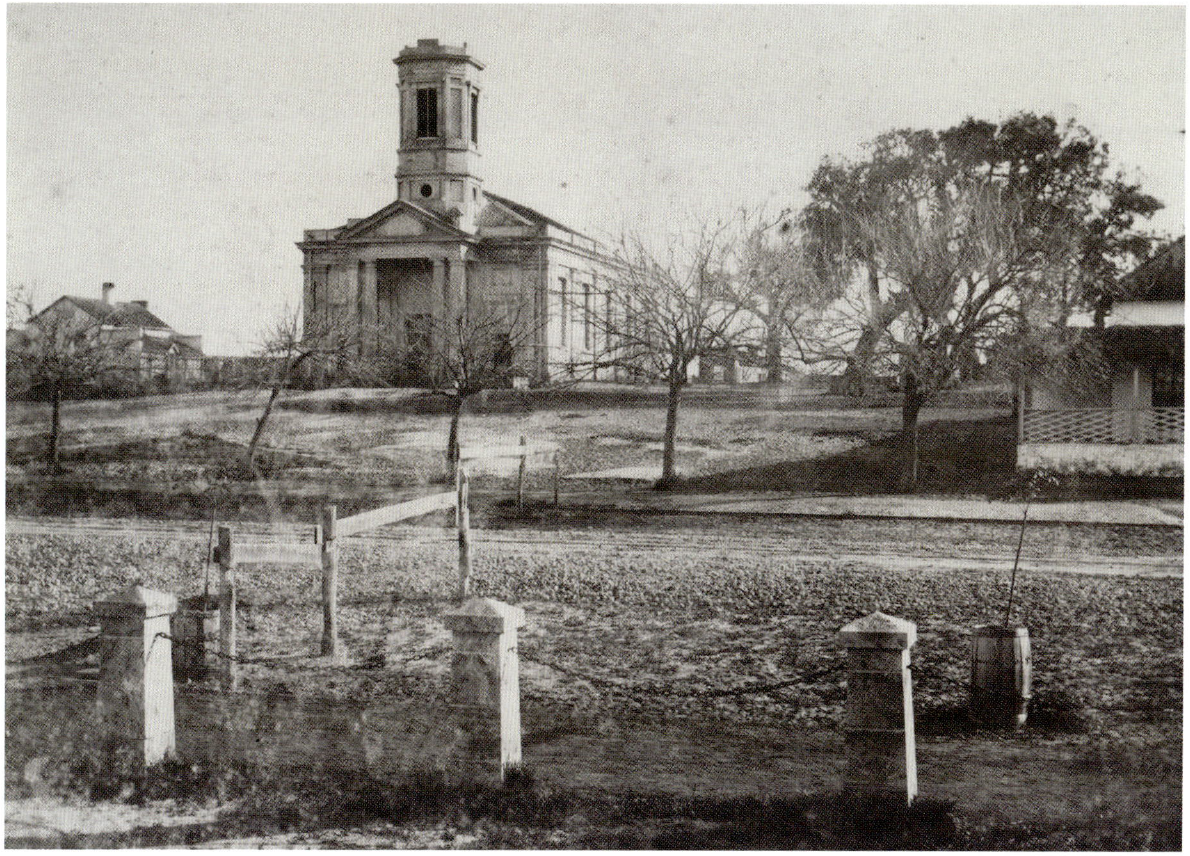

ABOVE St George's Church in 1860. The other two buildings were part of the barracks which previously occupied the site.

OPPOSITE St George's Church, c. 1870, showing the transept extensions of 1864 and the new Town Hall.

ALPHA COTTAGE

DEMOLISHED c. 1896

Having arrived in late 1829 as an enthusiastic young lawyer, Alfred Stone soon settled into life in the Swan River Colony and in the early 1830s was granted Perth Town Lot A2 on which to build his home. This lot was at the eastern end of St George's Terrace (now spelt without the apostrophe), not far from the dog-leg that denotes its junction with Adelaide Terrace.

At this time, St Georges and Adelaide Terrace were wide, sandy tracks, with only a few permanent buildings along their route. Stone's house was to be the first private residence of the street, thus its name: Alpha. Others soon followed, and by 1833 St Georges Terrace was a fashionable residential area. To ensure that it remained a respectable part of the town, a regulation was passed in 1833 requiring owners of lots on St Georges Terrace to build houses costing at least £200.

The plans for the house were drawn up by Alfred himself and show a spacious house, typical of the period, with two bedrooms, and a hall leading into a dining room and parlour. Next to this was an office, with its own porch and entrance, in which Stone could operate his legal practice. A separate building at a short distance from the back of the house, linked by a covered way, contained the kitchen, store, workshop, stable and servant's quarters. The separation of these two buildings was considered necessary to avoid fire spreading from the kitchen stoves to the main house during the hot, arid summers of Western Australia.

Once the property was established, Alfred drew another plan of the house and grounds in 1838, showing in detail the disposition of his beloved and productive garden. A large vineyard is shown at the back of the property and a smaller one at the front in which Muscat grapes were grown to be dried into raisins. The back garden had three fig trees, a peach tree and a vegetable patch, in which potatoes, radishes and other root vegetables were grown. For shade and utility, the front garden contained a lilac tree, two mulberry trees and a number of olive trees.

The Stone family continued to reside at Alpha Cottage past Alfred's death in 1873, and maintained their status as prominent members of Perth society, and the legal profession in particular.

It is not known exactly when Alpha Cottage was demolished, but the name Stone disappears from the St Georges Terrace listing in the Post Office Directory and is replaced in 1897 by the name Clarence H. Wilkinson. The arrival of Wilkinson, who would later become a prominent Perth architect, marked not only a change of owner but also the end of Alpha Cottage.

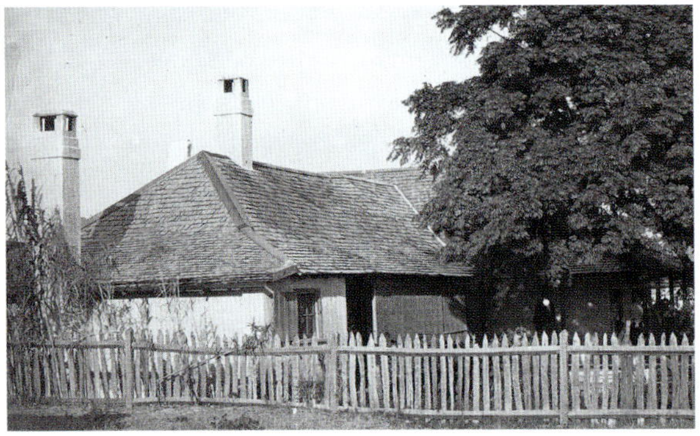

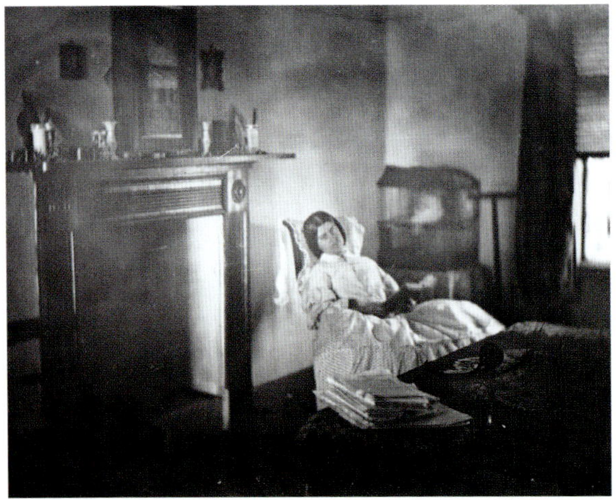

TOP LEFT Alpha Cottage as viewed from St Georges Terrace in 1860.

LEFT Fanny Stone (Alfred Stone's daughter) in the dining room of Alpha Cottage with the family's pet cockatoo "Cockie" in his cage (c. 1860).

OPPOSITE The back garden at Alpha Cottage in 1863.

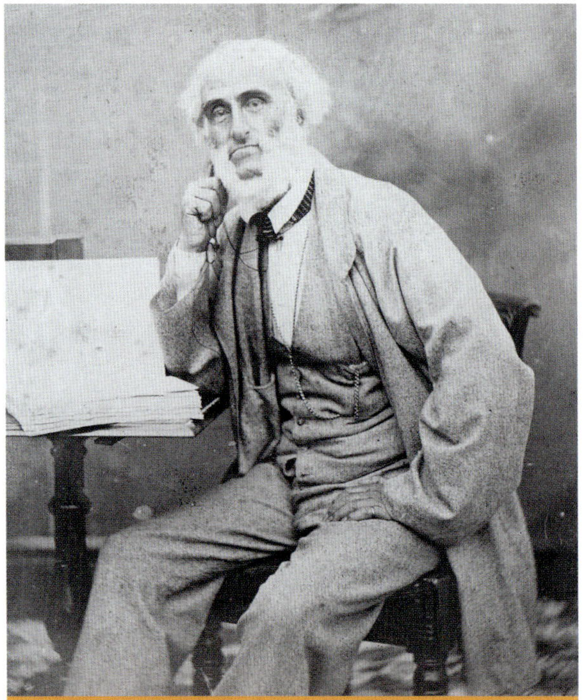

ALFRED STONE

Alfred Hawes Stone was born in Tunbridge Wells, Kent, in 1801. Having trained as a solicitor, he decided to try his luck in the newly formed Swan River Colony. He arrived in Western Australia on the *Caroline* in October 1829 and was appointed a Justice of the Peace three months later. During the following year, Stone held a number of other legal positions and in 1831 was issued a permit to practise law. In addition to his own legal practice, Alfred held a number of official appointments, including becoming Western Australia's first Registrar of Births, Deaths & Marriages in 1841. He eventually rose to the position of Attorney-General. In his private life, Stone was a keen musician, gardener and an avid photographer. Several examples of his photographs, which document the development of Perth during the 1860s and early 1870s, are included in this book.

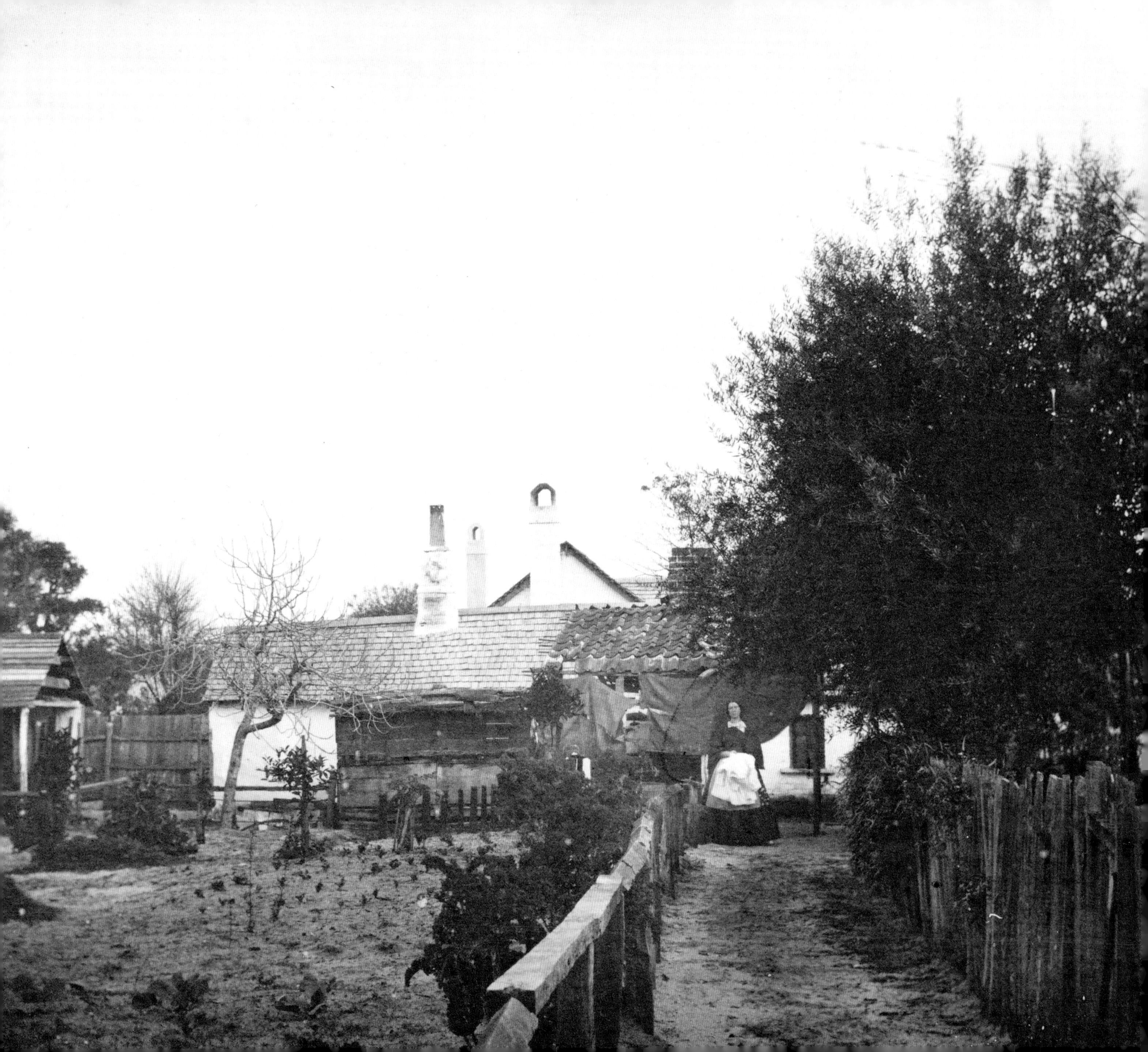

C. McNESS & CO.

DEMOLISHED 1896

Tinsmiths' shops were a common feature of most towns during the 19th century. Before the mass production of items such as jugs, mugs, forks, spoons, and candle holders, they offered an essential service to the working people of the community who could not afford the luxury of cutlery made of more valuable metals. Tinware was being produced in London by the early 1600s and became known as "Crooked Lane Ware" from the street where most of the tinsmiths worked.

It was with these skills that Charles McNess arrived in Perth in 1876, with the hope of setting up a successful business in a relatively new town. Soon after his arrival, he built a warehouse on the outskirts of the town, which he could rent out, and leased six plots of land at the corner of Twiss (now Hay) and Barrack Street from William Samson. Charles described the land as "the principal corner in Hay Street" and proceeded to build five galvanised iron shops there. One shop fronting on to Hay Street was his tinsmith and ironmongers, C. McNess & Co., the others being leased out.

Soon McNess was advertising his business in the local press: "Charles McNess – Proprietor. Furnishing and General Ironmonger, Tinsmith, &c. Wholesale and Retail. A large variety of Tinware, Ironmongery, and Spouting always on hand at lowest prices. Guns repaired, spouting fixed on shortest notice."

In addition to his interest in the ironmongers, Charles became a real estate agent, investing in city-centre properties, including a warehouse on Wellington Street, and purchasing a number of properties around Perth. The advent of the Western Australian gold rush in 1890 helped to increase McNess's fortune considerably. Not only did the value of his properties go up, but his shop did a positively roaring trade selling the necessary equipment to would-be prospectors as they started their long journey to the Eastern Goldfields around Coolgardie.

A dispute in 1895 between Henry Oakes and William Samson, owners of the land McNess leased on the corner of Barrack and Hay Street, led to a Supreme Court order to sell the land. The sale proved to be of great public interest, as it helped to give a clear indication of the value of prime city properties during the first gold rush. The property ordered for sale by the court was, in separate lots, the entire west frontage of Barrack Street from St Georges Terrace to Hay Street, which went for a total of £35,000.

McNess purchased a parcel of three lots of the Hay Street property for £12,550 and a year later moved his business to 365 Wellington Street, close to the railway. McNess & Co. was demolished in 1896 to make way for a more substantial development on the Hay Street site: the McNess Royal Arcade.

OPPOSITE McNess's Ironmongers Store in the 1880s.

RIGHT The McNess shop in the late 1870s with the Town Hall, which opened in 1870, behind.

BELOW Charles McNess (1852–1938).

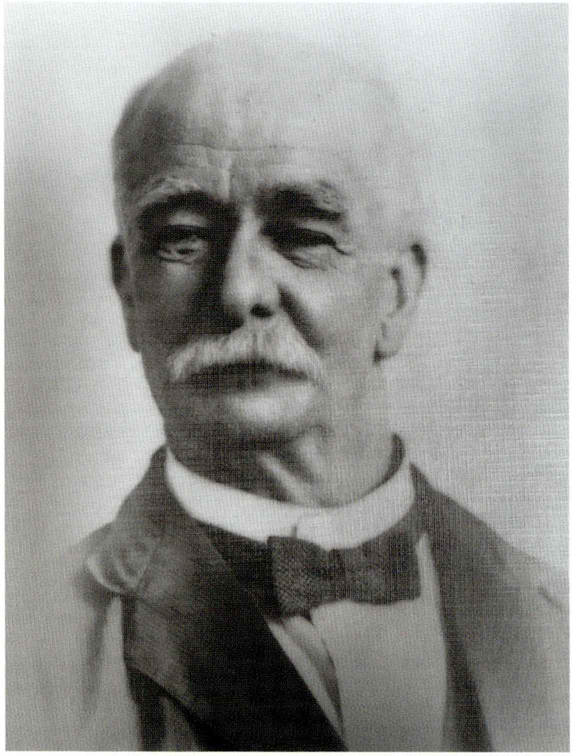

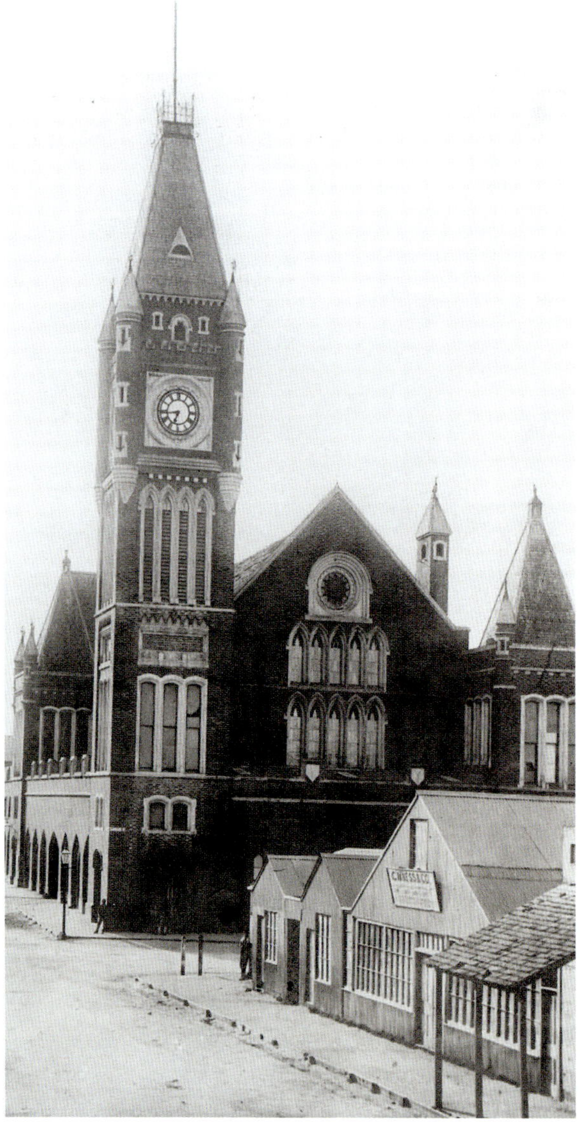

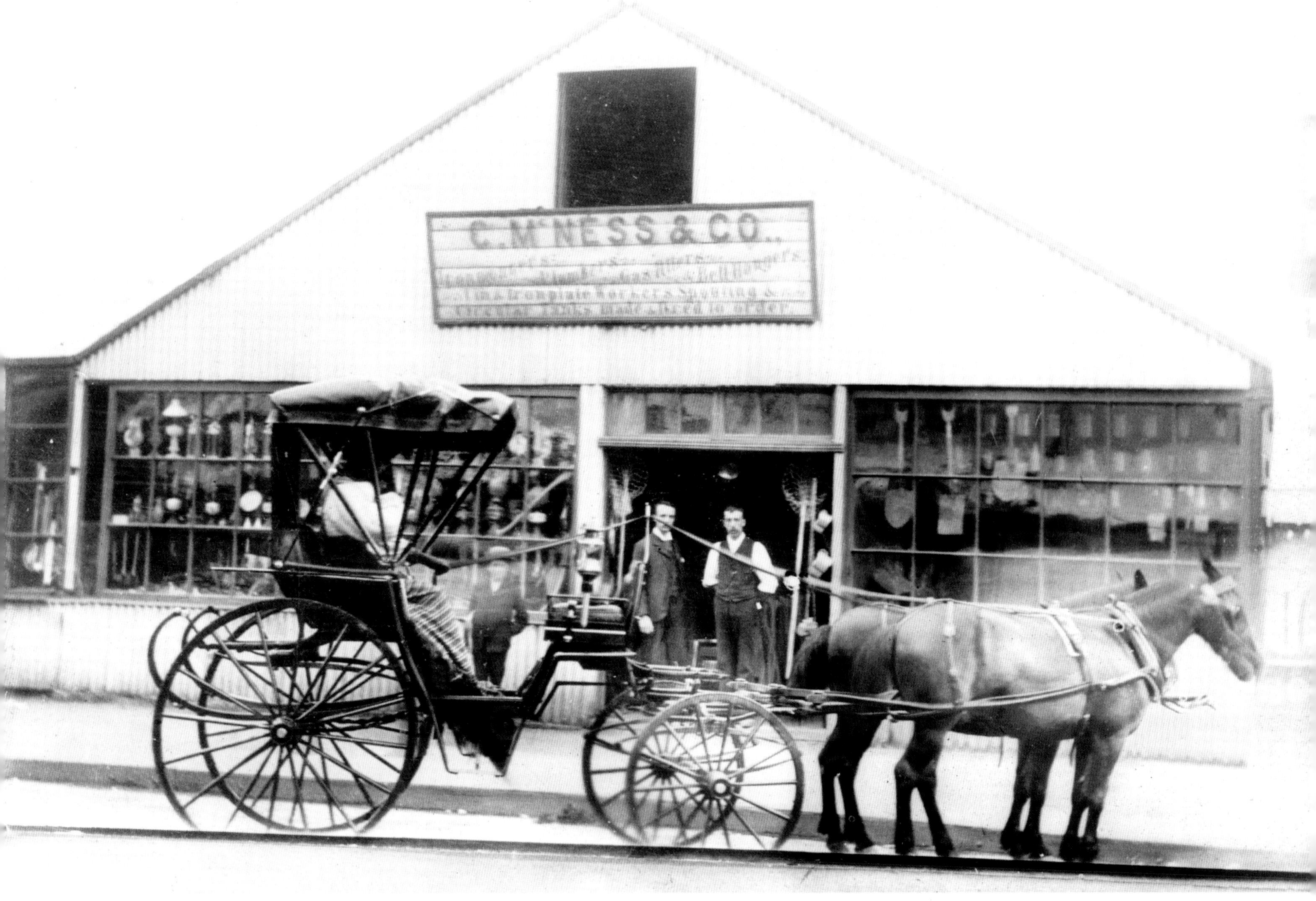
C. M^c NESS & CO.

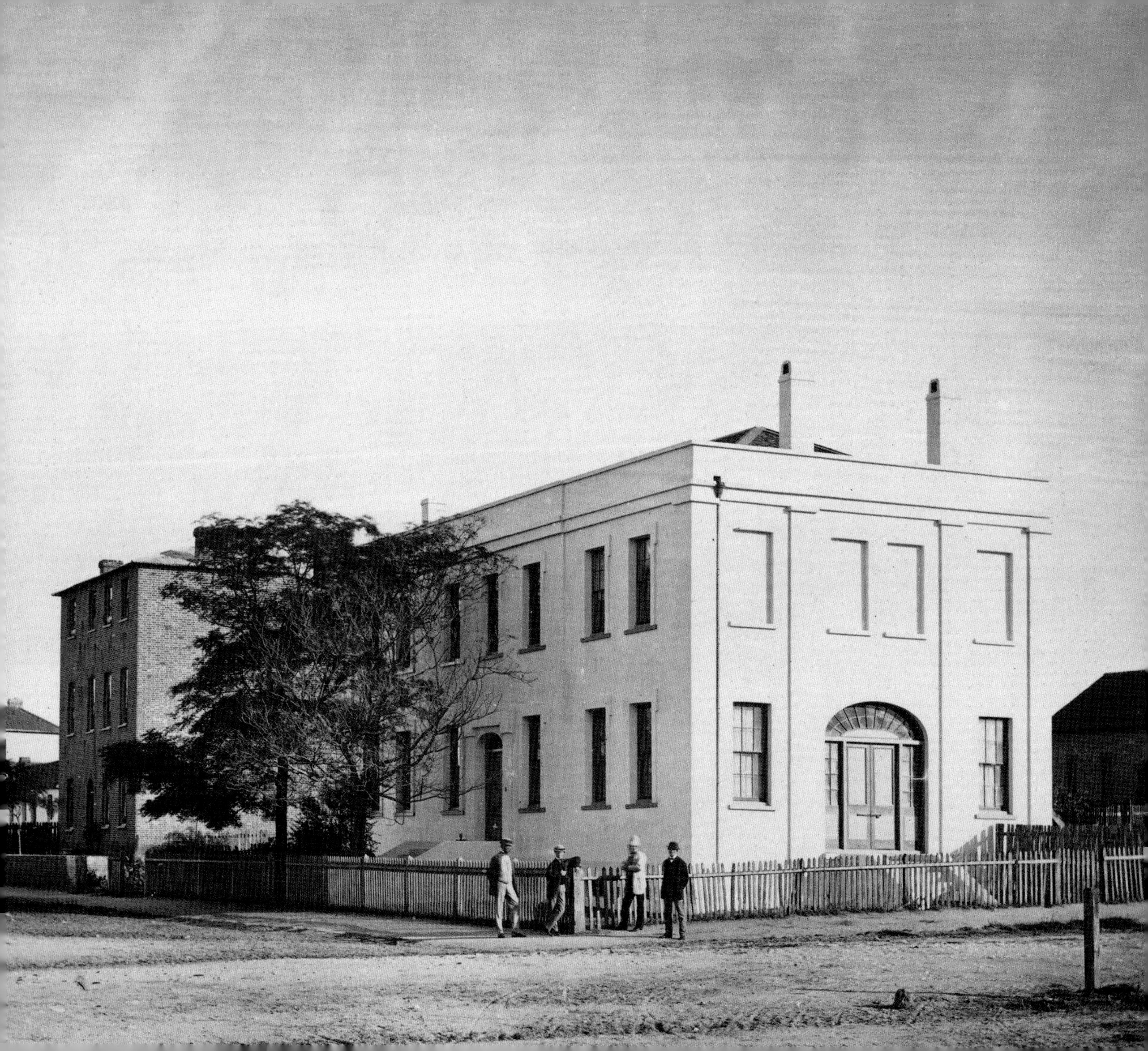

LIONEL SAMSON'S HOUSE

DEMOLISHED c. 1897

Lionel Samson, a merchant from a wealthy London family, arrived in Western Australia with his brother William in August 1829, just two months after the Swan River Colony had been founded. Almost within hours of getting off the boat, Lionel and his brother had unpacked the merchandise they had brought with them and set up a shop in Fremantle on what is now known as Bathers Beach. This was followed by the early establishment of a wine and spirit merchant, auctioneers and import business. (Lionel Samson & Son is now the oldest continuing family business in Australia.) For two years, from 1830, Lionel was also Postmaster of Fremantle and later added whaling to his commercial interests.

Samson took up several large land allocations in Perth, Fremantle and the Swan Valley. It was on one of his Perth lots, on the north-west corner of St Georges Terrace and Barrack Street, that he built probably one of the most substantial residences to be seen in the town at that time. According to the *Perth Gazette*, the new house was "more in keeping with the fashionable houses of Sydney than the simple dwellings of Perth", which, at a cost of more than £3,000, must have been the talk of the town. Lionel celebrated the completion of his elegant mansion in 1842 with an ostentatious supper and ball attended by 150. The Perth lawyer and diarist George Fletcher Moore reported that "almost everyone was there, and dancing kept up till sunrise."

A simple and elegant building, it had a handsome entrance, with fanlighting, pilasters and four bays, facing Barrack Street; and another fanlit entrance, with seven bays of windows, facing the Terrace. The building was finished in stucco, but at this stage there was no veranda.

When Lionel Samson moved out in 1875, the building was leased to the Weld Club as their clubhouse on an annual rent of £75. Named after Mr (later Sir) Frederick Weld, the Governor of Western Australia from 1869 to 1875, the Weld Club was founded at a meeting in Perth Town Hall on 8 August 1871 as an exclusive gentlemen's club. Members met to discuss politics, play billiards, invest in an informal stock exchange and read the latest news in British and colonial newspapers.

After some alterations, the Weld Club moved in to the premises it would occupy for the next 17 years. Weld Club historian T.S. Louch described the new clubhouse as a building consisting "of a basement and two floors and comprised two reading rooms, a billiard room, smoking room, dining room, bar, and four bedrooms; and in addition, quarters for the butler and his wife. Lighting was by kerosene lamps and candles, and water was obtained from a well in the yard. There was no plumbing, and the bathroom arrangements were primitive."

Following the Weld Club's move to its own custom-built premises in 1892, the newly formed Exchange Club moved into Lionel Samson's lavish home. Five years later, this club moved next door and the house was sold as part of a Supreme Court order to settle a property dispute, after which it was unceremoniously demolished and the site redeveloped.

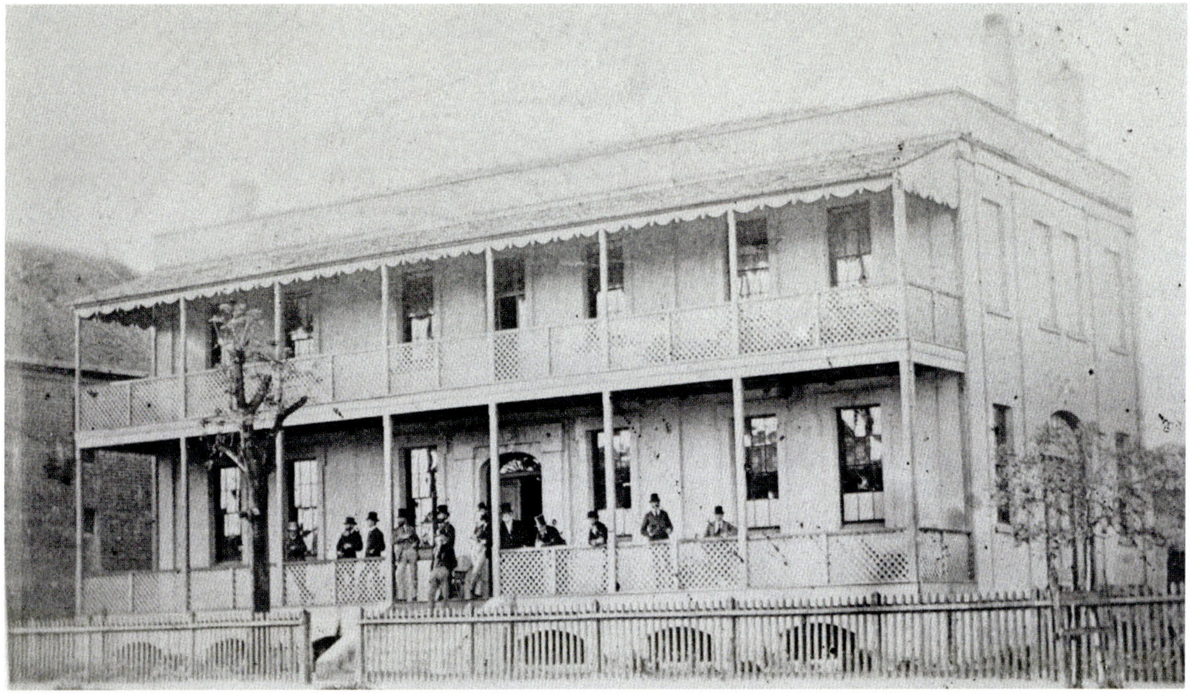

LEFT Some of the members of the Weld Club, standing on the veranda of their new club house soon after leasing it from Lionel Samson in 1875.

OPPOSITE Lionel Samson's house in 1868, before the veranda was added. Outside can be seen Will Samson, J. Parker and two nephews.

COMMISSARIAT STORES

DEMOLISHED 1901

Amongst the most important permanent buildings required by the fledgling Swan River Colony was a Commissariat Stores in which to keep government supplies. As reported in the *Perth Gazette*, construction started in June 1834: "The new Commissariat Stores at Perth are rising rapidly; the cellars are completed."

As with most other early public buildings in Perth, the store was designed by Henry Reveley, who had been recruited by James Stirling to be the Colonial Civil Engineer whilst working in Cape Town, where the first Swan River settlers stopped to victual their ship on the voyage to Western Australia.

The store had a large door opening on to the river, from which supplies could be transferred from riverboats. A rather diminutive classical portico on the other side of the building served as the main entrance. All did not go well with the construction, however, as the *Perth Gazette* reported on 22 November 1834: "Yesterday morning, about 11 o'clock, a terrible crash was heard in the direction of the new building erecting for the Commissariat, and it was soon ascertained that some few of the beams and rafters of the roof, which the workmen were putting up, had not been securely tied, and had fallen in. Although about 12 or 14 men were either under, upon, or near the rafters, providentially not one of them received the slightest injury. The damage is estimated at £20."

Eventually the building was completed in July 1835 and proclaimed to be, "the best, the cheapest, and the most substantial building in the Colony, and the work is creditable to the contractors."

The following advertisement for an auction at the Commissariat Stores in July 1836 gives some idea of the supplies stored there: "A quantity of damaged Flour, Ditto of Bran; Three Rifles and one Carbine (broken), Bayonets, Truck Wheels, Pickaxes, Pieces of Iron Windlass, Harpoons, Night-Caps, Drinking Cups, Knives, Forks, Spoons, &c.,-the property of Government."

The building continued as stores until it was converted in to a court building in 1879. However, working conditions in the former store were not comfortable, with complaints continually being made to the Legislative Council about how cold it was in winter and stuffy in summer. In 1883, one Member of Parliament reported an incident that demonstrated how uncomfortable the building was:

"The atmosphere in the Supreme Court last Friday was of the chilliest description...That most courteous of officers (the Sheriff) at once directed the caretaker of the Court to pile on the agony in the stove, in the shape of kindling a roaring fire to create a comfortable temperature. Mr Regan, as is duty bound, did as he was requested but the result was that the smoke poured out of the doors of the room in such volumes that when the Chief Justice entered the Court after the adjournment lunch, he had to grope his way through dense fog to his seat."

Parliamentary debate about the need, or not, for new law courts dragged on throughout the 1890s, with no firm conclusion being reached. The death knell for the Commissariat Stores was finally sounded in 1898 when Parliament was told the jury room was so badly constructed that their deliberations could be overheard all over the building.

In 1901 plans were made to construct a new Supreme Court building and the Commissariat Stores were demolished.

RIGHT The Commissariat Stores in about 1900, in use as the Supreme Court Building.

BELOW The front of the stores in the 1890s, with its somewhat diminutive main entrance.

BOTTOM The stores from Barrack Street Jetty in 1861, with a much larger doorway on this side of the building to allow the entry of goods from barges on the river.

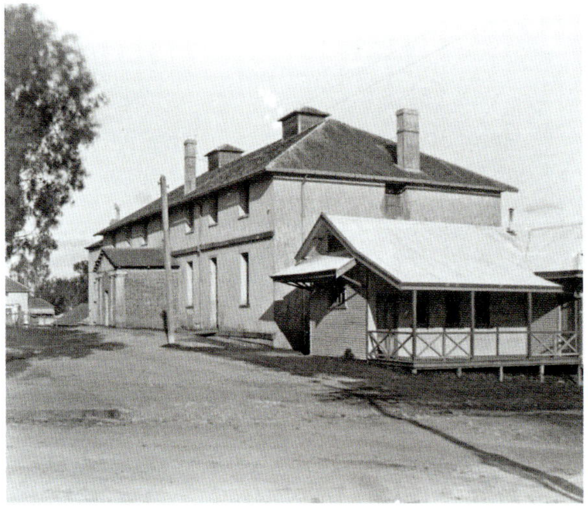

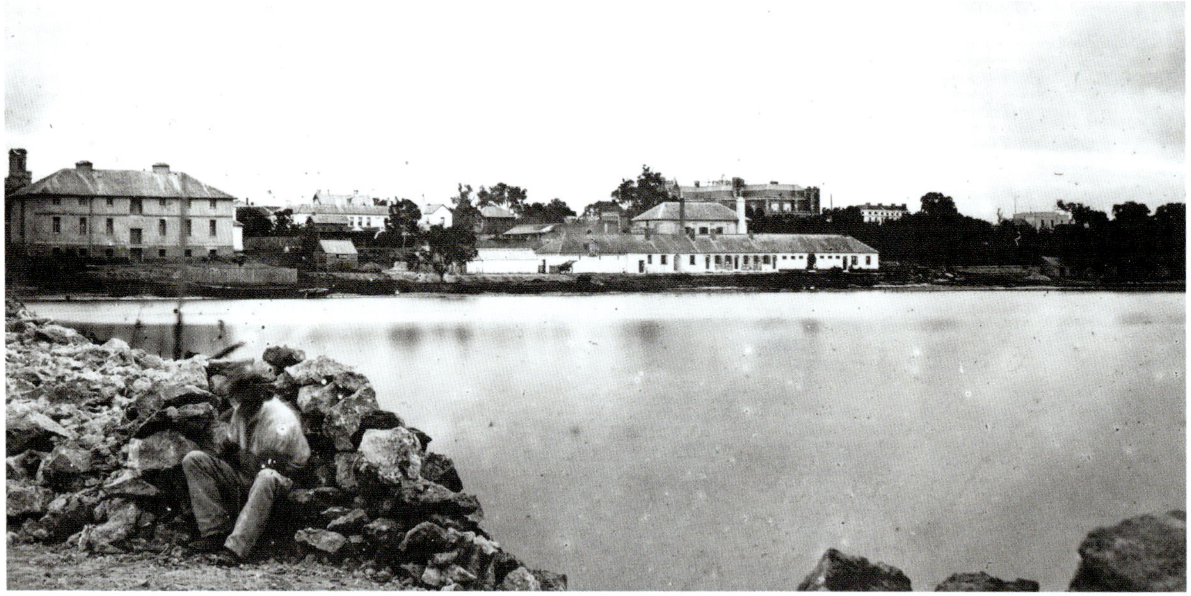

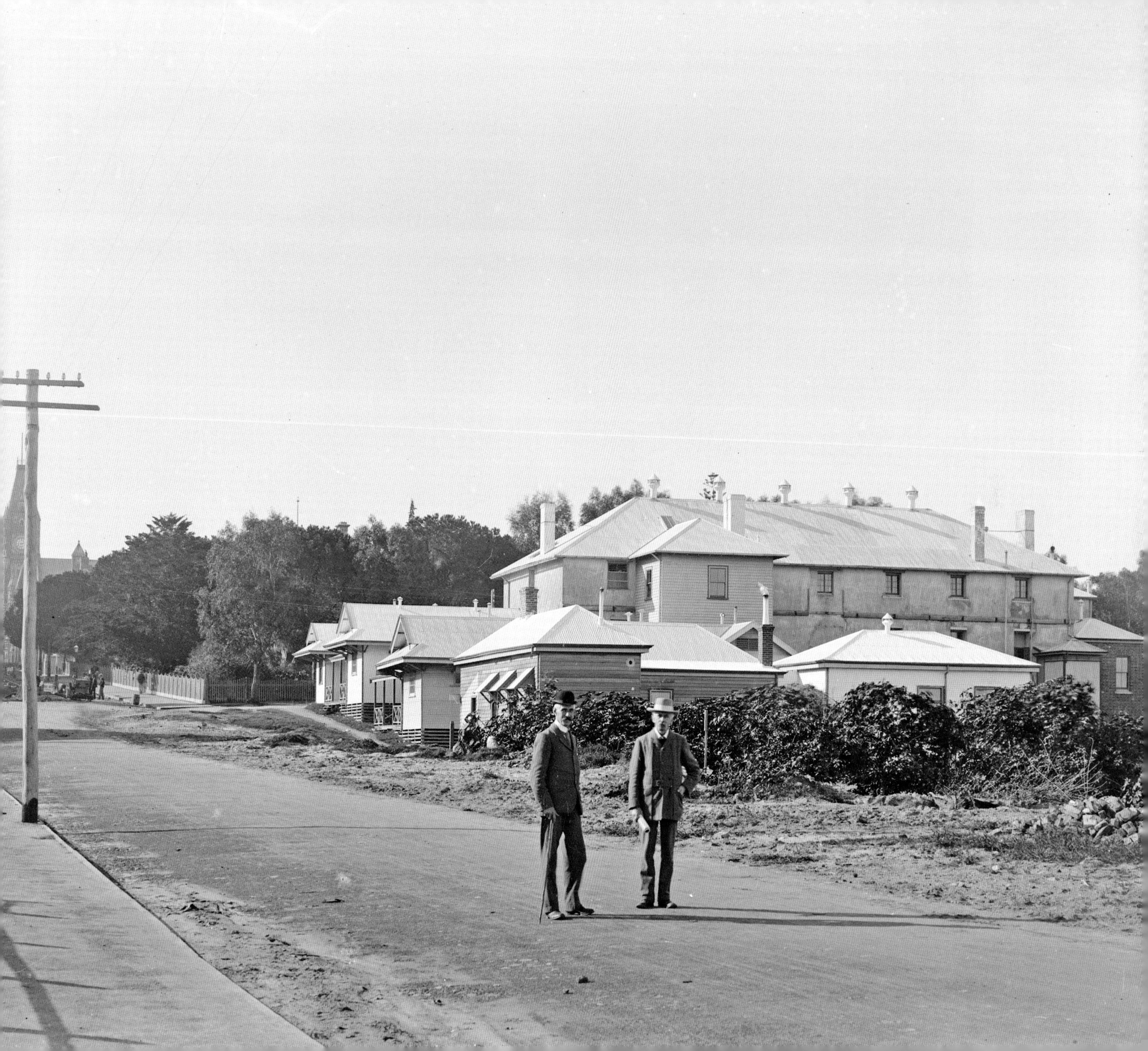

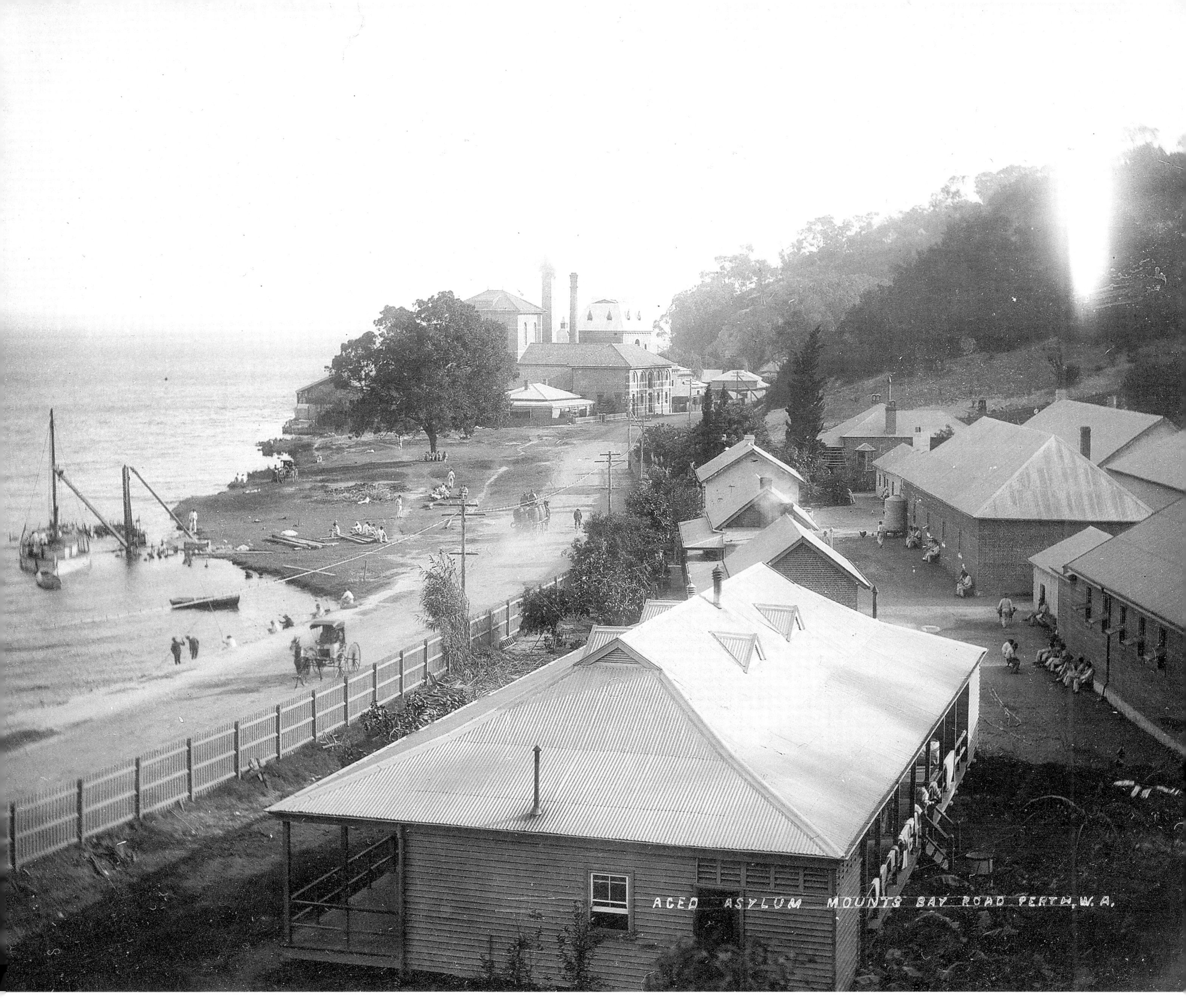
AGED ASYLUM MOUNTS BAY ROAD PERTH, W. A.

OLD MEN'S HOME

SOLD AND MOVED 1908

Unlike New South Wales and Tasmania, the Swan River Colony was intended at its outset to be a free colony. However, things did not work out quite as intended and by the 1840s the colony was struggling economically, not helped by a severe shortage of labour to build much-needed infrastructure such as roads and bridges. After much lobbying and debate, the British Government issued an Order in Council in 1849 declaring Western Australia a convict colony and the first 75 convicts (all male) arrived on 1 June 1850.

In order to house both the convicts and their guards, convict depots were erected at various locations around the state. To service Perth, one such depot was built just outside the city on the banks of the Swan River adjoining Mounts Bay Road. Records show a total of 223 convicts worked on the construction during February 1853. Of these, 15 carpenters and ticket-of-leave mechanics received the maximum pay allowed for such workers: 10d a week. Unskilled convict labour simply received their rations and no money.

The depot continued to be used by convicts, and the Pensioner Guard assigned to supervise them, until transportation ceased in 1868. After that, the building was occupied for a short period by the 14th Regiment. By 1869 the British Government handed over all the convict buildings to the Western Australian Government, who decided to convert the establishment into an asylum for old and incapable male paupers. According to the *Perth Gazette* of 19 March 1869, "The buildings under Mount Eliza lately occupied as a barrack by the detachment of the 2-14th Regt., have now been converted into an invalid depot, in which are placed invalid male paupers, chargeable upon the Colonial Revenue. There are now 39 incapables accommodated there under the medical charge of Dr Ferguson; out of those 39, we learn that no less than 33 are men who originally came into the colony as convicts."

Eleven years later, in 1880, a rise in the number of "incapables" and convicts led to a new ward being built with a dining area constructed on the site using rubble masonry.

Life for inmates was pretty tough and

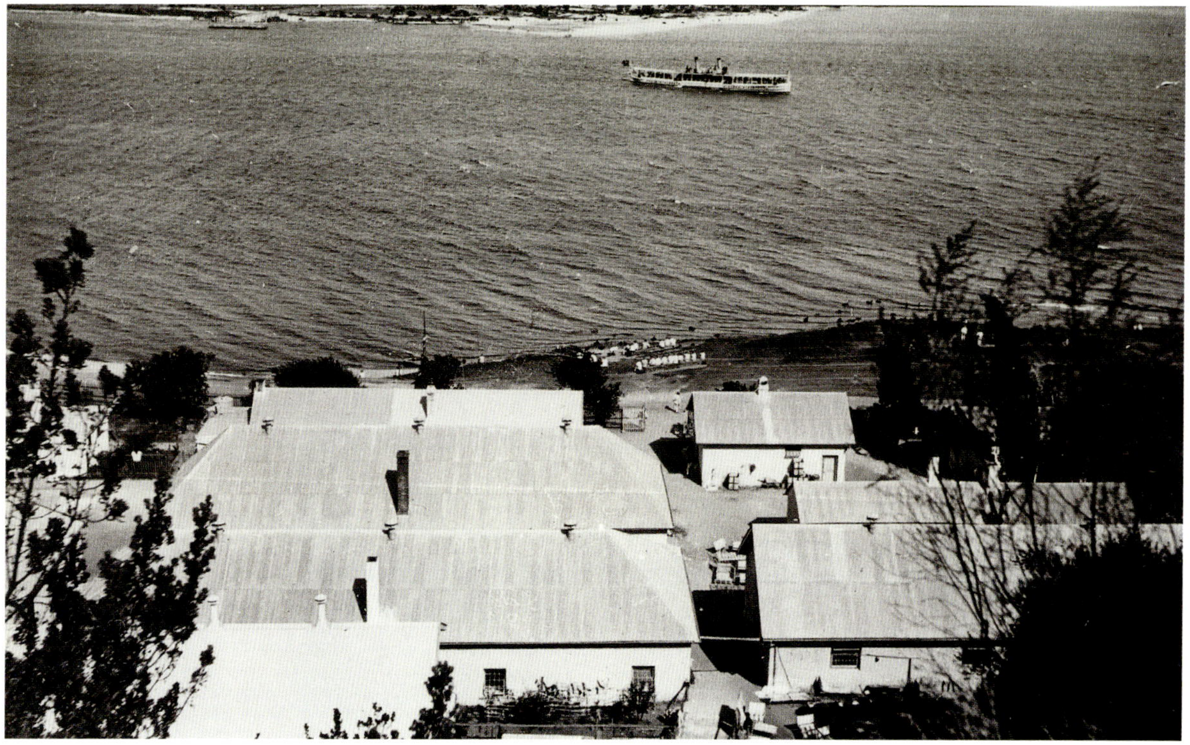

uncompromising. The Government Regulations for the Depot stated: "No idleness is allowed to exist amongst those able to work." Work for the paupers commenced at 8 a.m. and went through to 6 p.m., with an hour's break at noon. Most were employed in domestic duties around the buildings, but those who were skilled in trades, such as tailoring, were set to making and repairing uniforms and other garments, for which they received additional rations of beer and tobacco.

One of the more infamous inmates of the Invalid Depot, albeit for short periods because he kept escaping, was the bushranger serial jail-breaker Moondyne Joe.

By the end of the 19th century, the facilities at the depot were proving inadequate and in 1886 the Legislative Council explored the possibility of constructing a new building on a better site. This eventually resulted in a decision in 1904 to build a new Old Men's Depot on land in what is now the suburb of Dalkeith. On 11 April 1906, the *West Australian* reported: "The whole of the inmates of the Old Men's Home on Mount's Bay Road, have been transferred to the new establishment at Claremont. The old buildings have been handed over to the Public Works Department."

In 1908, the old buildings on Mounts Bay Road were sold, save one, which was transported in three sections to the new site, where it was isolated from the other buildings and used to house difficult and noisy inmates.

ABOVE A view over the roofs of the Old Men's Home to the river beyond in about 1900.

OPPOSITE Inmates taking a break from their labours at the Old Men's Home on Mount's Bay Road, not long before it was closed in 1906.

GOVERNMENT INDUSTRIAL SCHOOL

RELOCATED 1916

Industrial schools were developed in the United Kingdom during the 19th century, as a means of providing for the needs and education of orphans and "necessitous" children. In Western Australia, a number of these schools were established in the latter half of the 19th century, initially by the Catholic and Anglican Churches.

In 1874, the industrial schools were all brought under the Industrial Schools Act and set the task of imparting "a general handiness to the lads" and to ensuring that girls would be "well equipped for domestic work". With a marked increase in population in Perth during the last decade of the 19th century, the Inspector of Charitable Institutions proposed the government build an industrial school in Subiaco.

Plans were drawn by Robert Haddon, an English-trained architect employed in the Public Works Department. Late in 1896, tenders were called and a contract for building the school was awarded to H. Rhodes at a cost of £4,177, 1s and 7d, the completion of the project to be by September the following year.

The building, on Barker Road in Subiaco, was completed on time, but at the slightly higher cost of £4,500. The main building consisted of a large entrance hall and recreation room, two 16-bed dormitories, two large dining rooms, plus kitchens, a matron's quarters of two rooms, assistant matrons' rooms, an office, two bathrooms, sculleries, stores and larders. Additional to this was a detached laundry block, punishment cells and a wood store. On 6 October 1897, the "inmates" of the Government Receiving Depot were transferred from rented premises in East Perth to the new school.

Whilst originally intended to be an all-girl establishment, right from the outset the school was used as a mixed institution for boys and girls, who were sent there under Section 8 of the Industrial and Reformatory Schools Act. It had been hoped this would only be a temporary arrangement, but the school remained co-educational throughout its life.

A further 27 children were admitted to the school in December of the same year and, as a consequence, the staff was increased by the appointment of a schoolmaster and an assistant matron to assist the superintendent, Mr Fowler, and the matron.

Whilst the establishment was always referred to as a school, there appears to have been a fundamental flaw in the original design, as this 1897 report by the Superintendent of Relief and Inspector of Charitable Institutions reveals: "The buildings have a handsome exterior, but the interior arrangements are not so suitable as they might have been. There was no schoolroom arranged for, but by turning one of the kitchens, which is a good-sized apartment, into one, the difficulty has so far been got over; this room is also used for the purposes of a dining room."

As the building had been designed for training the girls, the laundry, washhouse, and kitchen were "well equipped with the necessary requisites", but there were no facilities for training the boys and the superintendent sought permission to erect workshops to enable shoemaking and carpentry to be taught. As a result, carpentry, tailoring and shoemaking shops, plus an instructor's quarters, were constructed, all of which have since been demolished.

In 1916 the Government Industrial School was relocated to Marquis Street in West Perth. The school's old building became the King Edward Maternity Hospital and was renamed Harvey House. Since 1985 it has been home to the Western Australian Medical Museum.

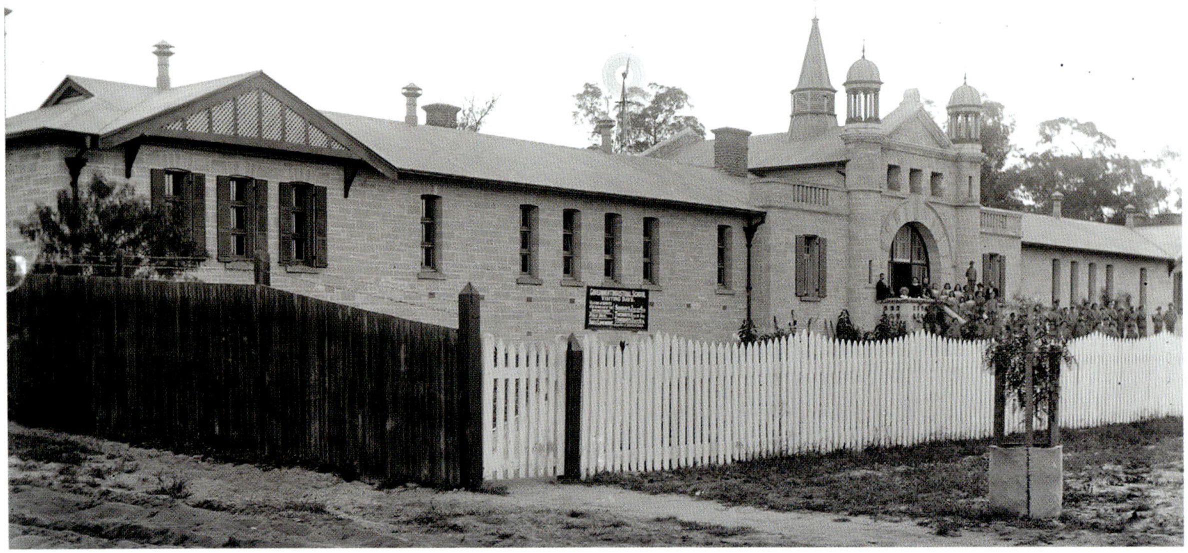

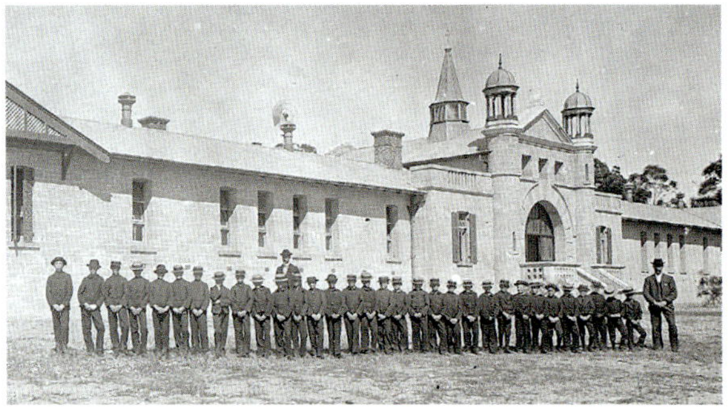

ABOVE Students line up outside the school soon after it opened in 1897. The building is now the Western Australian Medical Museum.

LEFT The Government Industrial School, on Barker Road, Subiaco, when it opened in 1897.

RIGHT The building in 1916, soon after it was converted into a 20-bed ward for the King Edward's Memorial Hospital and became the first government training school for nurses in obstetrics.

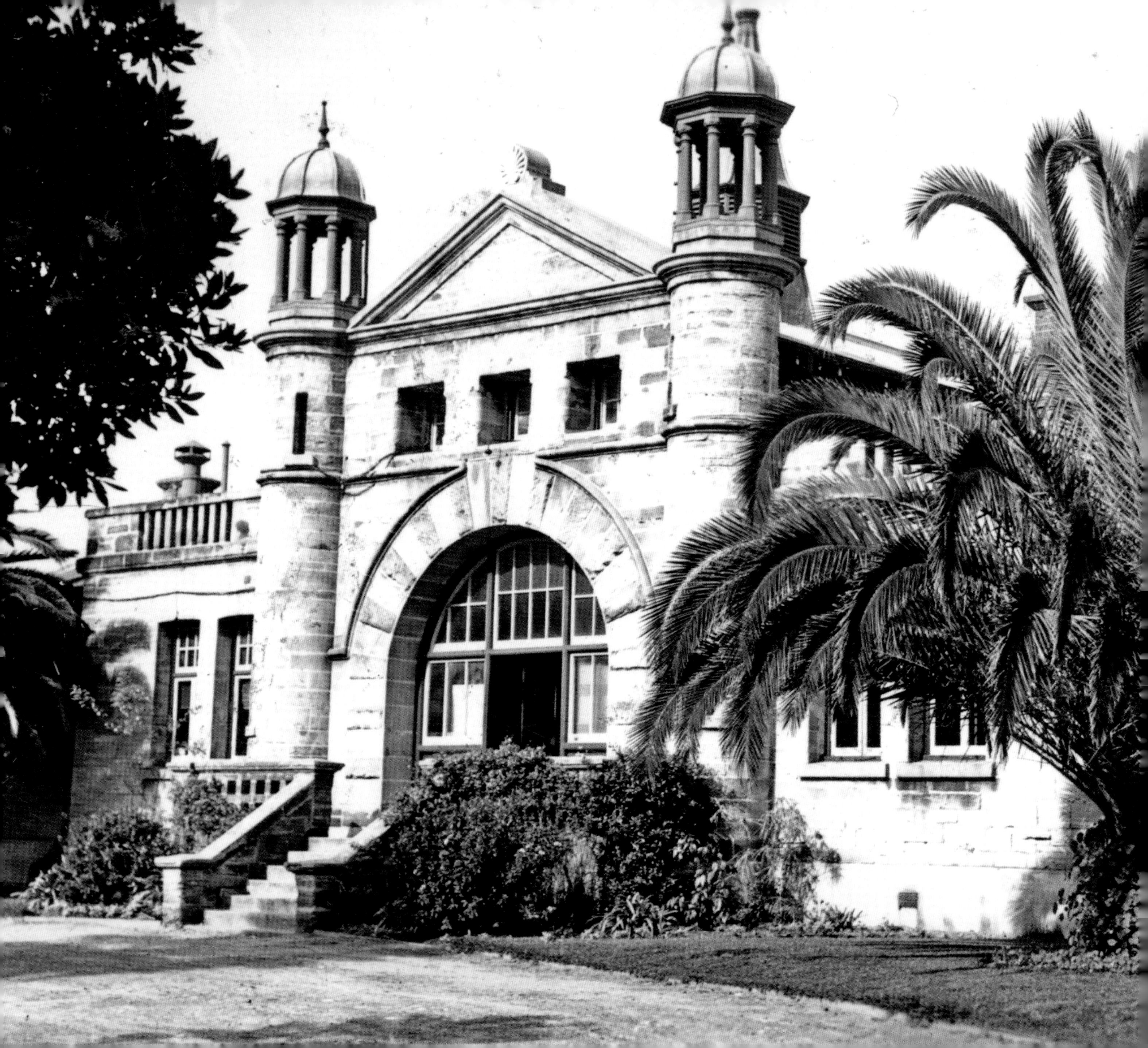

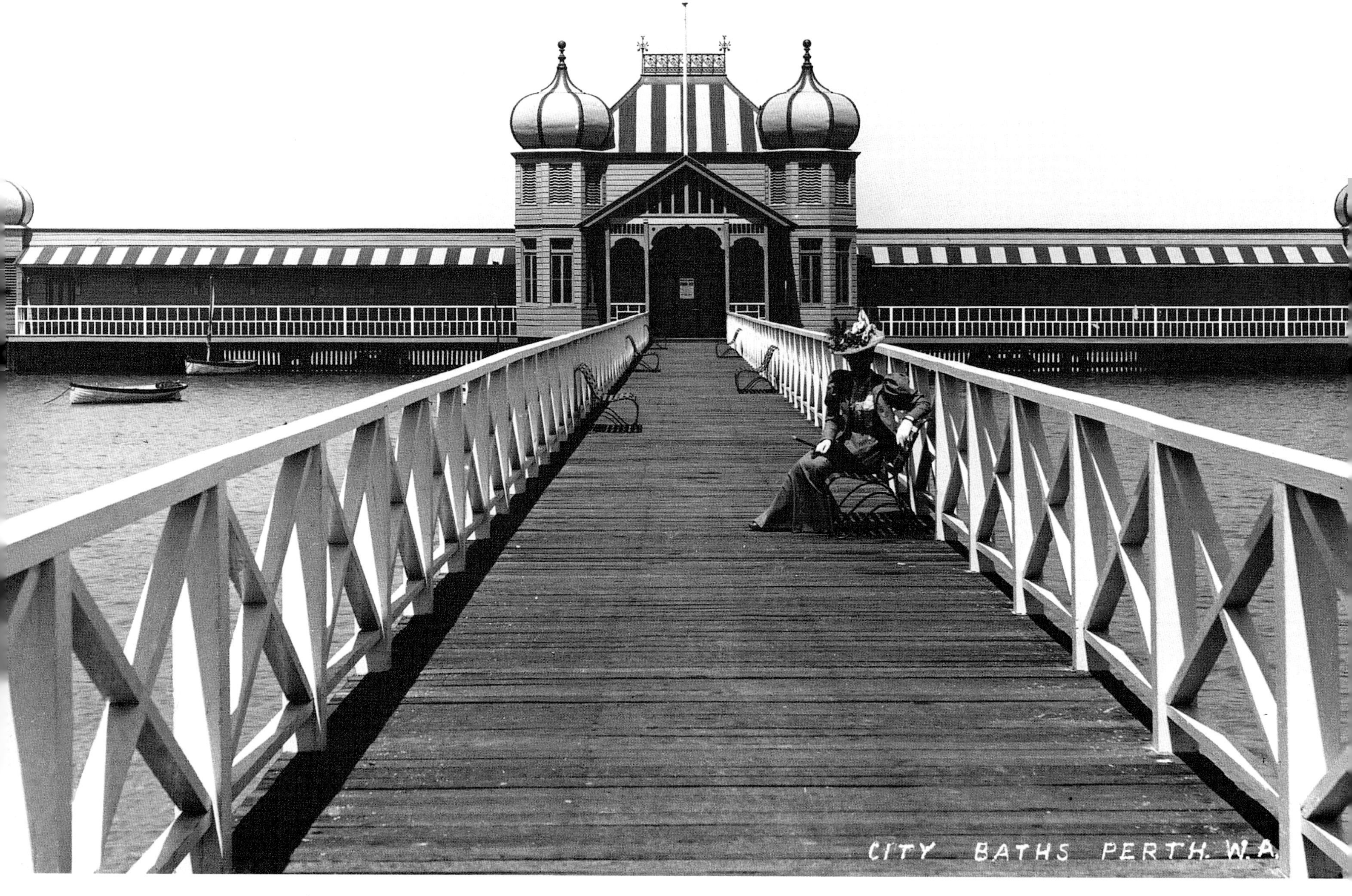
CITY BATHS PERTH. W.A.

CITY BATHS

DEMOLISHED 1920

Given the nature of the climate in Perth, people swam in the Swan River from the early days of settlement, but it was not until the 1870s that the community began to identify one of Perth's deficiencies as its lack of a public bathing facility. The *Western Australian Times* argued that "Individual attention to cleanliness, will go a long way towards promoting public, as well as individual health" and went on to suggest that neglecting to build swimming facilities "robs the city of one-half of its due modicum of health, besides denying to all, one of the most invigorating luxuries in a warm climate."

In 1884 a tin bathing shed with a water enclosure in the river was built between the William and Barrack Street jetties, but there were problems, as this report shows: "Swimmers' appearance, ungarmented, is objected to by persons ...they take particular delight in issuing from the screening walls of the bathing house to cut capers on the bridge and pay uncostumed visits to the mainland, for which they sometimes exhibit a preference as a dressing place to the shed so kindly provided for them. They do other things which may be mildly described as 'unrefined', and in particular, the language they address to one another in very high pitched tones is seldom free from epithets to which some listeners have been known to take exception."

The WA Police Act of 1892 sought to deal with these problems, with one section prohibiting bathing in a public place, except in proper costume between 6 a.m. and 8 p.m., but, despite prosecutions, the problem persisted and resulted in even more public pressure for the provision of a new and better bathing facility. To get this underway, a Perth Bathing House Fund was established in 1885 with government support, and new baths were eventually built at a cost of £2,600.

Constructed mainly of jarrah in an ornate Moorish style designed by G.R. Johnson, the City Baths were leased by the City Council and opened on 5 March 1898. In an attempt to avoid the muddy shallows of Perth Water, the lido was built about 60 metres out from the riverbank. Unfortunately, this was not far enough to ensure clear water and the silty conditions made swimming a less than pleasurable experience.

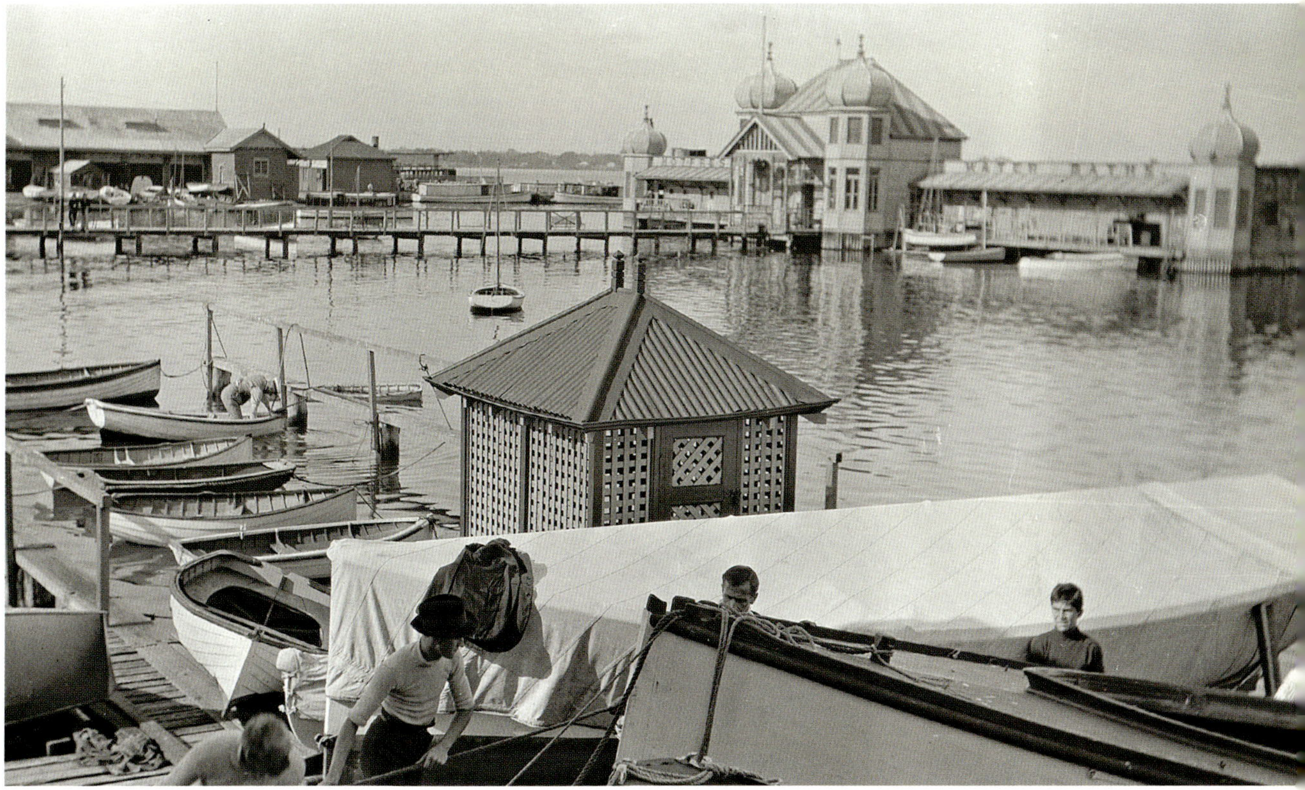

Within a few years new sites were being investigated and a move along Mounts Bay Road, which had always been a popular swimming spot, was suggested. The suggestion had its opponents because, it was argued, people walking in Kings Park would be able to see swimmers and, worse, those dressing and undressing. After much debate, the new City Baths in Crawley were opened on 7 February 1914 and the old City Baths were eventually demolished in 1920.

ABOVE The disused baths from the Royal Perth Yacht Club jetty just before demolition in 1920.

OPPOSITE City Baths on the Perth Esplanade in about 1900. The jetty connecting the river shore to the entrance was about 40 metres long.

RIGHT Boats belonging to Royal Perth Yacht Club moored up by the City Baths in 1899.

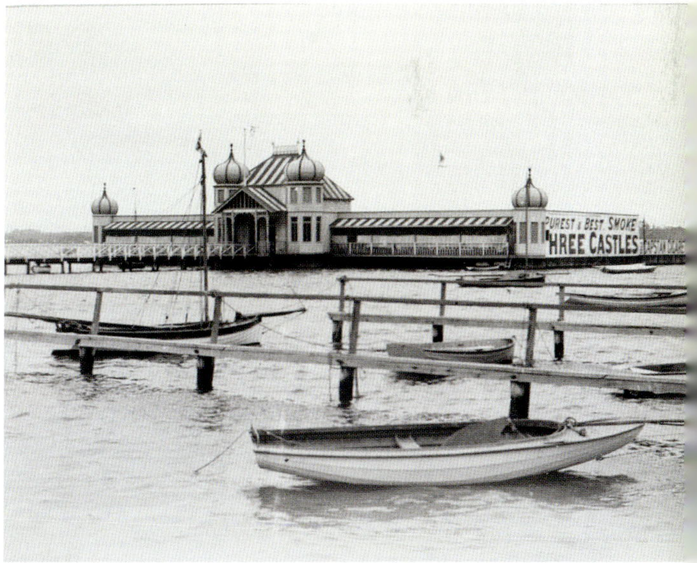

THE BUNGALOW

DEMOLISHED 1920

The Bungalow on Hay Street was the home of Sir John Forrest, a well-known explorer and politician, who lived there from 1876 to 1917. The land on which the Bungalow stood has a complicated history, which is typical of early land deals in Perth.

The site originally consisted of two blocks, owned by early settlers John Chipper and William Baker. In 1834 John Chipper acquired a portion of the land direct from Baker for £3. Baker's remaining land went through several further owners before Chipper finally purchased the remainder of the block, which then brought his holding to just over an acre. The house was originally built by John Chipper at an unknown date and subsequently tenanted by several members of the Wittenoom family.

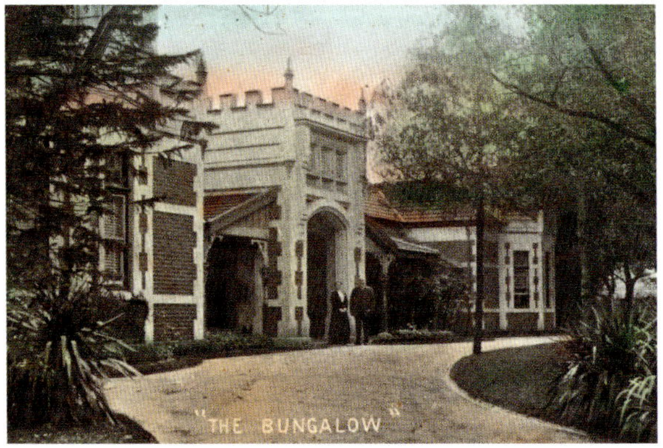

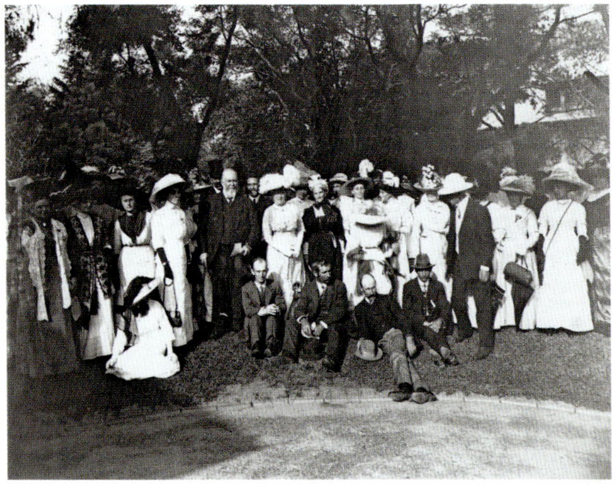

In 1867 the property passed, at a cost of £650, from Chipper to H. Ashton, who was Deputy Commissary General, and appears to have lived there for the rest of his life. Ashton died in 1874 and the property was sold to Edward Hamersley, the father of Lady Forrest, for £1,150. When Hamersley died, the property passed to Lady Forrest, and once in her and Sir John's hands the original house underwent a great many additions and alterations. The Forrests also completely transformed the gardens, which extended to Murray Street and were in their time renowned as among the most charming and beautiful gardens in Perth.

The Forrests carried on a long-standing tradition of lavish hospitality at the property. An article in the *West Australian* following the sale of the property in 1917 described how, like the previous occupants, the Wittenooms, Sir John and Lady Forrest would open their garden to local boys who were "let loose in the orchard to regale themselves with the peaches and other excellent fruits with which the place abounded."

The Forrests decided to sell the Bungalow by auction in 1917. The sale was held in Literary Institute Hall (on the corner of Pier and Hay Street) and was well attended. The property sold for £27,000 and was eventually demolished to make way for the Bungalow Building, which was built in 1920.

ABOVE LEFT Sir John and Lady Forrest at the entrance to the Bungalow in 1912.

LEFT A garden party in 1910 hosted by Sir John and Lady Forrest at the Bungalow. Sir John is standing on the left.

OPPOSITE The front entrance in 1910, a sanctuary from the hustle and bustle of nearby Hay Street during the first gold rush.

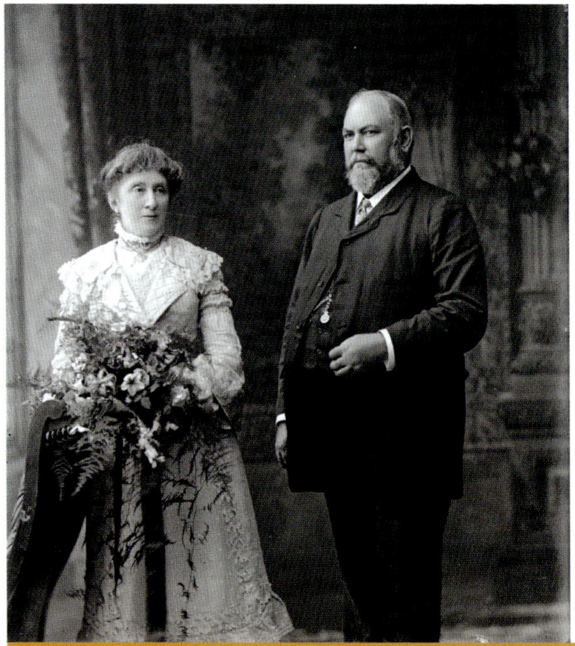

JOHN FORREST

John Forrest (seen here with Lady Forrest in 1903) was born at Picton, near Bunbury, in 1847. One of 10 children, he attended the Perth Church of England Collegiate School, from where he became the first man born and educated in the colony to qualify as a land surveyor. John worked for the Lands and Surveys Department and later became well known as an explorer. He led three expeditions to the interior of Western Australia and in 1869 carried out a fruitless search for the missing explorer Ludwig Leichhardt. In 1883, at the age of 35, he became the first native-born Western Australian to be appointed to the Executive Council. Not everyone was enthusiastic about the appointment, with some feeling that such posts were the exclusive domain of English government officials. Forrest became first Premier of Western Australia in December 1890 and, after Federation in 1901, he moved to federal politics, where he held a number of offices. John Forrest died at sea in 1918 on the way to London for treatment for skin cancer.

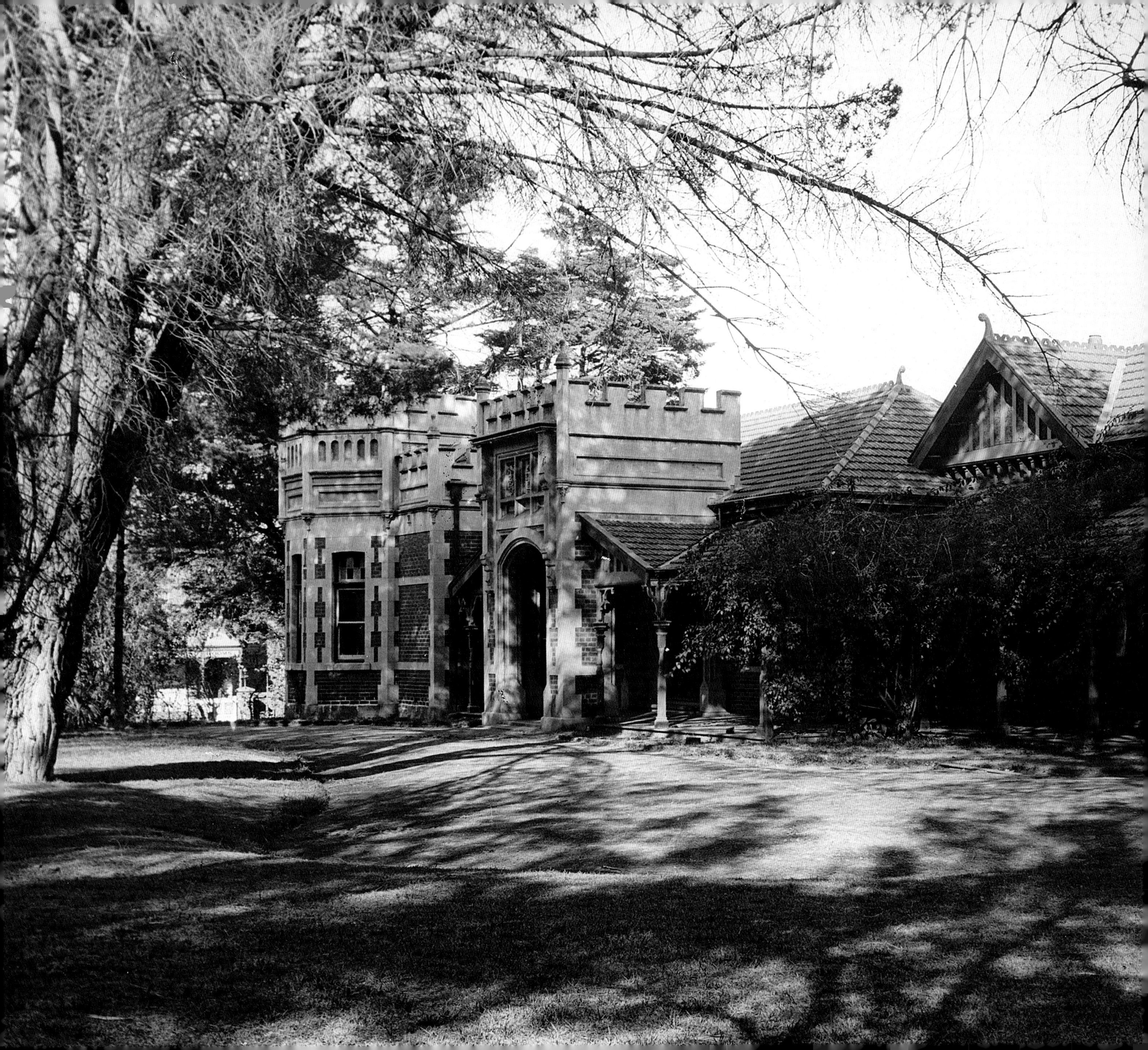

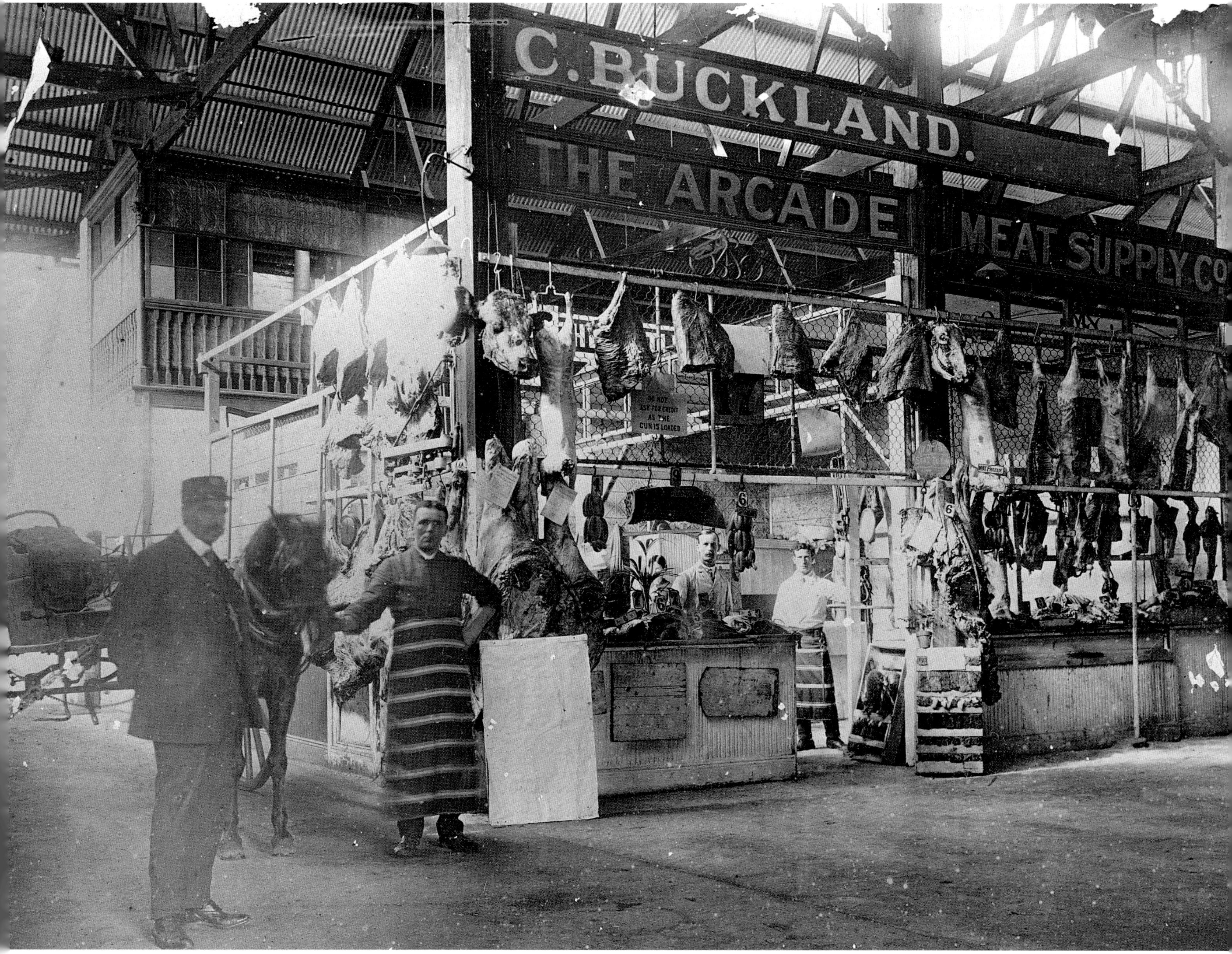
C. BUCKLAND.
THE ARCADE
MEAT SUPPLY Co
DO NOT
ASK FOR CREDIT
AS THE
GUN IS LOADED

CENTRAL ARCADE

DEMOLISHED 1922

Thanks to the hot, sunny climate, covered shopping malls have been a popular feature of central Perth since the opening of the McNess Royal Arcade in 1897.

Six years later a new arcade was being constructed on a lane formerly known as Station Street. Central Arcade was the brainchild of Robert McMaster, a Melbourne-born architect who came to Perth in the early 1890s. The arcade ran from Wellington Street, opposite the Railway Station, to Murray Street and construction commenced in 1903.

Under the title "Go Ahead Perth", a report in August of that year published in the *W.A. Record* spoke excitedly about the new development: "Quite a new and important development is proceeding in the midst of Perth almost as yet unnoticed by the general public. Mr. McMaster, with a busy staff of workmen, is transforming what has been hitherto known as Station Street, and which runs from Murray Street emerging into Wellington Street, opposite to the main entrance to the Railway Station, into an up-to-date Arcade."

The building was a tall barn-like structure, clad in corrugated iron, with glass skylights along the apex of the roof. A drawing of the Wellington Street frontage, published in the Christmas Day 1904 edition of the *Western Mail*, shows an elegant Federation-style façade with an iron canopy and balcony.

Although the arcade was not officially opened until 1906, adverts published late in 1903 indicate that one trader – the Commercial Trading Company, a well-known local firm of tailors – seems to have opened their shop before the building was anywhere near completion.

The arcade officially opened for business on 31 March 1906 and was heralded as a paragon of cleanliness and hygiene, with running water and mains drainage, as the report in the following day's *Sunday Times* shows: "The new Central Arcade was opened for business last night, and proved quite a feature in the amusement of the city. All the stalls completed up to date have been occupied, and Mr. McMaster expects that they will all be taken up by next Saturday. The air of absolute cleanliness about the place makes it look inviting."

Initially, instead of individual self-contained retail units, the building was divided into stalls, stable-like, from which each trader operated. With the stalls eventually replaced by shop fronts, the arcade thrived until the outbreak of World War I. It even boasted a live band giving a "discourse" of music on Saturday evenings.

After the war, there were reports from the City Council suggesting that the arcade was unhealthy. In order to improve the surroundings of the new GPO building, the Central Arcade was demolished in 1922.

The decision was not welcomed by all, as a report in the *Australian* of 18 August 1922 made clear: "The pulling down of the picturesque old Central Arcade to make way for the new GPO street has meant a general far-and-wide scattering of tenants who have been clustered together for many a long year. Most of these people run small businesses that do not advertise to any extent, so that they will be certain to suffer a considerable loss of clients by the break-up and unavoidable departure from a long-established site." The new street which took its place was officially named Forrest Place in 1923.

OPPOSITE A butcher's shop in Central Arcade soon after it opened in 1906. A sign hanging in amongst the meat says "Do not ask for credit as the gun is loaded!"

BELOW A horse removes rubble from the demolition in 1922.

BOTTOM The arcade from Wellington Street in about 1920, showing the Railway Coffee Palace and a chemist. Two vehicles parked outside are a 1918 Dodge tourer and a 1912 Ford tourer.

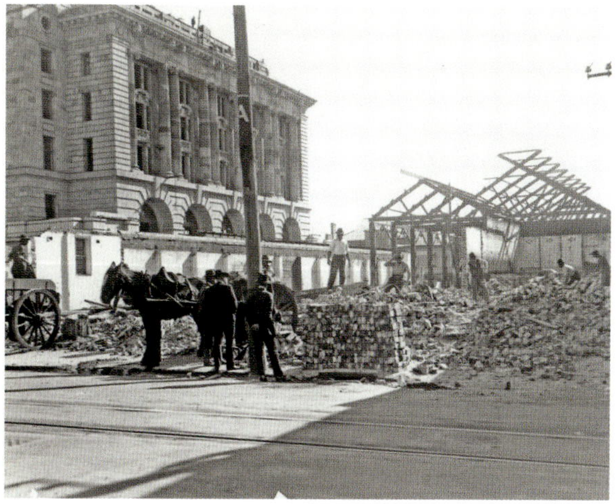

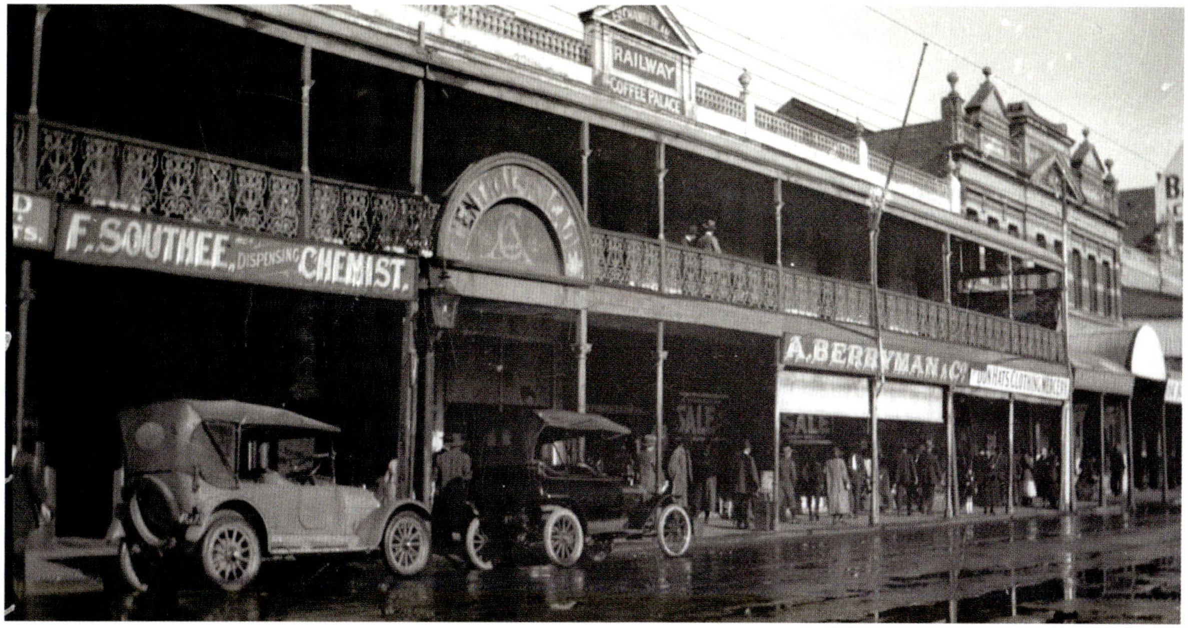

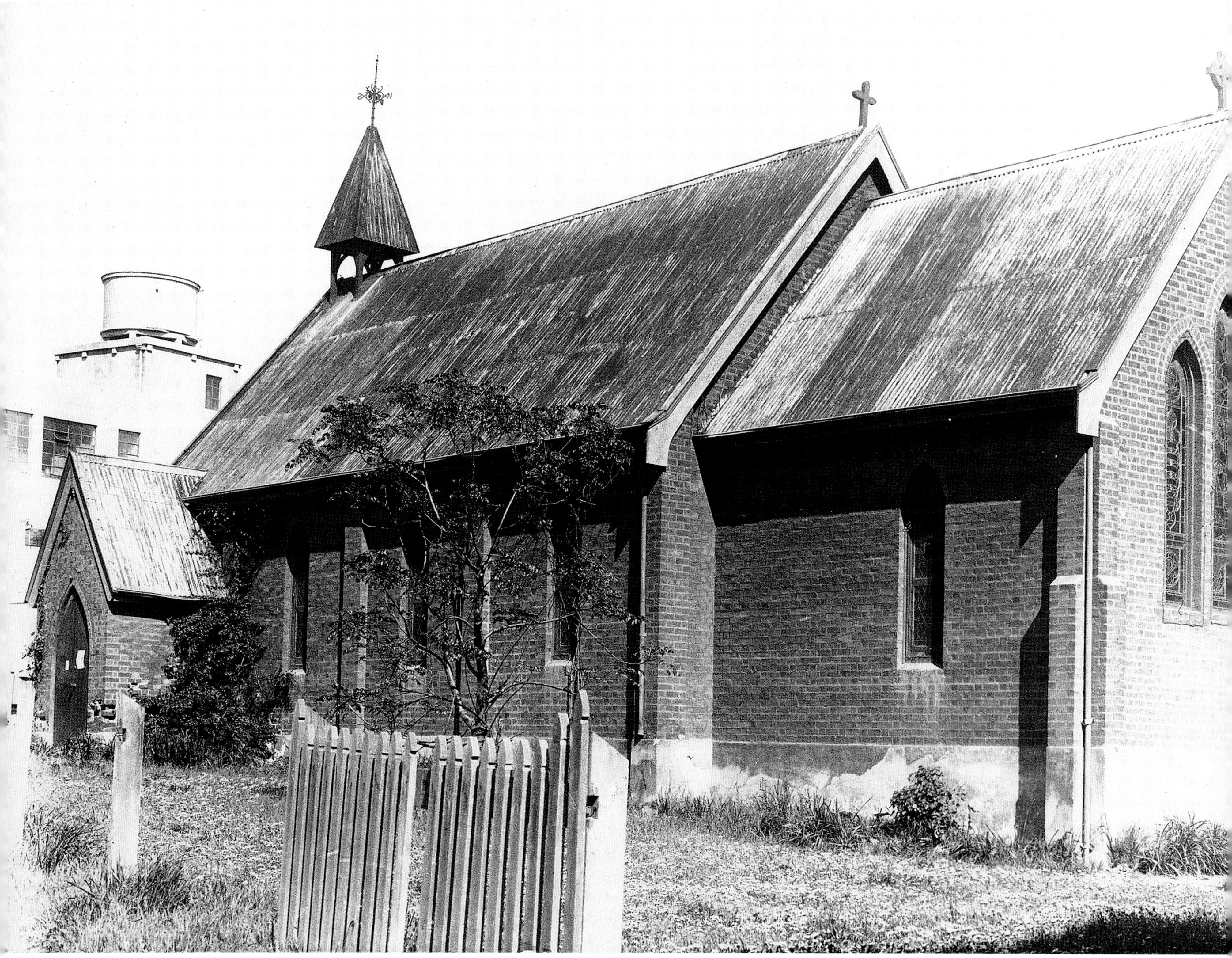

ST JOHN'S CHURCH

DEMOLISHED 1928

As the population of Perth grew in the late 19th century, churches of all denominations found it hard to keep pace with the growth in newly formed suburbs. This gave rise to a considerable building programme of places of worship to cater for a predominantly church-going society.

St George's Cathedral was the principal Anglican church (Church of England in those days) in the town, but by the end of the 1890s a number of "daughter" churches had been built in suburbs such as Highgate and Claremont to serve these growing communities.

One of these was the mission room on Melbourne Road (now Milligan Street) to serve the community in West Perth. Built in 1882, the Gothic-style building consisted of one large hall and porch with corrugated iron roofs. It was used as a Sunday school and meeting room, with a service held there every Sunday evening.

Early in 1888 a chancel was added and the older part of the building upgraded for use as a church rather than mission hall. On Sunday 24 June that year (the feast of the nativity of St John the Baptist), the chapel was licensed by the Bishop of Perth for divine service, under the name of St John the Baptist's Chapel, as a district church in the parish of St George's Cathedral. The Rev. James Allen, who had officiated at the services since 1882, was appointed curate in charge.

In 1890 an ancient stone font was acquired from England and shipped here together with a modern base and pedestal. The Anglo-Saxon font, dating from no later than the ninth or tenth century, was found near Peterborough Cathedral, where it was being used as a garden ornament. It is the oldest font in Australia and, together with its brass font ewer, was transferred to St Hilda's in North Perth when St John's was closed.

During the 1890s, the church attracted an influential congregation, many of whom patronised the church in preference to St George's Cathedral, which they considered to have undesirable "High Church" tendencies under Dean Frederick Goldsmith. The churchwardens during this period were Joseph Talbot Hobbs, the well-known Perth architect and army officer, and James Broun Roe, the son of Swan River Colony's first Surveyor-General, John Septimus Roe.

A church hall of galvanised iron with a brick front was built on vacant land next to the church in 1899 at a cost of £370. This hall was used as a Sunday School and for meetings and gatherings during the week.

Disaster struck in 1914, when the church was nearly burnt to the ground by a fire, which appears to have started in the neighbouring Bunnings wood yard. The *West Australian* of 22 January reported: "Not only the roof of the church but also some of the windows were broken, while the neatly-kept gardens surrounding the church also suffered a great deal, the grass and trees being withered up. The new fence, only just erected, was also damaged, owing to one of the falling telegraph poles coming into contact with it." The fire was estimated to have caused £150 worth of damage. Thankfully, the church hall was left unscathed by the fire.

The church was restored following the fire, but 14 years later a dwindling congregation, most of whom had migrated to the new St Mary's Church in West Perth, rendered the church unviable and it was demolished early in 1928. The hall remained in place until 1935, being used by a paint-spraying firm, but that too was demolished to make way for a garage, the building of which still exists as offices.

OPPOSITE St John's Church, taken about eight years before it was demolished in 1928.

BELOW LEFT The church from a strange photographic perspective (it was not built following the slope of the land) in 1920, clearly showing the church hall beside Wellington Street.

BELOW The nave, looking towards the chancel in 1920.

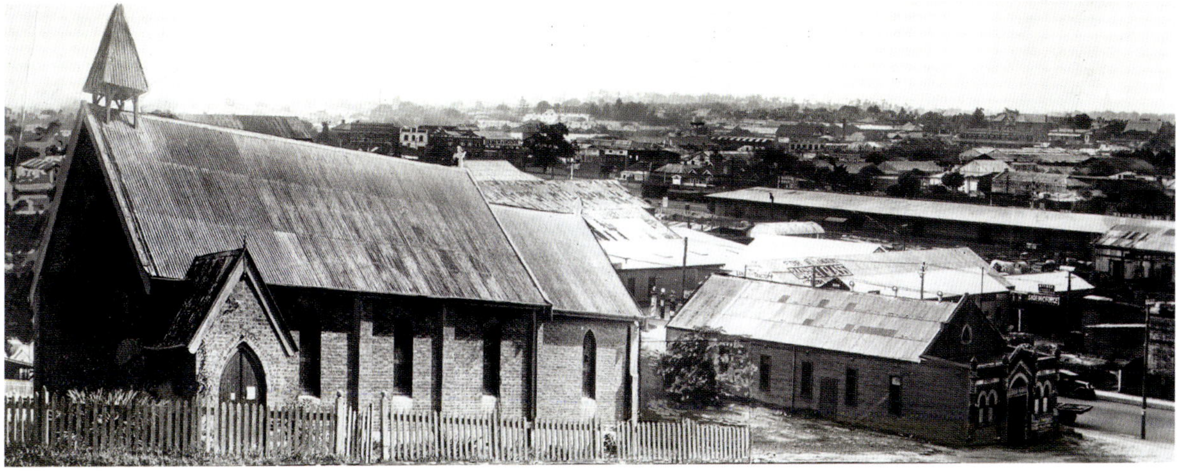

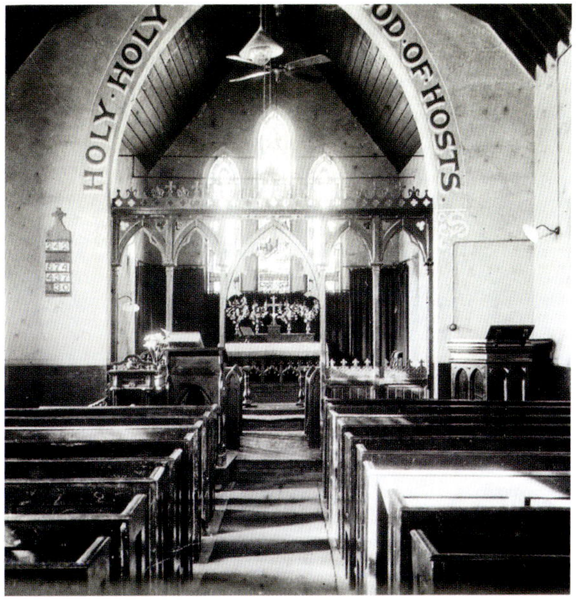

WHITE CITY

CLOSED 1929

White City, also known as "Cooee City" or "Ugly Land" was an amusement park originally based in the Supreme Court Gardens and established around the time of World War I. It was a popular place of entertainment for a wide section of the community and a venue that enabled various local charities to hold fundraising events there. The enterprise was often referred to as Ugly Land because the quirkily-named Ugly Men's Association (a charitable organisation established in 1917) was involved in the management of many events there.

Because the gardens were often used for other purposes, White City had to be dismantled and reassembled at regular intervals. The cost of constructing and demolishing structures frequently, and complaints about noise from near neighbours, resulted in the amusement park being moved in 1922 to a more permanent site on the western side of the Esplanade Reserve, at the bottom of William Street. The opening event was reported in the *Daily News* of 13 November 1922: "From Friday next, Carnival Square, at the foot of William Street, will be thrown open for the benefit of those in need of light amusement, fresh air and rest amidst pleasant surroundings and under comfortable conditions. 'White City' will be a representation of a big recreation park, where concerts, Punch and Judy, Pierrots, open-air dancing, hoop-la, and the latest American games, in addition to other forms of amusement, will be presented nightly. Light refreshments, cool drinks, ice creams, lollies and an endless variety of pleasant elements will be available."

There was always a real carnival atmosphere and amusements included wheels and swings, games of chance, boxing, log chopping, bands and dancing.

As was often the case with funfairs at that time, accidents were a fairly common occurrence. There were also more serious incidents, as the *Kalgoorlie Miner* reported in March 1929: "As a result of the recent deaths in connection with snake charming exhibitions, the secretary of the State Gardens Board has notified the tenants of White City that exhibitions of snakes and snake charming will not be permitted on the premises in future."

The venue was popular with Perth's Aboriginal people as well as the European population. This was something the Chief Protector of Aborigines, A.O. Neville, did not like and in 1926 reported that, "young black men were beating white men in boxing contests on the doorstep of the city and that they were being watched by black women." Sadly, the 1927 Prohibited Area declaration compelled Aboriginal people not on "lawful business" to leave the city and this gave Neville the excuse he needed to make the name White City poignantly relevant.

Following allegations of gambling, the reputation of White City continued to decline. The newly established Town Planning Commission called for its demolition, so that "beauty and healthfulness would replace squalor and the indulgence of vicious instincts." White City was closed in 1929 and within a matter of months it had been redeveloped as a gravel tennis court, with a tea room alongside. Today the area is the site of Esplanade Underground Station.

RIGHT An elevated view from 1928. The shed in the background belonged to Hudson Boatbuilders, probably one of the last boat builders on this stretch of the river.

BELOW Men line up at the soup kitchen, set up after White City closed in 1929. Run by the W.A. Housewives Association, it provided relief to the unemployed during the Great Depression.

BOTTOM The entrance to White City in 1922.

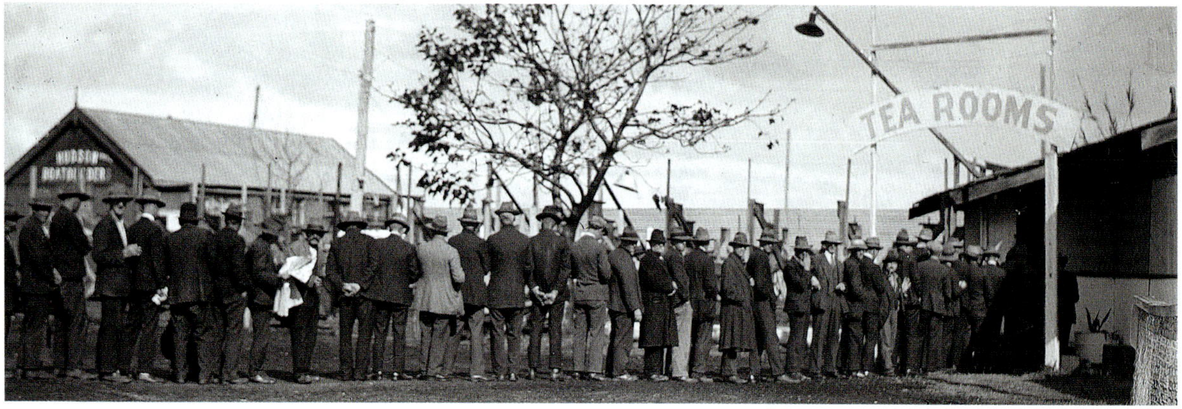

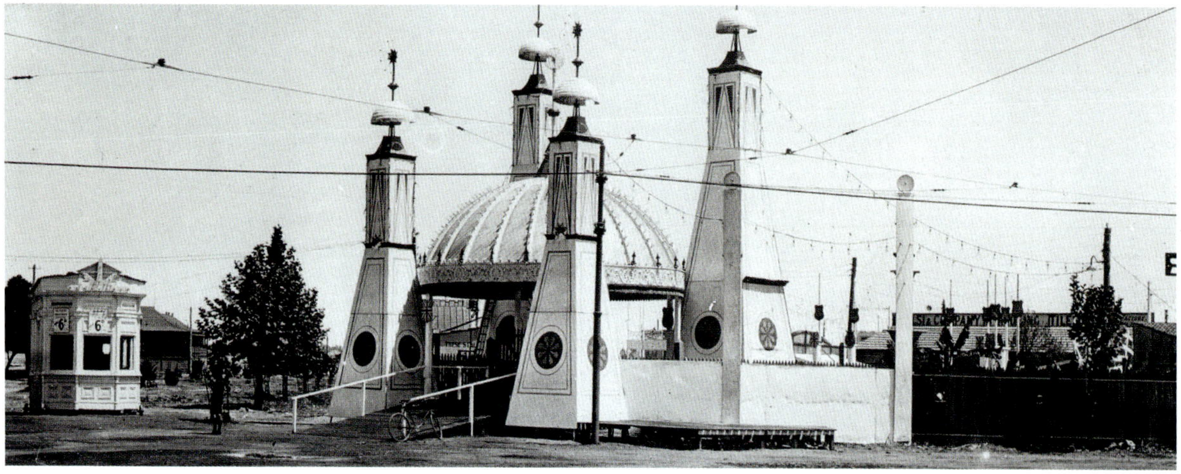

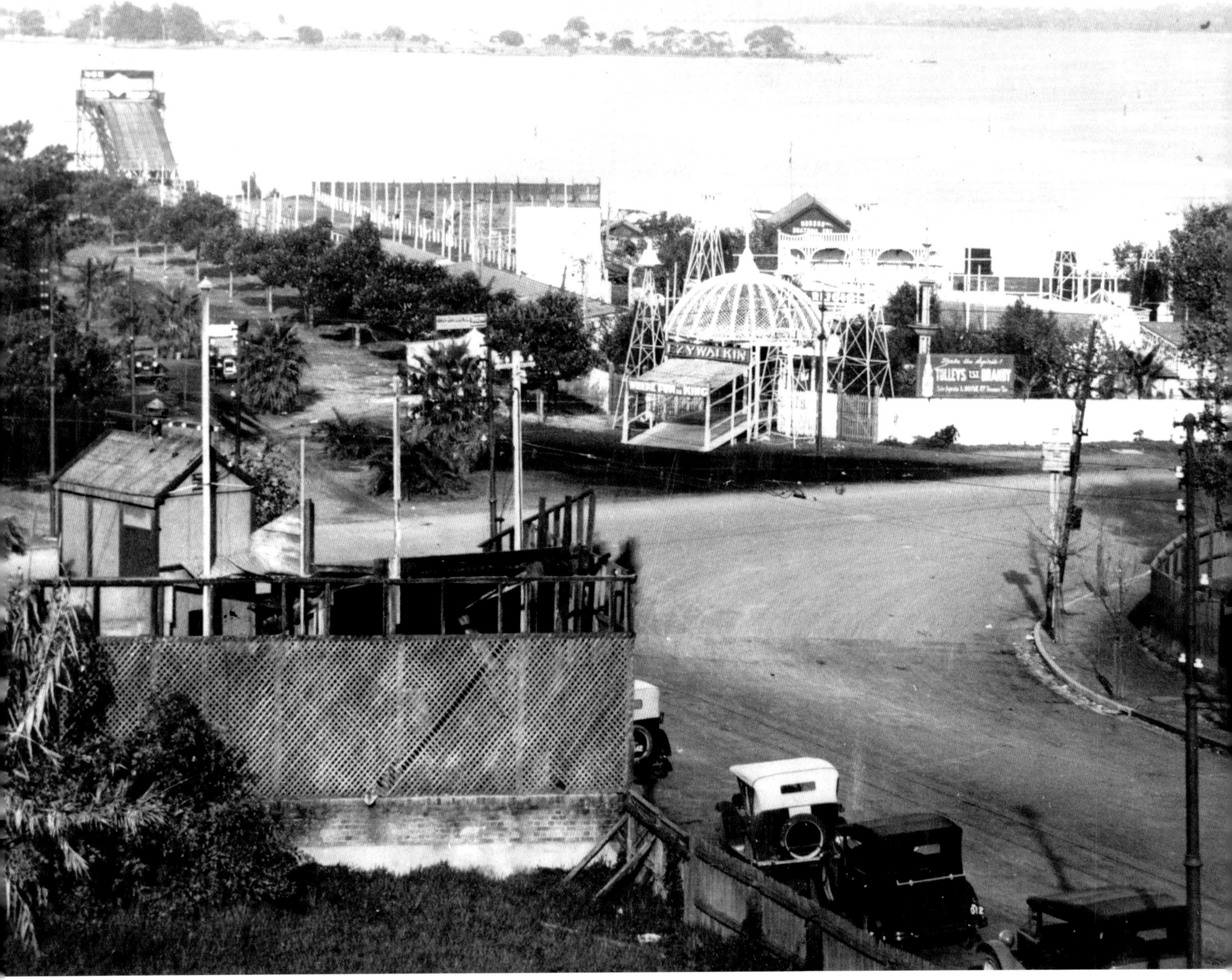
TULLEYS T.S.X. BRANDY

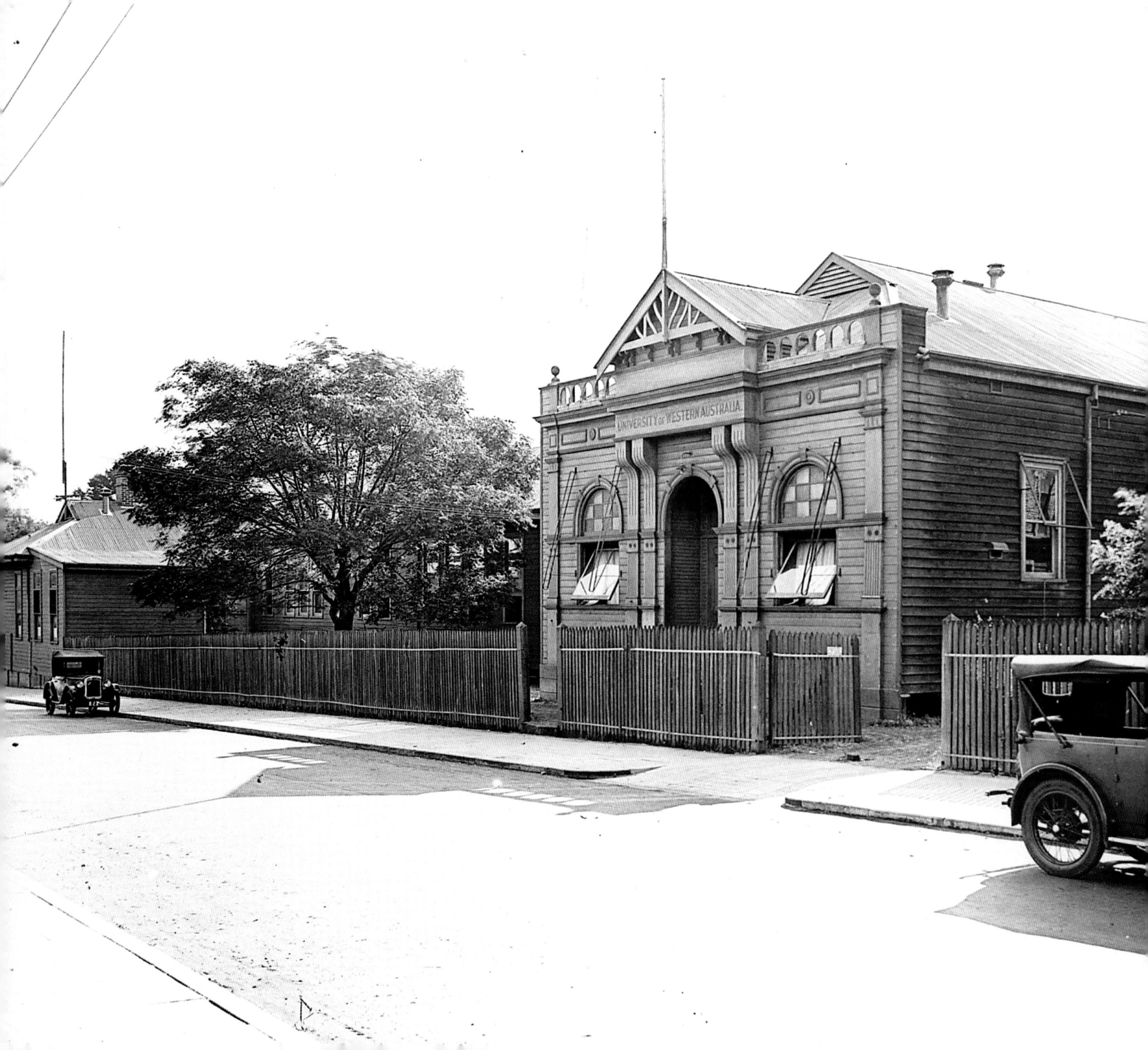
UNIVERSITY OF WESTERN AUSTRALIA

UNIVERSITY OF WESTERN AUSTRALIA

MOVED 1925–32

The Technical School on St Georges Terrace was the first place in Perth to offer tertiary educational courses in Western Australia. In 1905 the University of Adelaide formally affiliated it to enable students to sit undergraduate examinations in subjects including mathematics, geology, mineralogy and botany. Various degree courses continued to be offered under licence from Adelaide University until the University of Western Australia was founded in 1911.

At the end of February 1911 a bill was signed by the Governor of Western Australia to "establish, incorporate, and endow" the new University of Western Australia. From the outset this establishment had a special place in tertiary education history, as it was not only the state's first university, but also the first free university in the British Empire actively promoting equal access to tertiary education for everyone.

The university was established thanks to the passion and drive of Sir John Winthrop Hackett, proprietor and editor of the *West Australian* newspaper. Hackett, who chaired a Royal Commission that recommended the establishment of a university in Western Australia, was its founding chancellor and left over £425,000 in his will as an endowment.

In the following year there was much debate about the location for the new university, and in order to get things moving, temporary accommodation was rented in the city centre. In 1912 the administrative offices were housed in St George's Chambers, next to St George's Cathedral, and other locations were investigated for the teaching facilities. Eventually, the State Government made available a site of about an acre on Irwin Street, with frontages on both St Georges Terrace and Hay Street.

The first building to be constructed was a large timber-framed structure with a veranda, clad in weatherboard and capped with a corrugated iron roof. It was designed by the Department of Public Works and housed teaching facilities and further accommodation for administrative staff. Five years later the veranda was enclosed to provide yet more rooms. Slowly, other buildings were erected; some new and others relocated from different sites. One of the relocated buildings, the Workers' Hall, was transported 580 kilometres from Coolgardie. Its original location was where the Labor Party of Western Australia was founded. Other reused buildings brought to the site between 1917 and 1925 included the Oddfellows Hall from Leederville and two timber structures from the back of the Pensioner Barracks at the top of St Georges Terrace. Because most of these buildings had iron roofs, the site became known as "Tin Pan Alley".

The University of Western Australia opened for teaching on 31 March 1913 with 184 students. War intervened and it wasn't until 1925 that the university began the move to its designated permanent site at Crawley. In 1932 some of the Irwin Street buildings, including the one built for the opening of the university, were transported to Crawley. The original building was restored in 1987 and now sits beside James Oval, where it accommodates the Convocation Council Room, the university's archives centre and cricket club pavilion.

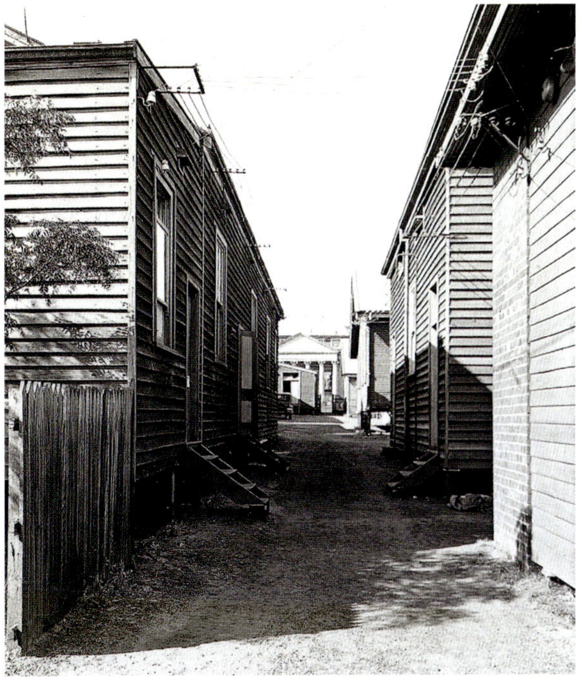

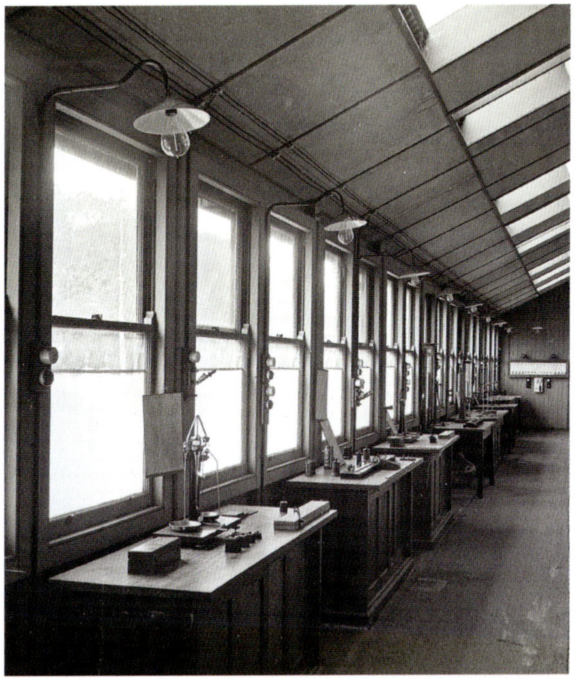

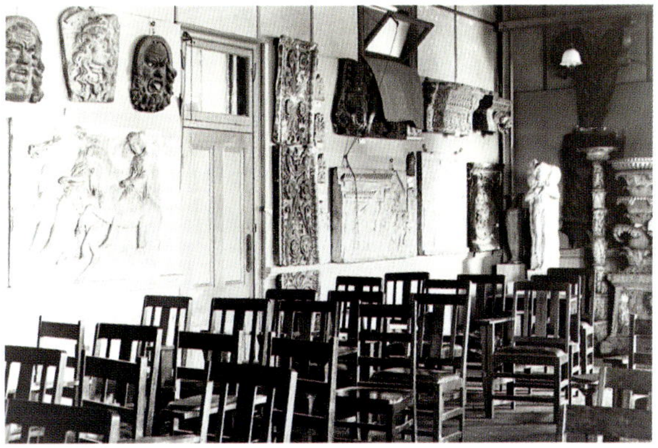

ABOVE The Fine Arts Lecture Room in the University's Irwin Street buildings in 1920.

LEFT A physics laboratory in Irwin Street.

FAR LEFT The Irwin Street buildings, taken from St Georges Terrace in 1920. At the end of the lane can be seen the front of the St George's Hall on Hay Street.

OPPOSITE The Administration Building on the corner of Irwin Street in about 1913.

LOMBARD CHAMBERS

DEMOLISHED 1935

The land on which Lombard Chambers stood was first owned by Frederick Sherwood, who arrived in the colony in January 1843. His land stretched from St Georges Terrace down to the river. It was in the middle of this slope facing the river that he built a brick house.

A surveyor and architect by profession, Sherwood seems to have been a man of many talents. He conducted a school in the house, which was attended by the children of some of the earliest Swan River colonists, and also built a brewery on his land, which would eventually become the famous Swan Brewery.

Lombard Chambers was built on the site in about 1880 and, at the time, was one of the most imposing buildings on St Georges Terrace. It was first used as residential quarters, but later became P.A. Gugeri's wine and spirit store. When Frederick Sherwood died, the property passed to his three children and was used by another member of the family, Harry Sherwood, as an aerated water and bottling works. Wine from vineyards in Maylands, beer from the brewery and aerated water made on the premises were bottled and delivered twice a week to customers between Perth and Guildford.

The *West Australian* was later to reflect on life in Lombard House in a retrospective from 1934: "For four years Mr. T.J. Briggs, of Claremont, worked for Harry Sherwood in the bottling works and delivered the liquor. He remembers well those days of free and easy licensing regulation when there was little more restriction on the brewery cart than there is on the baker's cart today. During the summer months when the demand for drinks was greatest, much of the work of bottling was carried out in the shade of a trellis of vines which ran down the hill from the front of Frederick Sherwood's old house. These vines were planted by Frederick Sherwood when he first arrived in the colony."

In 1895 the property was purchased by a syndicate of Perth businessmen, who converted the building into offices, which soon became the centre of the state's financial transactions. The first stock exchange was founded there by a committee including Alexander Forrest, G.T. Simpson, H.J. Saunders and James Cale. A portion of the ground floor was converted to make a dealing room, where many significant transactions from the early days of the first Gold Rush took place. Other floors were used by lawyers and stock brokers.

When electric lights were installed in the building during the first decade of the 20th century, it was found that the space between the ceiling and the roof contained a layer of seaweed as insulation.

In 1927 the St Georges Terrace end of the property was sold to the Norwich Union Fire Insurance Society. Subsequently, the entire holding was sold to Colonial Mutual Life Assurance Society Ltd., who demolished Lombard Chambers in 1935 to construct their magnificent CMLA Building.

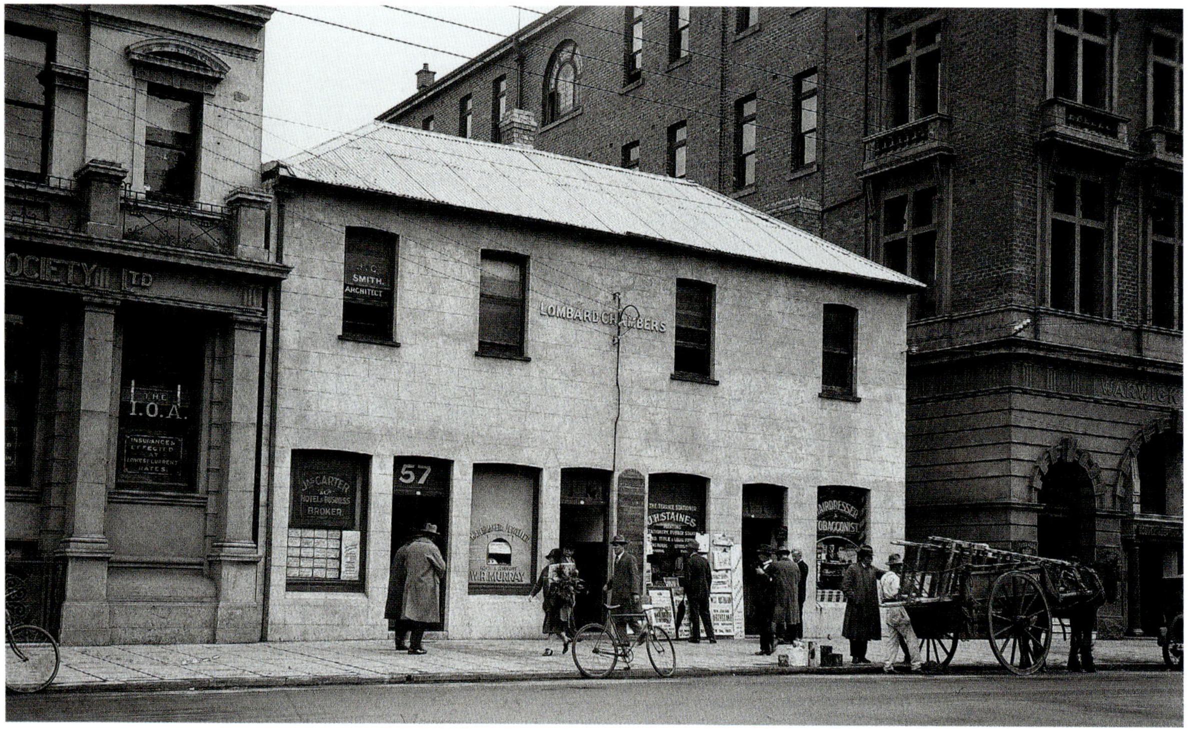

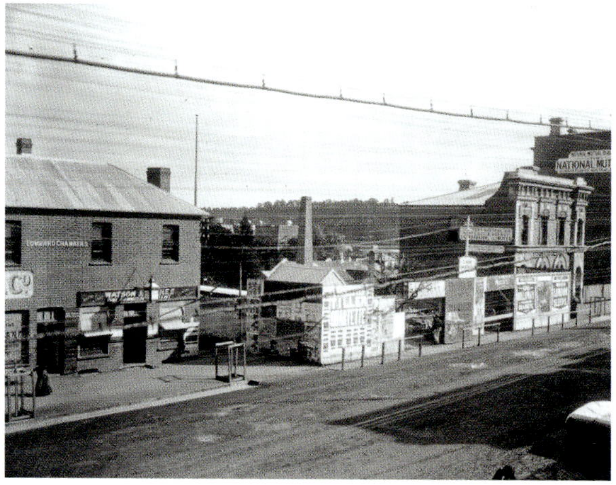

ABOVE View of the south side of St Georges Terrace looking west, with Lombard Chambers far left (1898).

LEFT Lombard Chambers in the 1920s. Companies based in the building included J.C. Smith, architect; Jas Carter & Co., hotel and business broker; W.R. Murray, watchmaker & jeweller; and J.H. Staines, stationer.

RIGHT The building decorated to celebrate the Coronation of King Edward VII in August 1902.

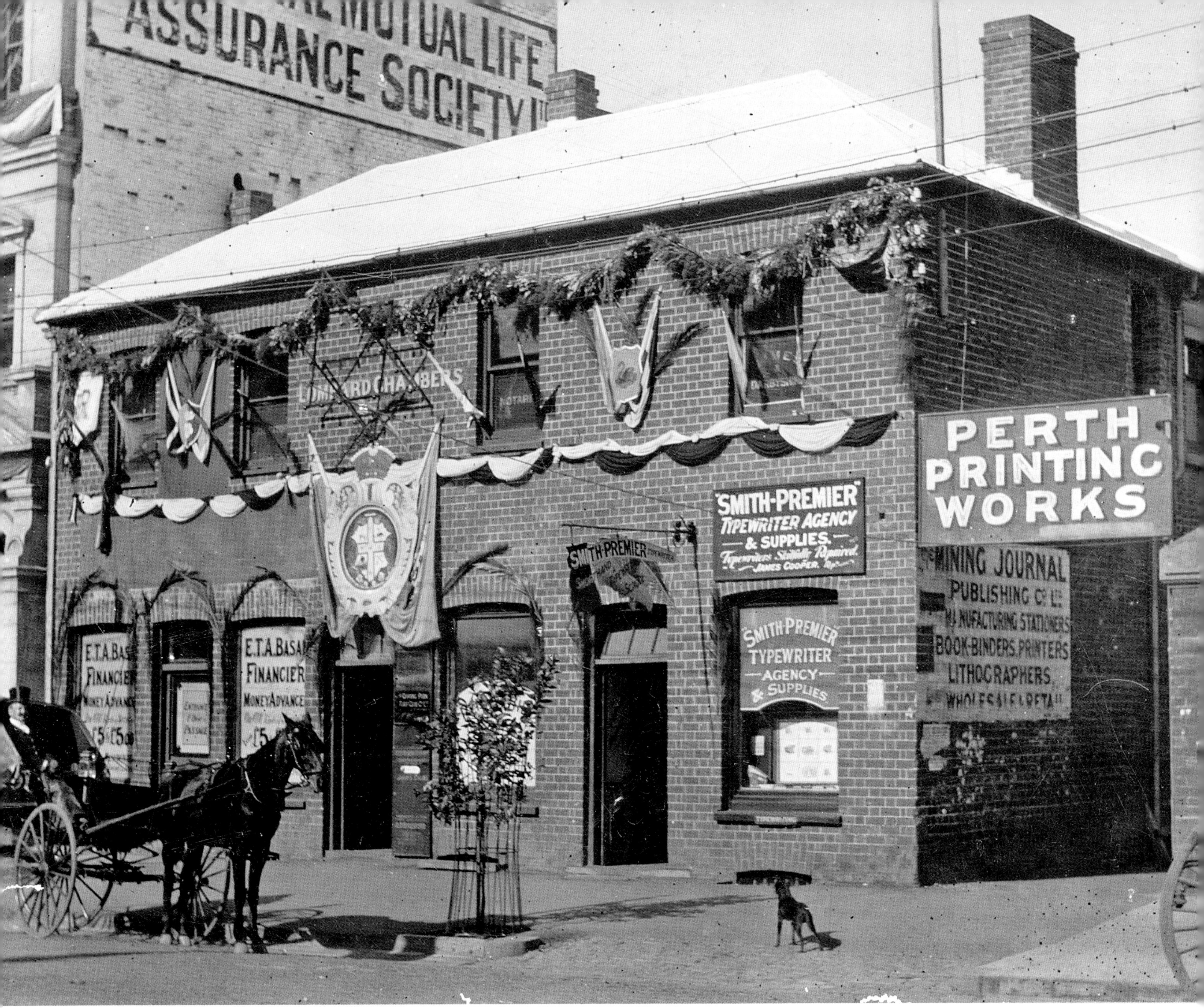

MUTUAL LIFE
ASSURANCE SOCIETY
LOMBARD CHAMBERS
"SMITH-PREMIER"
TYPEWRITER AGENCY
& SUPPLIES.
JAMES COOPER
PERTH
PRINTING
WORKS
MINING JOURNAL
PUBLISHING Co Ltd
BOOK-BINDERS, PRINTERS
LITHOGRAPHERS
"SMITH-PREMIER"
TYPEWRITER
AGENCY
& SUPPLIES
FINANCIER
FINANCIER

S

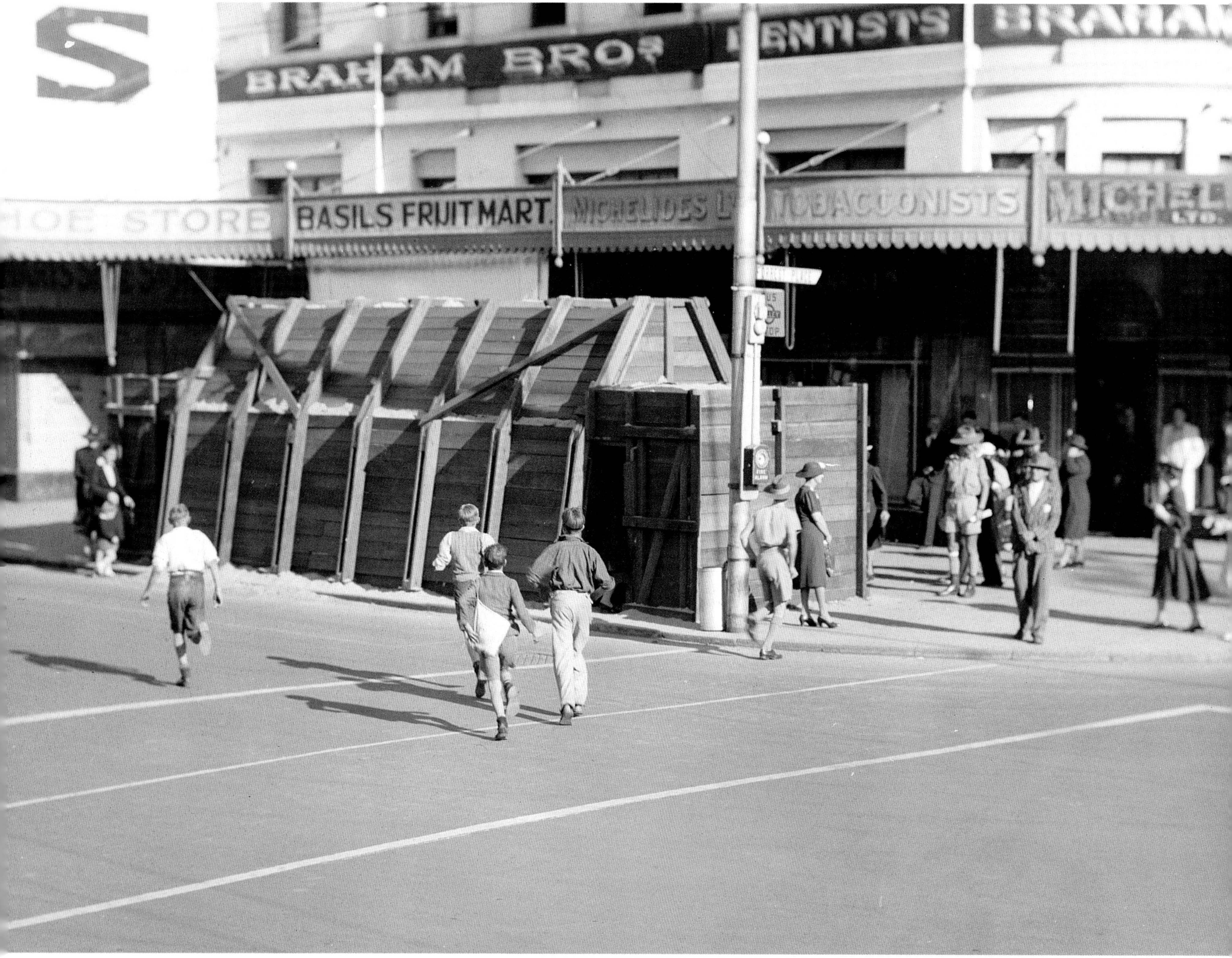

AIR RAID SHELTERS

REMOVED 1945

During World War II Perth City Council made a number of economic concessions, such as reducing general rates and fire levies, but their main focus for the war effort was digging trenches and building air raid shelters in central Perth. It initiated a war fund and also made the Perth Town Hall available as a recreation facility for thousands of visiting servicemen and women from Australia and abroad.

A special advisory committee was set up in 1941 to develop local defence measures. As the threat of hostilities in the Southern Hemisphere increased, the committee met daily to consider the risks to Perth from bombing raids. Plans were made to evacuate the most vulnerable communities living in coastal suburbs and health inspectors were given the task of finding rooms for 2,500 people in the safer areas of inland suburbs.

Throughout the community, volunteers, many of them women, were trained as ARP (Air Raid Personnel) wardens to help the public and guide them to shelters during the threat of air raids. Rescue plans were put in place and first aid kits were made widely available.

Owners of private buildings were required by law to provide suitable shelter for employees at their own cost. The responsibility to provide public air raid shelters fell with local government authorities. By April 1942 the city council had built 532 trenches to accommodate nearly 11,000 people. These included 47 Pyramid shelters, accommodating around 1,400; 30 Breastwork V's (usually an earth bank built to breast height to provide protection to defenders firing over it) to accommodate 600; and eight shop front shelters for 550 people. Accommodation for another 500 people in two basements was also completed and three more planned.

Not everything went to plan, however, and the management of Chas. Moore and Co. were taken to task for building an anti-bomb blast bund outside their department store on Murray Street without council permission. The council threatened to remove the bund and the firm responded saying, "As we erected the bund with the earnest belief that it would be approved by the council provided the necessary regulations were passed indemnifying the council against all claims for personal injury to the public, we feel that the council committee should be prepared to discuss the matter with us instead of resorting to such precipitate action."

The following day a large poster appeared outside the entrances to the shop, reading "The anti-blast protection, built for your protection on Murray Street footpath, will be pulled down after 6 o'clock tonight by the Perth City Council as there are no regulations permitting its erection. This will greatly reduce the safety of our air raid shelter!"

Blackout restrictions were in force in the city from the end of 1941 until October 1943. These made a huge impact on the community and reminded them that war was a real and imminent threat. Streetlights were subdued with black paint, shops were forbidden to illuminate their window displays and the clock face of Perth Town Hall was only dimly lit.

At the end of the war, shelters were slowly removed, trenches filled and life in Perth returned to normal.

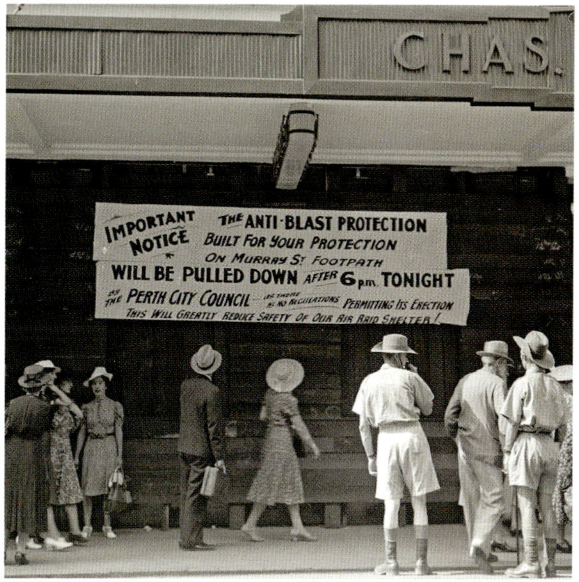

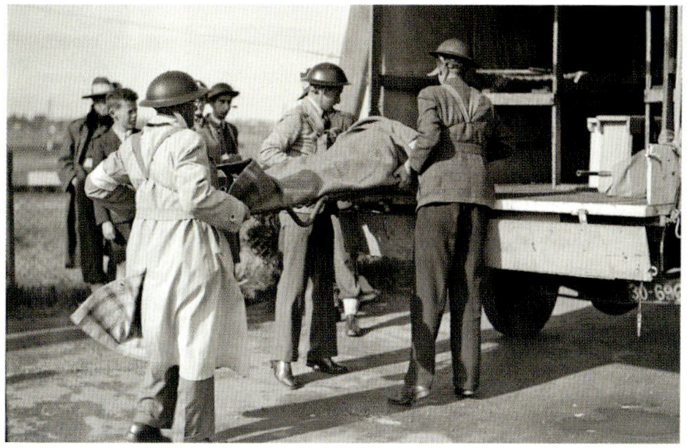

ABOVE An air raid precautions demonstration at the Ozone Hotel in July 1943.

ABOVE RIGHT A controversial air raid shelter provided for the public by Charles Moore & Co. in Murray Street, which was subject to a City of Perth removal notice in February 1942.

RIGHT The sand-bagged entrance to Australian Mutual Provident Society building in April 1942.

OPPOSITE People running towards a William Street air raid shelter during an ARP exercise in March 1942.

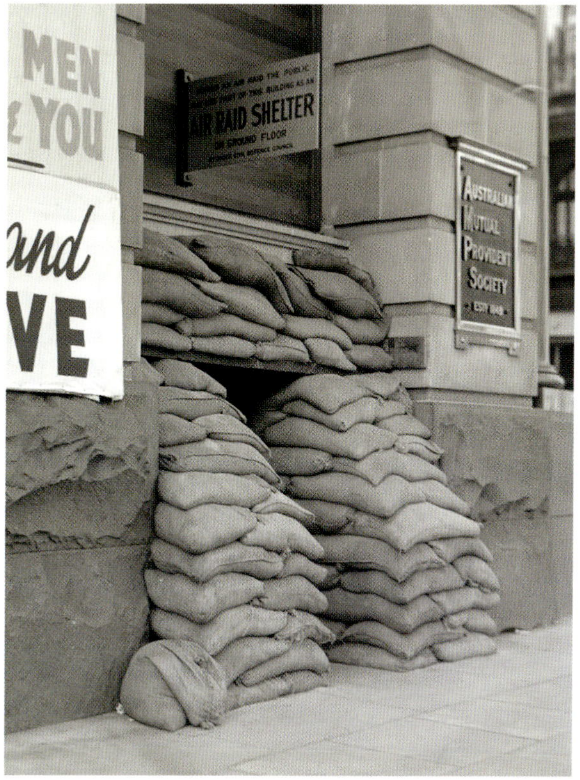

MARKET GARDENS

DISAPPEARED 1950s

The first settlers arriving in 1829 had travelled under the misapprehension they were coming to a land of milk and honey with plenty of fertile land at their disposal. They quickly discovered that promises of a river with a fertile flood plain were completely untrue. This had been the prediction of Charles Frazer, the New South Wales Colonial Botanist who accompanied James Stirling on his exploration of the Swan River in 1827. In the words of English author Anthony Trollope, who visited Perth in 1872, the soil was "eminently suitable for hour glasses".

Eliza Shaw, who arrived with her family in February 1830, wrote in her diary: "...out of 1,800 souls now come to this Colony in hopes of living, or at least of not being starved to death, there are not a dozen who know what to do or where they are to go. The people here look actually horror-struck one at another in absolute despair ...There are some who have been here nine months and have sown different seeds at different times, but they have all invariably died away and there is not one who has been able to raise either potatoes, cabbage or any other vegetable. That man who reported this land to be good deserves hanging nine times over ...Each side of the river is nothing more or less than sand – white sand – incapable of being made to produce anything for the sustenance of man!"

There were a few fertile areas, however, mainly along the riverbanks at the foot of Mount Eliza and to the north of the city around the lakes and swamps. By 1834 around 40 hectares had been planted with potatoes and other vegetables and an illustration from 1842 shows the land between the river and Mount Eliza, along what we now know as Mounts Bay Road, was a garden planted with vegetables and fruit trees.

With a large growth in the population of Perth between 1850 and the mid-1880s, a significant increase in food production was required, resulting in a proliferation of market gardeners in all available fertile areas of the town and its outskirts. During that period records show the number of families involved in market gardening increased from 63 to 97.

While many continued to take advantage of the good soil along the Swan River, substantial growth in the number of market gardens was only possible by draining some of the swampland to the north of the town, and gardens began to appear on the banks of Lake Kingsford in Roe Street and around Lake Henderson, where Palmerston Street now runs.

Many Chinese migrating to Australia in the 1800s came from rural backgrounds and brought with them agriculture and water management skills well adapted to the climate of Perth. From 1900 onwards the Chinese market gardeners were the principal fruit and vegetable producers in the Perth area. Up to the 1950s the Chinese gardeners were familiar figures around Perth, with their carts laden with fresh fruit and vegetables as they walked their regular delivery rounds. The introduction of artificial fertilizers and reliable irrigation systems enabled areas of poorer soil outside the city to be turned into land suitable for horticulture. This brought about the decline and the ultimate demise of city-centre market gardening.

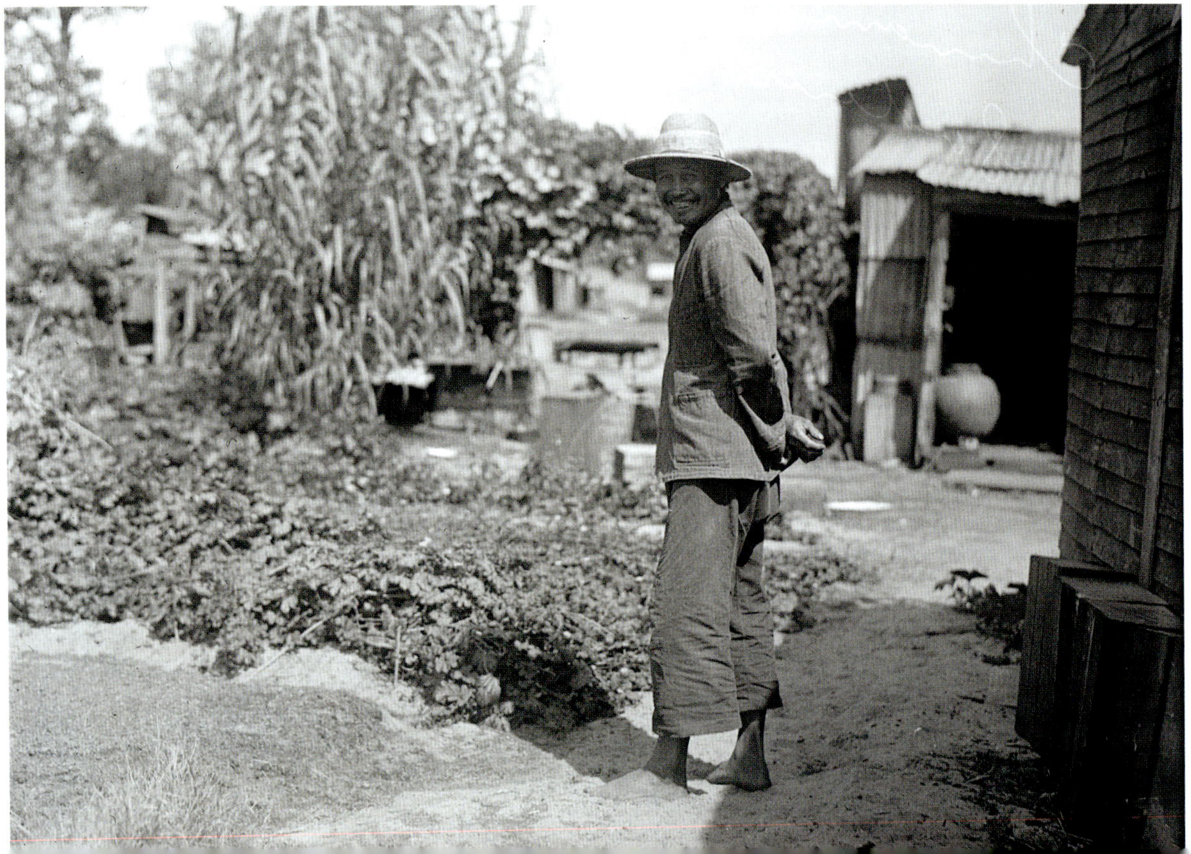

RIGHT The market gardens along the side of Mounts Bay Road, as viewed from Kings Park in about 1905.

LEFT A Chinese market gardener in his garden in 1928.

BELOW Looking over the market gardens towards the Narrows in 1900.

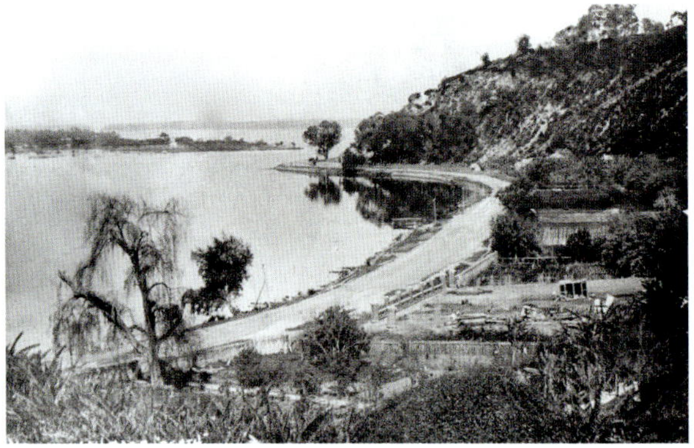

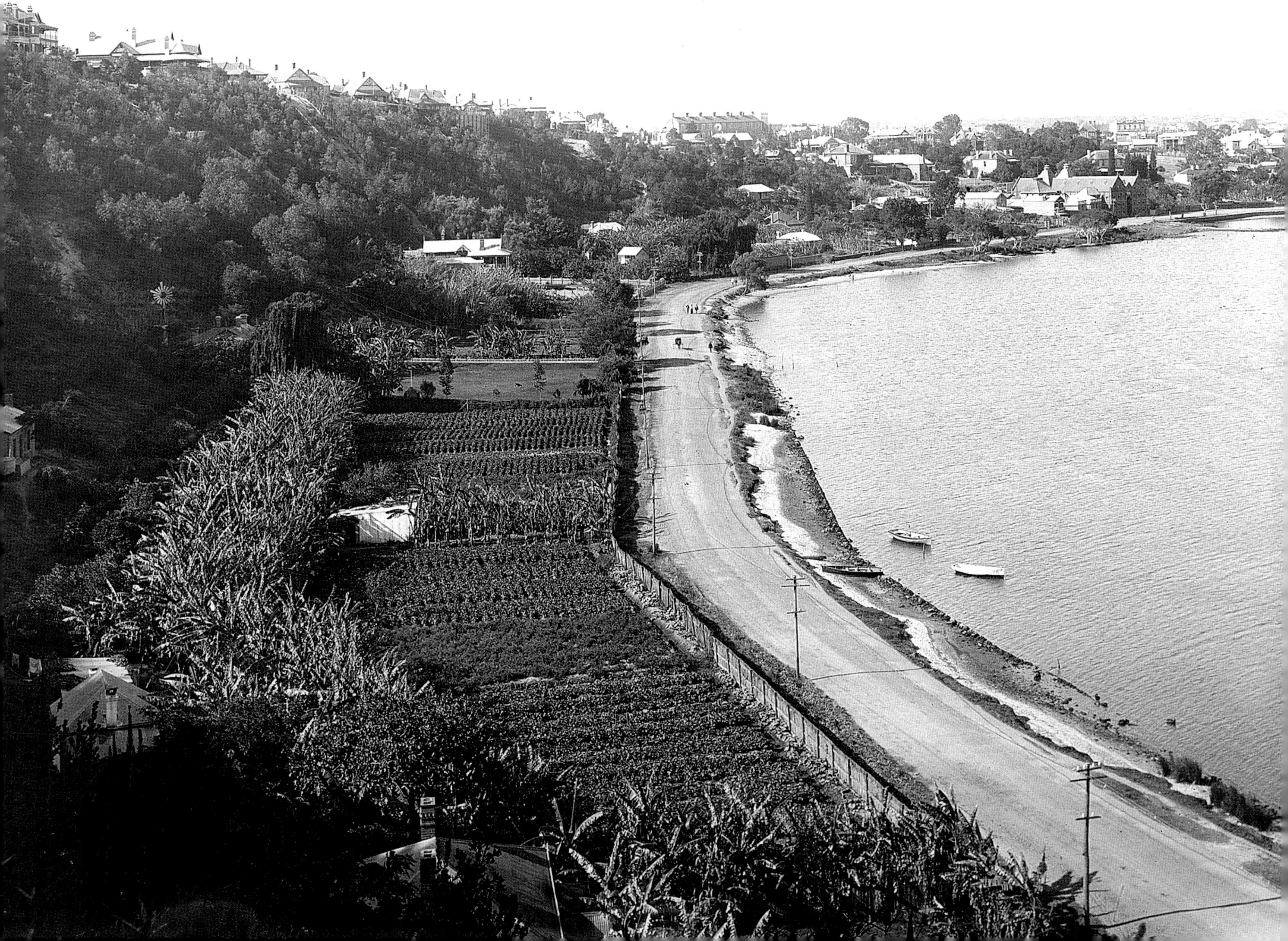

CAUSEWAY BRIDGE

FIRST REPLACED 1864; SECOND REPLACED 1952

When the first British settlers arrived in 1829, the land that we now know as Heirisson Island was a series of mudflats usually covered by shallow water. The Nyoongar name for the area, Matagarup, meaning "one leg deep", indicates why the area was a serious impediment to river navigation. With only flat-bottomed boats being able to get across to deeper water upstream, cargo would often have to be hauled across the mudflats by manual labour.

This navigational difficulty meant that land routes between Fremantle, Perth and Guildford were an obvious alternative, but with Perth having been settled on the north bank of the river rather than the south, a suitable crossing was required.

Not surprisingly, bridging the flats was an early priority, but lack of finance prevented a bridge being built until the 1840s. At a meeting of the Roads Board Trust in February 1839, a motion was passed for the erection of a bridge and causeway, which "would materially benefit the settlers throughout the Colony."

A design was prepared by the first Surveyor General of Western Australia, John Septimus Roe, and modified by Superintendent of Works, Henry Trigg, with tenders called in February 1840. The construction of the bridge, which consisted of two timber spans and associated roadway, took over three years and several contracts to complete. When it opened on 24 May 1843, it was the first time in the colony's history that a road connection had been established between Perth, Guildford, the Upper Swan Valley, York and Fremantle.

A toll was charged for almost everyone who crossed, including pedestrians, each head of stock and vehicles. Only officers and soldiers "in proper uniform", their horses, and mail carriers were exempt. At the time of opening, the *Perth Gazette* reported: "this communication with the interior presents one of the best public works constructed throughout the Colony."

By the early 1860s the bridge was reported to be in "a moribund state". Weakened by heavy use, it was almost completely submerged by winter floods in 1862. It was often bumped by heavily laden boats and accidents involving horses and carts were common, as were delays on the bridge. One example involved a Mr Loftie who was fined 40 shillings for causing an obstruction on the causeway. The herd of cattle he was driving took fright and wedged themselves between the railings of the bridge, taking over an hour to extricate them.

To address these problems, a new bridge was designed and supervised by Richard Roach Jewell, Superintendent of Public Works, and built by convict labour. The new bridge followed the same alignment as the old, but was raised by a metre and a third span was added.

Both bridges were constructed of jarrah and, for economy, a substantial amount of timber from the original bridge was reused. When the piles of the old bridge were drawn, they were found to be in extremely good condition and Jewell reported they "were as sound as when first used, upwards of 25 to 30 years; showing the superiority of the Swan Jarrah for engineering purposes of this kind over other known timber."

The new bridge opened for traffic in August 1865 and was officially opened by Governor Hampton on 12 November 1867. Whilst a great improvement on its predecessor, the new bridge was quite weak, uneven and narrow and had to be widened, altered and repaired many times during its life.

By the mid-1930s, the bridge was in poor condition, below standard for load-bearing capacity and often congested with traffic. War delayed the construction of a new bridge, but in 1949 work began on building a two-bridge, composite steel and concrete structure. The second bridge was torn down and the current bridge opened to traffic on 19 September 1952.

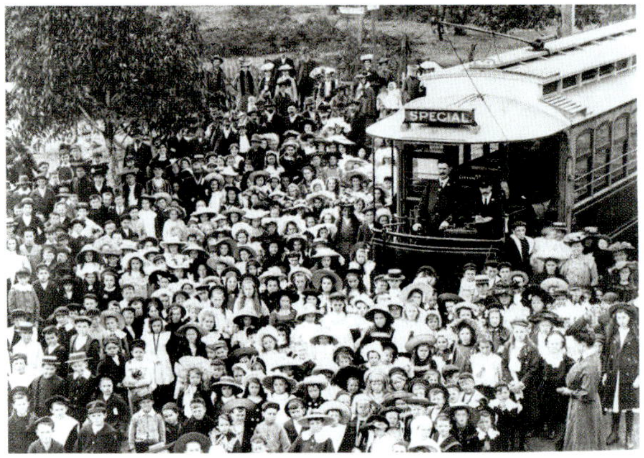

RIGHT The second Causeway Bridge, photographed by Alfred Stone soon after it was completed in August 1865.

BELOW The first Causeway Bridge in about 1860. Bumped by boats and over-laden by road transport, it was in a poor state of repair.

BOTTOM The causeway in the late 1920s, by which time it had been widened to accommodate tram tracks.

BOTTOM LEFT Children gather around a causeway tram to celebrate its inaugural crossing in 1905.

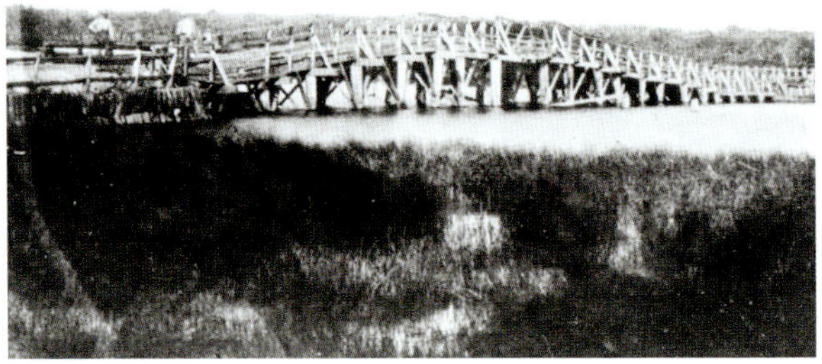

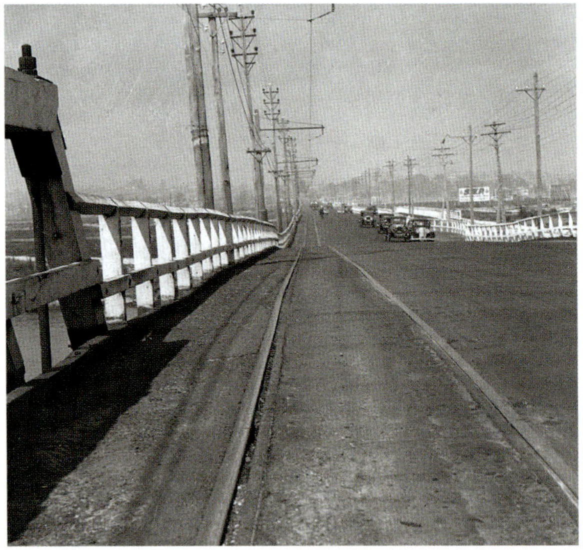

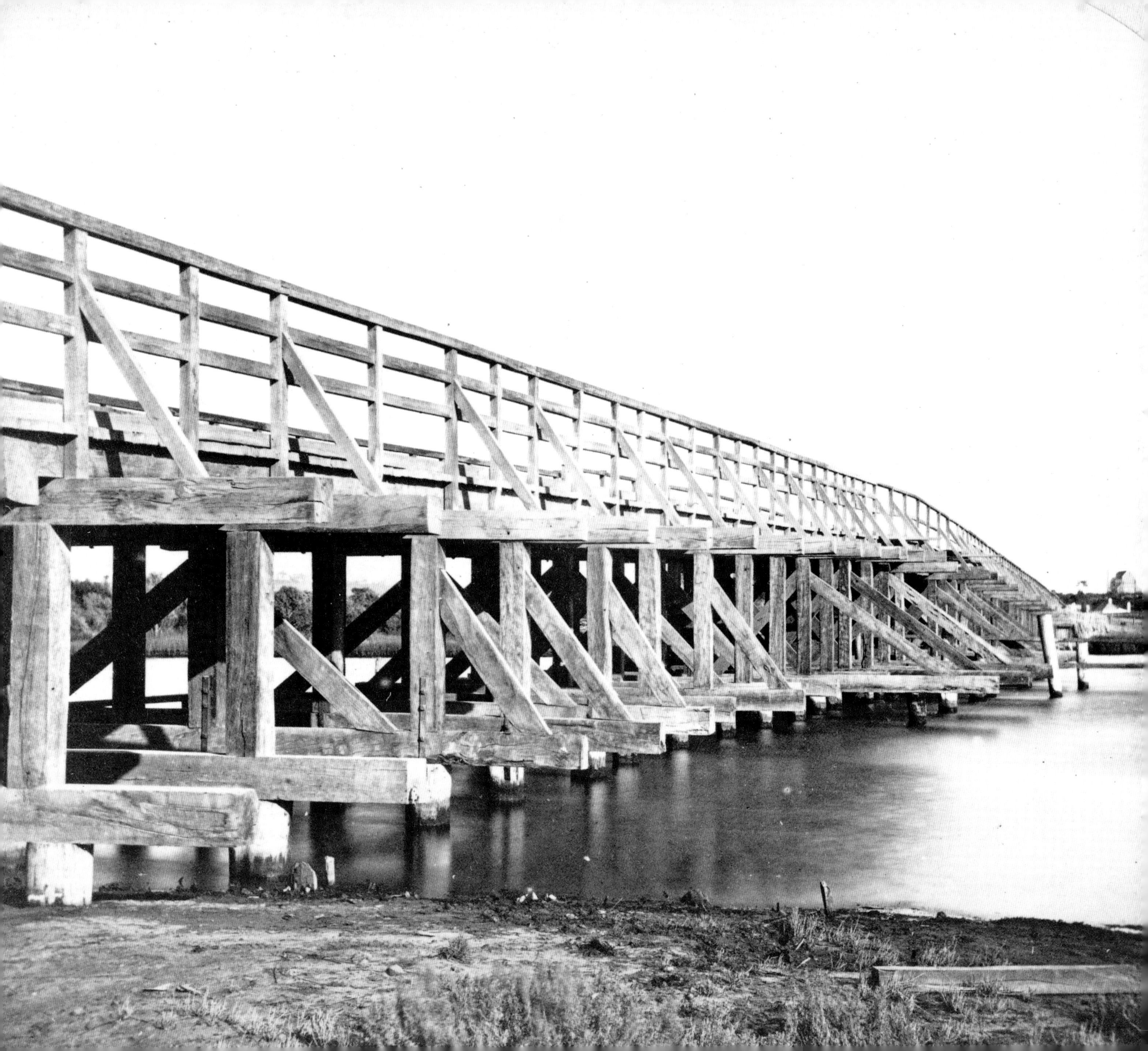

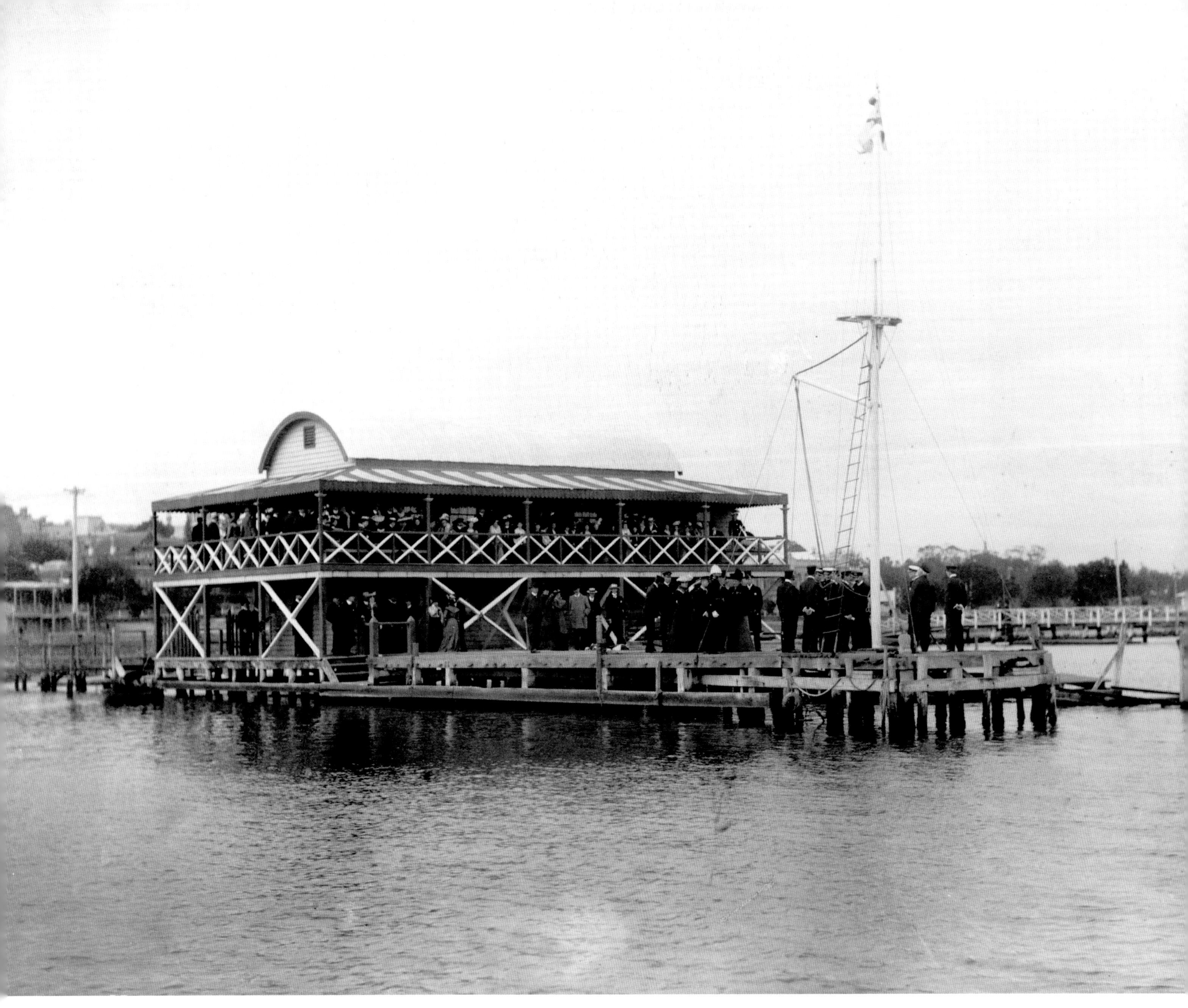

ROYAL PERTH YACHT CLUB

DEMOLISHED 1953

The first recorded sailing race in the Swan River Colony took place in June 1841, when a group of sailors staged a modest regatta to celebrate Foundation Day. However, it was not a roaring success as a report in the *Inquirer* newspaper of 9 June 1841 demonstrates: "In consequence of the unfavourable state of the weather on the 2nd, there was no sailing match that day; on the 3rd, however, two boats started for the second prize – one belonging to Jones and the other to Tuckey, and a very beautiful race ensued, won at last by Mr. Jones. The prize for large boats was awarded to Gibbs, who sailed the requisite distance without any competitor."

Foundation Day regattas included yacht races and gig rowing races, plus duck hunts, which were very popular with the public. Apart from this there seem to be few references in the papers to sailing, the manly sport of rowing being more to everyone's taste. However, a newspaper advert in May 1851 publicised four races, which were to take place the following month, one of which was for sailing boats. The race was a bit of a flop owing to a distinct lack of breeze (not a common complaint in Perth).

In the early 1860s a group of Swan River sailing enthusiasts decided to resurrect the regattas and each year formed a committee to run them. It was these sailors who formed the nucleus of a group which in 1865 became Perth Yacht Club.

In 1873 plans were made for the construction of a boathouse and moorings. These plans also included provision of a clubroom and quarters for a boat-keeper. As was so often the case during this period, lack of funds was the retarding influence and nothing got built.

By the late 1870s, the fortunes of the club were beginning to improve and in 1880 a jetty was built at the club's original location at the foot of William Street. Even then, the club had to take out an overdraft with the Western Australian Bank for 15 months on the security of the committee. This was followed by a clubhouse, which opened in 1889 and was described as a building that would "comfortably accommodate on its balconies 300 people and will serve all the purposes of a 'flag ship' on regatta days."

In 1890, on the recommendation of Governor Sir Frederic Broome, the club received the title and prefix of "Royal" from Queen Victoria. At the same time it was announced that the Lords of the Admiralty had granted the club the Royal Warrant to fly an undefaced Blue Ensign. As a result, a general meeting in 1891 unanimously decided to dispense with the old Perth Yacht Club burgee and adopt a new one forthwith. The design chosen was a white burgee – a triangular flag bearing a red St George's Cross and emblazoned with a St Edward's crown in the upper canton.

By 1938 plans were beginning to be formulated to move the club to a better location, as Perth Water was shallow and the accommodation cramped. The move was not popular with members who enjoyed popping down to the clubhouse from the city at lunchtime for a swift drink. However, the plan went ahead. The clubhouse was demolished and the club moved to its present site on Matilda Bay in 1953.

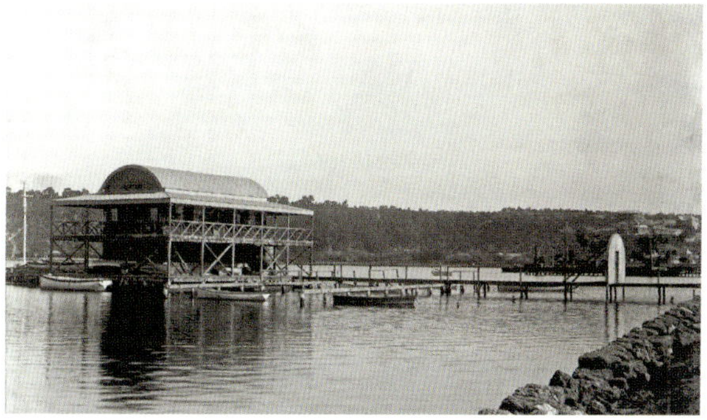

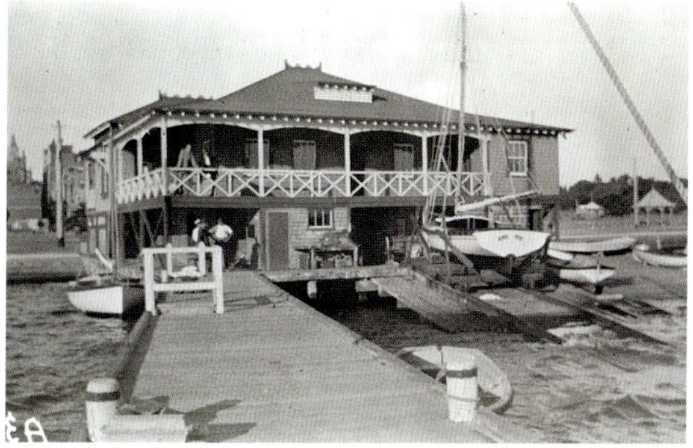

OPPOSITE A large crowd watches as the Governor, Admiral Sir Frederick Bedford, officially unfurls the new ensign for the first time in 1890.

BELOW Yacht *Wattle* coming alongside at Royal Perth Yacht Club in 1926.

BELOW LEFT The original clubhouse at the bottom of William Street, soon after it opened in 1889.

BOTTOM LEFT Taken in about 1922, after the clubhouse had been extended to enable the club to form the Western Australian branch of the Royal Australian Naval Volunteer Reserve.

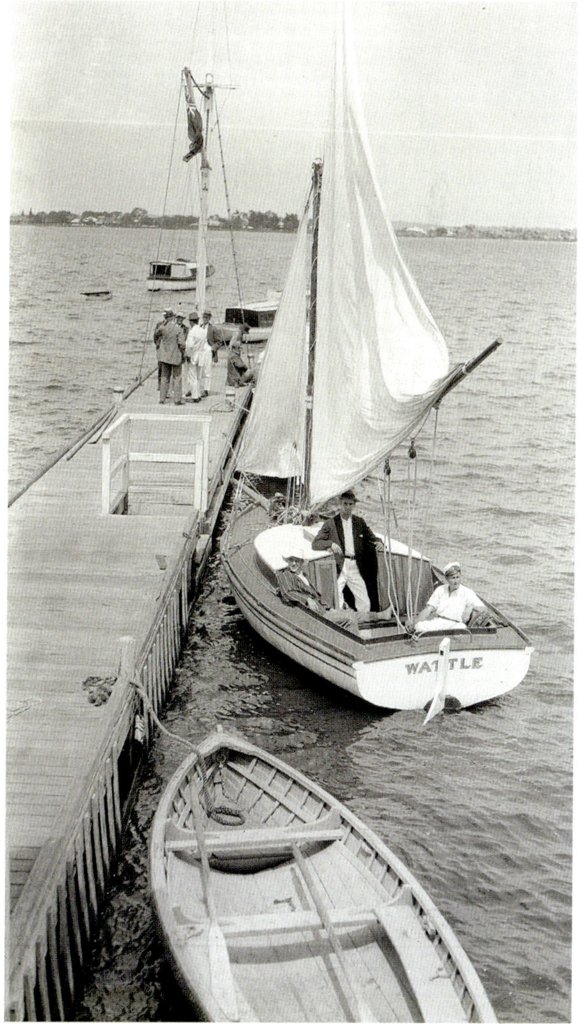

NICHOLSON'S MUSIC SHOP

CLOSED 1956

We have become so used to widescreen high-definition television with surround sound, and being able to access any style of music at the click of a button, that it is hard to remember our forebears did not have this luxury. For many families in Perth before the advent of radio and television, "home entertainment" meant granny playing familiar tunes on the piano and everyone gathering round to join in with the words. Consequently, music shops were an important commodity on every high street.

In Perth one of the largest retailers of music, musical instruments and, later, gramophone records was Nicholson & Co. Limited on Barrack Street. This firm was also one of the bridges between homemade and broadcast entertainment when it founded Perth radio station 6PR in 1931.

The firm was founded in Sydney in 1873 by James Nicholson, the son of an English organ builder whose factory in Malvern is still building church and concert organs for venues around the world. Nicholson had immigrated to Australia at the age of 22 in 1859 and got a job in the Melbourne music warehouse of Joseph Wilkie. In 1873 he joined Elmas Ascherberg to establish a music house named Nicholson & Ascherberg in Collins Street; a partnership which did well until Ascherberg returned to England for health reasons in 1879.

In 1878 the firm relocated to a fine six-storey building in Collins Street and created one of the biggest and best-known music houses in Australia. By 1880 every major city in the country, with the exception of Adelaide and Darwin, had a Nicholson store. The Perth branch, on the corner Barrack and Murray Street, opened in May 1894, offering a comprehensive range of instruments, sheet music, facilities for musical tuition and an early recording studio. The opening of the store brought about the following comment in the *W.A. Record*: "Perth has already received the name of the musical Mecca of Australia and the presence of a branch of such a leading musical firm as the above must assist to maintain its reputation as a music loving community."

Radio station 6PR was the third station to be opened in Perth and commenced broadcasting on 14 October 1931. Founded by Nicholson & Co. Limited, the station operated out of a studio at the Barrack Street music showroom. The station broadcast from 10:30 a.m. to 10:30 p.m. and provided a wide range of programmes, including a morning "women's session", "matters of general interest interspersed with music", local and interstate news reports and children's programmes for half an hour at 6:30 p.m. From those small beginnings, the station went on to be one of Perth's best-known talk-back radio stations, which now operates out of studios in East Perth.

When James Nicholson died in 1907, the business was passed down to his son. It remained a family concern until 1939, when it was sold to Allan's Music, who continued to trade under the Nicholson name. The Perth branch eventually closed its doors for the last time in 1956.

RIGHT The very elegant store interior in about 1932.

LEFT The exterior of Nicholson's Barrack Street store in about 1932. By this time radio station 6PR was operating from the premises.

FAR LEFT A Nicholson's window display advertising Maurice Chevalier's first talking film *Innocents in Paris* in 1930.

BELOW A display of Victor phono-radios in about 1932.

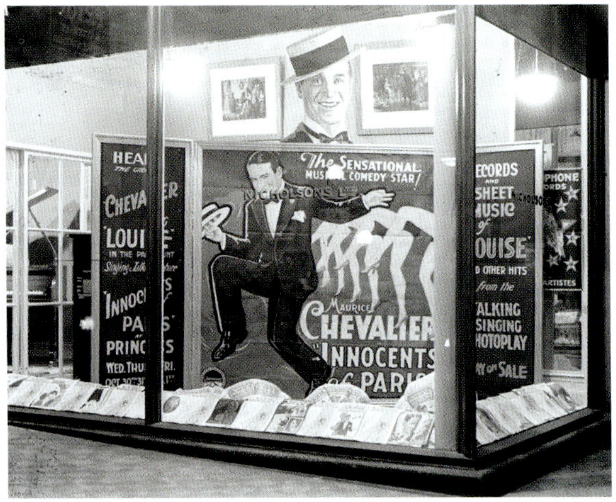

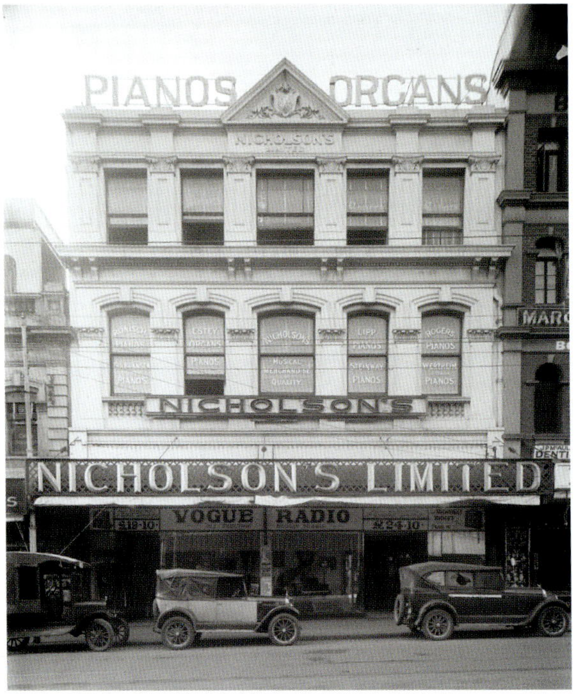

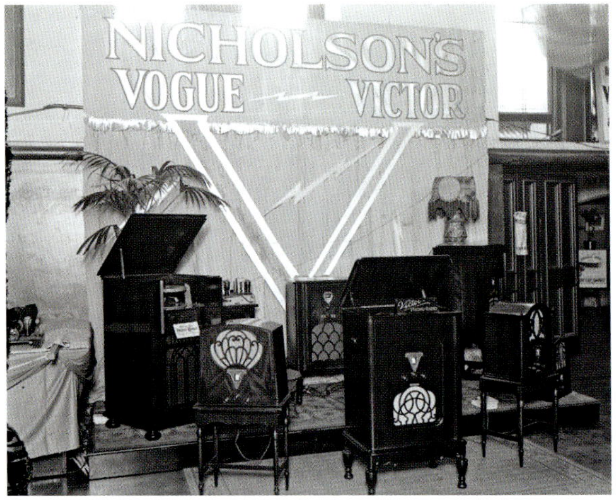

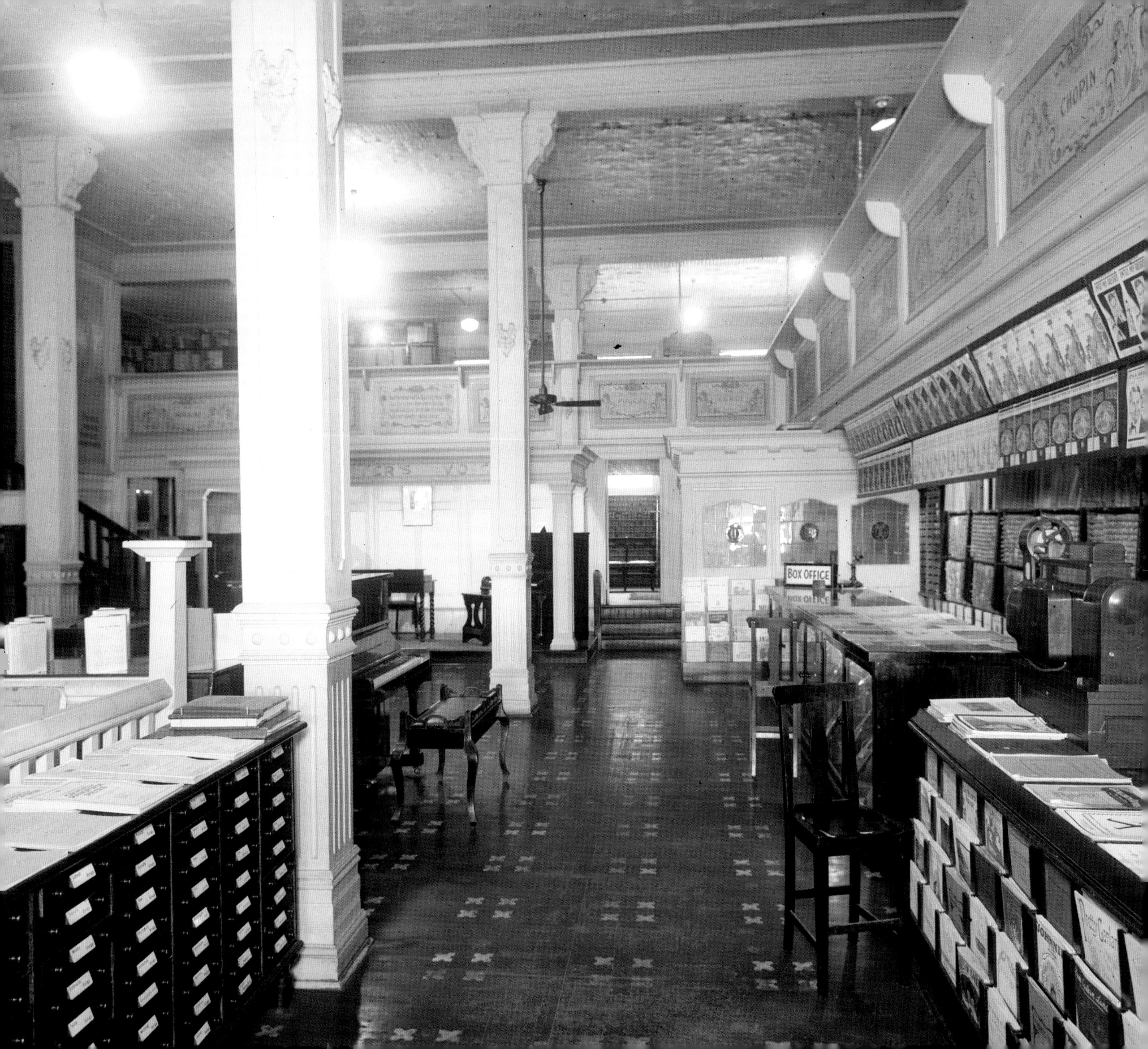
CHOPIN
BOX OFFICE

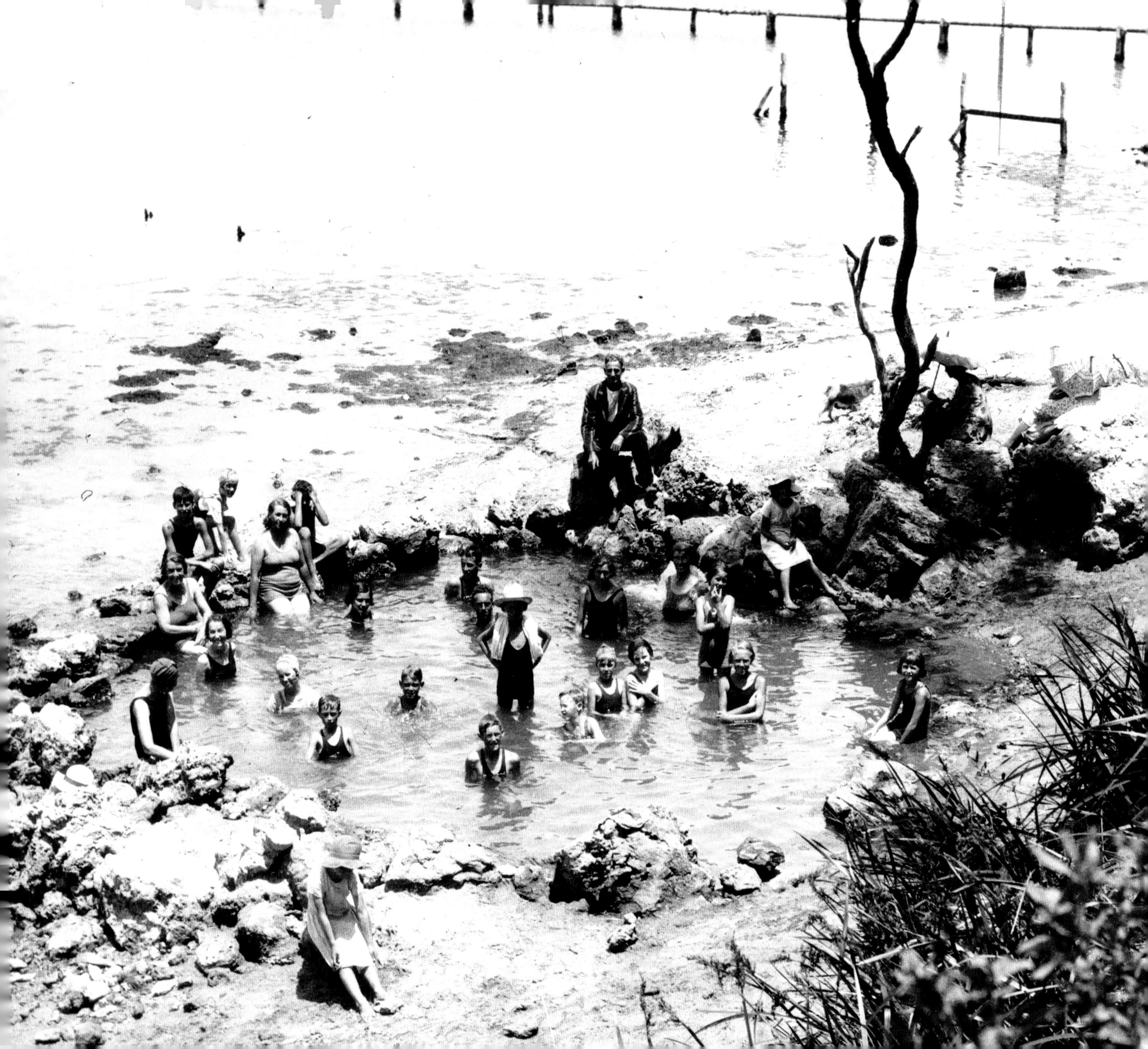

DALKEITH HOT POOL

FILLED IN 1957

The Dalkeith Hot Pool started its life as a hole that filled with hot water from a burst artesian bore on the river foreshore. The bore was discovered in the 1920s by a builder looking for water to supplement the supply for Sunset Hospital on the hill above. The bore went down 1,365 feet and the pressurised hot water it contained flowed up without assistance to a cooling tank near the hospital.

A problem developed when the tank became full and a cut-off valve caused back pressure, cracking the pipe. The water that escaped formed a large pool on the foreshore, which was promptly named the "Hot Pool" and rapidly became popular with campers, yachters and youngsters.

The pool soon started to be known as a spa, but analysis showed that besides traces of salt the water had no therapeutic qualities. Despite these findings, the pool was heavily used and it wasn't long before it gained a notorious reputation, thanks to the journalistic talents of the *Perth Mirror*. Published weekly from 1921 until 1956, the paper used scandal and titillation to increase sales.

With headlines like "High Jinks at the Hot Pool", the *Mirror* would cover the not infrequent court cases involving the pool. On 7 December 1935, the *Mirror* wrote under the title "Nudity at Dalkeith", "In the early hours of this morning the police descended on the hot pool at Dalkeith and there discovered two young men bathing in the nude. Also present were two girl companions, who wore only one minute garment each. The quartet was charged in the Perth Police Court this morning, when one of the men was fined £5 and the other £4. On one of the males also a further penalty of £2 was imposed for tendering a false name. The girls were fined £1 each." By 1938 the *Mirror* described the pool as being "notorious for its attraction to nudists and rarely is this secluded haven without its birthday-suitors at night and in the early hours of the morning."

During World War II the pool reached the peak of its activity, probably because the military were using the area for PT instruction, which would have introduced servicemen and women to the night-time possibilities of the pool. By October 1945 the military authorities had decided that enough was enough and were threatening to fill the hot pool in. Negotiations were entered between the Nedlands Road Board and the State Gardens Board for permission to control the reserve that included the pool. The negotiations were clearly successful, as newspapers in 1946 reported that a new hot pool large enough for swimming was to be constructed.

In the winter of 1950 the surrounding area was landscaped and repairs made to the changing sheds, while in November 1952 60 new Jehovah Witnesses were baptised in the pool.

Even with the improvements, there were still complaints of men swimming in their underpants and the pool finally closed in 1957 when an application to use water from the bore for swimming purposes had been refused by the State Government.

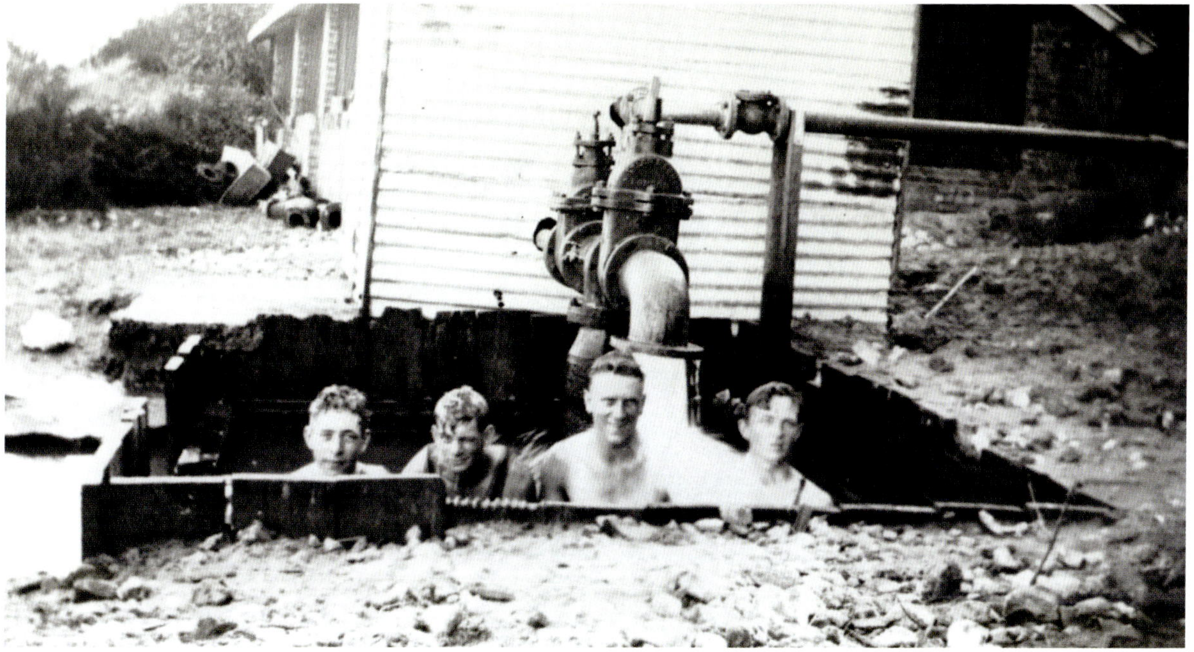

OPPOSITE Appropriately clad bathers enjoy the Hot Pool in the summer of 1935.

LEFT Four men enjoying the original Hot Pool in the early 1920s.

BELOW A makeshift camp alongside the pool, known as Howson's Hangout, in the early 1920s.

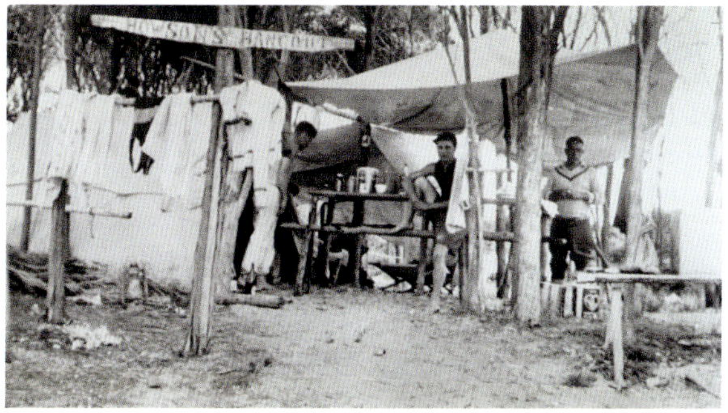

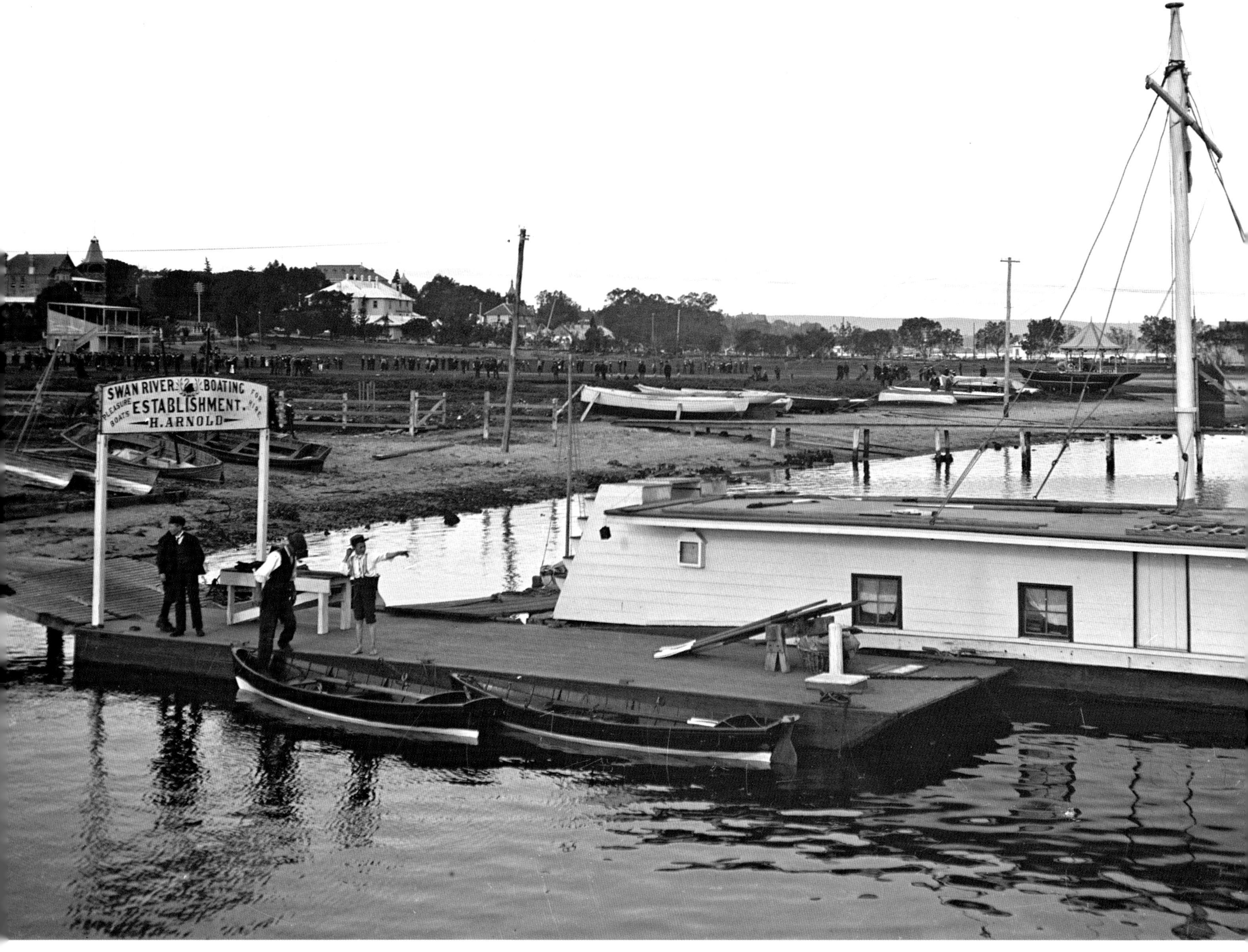
SWAN RIVER BOATING
PLEASURE BOATS
FOR HIRE
ESTABLISHMENT.
H. ARNOLD

WILLIAM STREET JETTY

DEMOLISHED c. 1958

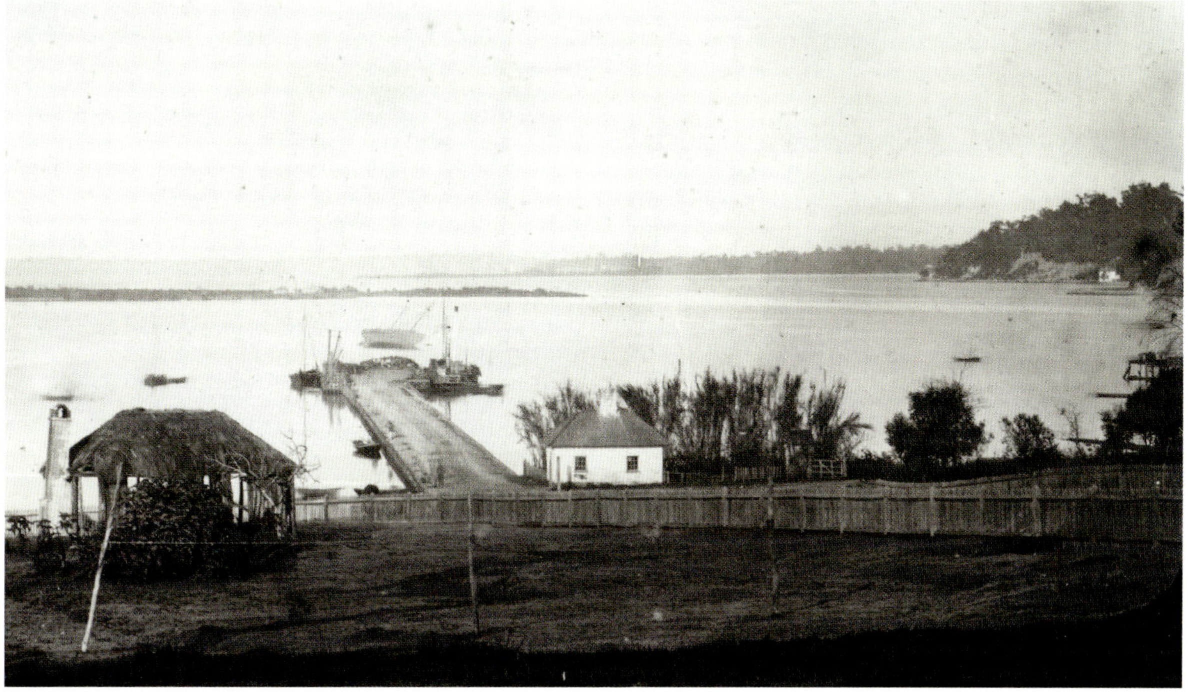

For the early settler, the Swan River was the equivalent of our modern-day freeways. As late as 1837, Governor James Stirling reported to the Secretary of State for Colonies, "At the present time it can scarcely be said that any roads exist, although certain lines of communication have been improved by clearing them of timber and by bridging streams and by establishing ferries in the broader parts of the Swan River."

The first jetty on the Perth foreshore was at Pier Street, built soon after the founding of Perth in August 1829. In 1858 Pier Street was closed off from the river by the construction of the new Government House and the Pier Street Jetty became a private jetty for the Governor's use.

The southern end of Barrack Street was the second location for a jetty and by 1845 it had been joined by jetties at William and Mill Street. Barrack Street Jetty was extended to take over the general cargo function previously using Pier Street Jetty, but slowly Barrack Street Jetty became the domain of the ferry operators and William Street Jetty handled most of the cargo coming up river from Fremantle and down from the agricultural area around Guildford. Mill Street Jetty became the centre of boat building, of which there is a long history on the river.

William Street Jetty was clearly a busy one, as the State Library contains a document from the mid-1850s setting out its management regulations. However, after the Fremantle to Guildford railway line opened in 1881, river use between the major towns reduced dramatically. By the following year there was only one licensed ferry on the river.

As commercial use declined, the river became popular as a place of recreation and the jetty was used by many private craft. These users, however, did not pay the same tolls and fees as the traders, which meant there was little money available for repairs. In 1888 a letter to one of the local papers complained that William Street Jetty was in a dangerous state, and that several holes almost large enough for someone to fall through had appeared in the planking.

The large increase in the population of Perth, brought about by the first Gold Rush in the 1890s, was a boon to river transport and business began to flourish again. Ferry services to Mends Street and Coode Street on the south bank were established in 1897 and William Street Jetty not only handled more cargo, but also began to be used by the pleasure cruisers going to Garden and Rottnest Islands.

By the early 20th century, the increased river traffic and the berthing of growing numbers of large steamboats necessitated better wharf facilities on Perth's foreshore and the existing jetties, including William Street, were repaired and some widened.

After World War II, cargo transport on the river diminished and the jetty was reported to be in a poor state of repair. It was eventually removed to allow for the widening of Riverside Drive and the creation of an intersection with the new freeway in about 1958.

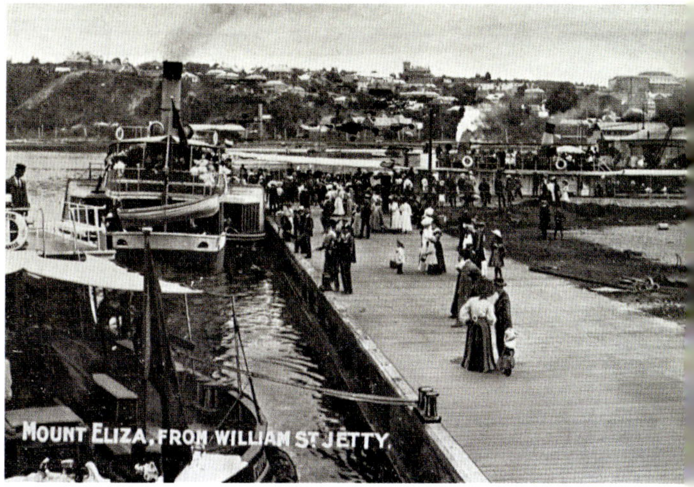

OPPOSITE A 1900 photograph of Henry Arnold's boat hire business, which he ran from William Street Jetty until it was sold in 1902.

TOP William Street Jetty as photographed by Alfred Stone in 1861.

ABOVE A busy William Street Jetty in 1907.

TRAMS

LEFT THE RAILS 1958

In September 1885 the Legislative Council passed a new Tramways Act. This enabled municipal councils to create a new public transport system, on the condition that it did not "cause any impediment to the ordinary street traffic and that the public shall at all times be entitled to the free and uninterrupted use of every part of the streets which these tramways may traverse."

The legislation had been brought about by a group of Perth businessmen who wanted to construct a tramway but discovered that the local council had no authority to alter streets and roadways in any manner.

Like many grand schemes in Perth during the 19th century, there was a long delay between the passing of the legislation and the start of any works. Proposals came and went, but none ever got under way. The growth of Perth during the first Gold Rush, however, gave rise to a great many new suburbs for Perth. Those not near enough to the Fremantle to Guildford railway line to be of use to the residents needed connections with other suburbs. This led to renewed calls for a better integrated public transport system.

Eventually, the call was answered by Charles Dickinson, who in 1897 put forward a proposal to Perth City Council to build an electric tramway in the centre of Perth. Agreement was given to this scheme and negotiations started to sort out the fine detail of the plan. While this project faltered for lack of capital, the city council used Dickinson's plans for a tram system centred on Perth and radiating out into the suburbs of the city. To fund the project, the city invited the newly formed Perth Electric Tramways Limited to build a tram system. The company had been registered in London in February 1898 and involved a number of people experienced in running similar ventures in England.

The first line was planned to be from a car barn in East Perth, 4.8 kilometres along Hay Street to its junction with Thomas Street in the west, with a spur line along Colin Street to serve residences and give access to Kings Park. Track construction started in January 1899 and services officially started on 28 September that year.

The following day, the *West Australian* reported: "The principal event in the city yesterday was undoubtedly the opening of the Hay Street tram cars to traffic ... The comfort and convenience of the trams, coupled with the speed at which they travelled, formed an almost universal topic of conversation amongst the passengers."

Over the next few years, the system grew to meet the demands of growing communities outside the city. Many of the lines were lengthened a few hundred metres at a time to service newly developed areas. Some of these extensions were paid for by property developers who were keen to advertise their proximity to "frequent tram services to the city", which became a key selling point in suburbs such as Mount Lawley, Maylands, Nedlands and Osborne Park.

The system also catered for leisure activities and the ever-popular Perth Zoo could be reached either by the South Perth tram across the Causeway, or via Barrack Square to the ferry across the river. After several extensions, the tram along Mounts Bay Road serviced Crawley Baths and Matilda Bay, where many a Sunday afternoon picnic could be enjoyed.

Privately run tramways could be very profitable, but the capital for further expansion was often a problem. To create a more structured approach to public transport and ensure its growth, the state government decided to purchase the tram system and operations under government control began in July 1913.

The Great Depression of the 1930s had an adverse effect on every aspect of life in Perth and use of public transport was no exception. After three decades of steadily increasing patronage, there was a dramatic drop in the use of the tram system. This, combined

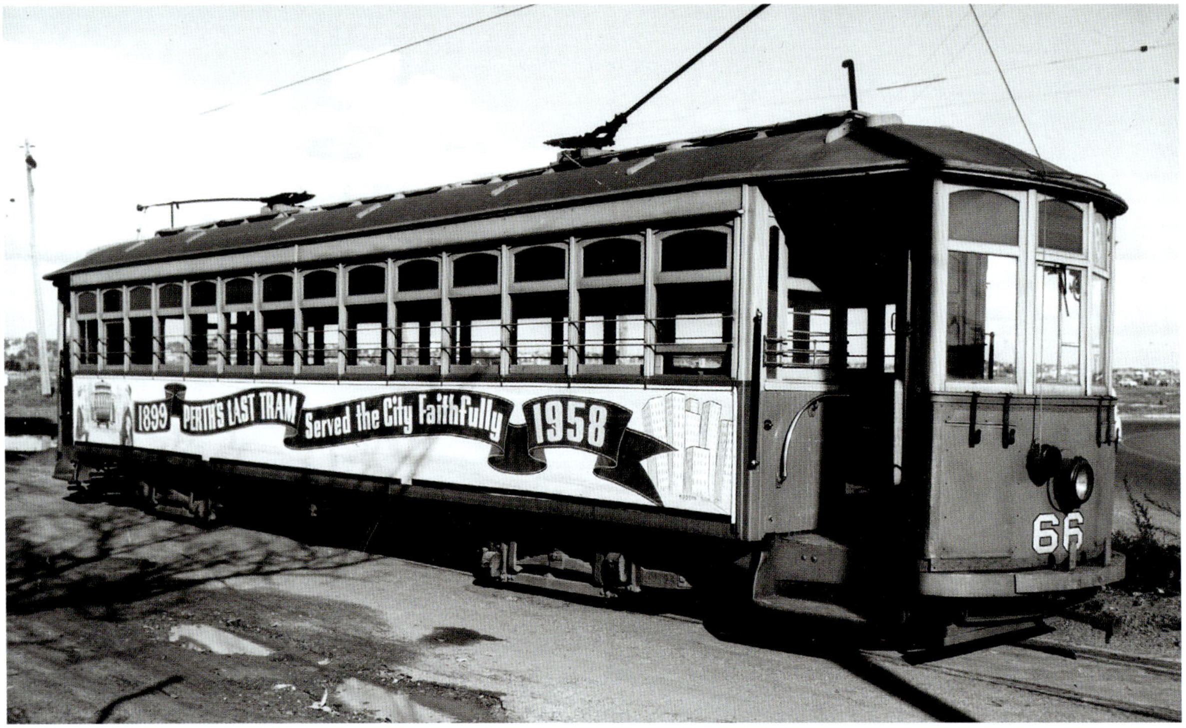

RIGHT The official opening of the William and Wellington Street service on 3 May 1902. E.E. Rogers, the tramway company manager, stands to the left of the driver.

LEFT Tram number 66, the last tramcar to run in Perth, July 1958.

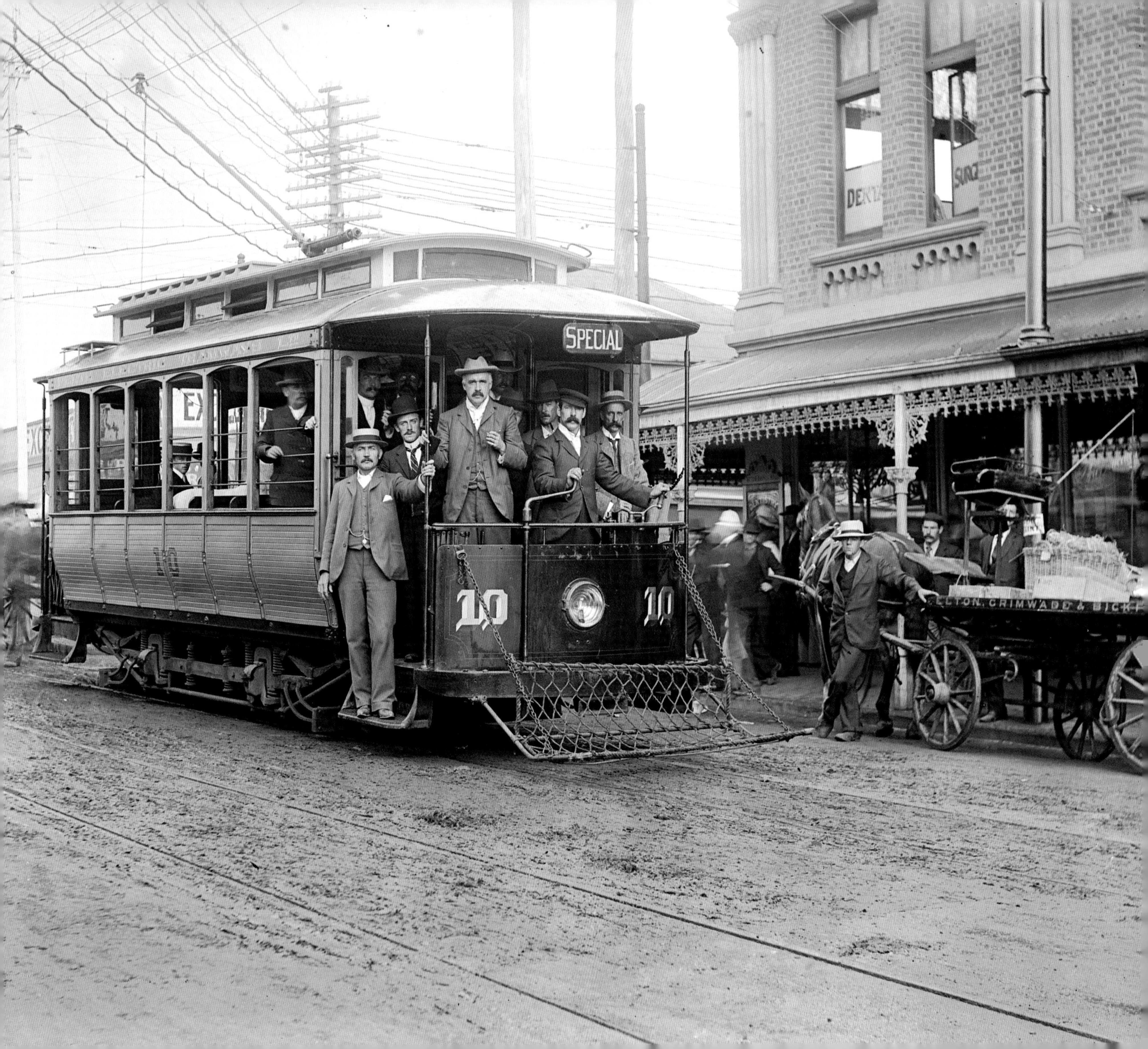
SPECIAL
10
10
10

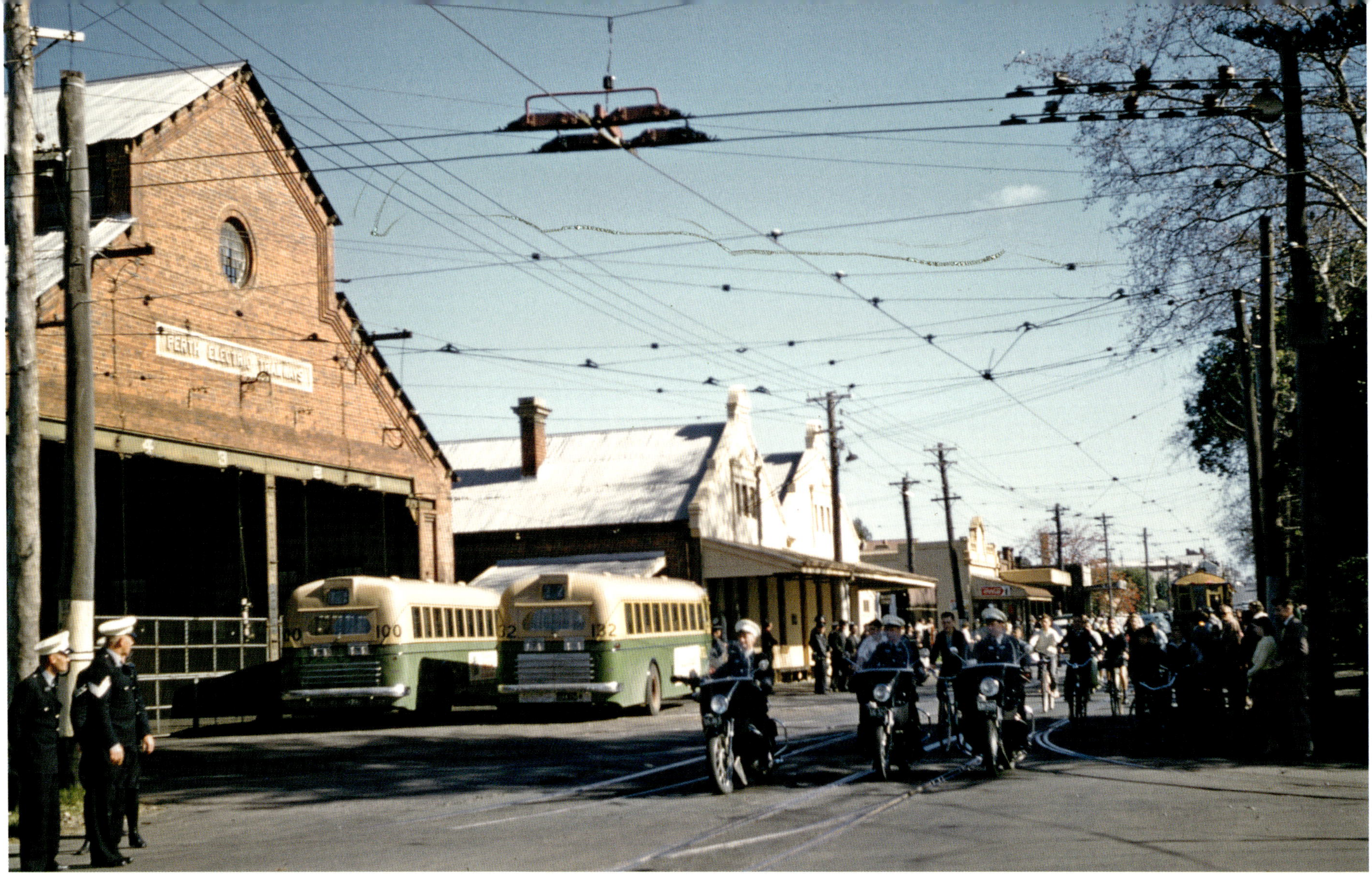

with a 1933 amendment to the Tramways Act, permitting trolley buses to use the tram routes, meant the writing was on the wall for Perth's trams.

After World War II, Perth, in common with many other parts of the world, considered its trams to be old-fashioned and their overhead wires unsightly. The system was also under-maintained, with much of its infrastructure in need of replacement. Increased ownership of private cars reduced the use of the trams, which were also considered a hazard by car drivers.

As a result, on 19 July 1958 Tram No. 66 ran down Route 18 for the very last time, accompanied by a Mounted Police escort. The following day the *Sunday Times* wrote: "End of the Line. After 115 million miles and 1,112 million passengers, Western Australia's trams yesterday went to their rest in a blaze of glory. WA has become the first Australian State to dispense entirely with trams." By this time the whole system had been superseded by buses and trolley buses.

ABOVE Tram No. 66 receives a police escort on its last trip back to the car barn in Hay Street, East Perth, on 19 July 1958.

RIGHT The tramways workshops in Hay Street, East Perth, in 1958. The car barn was to the right of this building, on the opposite side of Bay Street.

OPPOSITE A tram travels along Hay Street, just before the intersection with Kings Street in about 1955. Seen on the right-hand side is the Hotel Rex, which in 1951 had sold for a record £105,000.

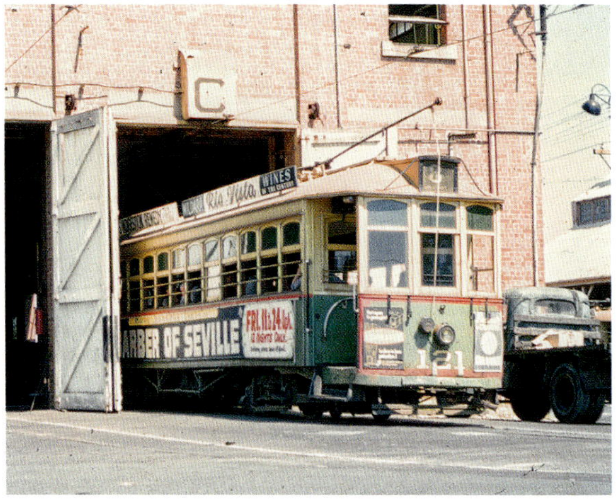

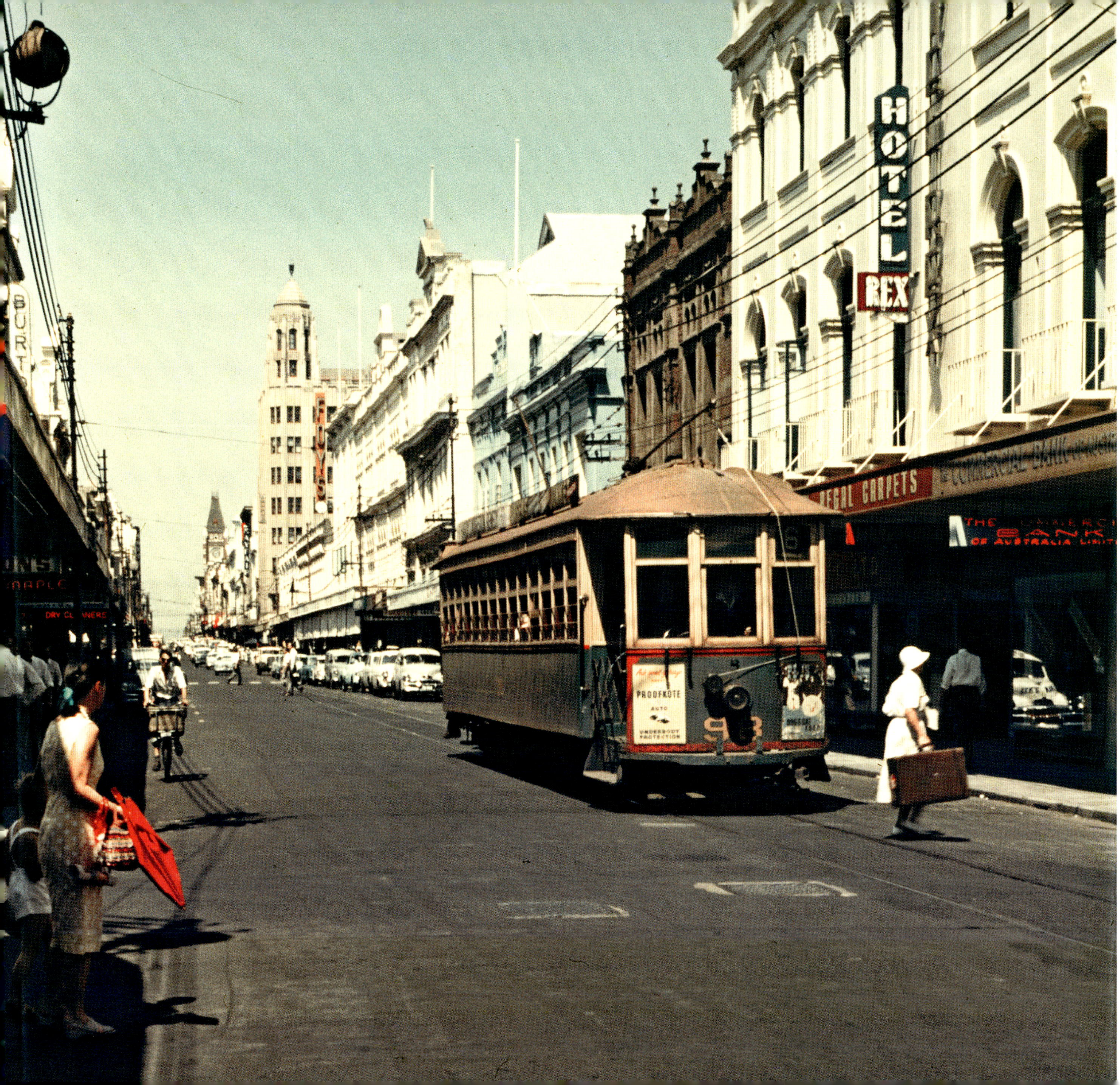
HOTEL
REX
REGAL CARPETS
PROOFKOTE
UNDERBODY PROTECTION
DRY CLEANERS

MOIR CHAMBERS (T&G CHAMBERS)

DEMOLISHED 1960

Strictly speaking there have been two losses on this site in the last 120 years. Prior to the construction of Moir Chambers (later T&G Chambers), the site was occupied by two buildings: the National Bank of Australasia and the United Service Tavern Hotel. In the early days of the Swan River Colony there was insufficient collateral to start a bank and it was not until 1837 that the Bank of Western Australia was founded. This was followed in 1841 by the National Bank of Australasia, which opened a branch on the corner of St Georges Terrace and Barrack Street, and ultimately caused the demise of the Bank of Western Australia.

The bank and the hotel survived until the site was purchased by Herbert Moir, a mining speculator from London who made a large amount of money in the first Western Australian Gold Rush. He contracted Sir Joseph John Talbot Hobbs to design and oversee construction of Moir Chambers, which was built for around £18,000 by Messrs Hewett and Wright and completed in 1897. The five-storey building also included a basement and a two-storey corner tower.

The building was roofed in American Vermont green slate, the base was of massive moulded Malmsbury bluestone and the front and side elevations were constructed in a cherry red Northcote brick imported from Melbourne. The windows and entrances on the ground floor were ornamented with clusters of polished red Aberdeen granite – all richly ornamented with elaborate cement dressings, decorative cornices and ornamental carvings made by Gallagher and Jose, a specialist building and sculpting company in Perth.

Moir Chambers quickly became one of the most popular buildings in the city and the Bank of New South Wales took immediate tenancy of the ground floor offices fronting St Georges Terrace, with the Agricultural Bank and Forestry Department leasing the entire first floor.

Though the property was valued at £34,000, Moir sold the building in 1908 for £27,000 cash to the Australasian Temperance & General Mutual Life Assurance Society of Melbourne and it was then renamed T&G Chambers. After this, the back of the building became the headquarters of the Women's Christian Temperance Union, which was founded in 1892 to create a "sober and pure world".

The elegant T&G building survived until 1960, when the need for more office space drove the owners to demolish the building and construct what was, for some 10 years, the tallest building in central Perth, now known as Citibank.

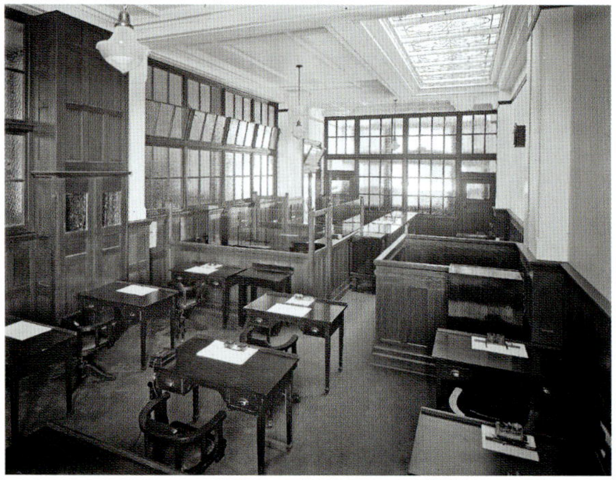

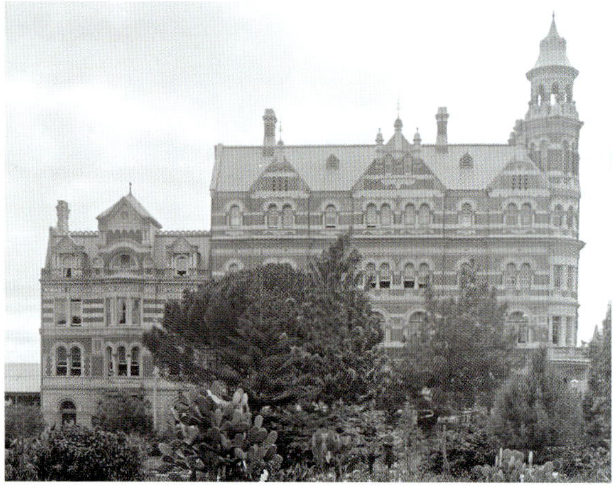

ABOVE Moir Chambers, seen from Government Gardens in 1908. At the left-hand end of the chambers is the headquarters of the Women's Christian Temperance Union.

LEFT Later known as the T&G Chambers, this photograph shows the interior of one of the offices in 1932.

OPPOSITE The imposing architecture of J.J. Talbot Hobbs, as seen in 1932.

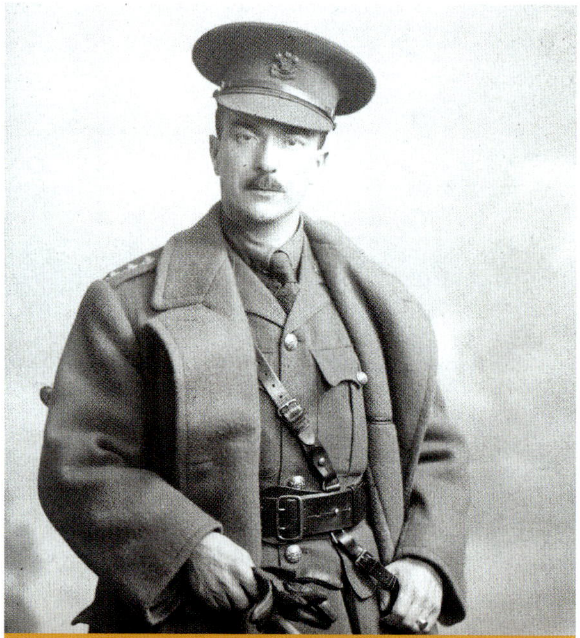

J.J. TALBOT HOBBS

Joseph John Talbot Hobbs was an exceptional man who very successfully combined a career as a talented architect with one as a much respected army officer. Born in London, he worked as an architectural draftsman before migrating to Perth in 1887 at the age of 23. He initially worked as a carpenter before setting up his own architectural practice. Recognition came when he won a competition to design the new Weld Club building. This brought a stream of commissions for many new buildings in Perth and Fremantle and, as a result, he set up the firm Hobbs, Smith & Forbes, of which he was the senior partner. As an army officer, he gave distinguished service during World War I. Renowned for his justice and integrity, he rapidly won the affection and loyalty of all who served under him. He retired from the army in 1927 and returned to his architecture practice. Hobbs died in 1938 whilst en route to the unveiling of a war memorial he designed at Villers-Bretonneux.

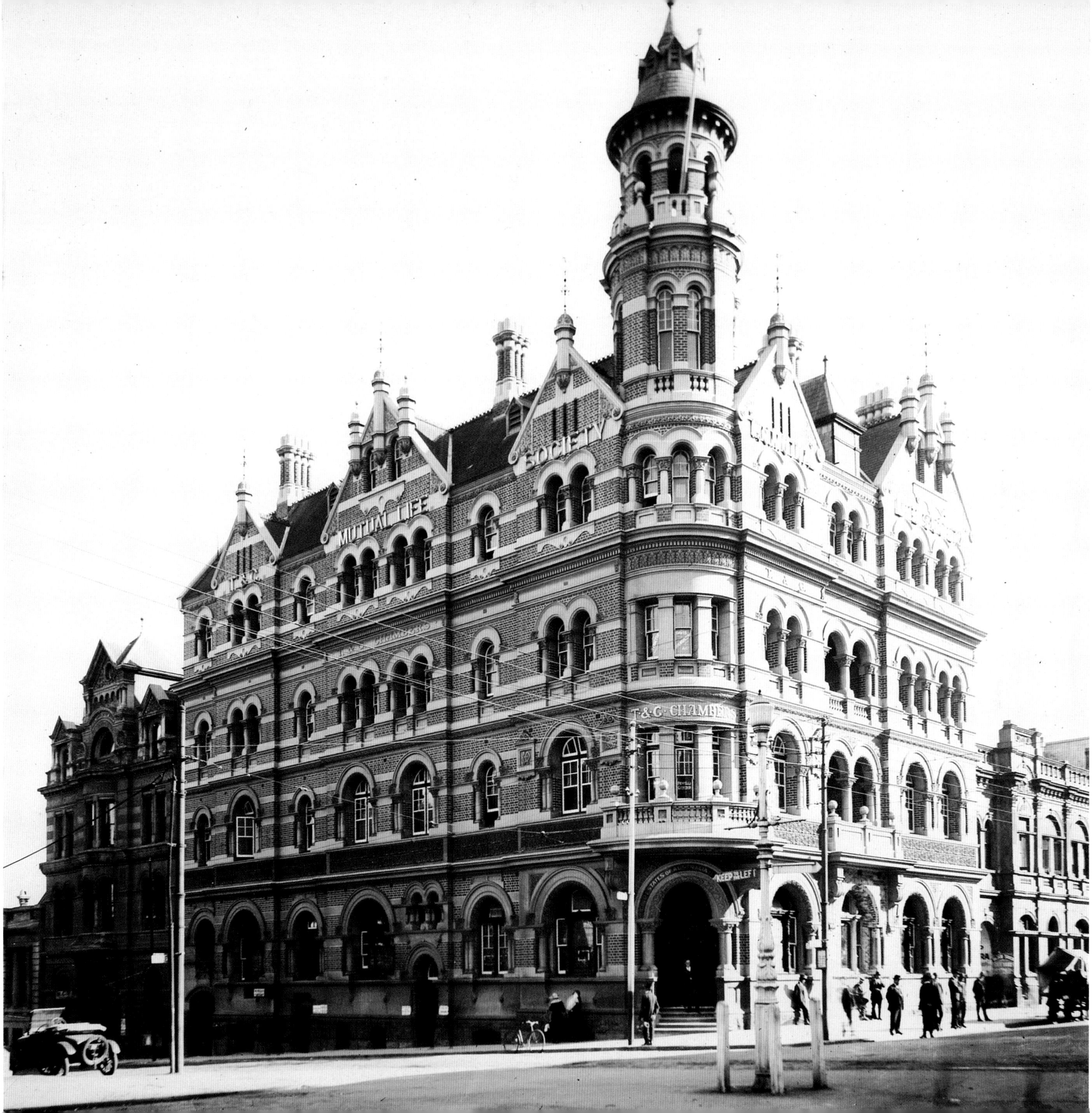
MUTUAL LIFE
SOCIETY
T.&G. CHAMBERS

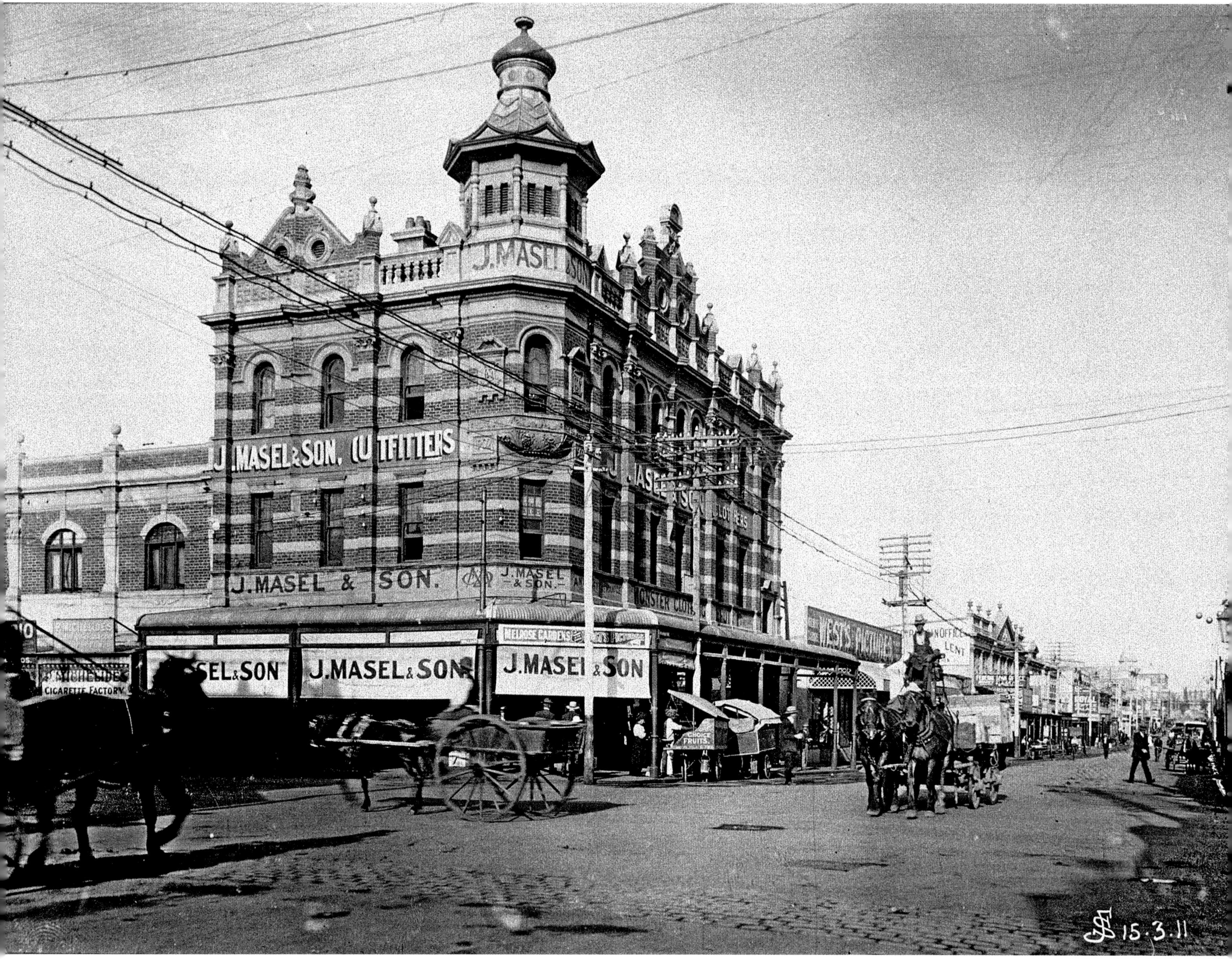
J.MASEL
J.MASEL & SON, OUTFITTERS
J.MASEL & SON.
J.MASEL & SON
CIGARETTE FACTORY
J.MASEL & SON
J.MASEL & SON
MELROSE GARDENS
CHOICE FRUITS.
WEST'S PICTURES
15.3.11

J. MASEL & SON

DEMOLISHED 1960

Sketch plans for the development of the north-eastern corner of William and Murray Streets were drawn up by Perth architect Thomas Jackson in 1896 for owners John Mitchell and his wife Harriet.

When eventually built in 1902, the well-proportioned building was three-storeys tall with a tower on the south-western corner extending it to four storeys. It was designed with retail space on the ground floor and offices above. Initially known as Mitchell Chambers, newspaper advertisements suggest it was up and running by December of 1902.

The first retail tenant, with frontage on both William and Murray Street, was J. Masel & Son, who already had a store in Fremantle. Their shop, which sold toys, jewellery and "fancy merchandise", also advertised themselves as the "Best place for Boys' and Men's Clothing". As a result of their presence, it was not long before the building became known as Masel's; a name which stuck for the next 30 years. In 1932 another firm with the name Masel opened in Perth, so to avoid confusion, J. Masel & Son changed its name to Gaynes.

Next to Gaynes on Murray Street was the Prince of Wales Theatre and Bairds Department Store. Opened in 1922 and seating 2,300, the Prince of Wales Theatre was Perth's first genuine picture palace of the silent era. At the time of its opening, its competitors were much smaller and far less ostentatious, despite their names: Britannia Theatre (1915), Grand Theatre (1916), Majestic Theatre (1917), Pavilion Theatre (1921) and Palladium Theatre (1921). Built by Sir Thomas Coombe – one of Perth's early cinema promoters – on the site of the former Melrose Theatre (named after Coombe's place of birth in South Australia), the Prince of Wales was an elaborately decorated theatre. It boasted its own orchestra and was, in 1929, the first cinema in Perth to install the equipment to show talking pictures. At one stage it only showed British films and was advertised as "Perth's All British Theatre".

In 1935 the theatre was demolished and a Bairds department store was built in its place. Bairds, which opened its first store in Coolgardie in 1896, purchased the building next door to the Prince of Wales Theatre in 1919 and redeveloped it into a shopping arcade and hardware premises, with the ground on which the theatre stood being used to enlarge the store.

The fine tower and elaborate original façades were removed after suffering severe storm damage in early 1957. By the late 1950s the Gaynes building was purchased by Bairds and demolished in 1960 to make way for an even larger store. The entire block was redeveloped from 2006 to 2010 to create the new One40 William Street complex of retail, offices and Perth Underground Station.

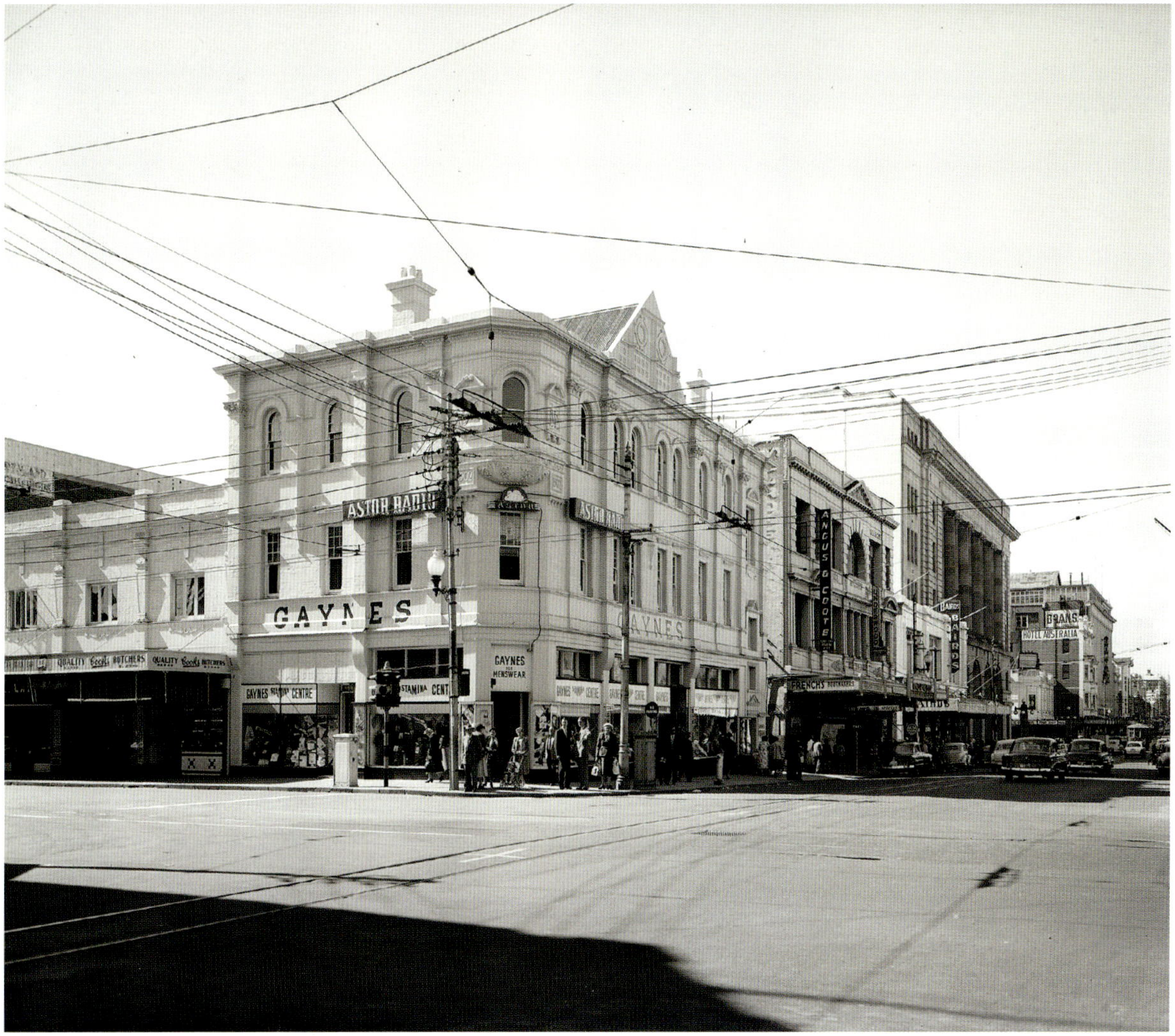

ABOVE Gaynes menswear store, shown not long after the removal of the storm-damaged tower in 1957.

OPPOSITE J. Masel & Son, on the corner of William and Murray Streets in 1911. Next along Murray Street is Melrose Theatre, run by West's Pictures.

FLOWER DAY

WILTED EARLY 1960s

The wild spring flowers in the south-west corner of Western Australia produce one of the most spectacular displays of colour and variety of any floral display anywhere in the world. In the early 1950s one Perth charity took advantage of this, and its supporter's horticultural talents, to produce an extravaganza of flowers that became one of the most popular events of its time.

Silver Chain, which helps people of all ages to receive the medical care they require in their own home so they can continue to live independently, was started with the establishment in 1894 of the Royal District Nursing Service of South Australia. The West Australian Silver Chain Nursing and District Bush Nursing Association, which was initially set up to care for sick or neglected children, came into being in 1905. From those small beginnings, Silver Chain has become a major charity healthcare provider in all Australian states and territories.

South Australia's Silver Chain volunteers started National Flower Days in Adelaide to raise funds for the charity in the early 1930s by covering every possible city space with floral displays and selling flower buttons to passers-by. The concept proved very successful and the idea of a similar festival being staged in Perth was first mooted in 1949.

Plans began to be made for a festival to be held on 15 September 1950, when around 200 representatives of participating organisations met in the Shell Building on St Georges Terrace to begin the process of creating the largest flower show the city had ever witnessed. Floral displays were constructed at the foot of selected trees on St Georges Terrace, in the park on the corner of St Georges Terrace and Mount Street, on the steps of Trinity Church, at the entrance to Government Gardens (Stirling Gardens), near the Alexander Forrest memorial, in front of the Perth Railway Station, on the lawns adjacent to Wesley Church, along the Commonwealth Bank in Murray Street and in a garden at the foot of Howard Street. Additional decorated stalls were to be positioned on as many city intersections as possible.

Flowers, both wild and cultivated, were sent to Perth from all over Western Australia, their transport being provided free by the Government Railways and the Midland Railway Company. Despite blustery winds on the previous day, almost every building in the city centre made an effort to contribute to the colourful display. The *West Australian* described the event: "All forms of transport were heavily taxed yesterday morning and the streets were soon crowded with sightseers. As the day advanced, schoolchildren flocked into the city to see the displays." The day raised £2,500, primarily through the sale of floral badges and buttons, and was deemed a great success.

Over the following years, the festival grew in size and not only spread to the Perth suburbs, but also to other Western Australian towns. By the mid-1950s the event was raising in excess of £5,000, but by the late 1950s the format changed to a flower show, which was eventually subsumed by other Silver Chain public appeals.

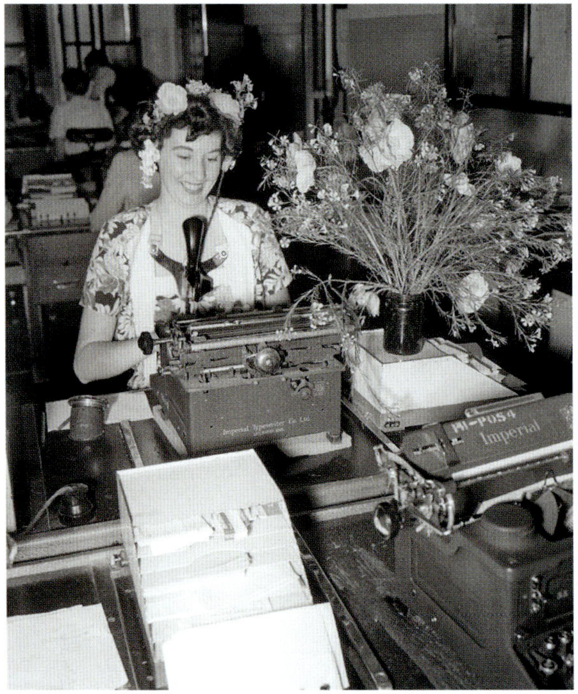

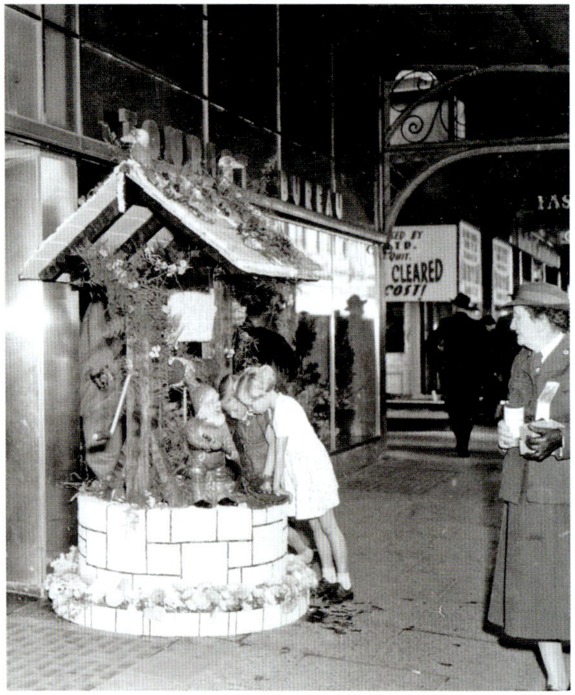

RIGHT A Gold-Tone Holden taxi enters into the spirit of things during Flower Day, 1954.

LEFT A child makes a wish at the floral wishing well outside the Tourist Bureau at the Winterbottom Motor Company premises on St Georges Terrace in 1953.

FAR LEFT A city-centre secretary enjoying Flower Day in 1952.

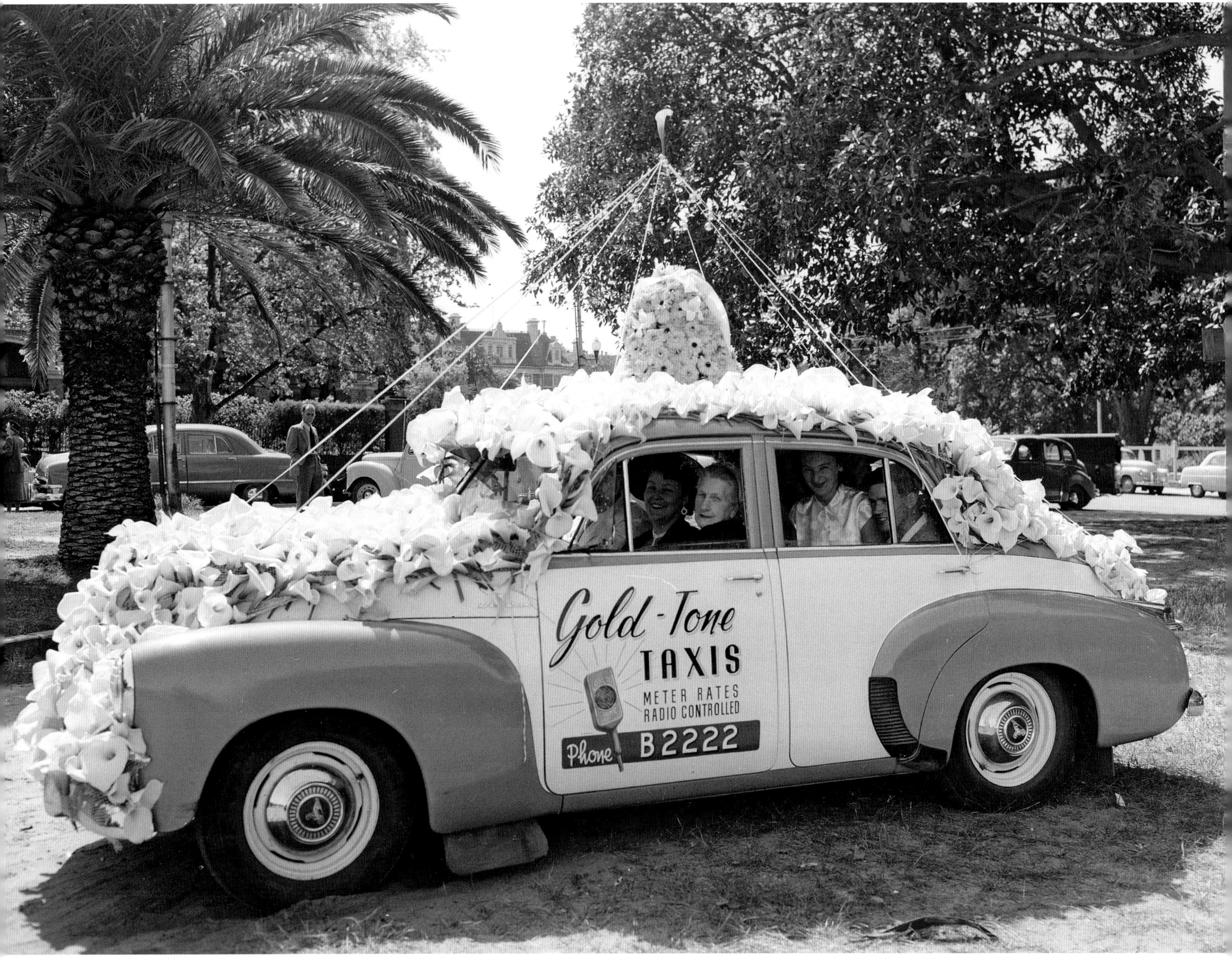
Gold-Tone
TAXIS
METER RATES
RADIO CONTROLLED
Phone B2222

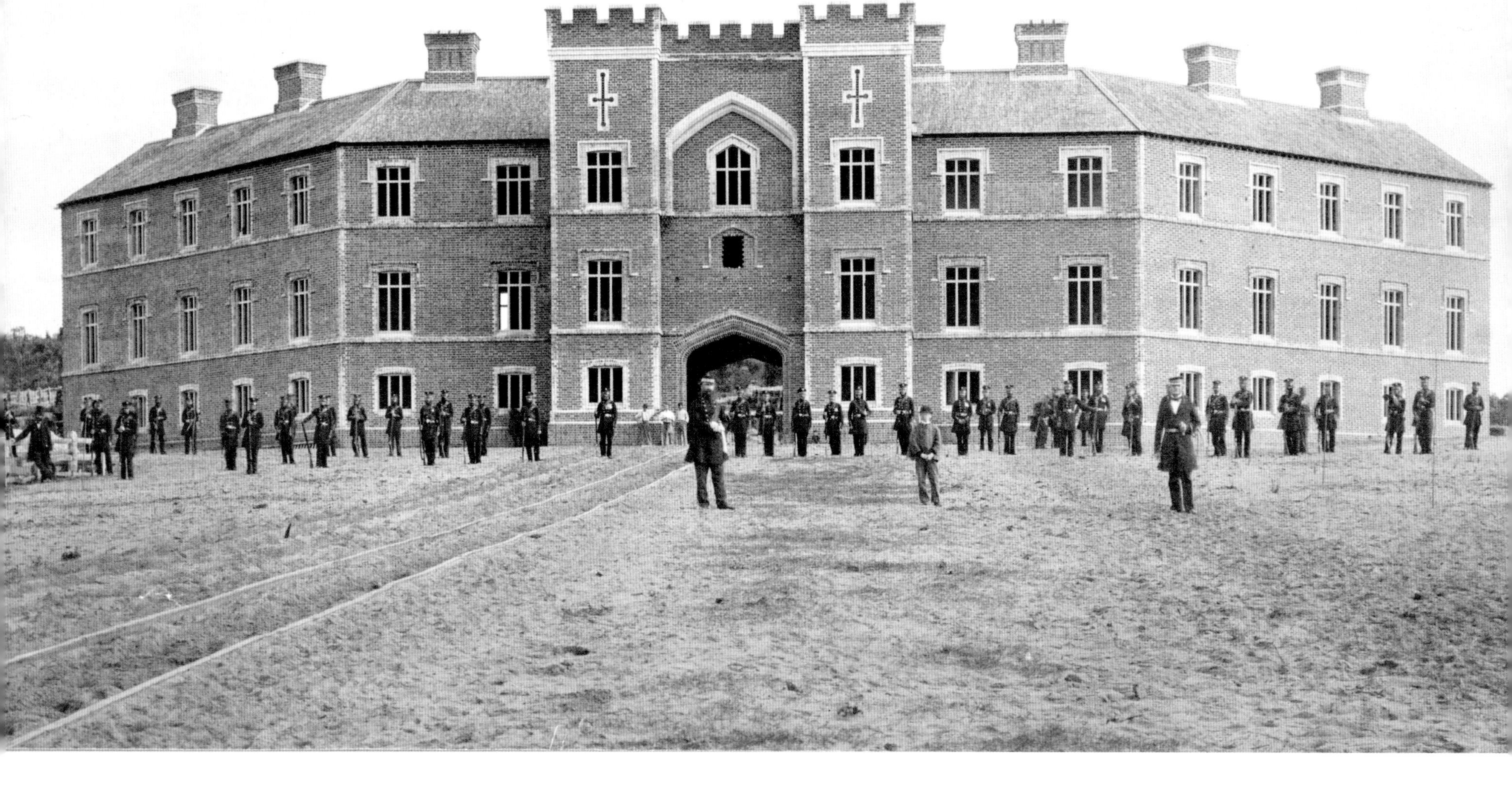

PENSIONER BARRACKS

PARTLY DEMOLISHED 1961

In May 1849 an Order-in-Council was passed by the British Parliament declaring Western Australia a penal colony. The first ship, carrying 75 convicts, arrived in Fremantle on 1 June 1850, but the colony was totally unprepared as the ship had overtaken the dispatch announcing its arrival.

Between 1850 and 1868, nearly 10,000 convicts were transported to Western Australia, and with them came around 2,500 free citizens employed as guards and supervisors. Many were members of the Enrolled Pensioner Force, who arrived as guards on the convict ships. On arrival, they were offered either a grant of 10 acres of land or to continue guard work. Initially most of the convict projects were in Fremantle, but by the 1860s they were deployed on work in Perth. As a result there was a need to accommodate many Enrolled Pensioners and their families in the city.

To create accommodation, Richard Roach Jewell designed a Pensioner Barracks at the western head of St Georges Terrace in a style resembling an English medieval castle. The building was brick, rather than more expensive stone, with horizontal lines of lighter coloured bricks to emphasise features such as windows. Work commenced in February 1864 and by April the *Inquirer* newspaper was able to report that "The Pensioner Barracks is beginning to make a show, the walls being several feet high."

It was finished in 1866 and each family was allotted an apartment of two rooms, each about 13 by 11 feet, with at least one fireplace. Communal facilities in outbuildings included a cook house, firing range and gun room, wash house, stores and stables. Later a fives court was created.

A fire in 1887 destroyed flooring in the east wing and the second floor of the central section. To fight the fire, water was pumped from the Swan River with hand pumps and carried to the conflagration in buckets by a chain of volunteers. The damaged sections were later restored.

The Pensioner Guard Force was disbanded in 1887 and the barracks were converted to offices for the Public Works Department. The fives court housed the drawing office, which was connected to a mid-1920s addition for the Metropolitan Water Supply, Sewerage and Drainage Department.

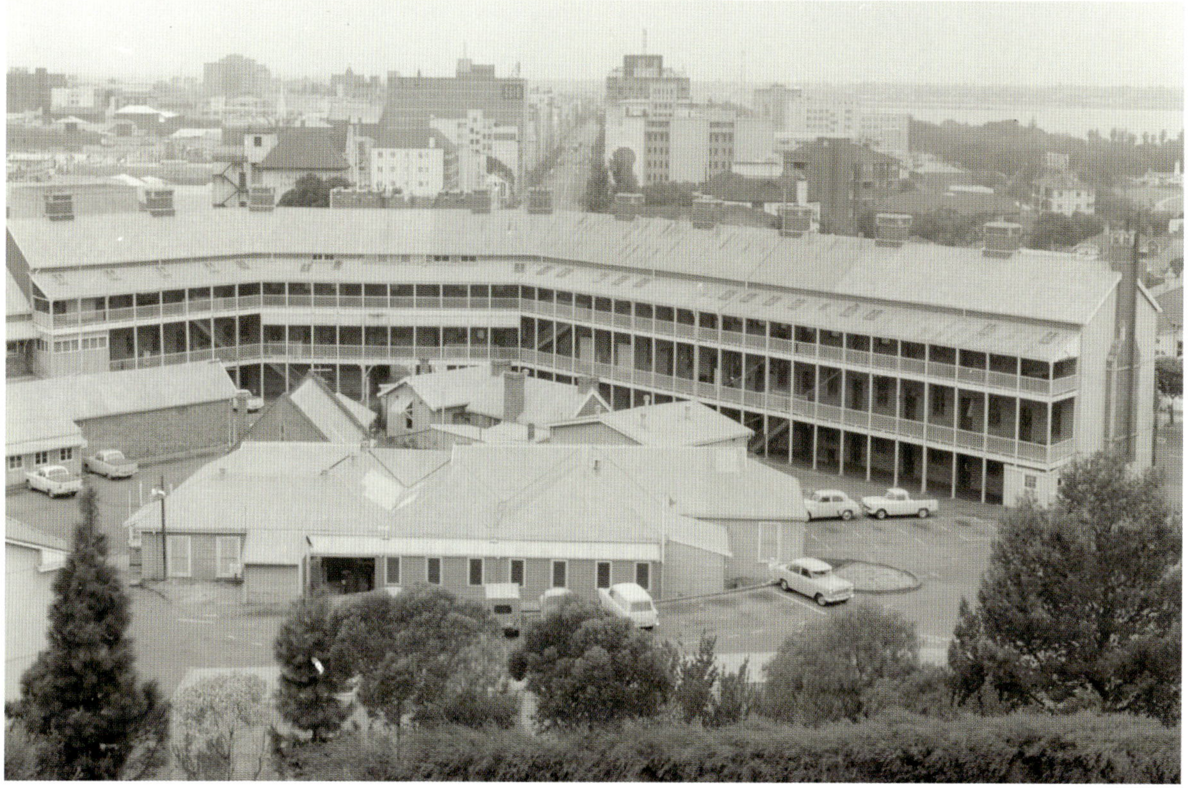

In the early 1960s all departments were moved to nearby Dumas House, and the government intended to demolish the barracks to make way for a freeway. The Royal Western Australian Historical Society formed a Barracks Defence Council in 1961 and joined the public outcry against demolition.

The Defence Council campaigned to save at least the arch and five bays of windows either side. Meanwhile, demolition proceeded, with a large section demolished and cleared. Such was the outcry at the demolition that opinion polls were conducted to gauge the public's preferences. In a poll conducted by radio station 6IX, 97 per cent voted to retain the arch and a similar poll in the *West Australian* recorded 87 per cent for retention. Cabinet authorised a Gallup poll, which showed 49 per cent for retention, 35 per cent against, 11 per cent no opinion, and 5 per cent for moving the arch elsewhere. The Premier, Sir David Brand, interpreted the results as indecisive and declared parliament would decide on the arch's fate on a non-party basis. On 19 October 1966, a motion to demolish the arch was defeated by 26 votes to 18.

The arch is now all that remains of the impressive Pensioner Barracks and is sometimes affectionately referred to as Perth's answer to the Arc de Triomphe.

ABOVE A view of the rear of the barracks showing various ancillary buildings, just before demolition began in 1961.

OPPOSITE Pensioner Guards on parade outside their nearly completed barracks in 1866.

CRAWLEY BATHS

DEMOLISHED 1964

Having made the decision that the old City Baths on the Esplanade were not satisfactory, a search began to find a suitable alternative location within a reasonable distance of the city centre. Attention for this search focussed on the foot of Mount Eliza, along Mounts Bay Road in Crawley, which had been a popular swimming spot for many years.

A suitable location, not far south-west of the Swan Brewery, where the river bed was sandy, was chosen. However, the council then faced fierce public opposition to the scheme for a swimming pool, on the grounds that seeing people undress, swim, or dress would upset the sensibilities of those enjoying the tranquillity of Kings Park further up the nearby escarpment.

Those fears allayed, the next complaint was the distance the baths would be from the city centre and the lack of public transport to the location. This complaint brought about the following comment in the *Western Mail*: "For the immediate present bathers may take the Mount's Bay road tram and walk to the baths from the terminus. They will hardly grudge the walk, if, indeed, they have time to notice and consider it, for the park on the one hand and the river reaches on the other offer scenic beauties which none but a barbarian could fail to feel soul-satisfying."

Work on the construction commenced early in October 1913, with a large area of the river being enclosed by a submerged wooden barrage. The incomplete swimming pool was made available to swimmers free of charge over the Christmas 1913 period and the *Western Mail* suggested the opening of the new pool would "almost immediately shake-off the disrepute which deservedly attaches to a city having no swimming baths."

The total cost of the new facility was £5,000 and the baths were the largest enclosed body of water in the Southern Hemisphere. The official opening was carried out by Premier John Scaddan on 7 February 1914, with a major swimming carnival and displays of life saving.

The event was recorded in the *Sunday Times*: "The long-sustained efforts of the City Council to provide for its citizens an area in which they can disport themselves in aquatics and enjoy the pleasures of the water so handy to them were brought to a happy consummation yesterday, when the Premier (Hon. J. Scaddan) at 3 o'clock declared the new Crawley baths open."

With the opening of the new swimming pool, the *West Australian* declared that provision of public baths had characterised every forward civilisation of which history has record and, "At last Perth had the chance to achieve greatness."

The baths were reconfigured in 1933 to create an Olympic length pool and throughout their history were a popular recreational facility where thousands of Western Australian children were taught to swim. Conditions were not always ideal, however, and many former patrons recalled days when the water was freezing cold, murky and sometimes swarming with large brown jellyfish.

Crawley Baths were demolished in 1964, following the opening of the new state-of-the-art swimming pool at Beatty Park for the 1962 Empire Games.

RIGHT The entrance in 1955. The *West Australian* once wrote, "The raffish elegance of the Crawley Baths belied the sting of the jellyfish that lurked in its swimming lanes."

BELOW Diving at Crawley Baths in March 1940.

BELOW LEFT A water slide, 1920s-style.

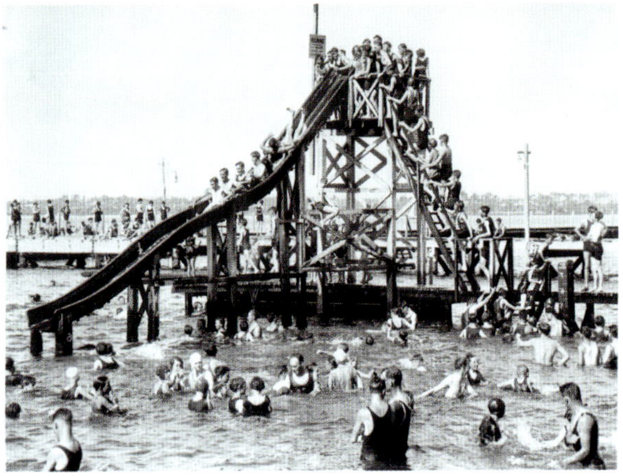

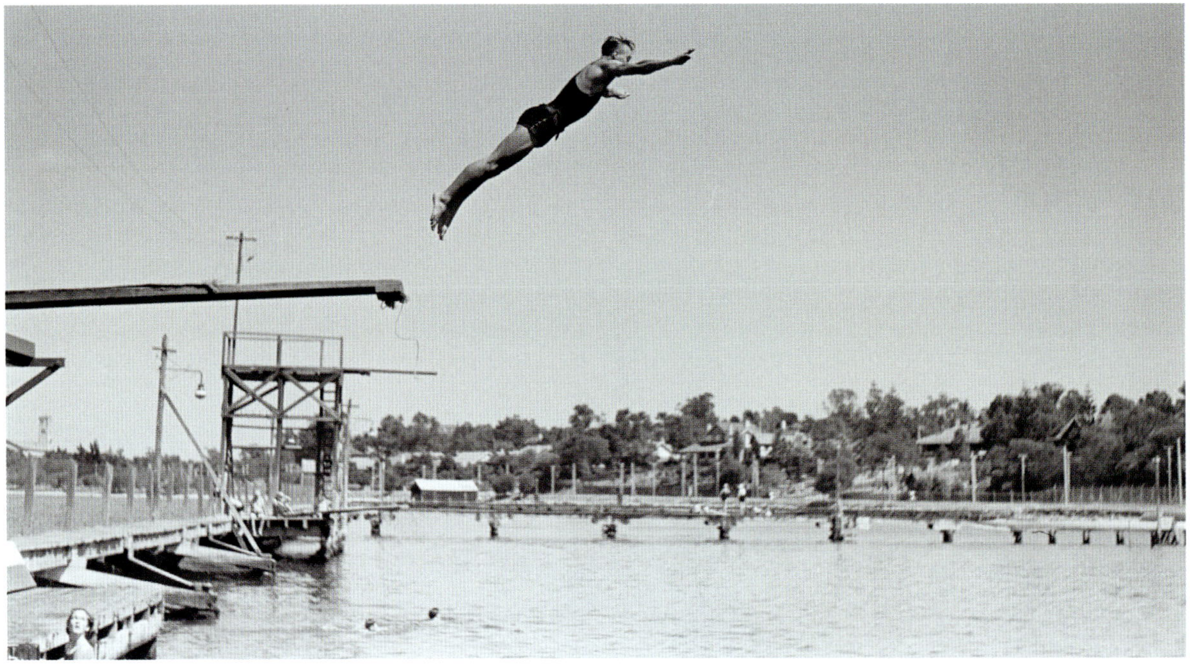

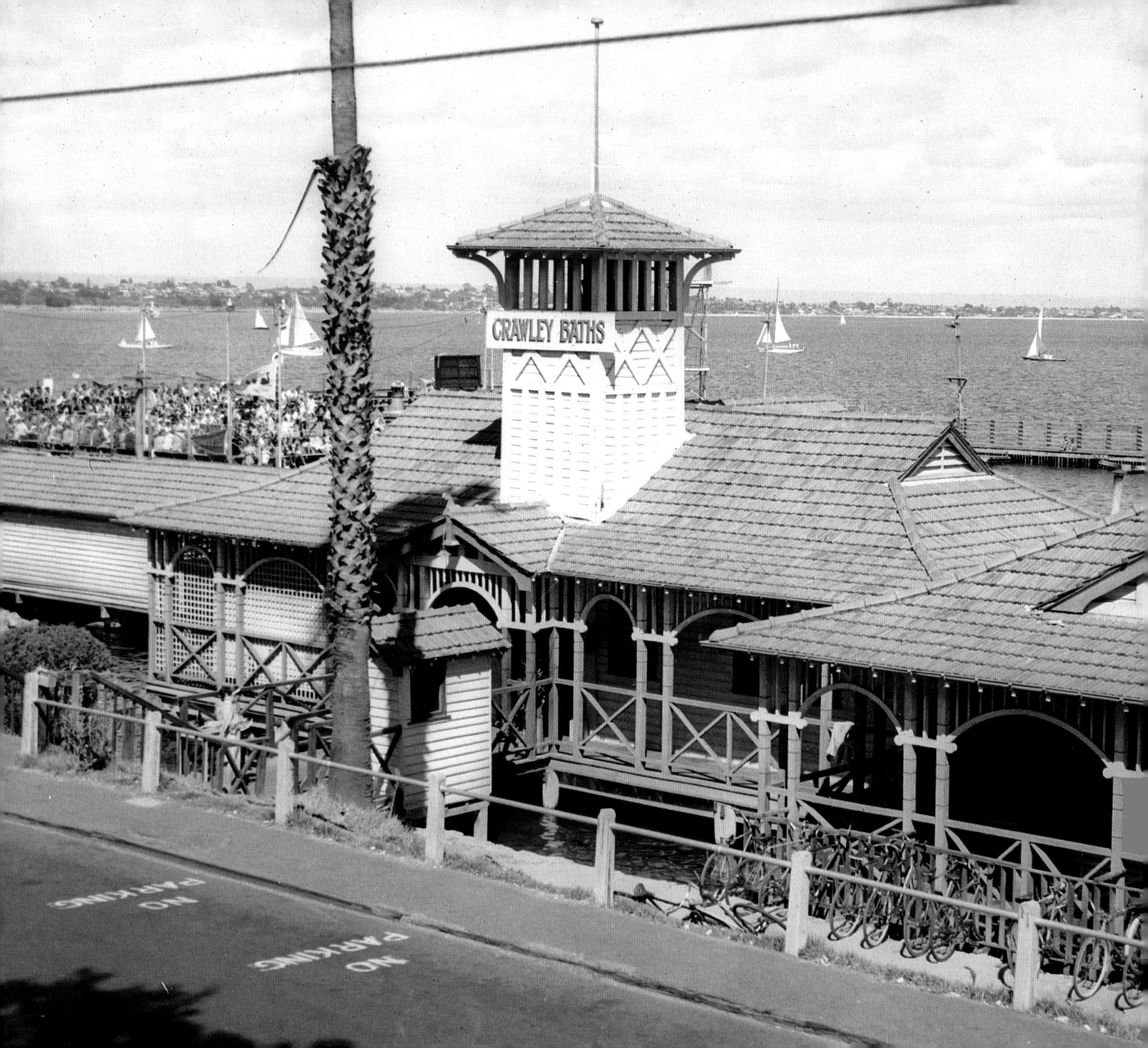
CRAWLEY BATHS
NO PARKING
NO PARKING

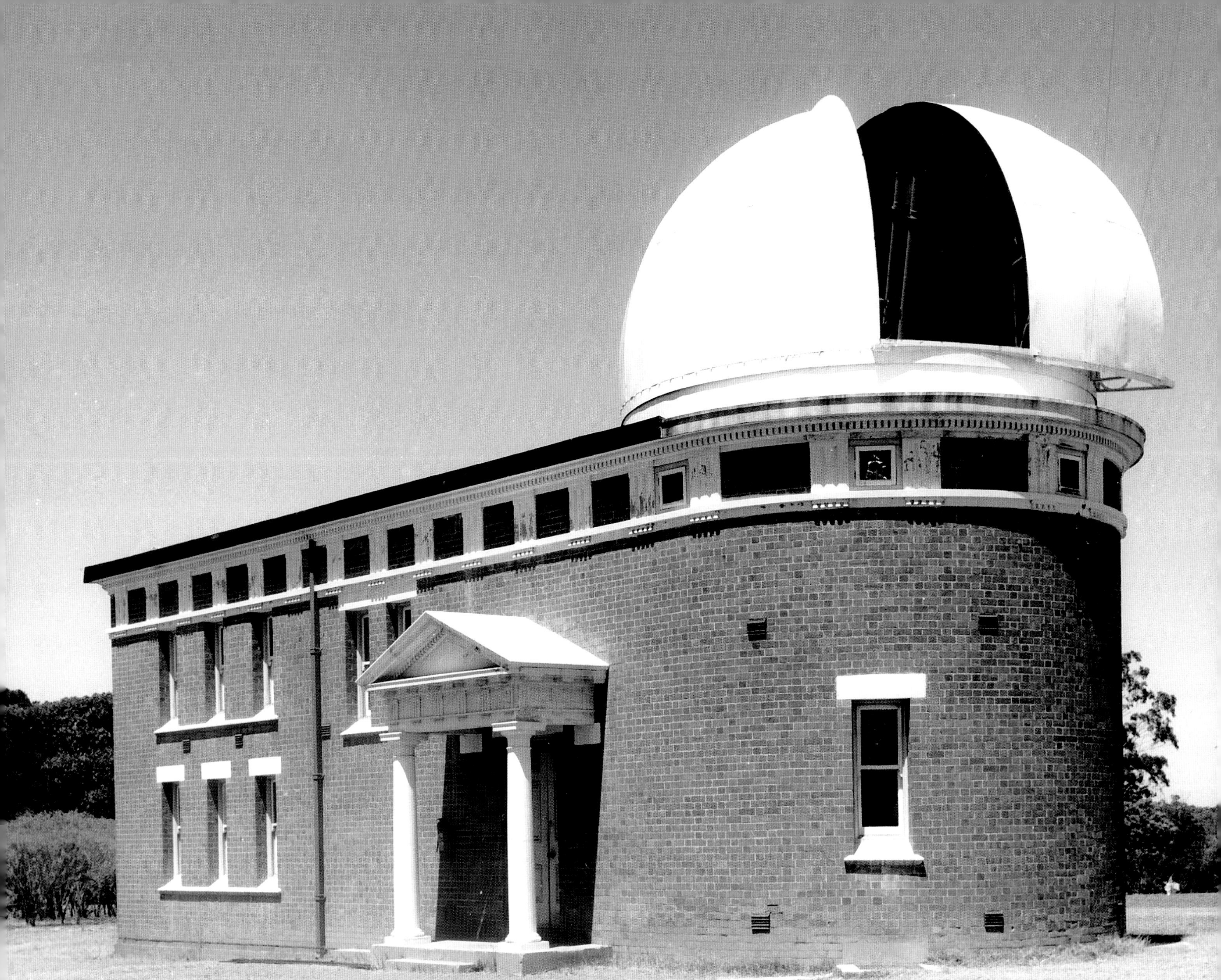

OBSERVATORY

PARTLY DEMOLISHED 1964

The first public clock was erected on the Public Offices building in St Georges Terrace (now the site of Council House) in 1838. Until then, a bugle had been used to help the early settlers know the time at set hours of the day. The first clock was superseded in 1870 by the clock in the new Perth Town Hall, which was then transferred to the Courthouse in Guildford, where it was once again usurped in 1901 by the new Post Office clock.

Until the appointment of the first Western Australian Government Astronomer, William Cooke, in 1896, timekeeping in the state was a somewhat haphazard affair, relying mainly on local solar observations. On arrival in Perth, Cooke's first task was to determine the exact latitude and longitude of Perth, which would enable accurate time to be calculated.

Another early task of Cooke's was to oversee the building of an observatory, of which part still remains to this day on Mount Eliza, opposite the entrance to Kings Park. Constructed in 1896, the buildings (there were three) were designed by Colonial Architect, George Temple-Poole. The complex was officially opened in 1900 by John Forrest, the first premier of Western Australia.

The observatory was responsible for weather forecasting, navigation, astronomy and seismology, as well as state time keeping. The original three buildings were a transit circle building, which housed a meridian telescope for taking accurate measurements of the position of the stars; the dome, which was a steel dome, similar to one at the Royal Observatory in Greenwich, used for taking telescopic photographs of the night sky; and the government astronomer's working office and family residence. This building, of grand design, is the one still standing.

The determination of the precise latitude and longitude of Perth having taken place early on in the life of the new observatory, a standard time for Western Australia was established. The *West Australian* noted on the introduction of standard time, "It seems scarcely credible that only six years ago there was absolutely no correct time throughout the State, and the amount of confusion caused thereby, especially to travellers, was the cause of much profanity. To revert to the former condition would be intolerable".

The correct time was displayed from 1899 on a clock at the observatory gates, noted in 1902 as "the first public clock in Western Australia to know the correct time." From the middle of November 1900 the signal was also sent electrically to a "time ball" on Arthur Head in Fremantle Harbour and a large ball dropped daily at 1 p.m. so that maritime clocks could be set to the exact time. Another means of signalling the time was by the firing of a six-pounder canon as a time gun, which could be heard all over the city. The gun, fired from the observatory, went off on weekdays at 1 p.m. and at noon on Saturdays, but not, apparently, on Sundays.

By the early 1960s, increasing light levels at night from the city below meant the observatory was becoming less and less useable, so it was dismantled and the telescope was moved to the new location at Bickley in the Perth Hills. The transit circle building and dome were demolished to make way for Dumas House and the astronomer's house became the headquarters of the Western Australian National Trust.

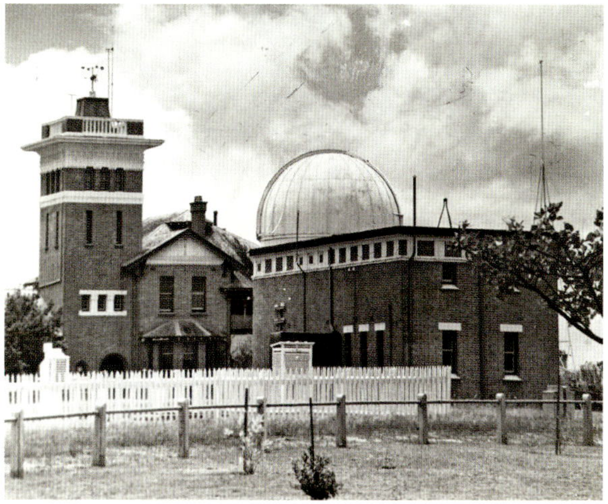

ABOVE The observatory shortly after it opened in 1900. The white fenced area contained the meteorological measuring instruments.

OPPOSITE The dome telescope building in 1961, not long before it was demolished to make way for Dumas House.

BELOW Premier John Forrest laying the foundation stone of the Perth Observatory on 29 September 1896.

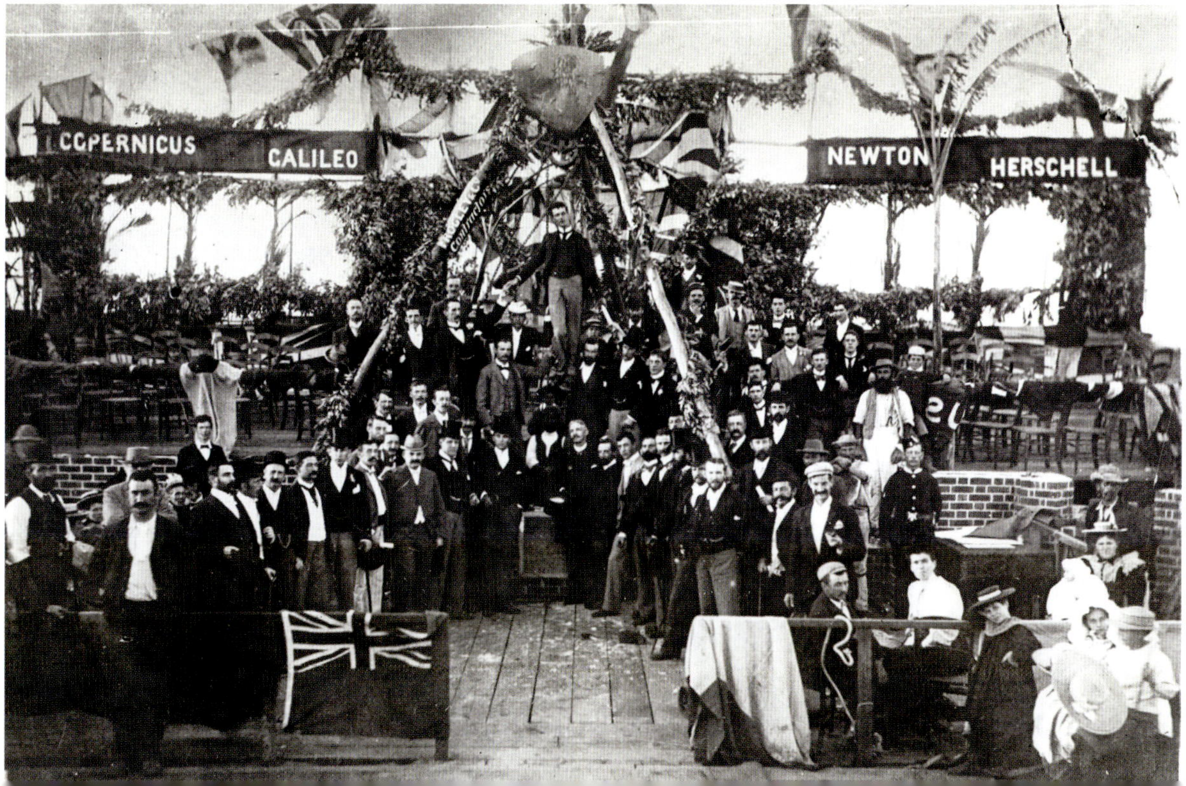

CHRISTIAN BROTHERS' COLLEGE

DEMOLISHED 1965

The Christian Brothers, a Roman Catholic order, was established in Ireland at the beginning of the 19th century to work amongst the poor and educate the young. They were first invited to Western Australia by Bishop Matthew Gibney to help address the lack of Catholic schools in the colony. At that time the only Catholic schools in Perth were the Sisters of Mercy School, founded in 1846 (which later became Mercedes College on Goderich Street), and St Patrick's Boys' School on Irwin Street, which opened in 1878.

On arrival in 1893, the Brothers purchased a 3-acre block on the corner of St Georges Terrace and Victoria Avenue from the Catholic Church. This block included a substantial brick building that had originally been owned by the first Colonial Secretary of the Swan River Colony, Peter Broun. This house was used as their residence and another "wretched brick structure" was very soon converted into a school and opened on 1 February 1894 with 13 students.

By the beginning of the school year in 1895 the roll had increased to 75 and the old building was found too small for the demand. To address the problem, plans were made for a new school building to be constructed, which was eventually built in three stages. The first was the West Wing and the foundation stone was laid by Bishop Gibney in November 1895. In order to fund the new school, one of the Brothers went round the goldfields asking for donations and raised £2,000 in the process. The architect for the project was Michael Cavanagh, who designed many other buildings for the Catholic Church during this period.

During 1897 Peter Broun's house was demolished to make way for the second stage of the new building, the central section, which included an impressive water tower. Finally, the East Wing of the building was opened in August 1911 with over 1,000 people attending the opening ceremony.

In 1938 boarders and some day students were moved from Perth to the new Aquinas College at Salter Point. The Perth campus continued as a day school until 1961 when Perth City Council acquired the site, at which time staff and students were transferred to the college's present location in East Perth, where it was renamed Trinity College.

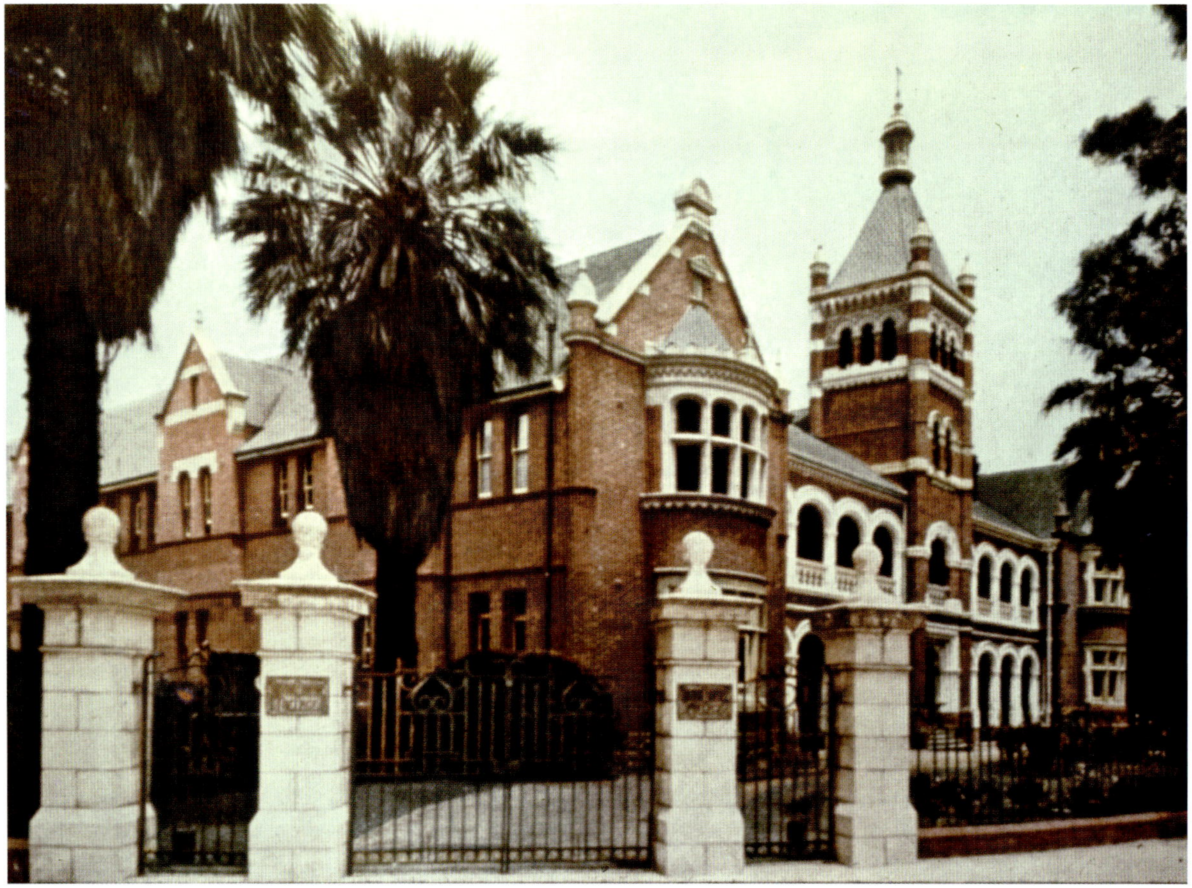

The original intention for the St Georges Terrace site was to erect a hotel to service the forthcoming Empire and Commonwealth Games. Instead, the land was sold to the Commonwealth Government, who demolished the imposing school buildings in 1965 and built a high-rise Taxation Office. In 1996, the Taxation Office was also sold and converted into the Duxton Hotel.

ABOVE The college building in 1960, one year before the school was closed.

RIGHT The college in 1910, just before work commenced on the east wing.

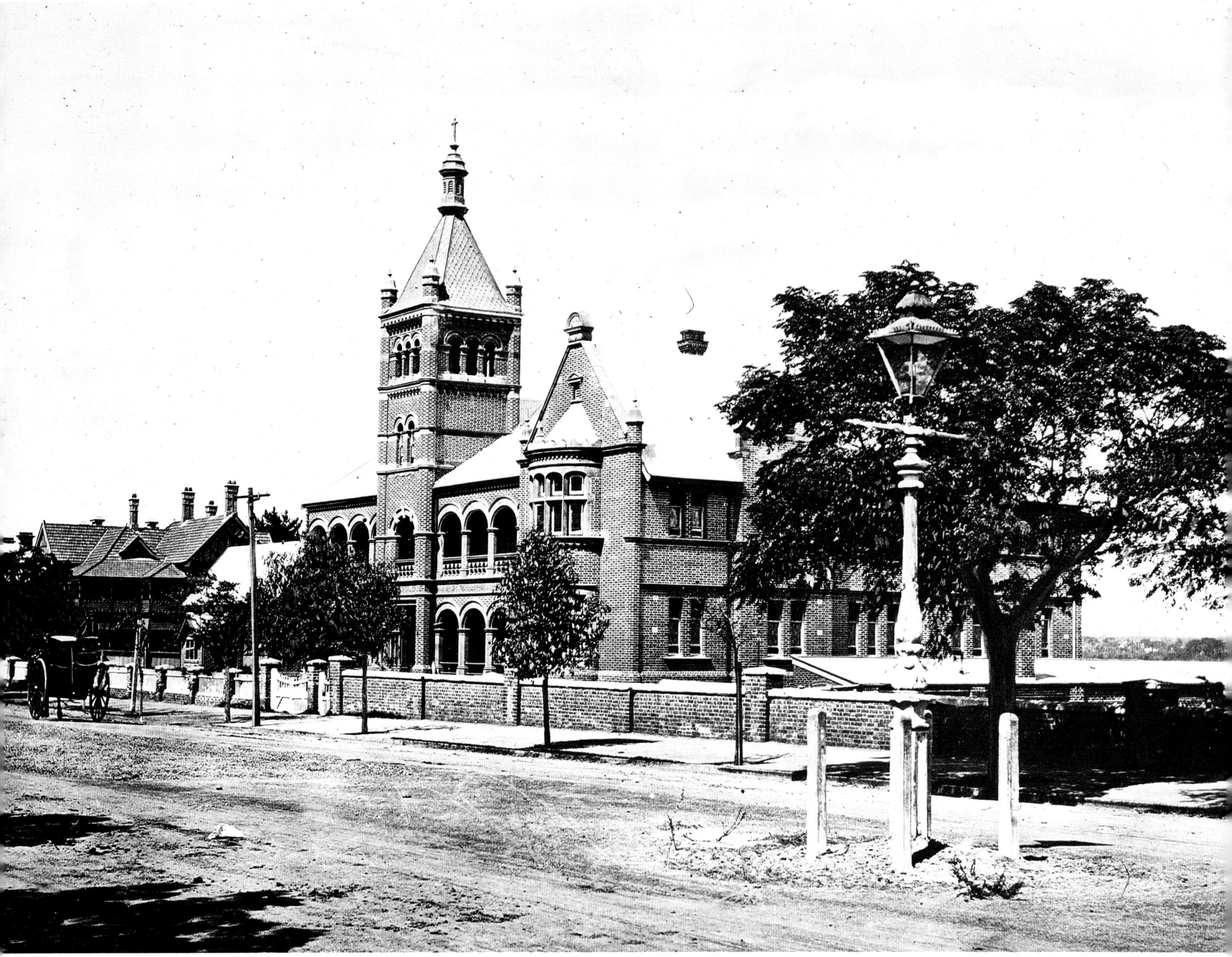

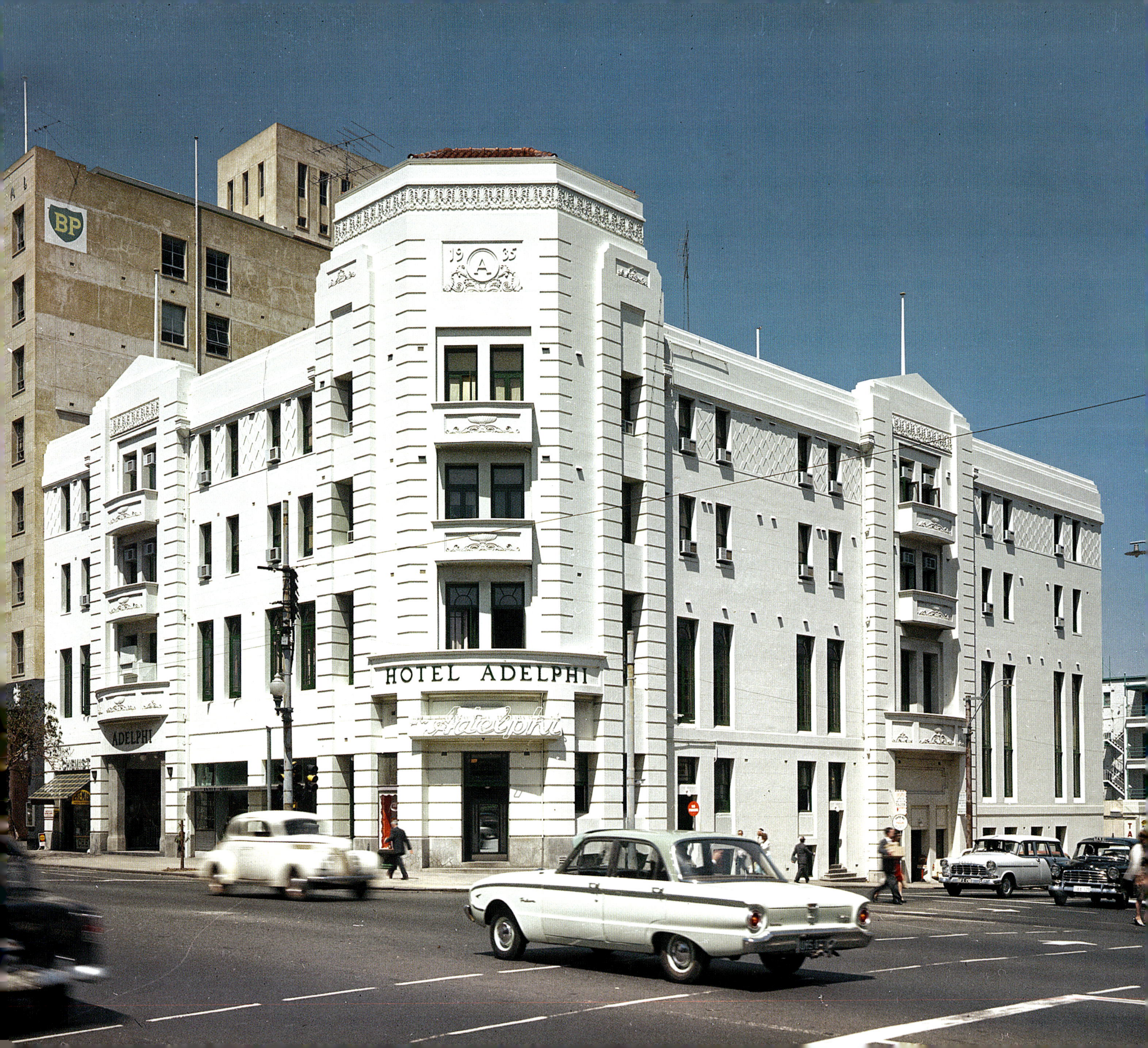
BP
19 A 35
HOTEL ADELPHI
Adelphi
ADELPHI

ADELPHI HOTEL

DEMOLISHED 1967

According to a *West Australian* article from 1935, the site on which the new Adelphi Hotel was about to be constructed had been occupied by a cottage built in the 1850s. Known as "Honeymoon Cottage", the house was part of an adjacent water mill and became a popular boarding place for newlyweds.

In 1933 Foy & Gibson, one of Australia's earliest department store chains, purchased the land on which the cottage stood (by then a Chinese laundry), which was adjacent to their factory. Not long after, the land was resold for £14,500 to gold miner and Perth hotelier Gordon Dunleavy, who intended to build a luxury hotel on the site.

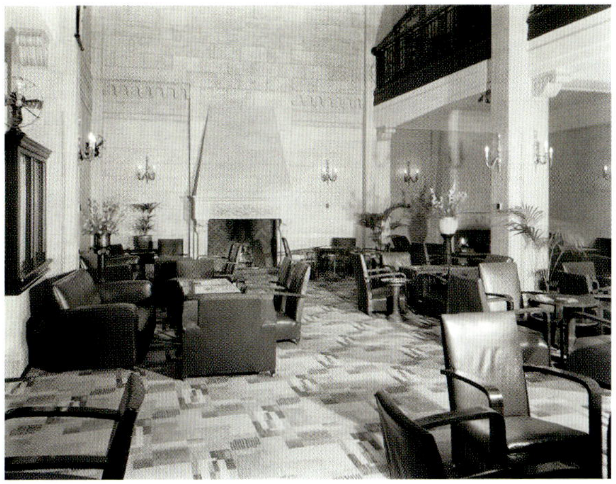

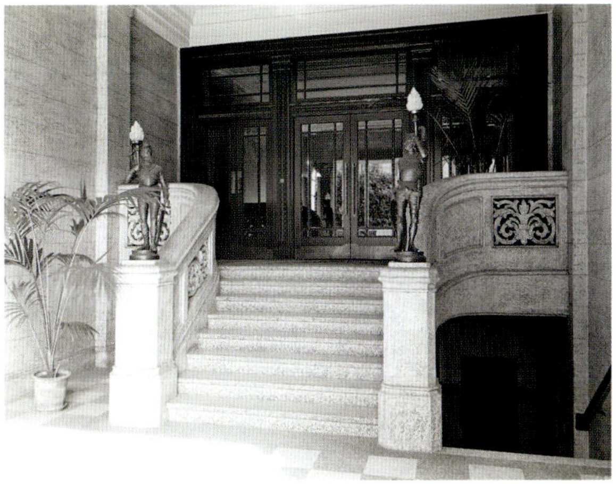

Perth architects Oldham, Boas & Ednie-Brown designed a four-storey hotel in the fashionable Art Deco style, which was built by Finlay and Stoneham at a cost of around £58,000. The hotel design was described in great detail in the *West Australian* in January 1936 just before the opening. According to the article, the basement contained a beauty parlour, men's hair salon, swimming pool (Perth's first hotel pool), a Turkish bath and gymnasium. The hotel also included a roof garden tea pagoda that allowed guests to view the city skyline.

The interior of the hotel was designed by Margaret Pitt Morison, Western Australia's first female architect, who at the time worked for Oldham, & Boas Ednie-Brown. Most of the furnishings were supplied by Boan Bros., who, amongst other soft furnishings, supplied 2.5 acres of Axminster carpet. Pitt Morison's designs clearly impressed one journalist, who described the interior as a "triumph of intelligent planning".

In the two days before the grand opening on 18 January 1936, a lunch, open to the public, was served and the following day a bridge and dance evening was held, organised by the West Perth branch of the National Party, with a buffet supper served to around 300 guests. Among other facilities, the hotel boasted two "mixologists", who claimed to have 800 cocktail recipes up their sleeves.

After the opening, the *Mail* newspaper reported, "Expressions of admiration were heard on all sides ... The ballroom was used for the first time, dancers declaring the floor to be first class, whilst numerous card players occupied the rooms and lounges. The lighting called for special comment, and the supper showed what can be done in the cuisine department."

The hotel's Adelphi Grill Room restaurant opened a few months later and rapidly became the restaurant of choice among Perth's high society. The hotel even became popular with honeymooning couples – a reminder of the site's humble beginnings.

Throughout its life, the hotel remained one of the most luxurious in the city, frequented by many famous people such as H.G. Wells and Robert Menzies. The hotel was demolished in 1967 to make way for Parmelia House, a 19-storey office building.

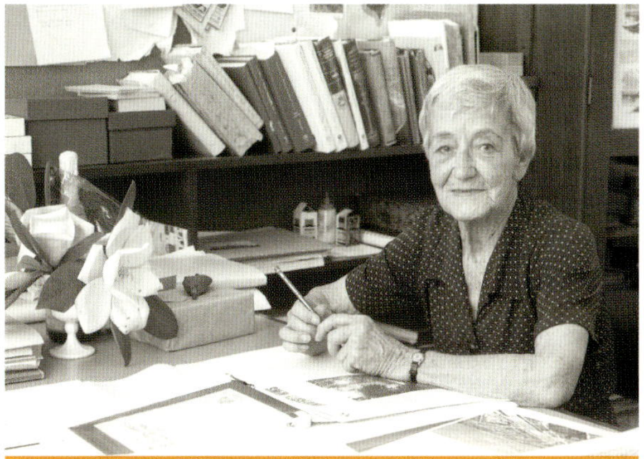

MARGARET PITT MORISON

Margaret Pitt Morison was Western Australia's first female architect in an era when such jobs were considered unsuitable for women. She was the daughter of artist George Pitt Morison, who is probably best known for his painting *The Foundation of Perth 1829*, commissioned for the centenary of the founding of the city. After leaving school in 1920, Morison was articled to Perth architect Geoffrey Summerhayes, completing her training with the firm of Eales & Cohen. She registered as an architect in October 1924. Later she set up her own design studio, but the practice had to close at the outbreak of World War II. After the war, she taught architecture at Perth Technical School until 1962 and later joined the University of Western Australia's School of Architecture and Fine Arts as a research officer, where she remained until her death in 1985.

TOP LEFT The hotel lounge in 1936.

LEFT The grand entrance on St Georges Terrace in 1936.

OPPOSITE The Art Deco elegance of the Adelphi Hotel in 1961.

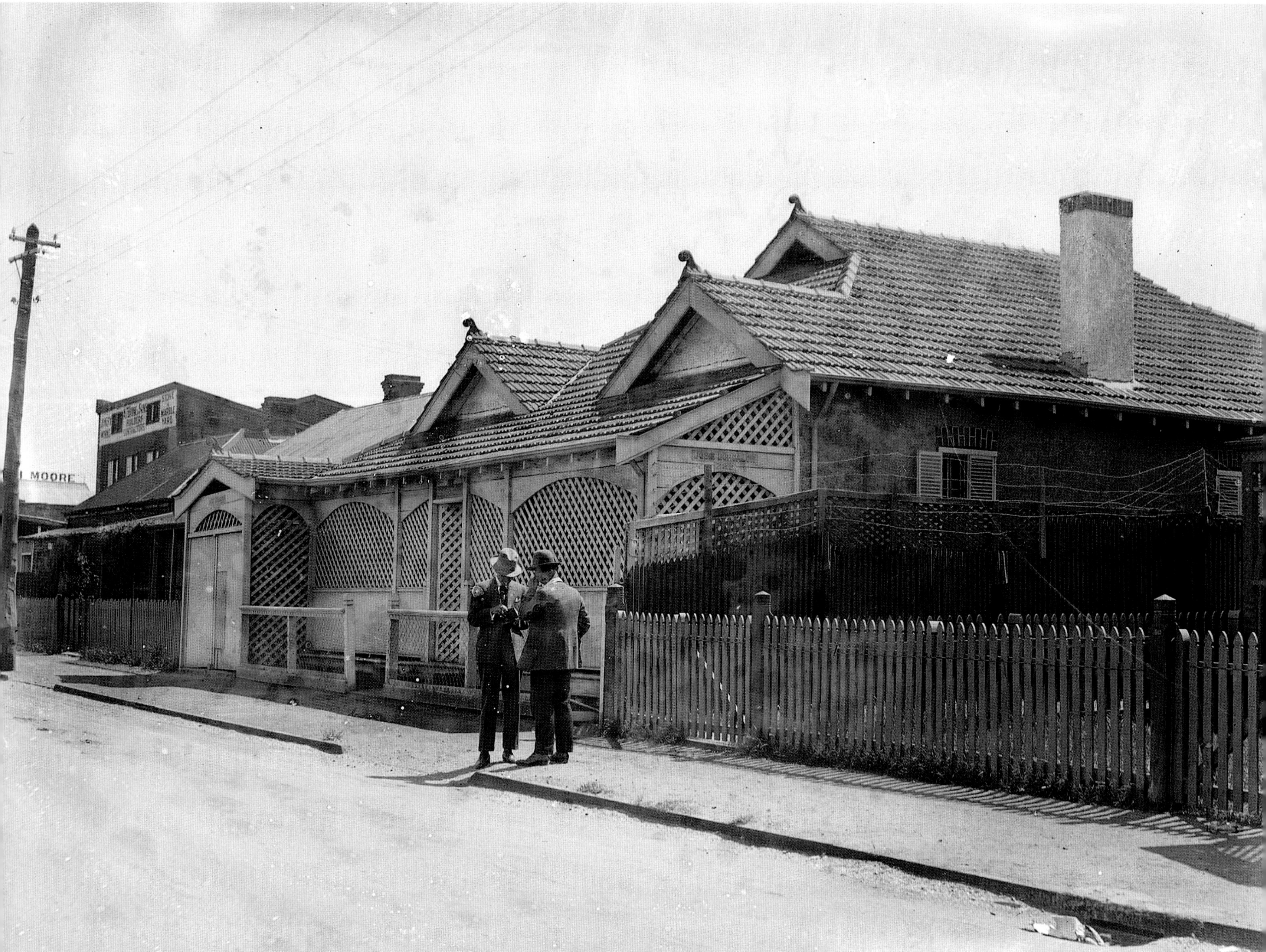

BUILDERS
CONTRACTORS
STONE & MARBLE YARD
MOORE

JOSIE BUNGALOW

DEMOLISHED c. 1967

One of the first references to prostitution in Australia comes in the Bigge Inquiry Report of 1822, which refers to brothels in New South Wales. Some of the women transported to Australia had previously worked as prostitutes, while others were forced into it by economic circumstances and a severe imbalance of the sexes in the colony.

The earliest direct reference to prostitution in the Western Australian newspapers appeared in the *Perth Gazette* of October 1869, where the report of a murder trial claimed the victim to have been a Perth prostitute. The report of a Fremantle divorce case in the *West Australian* of 20 November 1885 also shows evidence of the existence of brothels: "It appeared from the evidence, which was very uninteresting and very unromantic ... He [the accused] had also been seen frequenting brothels of a low description, in the town, and observed to leave these houses at the hour of one and two in the morning."

Given the vast increase in population Western Australia experienced during the first Gold Boom, there is no doubt that "service industries" increased proportionately.

Whilst prostitution itself was not illegal in WA, the Police Act of 1892 prohibited activities such as street soliciting and operating brothels. Historically, the police have used an unofficial containment policy to control the number and location of brothels. By the beginning of the 20th century police records show that brothels were located throughout the centre of the city, particularly along Murray Street. However, at some point they began to migrate north, across the railway line into Roe and James Streets.

The first to move seems to have been "Auntie McKenzie", who opened a brothel on the corner of Roe Street and Melbourne Road (now Milligan Street). Auntie's establishment seems to have gained a high degree of notoriety in the area and was run by Ms McKenzie right into the 1930s, by which time she was in her 80s and pretty much deaf and blind.

In a police report of 1911, 75 houses around Roe, William, James and Aberdeen Streets were identified as brothels.

This situation seemed to continue right up to World War II, as the caption to a photograph in the *Truth Newspaper* in 1929 demonstrates: "Josie Bungalow, brothel in Roe Street that allegedly lures married men to folly and infidelity and the secret entrance from James Street."

Josie was one of Perth's best-known madams who ran a brothel towards the west end of Roe Street in the first decades of the 20th century. The secret entrance to Josie's den of iniquity was in the back of a petrol station on James Street, giving gentlemen the perfect cover for their clandestine activities. It was here in 1919 that Josie De Bray was wounded in a shooting during the early hours of the morning, when she refused entry to some over-eager customers.

Perth City Council records show the council came under considerable pressure in the early 1940s for the Roe Street brothels to be closed and this eventually happened in 1958. Josie's Bungalow was demolished almost 10 years later.

OPPOSITE The caption to this photograph in the *Truth* newspaper read: "Josie Bungalow, brothel in Roe Street, that allegedly lures married men to folly and infidelity ..."

BELOW The infamous Roe Street brothels as photographed for the *West Australian* in May 1958, three months before they were all closed.

BOTTOM There was a secret entrance through the service station in James Street to Josie Bungalow for those who needed to be discreet about their visits.

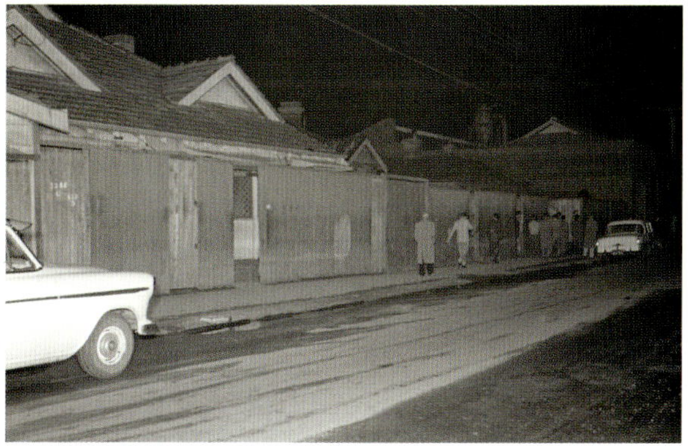

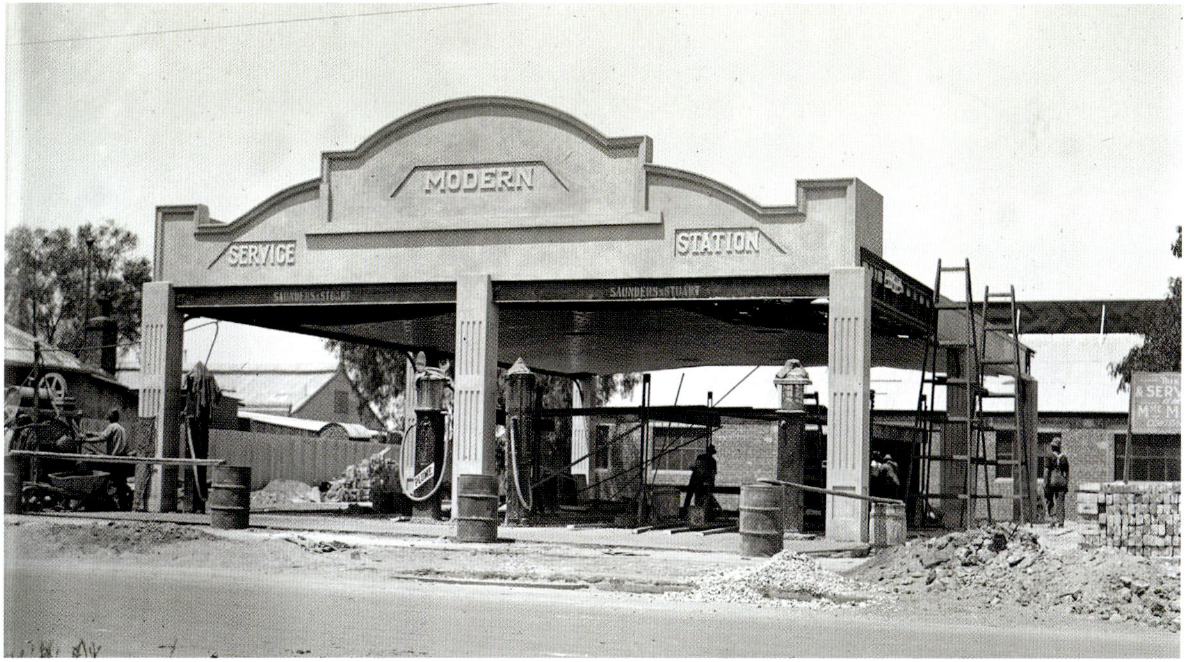

LEGISLATIVE COUNCIL BUILDING

DEMOLISHED 1968

The first legislative council in Western Australia was convened in 1832 and consisted entirely of those who held public office, such as the Surveyor General and Colonial Secretary. Six years later, an additional four members, who did not hold public office and were appointed by the governor, were added to the council.

In 1850 the British Parliament passed an act permitting the Australian colonies to establish legislative councils, which were one-third nominated and two-thirds elected. This authority was given, however, on condition that the colonies took responsibility for the costs of their own government. Western Australia, having one of the most precarious economies of any colony in the country, was not enthusiastic about this clause and so it was not until 1867 that the governor responded to public demand and held unofficial elections. Following these elections, he had to nominate each elected representative to the council. In 1870 representative government was finally officially adopted and the legislative council was changed to consist of 12 elected members and six members nominated by the governor.

Despite the time taken to reach this point, a legislative council of 18 members appears to have caused an accommodation problem and hurried arrangements had to be made to create a venue for the meeting.

Luckily, Governor Hampton had decided in 1866 to build a town hall for Perth as part of a public works programme set up for the convict colony to carry out. This new hall was designed by the Superintendent of Public Works, Richard Roach Jewell, who was the first trained architect in Western Australia.

The laying of the foundation stone on 24 May 1867 was meant to have been accompanied by great pomp and circumstance, but the weather was foul and the ceremony much truncated.

Overseen by the Clerk of Works, James Manning, much of the construction work was carried out by convicts and was planned to take 12 months to complete, but this was a gross underestimate and the building was eventually finished three years later.

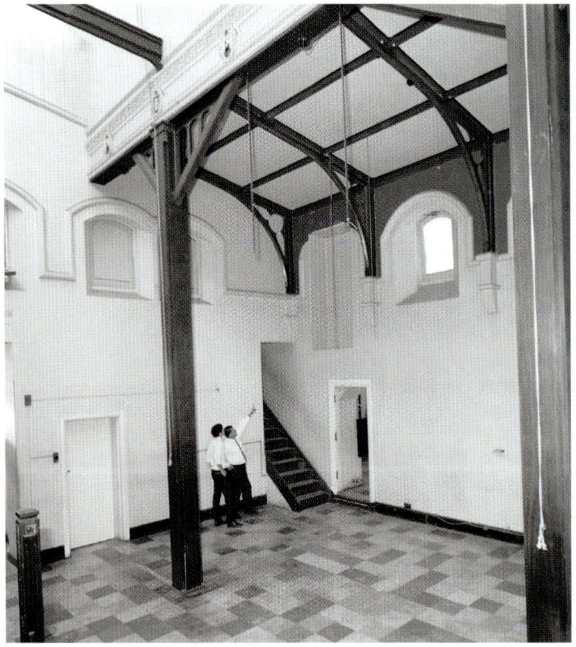

Governor Weld officially opened the Town Hall on Foundation Day, 1 June 1870, and a few days later a Monster Tea Party was held, with over 900 people in attendance.

To alleviate the problem of where to house the legislative council, Richard Jewell designed a temporary extension on the eastern end of the Town Hall in an area originally intended as a courtyard. The legislative council held its first meeting in the new extension on 5 December 1870, a month before the city council held their first meeting in the main hall next door.

The temporary accommodation lasted until 1904 when the Parliament Building on Harvest Terrace was opened and the legislative council moved in. After this the Town Hall extension was used as offices, with the last tenants being the Commonwealth Bank. The Old Legislative Council Building was acquired by the R&I Bank in 1968, who controversially demolished it to build a 14-storey extension to their existing Barrack Street head office. This building was in turn demolished in 1994–95.

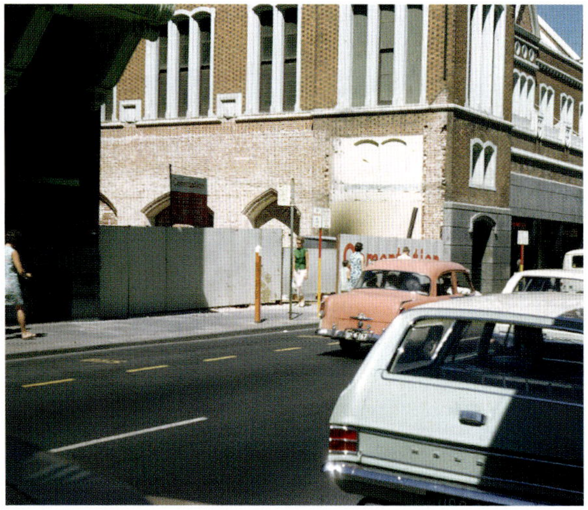

ABOVE This photograph from December 1968 shows an empty block of land where the old Legislative Council Building had been.

LEFT The interior of the building just before it was demolished.

RIGHT The last tenants of the building were the Commonwealth Bank, who vacated in 1968 to allow the R&I Bank to demolish the building.

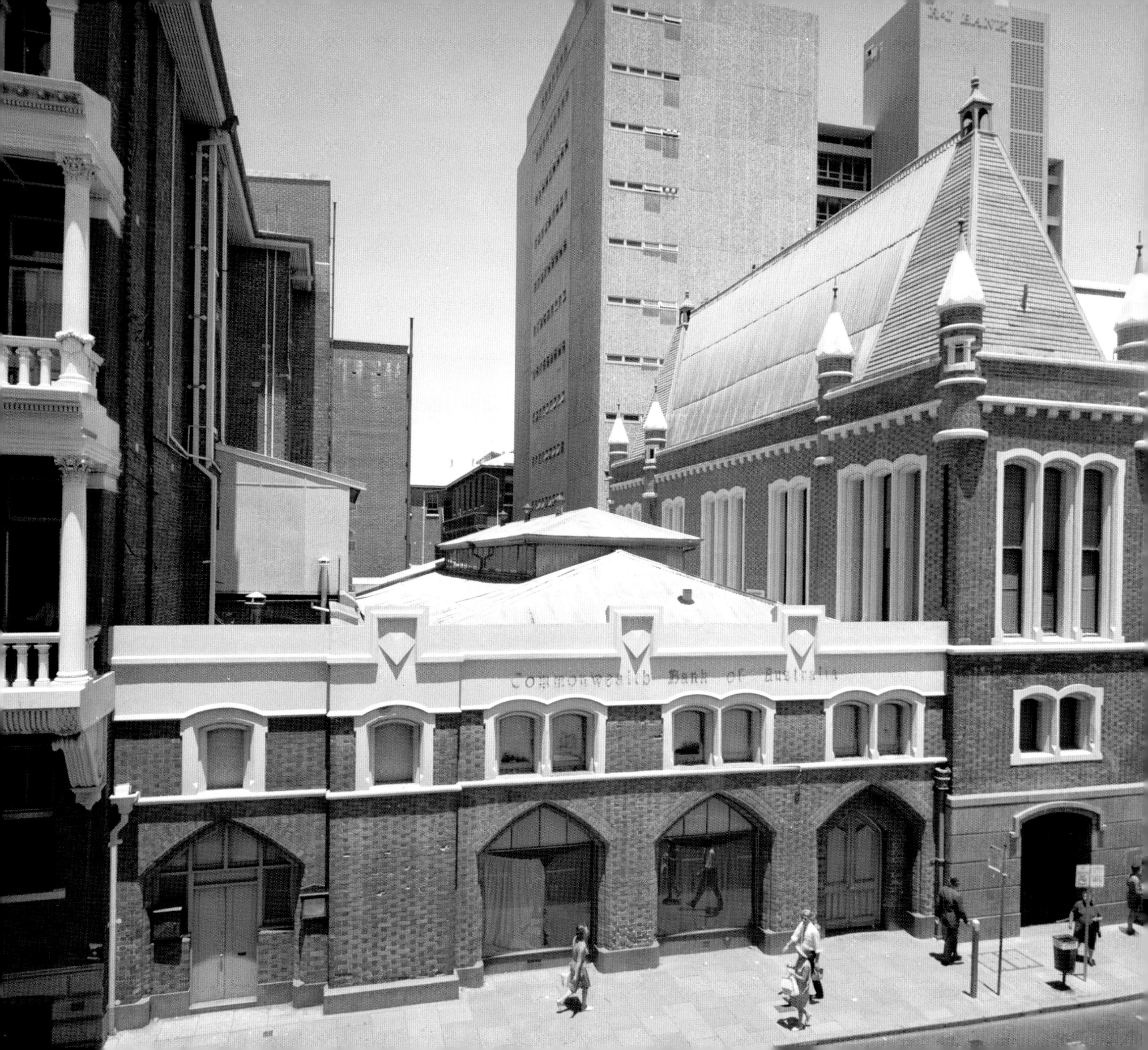
Commonwealth Bank of Australia

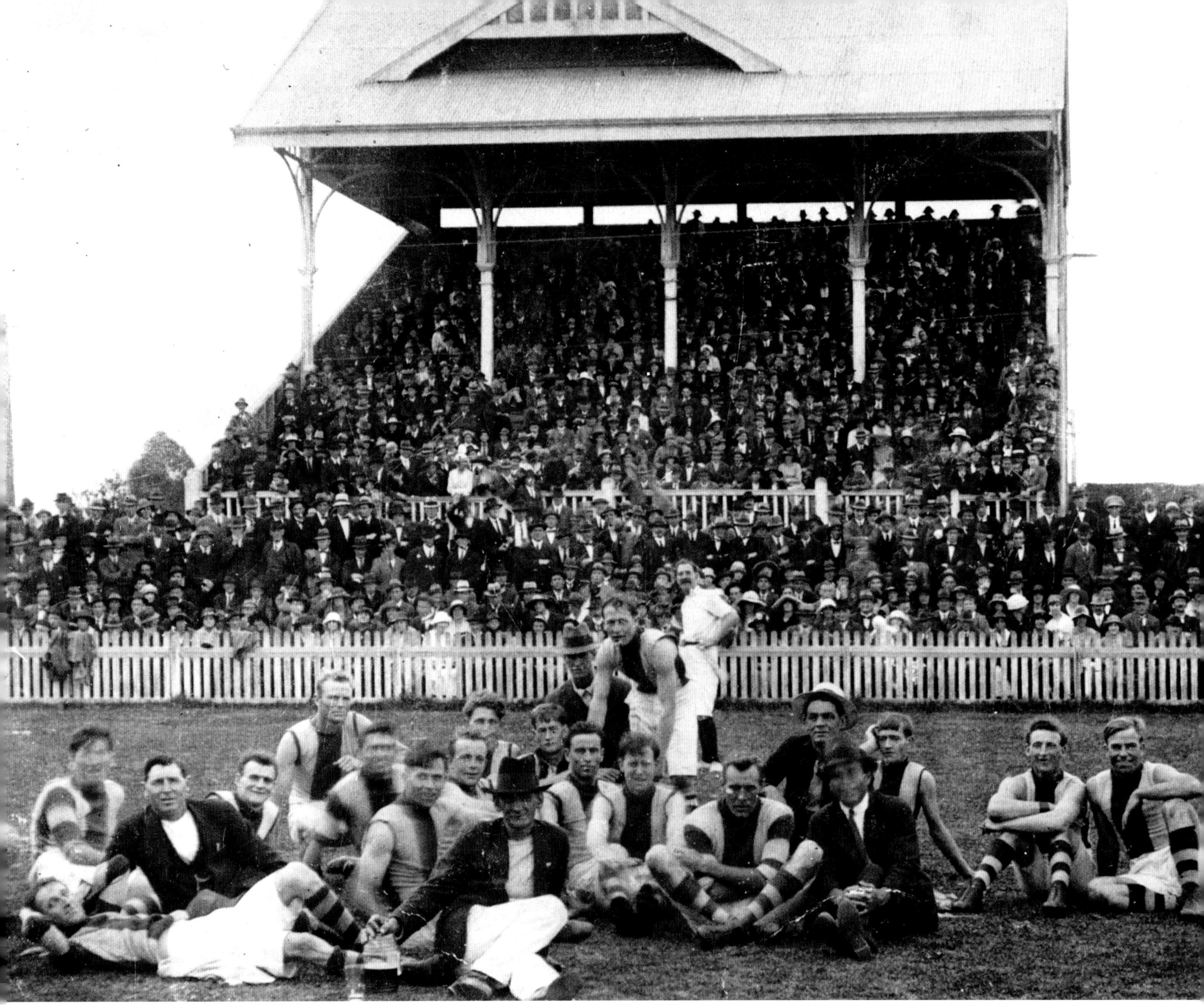

FIRST GRANDSTAND, SUBIACO OVAL

DEMOLISHED 1968

From very humble beginnings on a patch of sand where some of the early games of Australian Rules Football were played in Perth, a stadium known throughout Australia developed and became the headquarters of the Western Australian game.

In 1896 Subiaco played in the First Rate Juniors Competition and their first official match was against Fremantle Imperials. Subiaco's first game on the "sand patch", which was a scrubby piece of land on Mueller Road (renamed Roberts Road during World War I), took place on 4 July 1896, again against Fremantle Imperials. No other games appear to have been played on the sand patch that year, but the team continued using the ground throughout 1897.

After this they abandoned the ground and, along with the cricket club, for the next 10 seasons, moved to a new recreation ground which had been created in West Subiaco (later renamed Shenton Park). The new venue, whilst scenically attractive, being on the banks of Lake Jualbup, proved to be a real handicap to the club, as in winter it became part of the surrounding swampland. This made training impossible and home games out of the question, with home fixtures having to be played on borrowed ovals in Fremantle.

By 1906 some junior football was again being played at the sand patch, the ground having been cleared of scrub the year before, principally to deter miscreants who were using the area as a hiding place. In July of that year, Subiaco Council resolved to allocate £350 for the improvement of the Mueller Road Reserve, with the object being that it should be used for football and cricket. Earlier in the year a request to the council had been made by the local rifle club for permission to use the sand patch as their headquarters, but football and cricket won the day.

It was clear to everyone that with a good home ground the Subiaco teams had a chance of stardom and so work on the development of the Mueller Road sand patch commenced as a priority. The improved ground, later known as Subiaco Oval, was not ready for use, however, until 1908.

Once the grass was judged as capable of use, Subiaco hosted Cottesloe Football Club (later Claremont FC) in a practice game in April 1908, the first recorded game on the new pitch. After a close inspection, league officials stated "as a recuperative green in wet weather, it ought to prove the equal to Fremantle Oval." A month later Subiaco defeated East Perth in the first league game at Mueller Park.

Subiaco Council deferred an official opening until after the erection of a grandstand, which was constructed early in 1909, allowing the grand opening to happen on Saturday 17 April 1909, two weeks before the first match of the season.

The principal entertainment was a fancy dress football match between the residents of Subiaco and Leederville, all proceeds being donated to the nearby Children's Hospital (later renamed Princess Margaret Hospital). A crowd of some 6,000 people gathered to witness the comical exhibition and at half-time Subiaco Mayor, Shirley White, invited Lady Forrest, wife of Sir John, the federal parliamentarian and former premier, to formally open the grandstand.

By the 1960s the grandstand, which was constructed of timber, had become too small to safely accommodate the large crowds that gathered for matches at Subiaco Oval. As a result, it was demolished by 1968 to make way for a much larger, three-tier concrete grandstand which opened in August 1969.

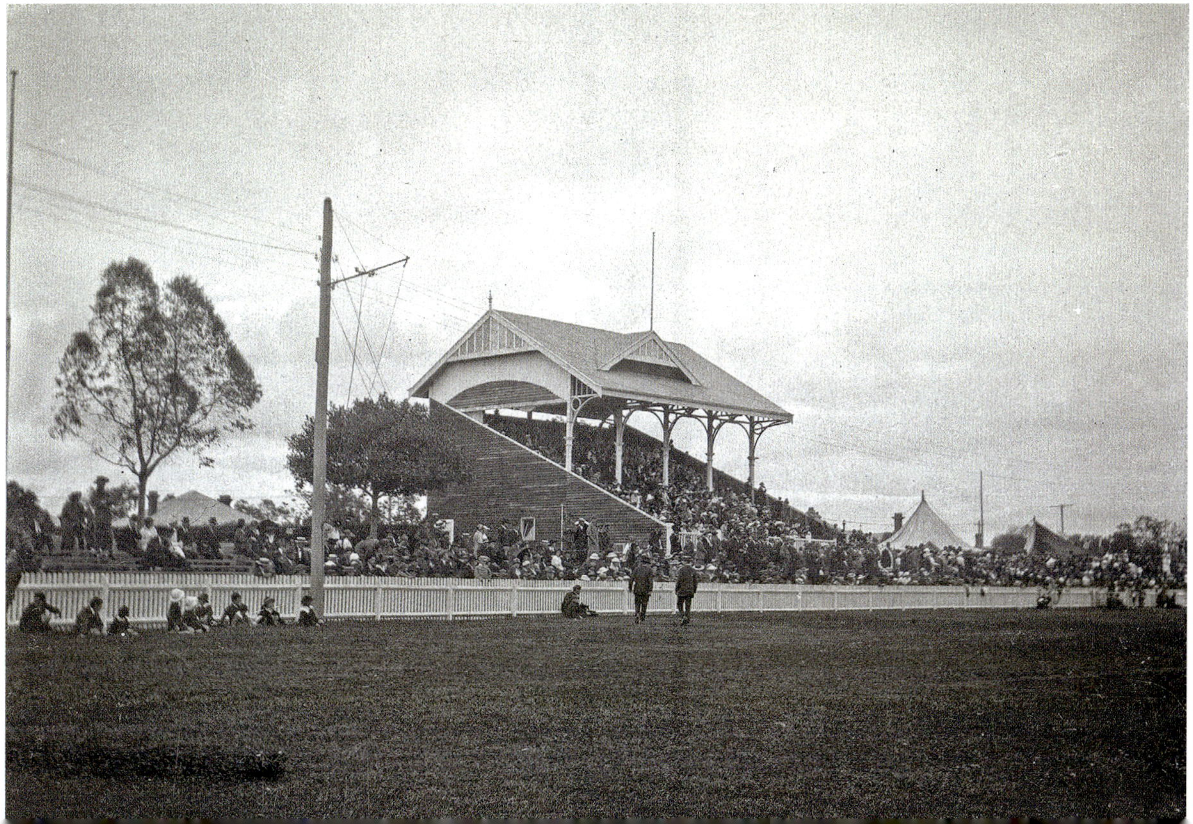

LEFT The grandstand in the early 1920s. Those not wishing to pay to see a match would often climb the tree on the left to get a glimpse of the action.

OPPOSITE The caption to this photograph of the grandstand from *Weekend News* in 1920 reads: "Tom Lewis, trainer in black suit, no hat."

COUNCIL CHAMBERS

DEMOLISHED 1970

Perth City Council was formed in 1858, but it was not until 1871, when Perth was declared a municipality, that the council was given a permanent home at the new Town Hall.

By the beginning of the 1920s the number of staff employed by Perth City Council had reached a point where they were struggling to find sufficient space in the Town Hall. So began the search for an alternative building to use as council offices.

The search identified the Strelitz Building, which was on Murray Street, close to what is now Forrest Place. This building, "a large business premises", had been designed for the Strelitz Brothers, Paul and Richard, in 1907 by Joseph Allen.

The German brothers initially immigrated to Victoria, but the lure of the Gold Rush brought first Richard and then Paul across to establish Strelitz Brothers, Merchants and Shipping Agents of Fremantle and Kalgoorlie. As their business flourished, they decided to open another branch in Perth. In addition to their core business, Paul was appointed the Western Australian Consul of the Netherlands and his brother the equivalent for Denmark and Sweden.

Todd Brothers gained the tender for the construction work. It was said at the time that the quantity of bricks required for the construction of the project was second only to the Supreme Court building in what is now Stirling Gardens.

Consisting of two separate buildings, one fronting on to Hay Street and the other Murray Street, the complex was joined in the middle by common warehouse facilities and a yard. The combined floor area of the buildings was nearly 12,000 square metres.

The British General Electric Company leased the Murray Street end when it was completed in 1908, while the Optical and Photo Supplies Company (taken over by Kodak in 1924) leased the Hay Street building.

Perth businessman William Padbury, who owned the entire eastern side of the new Forrest Place (on which he built his Padbury Building in 1925) approached the Strelitz brothers to buy their Murray Street building in August 1924. Having purchased the property, he resold it within a week to the Perth City Council for £37,500, making a profit of £2,000 on the deal.

There were some members of the council who thought the price paid was far too high, but it was finally accepted and they resolved to engage architects Hobbs Smith & Forbes to build extra offices and council chambers on the site of the old warehouses and yard behind the Murray Street building. This they achieved by creating a basement and two floors in the yard space.

To fund the project the city ordered alterations to the ground floor of the Town Hall to create shops, the rent from which would service the loan for the new building, plus a profit of £1,230.

The council remained in the Strelitz building until the new Council House building was completed in 1963. The Murray Street building was demolished in 1970 to make way for the Carillon City shopping centre.

BELOW AND RIGHT The newly opened Council Chambers in 1925.

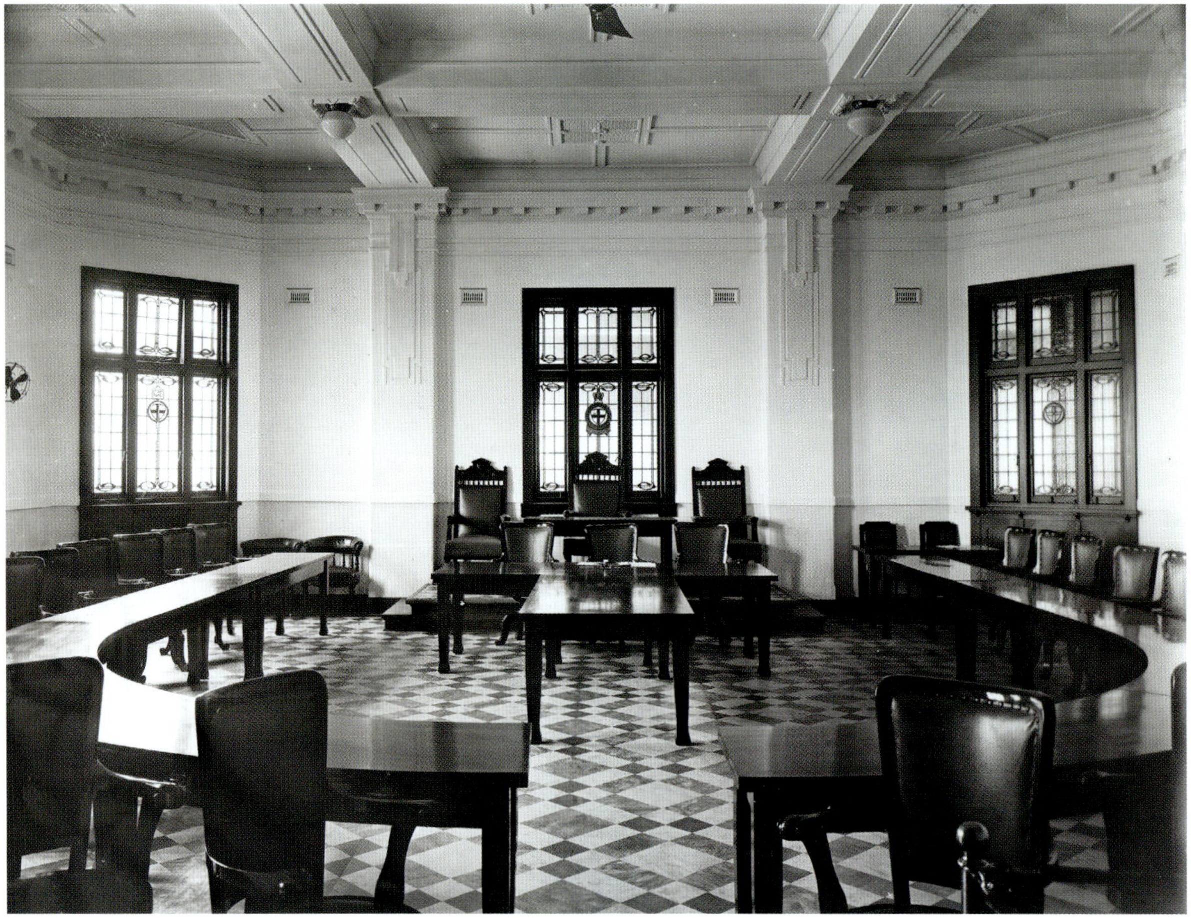

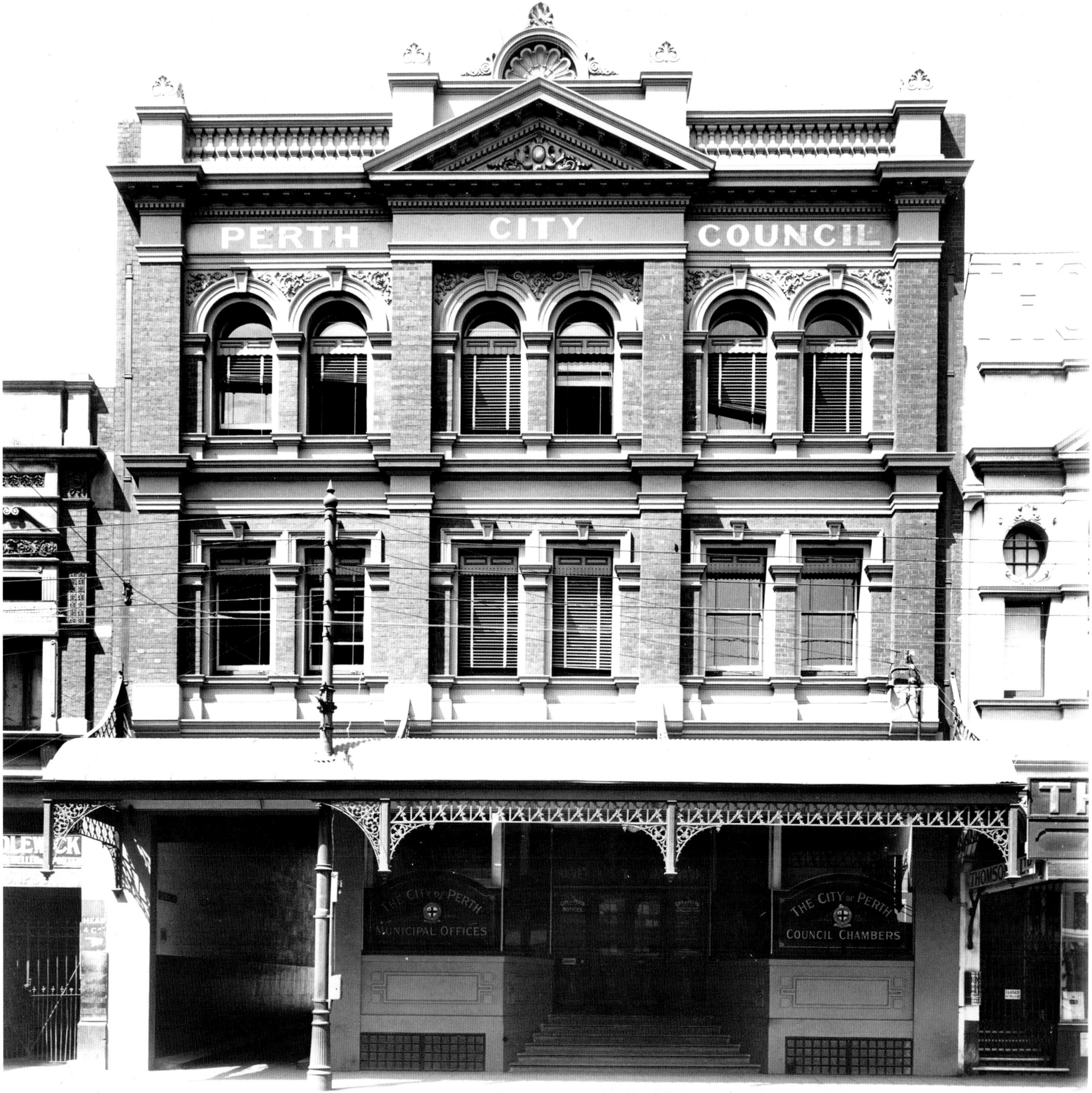
PERTH CITY COUNCIL
THE CITY OF PERTH
MUNICIPAL OFFICES
THE CITY OF PERTH
COUNCIL CHAMBERS

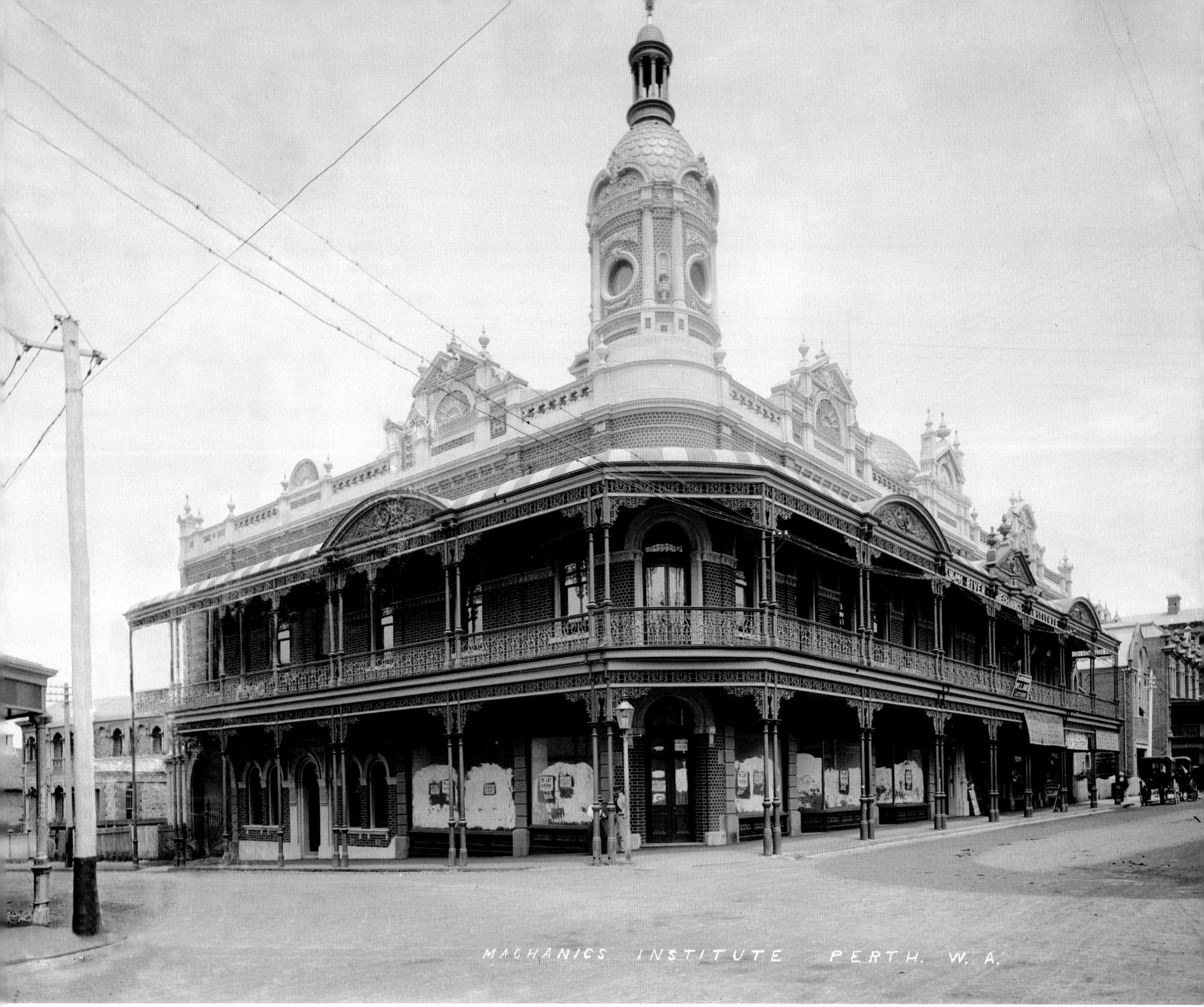
MACHANICS INSTITUTE PERTH. W. A.

MECHANICS' INSTITUTE

DEMOLISHED 1970

The first Mechanics' Institute was established in Edinburgh, Scotland, in 1821 and was devised as a means of providing instruction for tradesmen (mechanics), many of whom had not received a childhood education. The first Mechanics' Institute in Australia was established in Hobart in 1827, followed by the Sydney Mechanics' School of Arts in 1833.

In Perth, the Swan River Mechanics' Institute, which was the first in Western Australia, was established in January 1851 and its founding president was Surveyor-General John Septimus Roe, who held the position until his death in 1878.

During its first year it established a library and hosted well-attended lectures in subjects as diverse as astronomy, English literature and Assyrian sculpture.

Although established to benefit the working classes, the Swan River Mechanics' Institute was predominantly frequented and run by men from the upper echelons of Perth society, who tended to treat it as their club. Institute rules did not allow the discussion of political issues and in 1856 one working-class man was expelled for criticising government policies.

Ex-convicts were barred from being members, prompting the formation of a number of alternative working men's associations, such as the Western Australian Working Men's Association, which met in Fremantle during the mid-1860s. These groups had less restrictive entry requirements – to become a member one had to be seen as a respectable member of the community.

Early meetings of the Mechanics' Institute took place at the Court House and lectures were held in the Murray Street Boys' School. Eventually, a site for a permanent building was granted by the legislative council in Howick Street (now Hay Street) and the foundation stone for the new building was laid by Governor Fitzgerald on 25 May 1852.

In 1898, an impressive new building was designed by William Wolf to replace the original building. The foundation was laid by the Premier, Sir John Forrest, in June and the building was completed by the following year. It was designed with a concert hall capable of seating 400, complete with a platform and dressing rooms. There was also a spacious library and accompanying reading room.

The organisation changed its name to the Perth Literary Institute in 1909. At that time, an inventory showed the library contained nearly 10,000 books. In 1957 the institute became City of Perth Library, which was moved to the lower ground floor of Council House in 1963 and the very fine institute building was sadly demolished in 1970, it being one of many such buildings in the city to have disappeared without fuss during this period, being considered old-fashioned rather than of historic interest.

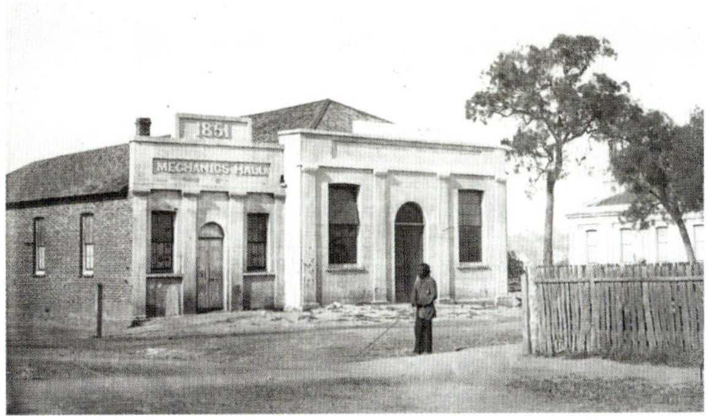

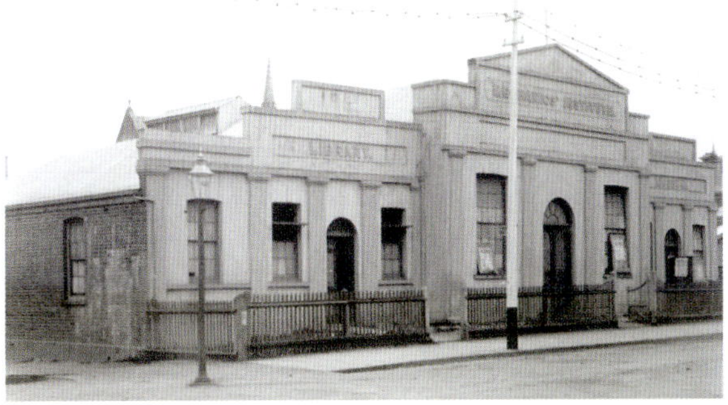

ABOVE LEFT The original Mechanics' Institute building as photographed by Alfred Stone in 1861.

LEFT By the 1880s extensions had been added to the original building, to house a library at the eastern end and a museum at the other.

OPPOSITE William Wolf's exuberantly detailed 1898 Mechanics' Institute building.

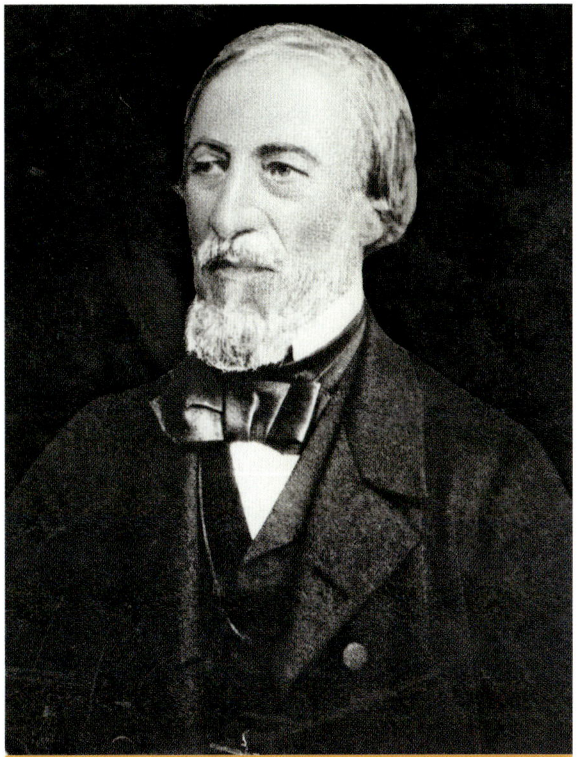

J.S. ROE

John Septimus Roe was born in 1797. The seventh son of the Rector of Newbury, Berkshire, UK, he was educated at Christ's Hospital, London. When 16 Roe joined the Navy and was appointed a midshipman. In 1817 he passed examinations in mathematics and navigation and was posted as master's mate to the surveying service in New South Wales. In 1828, whilst recuperating from illness, he was offered the post of surveyor-general to the new Swan River Colony. To enable him to accept the position the Admiralty gave him two years' leave; later extended to over 40. From the time he arrived in June 1829 until his death in 1878, Roe was influential in many aspects of the development of Western Australia. He retired in August 1870 and one of the last entries in his diary says, "I have not been an idle man in my generation."

VIKING HOUSE

DEMOLISHED 1970

Viking House, or the Viking Buildings as it was originally named, was a development project of the Strelitz Brothers, Merchants and Shipping Agents of Fremantle and Kalgoorlie. How the building's name was chosen is unclear, although it is likely to derive from the brothers' diplomatic links with Scandinavia. To represent the theme, the stern head of a Viking warrior was carved above the main entrance on William Street.

The building was designed by Joseph Allen, who seemed to be the Strelitz brothers' architect of choice, having worked on a number of their development projects around the city. The building stood 115 feet tall and was described as a skyscraper by the newspapers at the time of its opening. All terms are relative and although modest by today's standards, the building outstripped everything else in the city in the early 1900s.

The building, which cost £25,000 to build, had over 50 offices, either suites or single occupancy, each with its own strong room. Each floor had its own modern bathroom facilities and a caretaker lived on the premises in a three-room apartment. The main entrance and foyer had a nautical look with decorative tiles featuring ships and the top floor, leased by the Amateur Sports Club, had an ornate oak ceiling, with complementary furnishings. It also had one of the first automatic lifts in Perth.

On 10 January 1913, during the final stages of construction, a tragic accident occurred involving the new lift. David Carlton, a talented local artist and prolific writer, was preparing to move into the art studio he was renting on the second floor. The lift was coming down from the fourth floor and although the lift's motion bell was ringing, Carlton apparently did not hear it or ignored it, put his head through an opening at the side of the lift shaft to speak to someone below and was struck by the passing lift, which killed him instantly.

On a more cheerful note, the building was the venue for Perth's first nightclub, the Miami Club, which opened in August 1937, by which time the building was known as National House. It must be said, however, that the concept of a nightclub in the 1930s was somewhat different from the current examples. The *West Australian* described the club's inaugural dinner and dance: "The ballroom, in which dinner was served on long-tables gay with vases of Iceland poppies, was an attractive place, with walls of cream and gold and furnishings to tone. Effective lighting came from large square-shaped, indirect lights in the ceiling and small candle-shaped brackets on the walls. Palms were the only other decoration used. During dinner the Miami Orchestra played several numbers ... At the conclusion of dinner the guests were shown over the other rooms of the club while the ballroom was cleared for dancing."

A week later, the *Mirror* featured the headline, "The Miami Night Club Is A Perth Man's Dream Realised – somewhere to go for supper and to have a cheery dance with attractive appointments and luxury surroundings."

National House continued to be a mixed-use building, with offices and club rooms, such as those of the Naval, Military and Air Force Club, until it was demolished in 1970 without fuss. The site remained vacant for 16 years. In 1986 the entire site was acquired by the Superannuation Board of Western Australia, Bond Corporation and Laurie Connell and Partners who planned a 51-storey skyscraper. The AMP Building plaza and Western Australian Visitors' Centre now occupy the space where Viking House once stood.

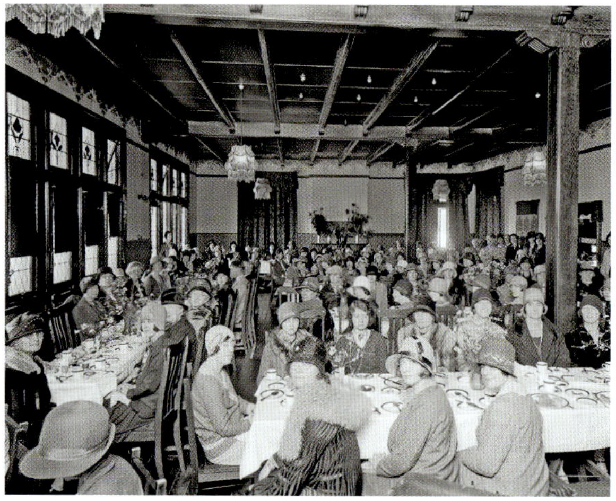

ABOVE Interior of building, as seen at a Women's Service Guilds luncheon held on 27 August 1929. The organisation's offices were in Viking House.

LEFT A Viking figurehead on the arch at the entrance to Viking House.

RIGHT Architect Joseph Allen's clever use of strong vertical lines made Viking House look much taller than it really was, as can be seen from this 1920 photograph.

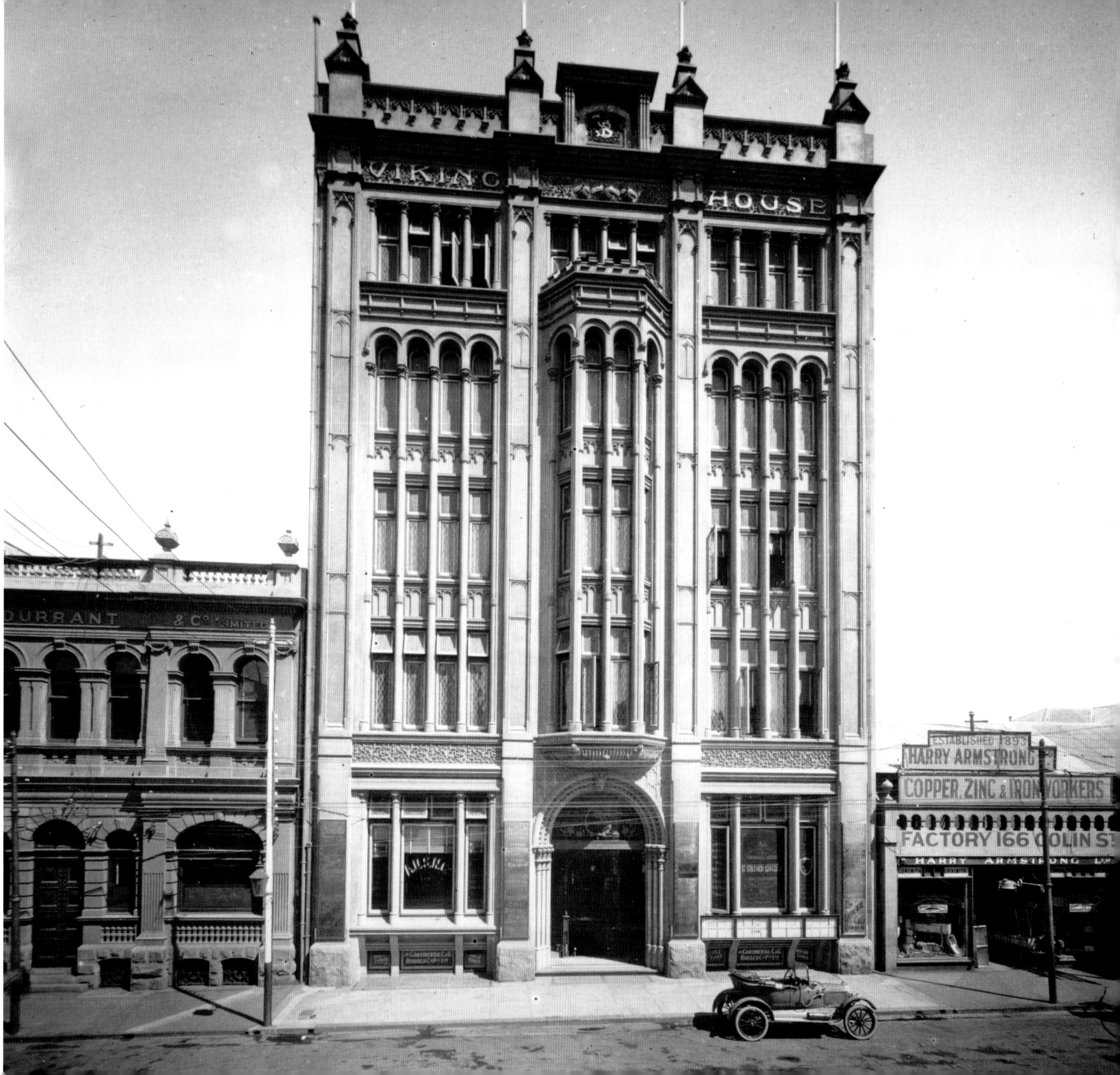
VIKING HOUSE
DURRANT & Co LIMITED
ESTABLISHED 1893
HARRY ARMSTRONG
COPPER, ZINC & IRON WORKERS
FACTORY 166 COLIN ST

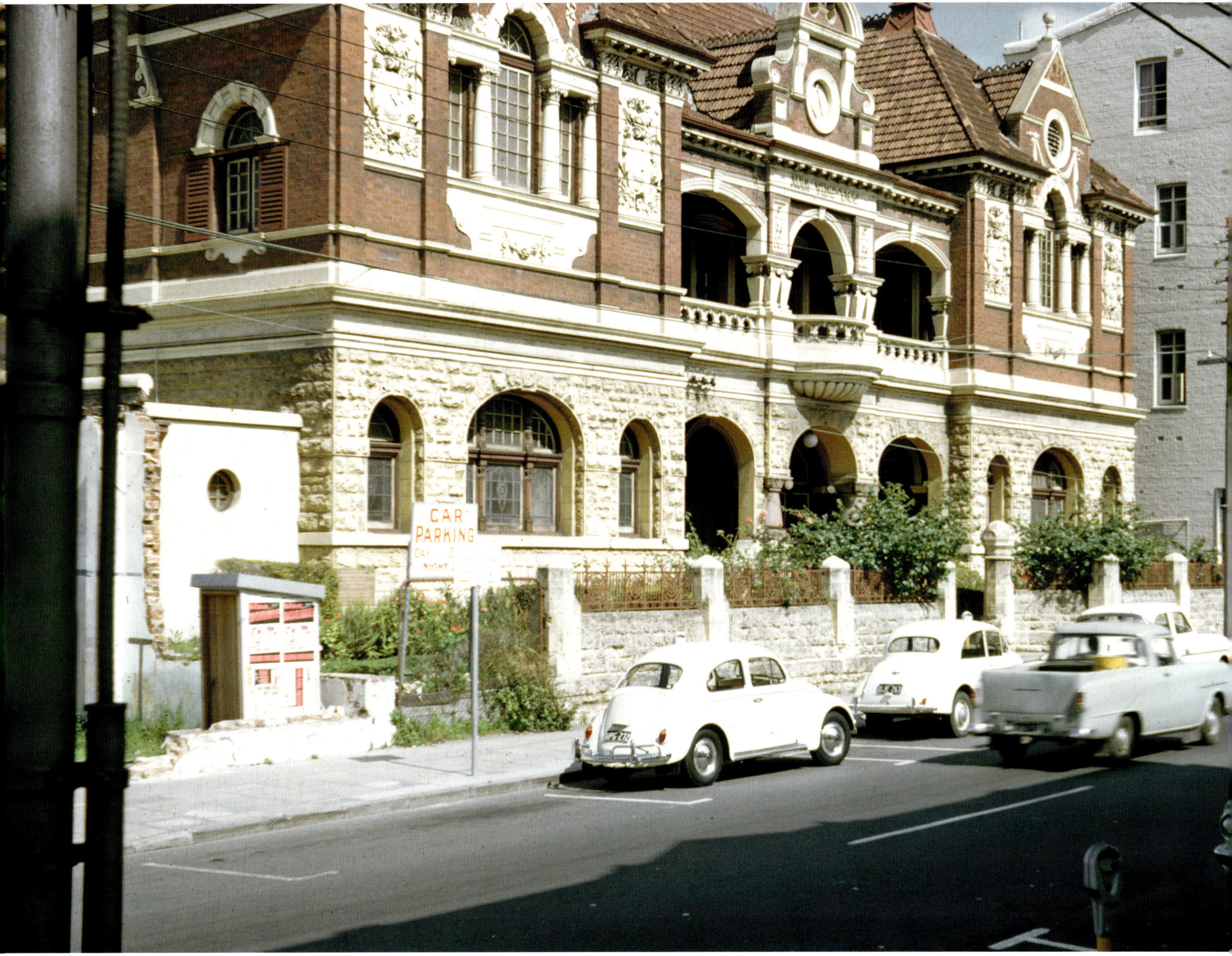
CAR
PARKING

MASONIC LODGE

DEMOLISHED 1971

Freemasonry is an ancient fraternal organisation that traces its origins back to the European medieval craft guilds. Its objectives are stated as, "the improvement of society and teaching of the three main principles of brotherly love, charity to those in need and a belief in one true God." Organised into lodges, which may have general membership or be based around a particular occupation such as law or a traditional craft, the first Freemason Hall to house a lodge was opened in London in 1776.

The first Masonic lodge in Western Australia was inaugurated at a meeting in the old Government House on 1 September 1841. On that day, Governor John Hutt, himself a Freemason, met with six others from the fraternity, including the then Colonial Secretary, Peter Broun to begin the process of setting up a lodge. A request was sent to London a few days later for a charter of establishment and the new Lodge of St John met officially for the first time in April 1843.

Several meetings of the new lodge were held at Government House, but this was considered inappropriate use of a government facility and so moved to Leeder's Hotel on St Georges Terrace (now the site of the Palace Hotel). In 1845 the proprietor, William Leeder, built an extension to the hotel to better accommodate the lodge and the building soon became known as the "Freemasons' Hotel". The *Inquirer* newspaper reported: "The first stone of the new portion was laid on Friday last, and as part of the building is designed for a new masonic lodge (the first ever constructed in this colony), the stone was laid by the Hon. P. Broun."

When accommodation at the Freemasons' Hotel became inadequate, a block of land was granted by the government on Howick (now Hay) Street, next to the Mechanics' Institute and just east of the Town Hall. Here, in 1867, the lodge constructed its own building in a Tudor Gothic architectural style.

By the 1890s the brethren had outgrown their hall and in January 1896 it was announced that the state government had purchased the building with a view to housing their mines department there. The Freemasons acquired a new plot of land on Howick Street, just east of Pier Street, and here erected a temporary building at the back of the block. Designs for a new, two-storey building of "an imposing nature" were drawn up by J.J. Talbot Hobbs and the foundation stone was laid by the Governor in September 1896.

Initial estimates that the building would be completed in eight months, with the ground floor available for use earlier, proved rather optimistic, as reports of the opening did not appear until December 1897.

The growth of Freemasonry in Western Australia during the first Gold Rush warranted the formation of a Grand Lodge of Western Australia and this came into existence in February 1900. They later purchased the Hay Street site and buildings from the Lodge of St John, paying £1,000 and taking over the mortgage. The organisation vacated the building in 1967, moving to premises in Terrace Road, and the old Masonic Hall was demolished in 1971, becoming another victim of the "modernise our city" trend, which was not unique just to Perth.

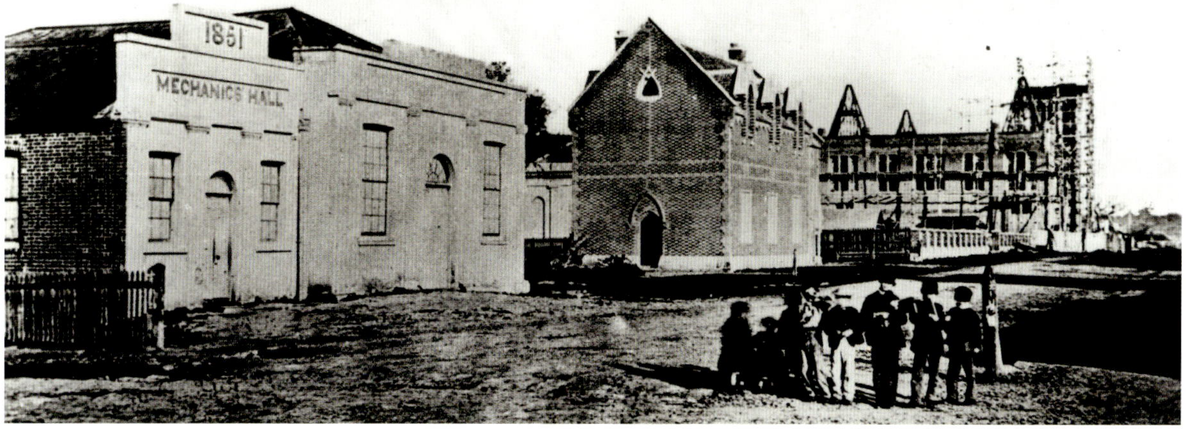

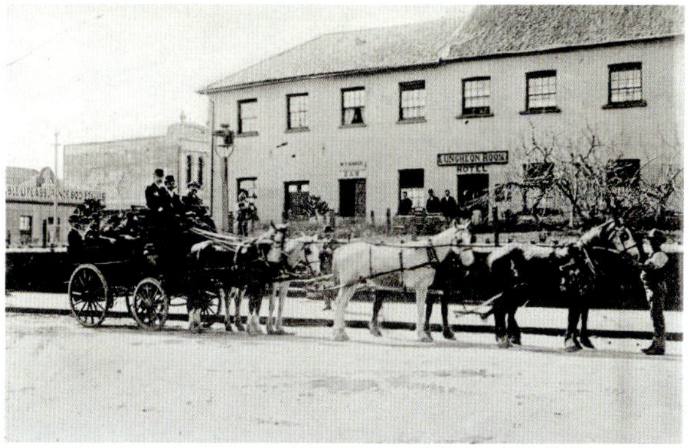

TOP The Masonic Lodge, next door to the Mechanics' Institute, in 1868. In the background can be seen the Town Hall under construction.

ABOVE The first home of the Lodge of St John, Leeder's Hotel on St Georges Terrace, which soon became known as the Freemasons' Hotel.

OPPOSITE J.J. Talbot Hobbs' elegant Masonic Lodge opened on Hay Street in 1897. This photograph was taken four years before its demolition in 1971.

FEDERAL HOTEL

DEMOLISHED 1972

A "palace" is an apt description of this magnificent example of Perth's opulent building designs of the late 19th century.

Initially named Stein's Coffee Palace, the Federal Hotel was located on the corner of George and Douro (later Wellington) Streets. It was designed in 1896 by J.W. Wright & Co., a well-established Perth architectural firm of the time, and built by G. Nicol in 1897 for Bernard Stein.

Stein arrived in Western Australia as a convict in 1867, having been convicted of larceny in the UK. Sentenced to 10 years' penal servitude in Western Australia, he obtained his ticket of leave in 1872 and opened a bookshop on the corner of Howick (now Hay) and Barrack Streets. In 1873 he was once again imprisoned for theft, but absconded with another convict whilst working with a road gang. They eventually found their way to Port Adelaide, where they were apprehended almost two years later and sent back to Perth to complete their sentences. On his release he resumed his book business and, after marrying Ann Barnard in 1884, appears to have been a law-abiding citizen.

In the 1880s he expanded his business property to include offices and more retail space, which became known as both Stein's Chambers and also Bernard Stein's Book Arcade. The success of this venture led him to open several more profitable arcades in Kalgoorlie, Coolgardie and Boulder. His growing fortune allowed him to become a developer, building shops and offices in prime locations in Perth and Fremantle, as well as several houses in Claremont.

The foundation stone of Stein's Coffee Palace was laid in November 1896 and construction continued over the next eight months. Flanked by shops on either side, it had a basement accessible from George Street, with billiard room and storage, verandas over both George and Wellington Street footpaths and an imposing corner tower with a lookout at the top. Externally, the tuck-pointed red brick façade featured decorative moulded cornices, pediments and balustrades, which all added grandeur to the building.

According to reports from the time, internal proportions were grand and designed to be light and airy. The ground floor, with 15-foot ceilings and a 12-foot-wide entrance, featured a 150-seat dining room, plus comfortably furnished reading and smoking rooms. Each of the 52 bedrooms opened onto the verandas, with well-appointed bathrooms and sitting rooms on each floor. The building cost Stein £13,000 and when completed it was one of the largest hotel buildings in Perth.

Coffee palaces were also known as temperance hotels and did not sell alcohol of any kind. However, a liquor licence was obtained for the site in late 1897 and the property was officially reopened as the Federal Hotel in January the following year.

The Federal became a popular Perth watering hole, which offered both short and long-term accommodation and remained so until it was acquired in the early 1960s by the government in preparation for the construction of the Mitchell Freeway. The contents of the hotel were sold off by auction, the tower was removed in 1969 and the rest of the building was demolished in 1972. The hotel's foundation stone was saved from destruction and is now in the possession of the Royal Western Australian Historical Society.

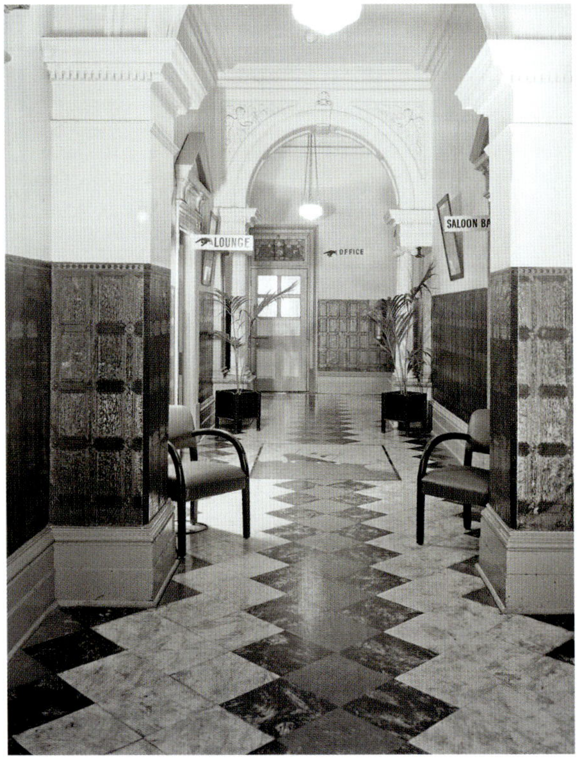

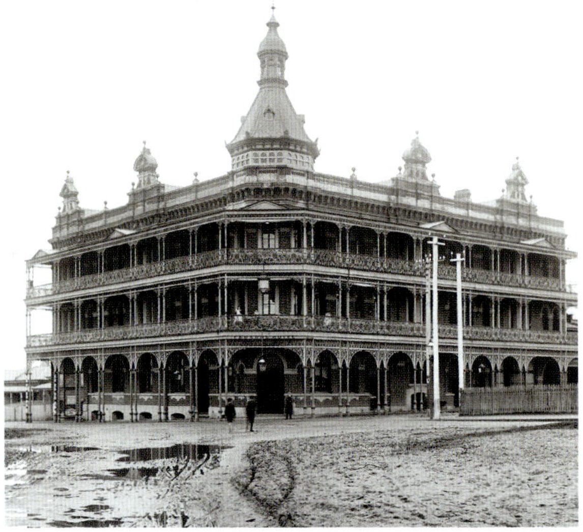

RIGHT Taken in the early 1960s, the banner on the hotel reads: "Important auction sale. Contents of Federal Hotel. Wed. Jan. 22nd at 10.00 a.m."

LEFT The magnificence of the Federal Hotel on a rainy day in about 1905.

FAR LEFT The hotel hallway in 1953.

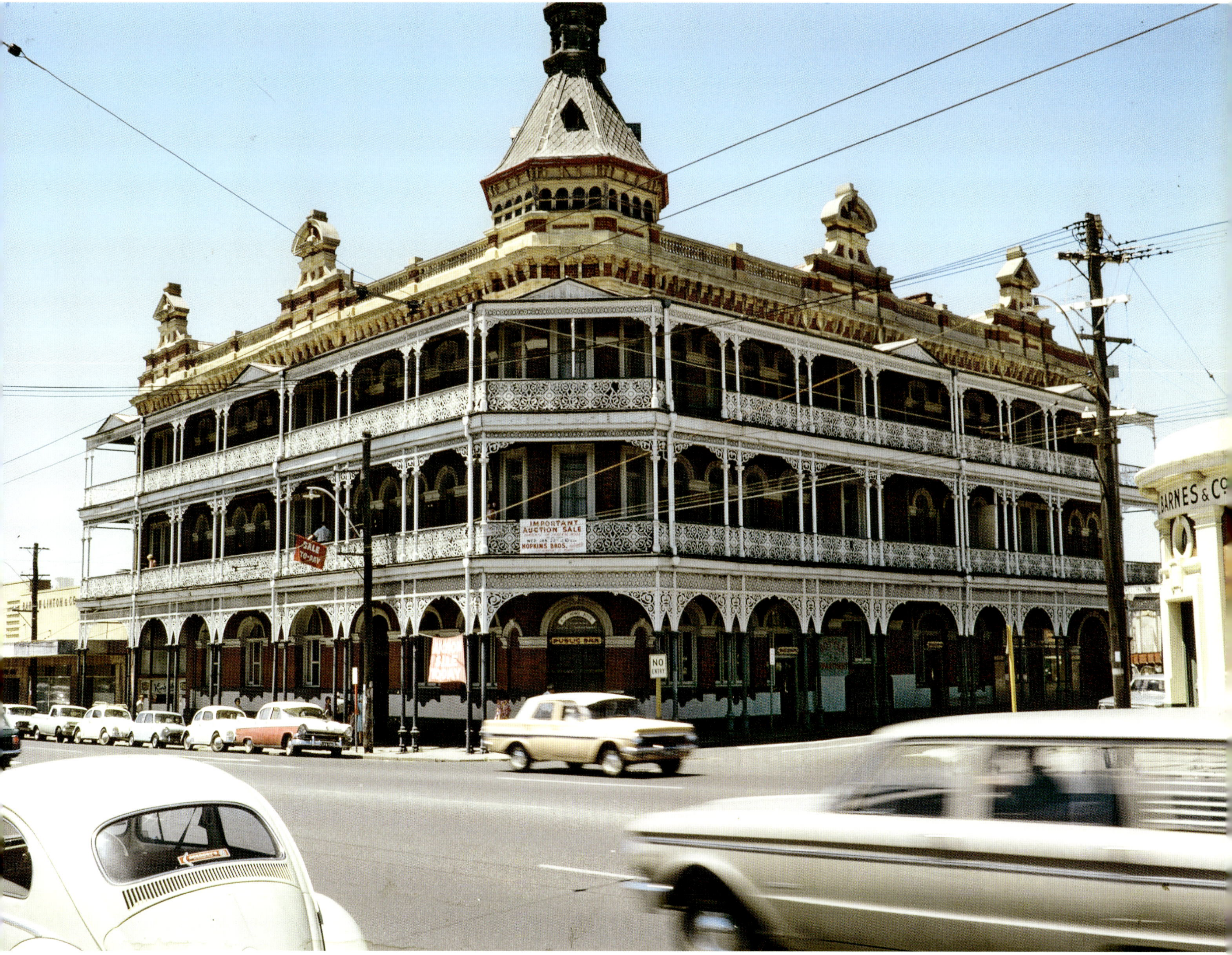
IMPORTANT
AUCTION SALE
HOPKINS BROS.
PUBLIC BAR
NO
ENTRY
BARNES & Co
SALE
TO-DAY

AMBASSADORS THEATRE

DEMOLISHED 1972

On 28 June 1927, the *West Australian* wrote excitedly, "A magnificent theatre, capable of seating from 2,500 to 3,000 people is about to be built on the eastern side of the Theatre Royal in Hay Street."

Construction of the Ambassadors started almost immediately and created one of the most ostentatious theatres in Perth's history. Funded by Sir Thomas Coombe, in partnership with Union Cinemas, the new theatre was to be an "atmospheric" cinema. The idea was born during a visit to America by Union's managing director, Stuart Doyle, who was impressed with similar theatres in San Francisco. He later described an atmospheric cinema as being "A long, long way from the old open-air enclosure, where flickering motion pictures allied to music from an out-of-tune piano, thrilled one and all, to the million-dollar temples of the cinema with their mammoth orchestras and superlative presentation plans." The philosophy of these theatres was for patrons to suspend reality on entry and be whisked back in time to a classical courtyard somewhere in Southern Europe, complete with a starlit sky ceiling.

The Ambassadors was Australia's second atmospheric theatre, being preceded by the Capitol in Sydney, which opened a few months before. Construction was rarely out of the news during the rest of 1927 and early 1928. From the lifting of 90-foot steel beams, weighing 28 tons, to hold up the auditorium roof, to the installation of a magnificent Wurlitzer theatre organ, the largest in the Southern Hemisphere, all was reported in the minutest detail.

The opening took place on 29 September 1928 and for several days the Perth newspapers featured little else than talk of this extravagant project. A few days later, the correspondent sent to cover the opening by the *West Australian* described his first impressions as the guests entered the auditorium, "Among the first of the marvels to catch the eye as one joined the human stream ascending the grand stairway was the atmospheric 'sky.' Sceptics admitted conversion. Undeniably, the effect was wonderful. Immeasurably distant, seemingly, the deep blue vault of heaven arched above as, having inspected the diverse art objects shrined in the wide, luxurious balconies, one emerged on to the Florentine garden, which is the theatre's amazing auditorium."

The theatre immediately became popular with cinema-goers and the theatre orchestra and organ were featured almost on a daily basis on local radio stations. However, just over a year later, the Wall Street Crash plunged the world into a deep recession and the Ambassadors was hit by dwindling audiences. The orchestra was scrubbed and the theatre closed for some months in 1932, reopening the following year under new management.

Further changes took place in 1937 when the theatre was redesigned in an Art Deco style. The theatre was a popular venue throughout World War II and in 1953 became the first cinema in Western Australia to show a Cinemascope film. With the rising popularity of television in the early 1970s, audiences dwindled. The cinema closed with a final showing of *Diamonds Are Forever* on 2 February 1972 and was demolished later that year.

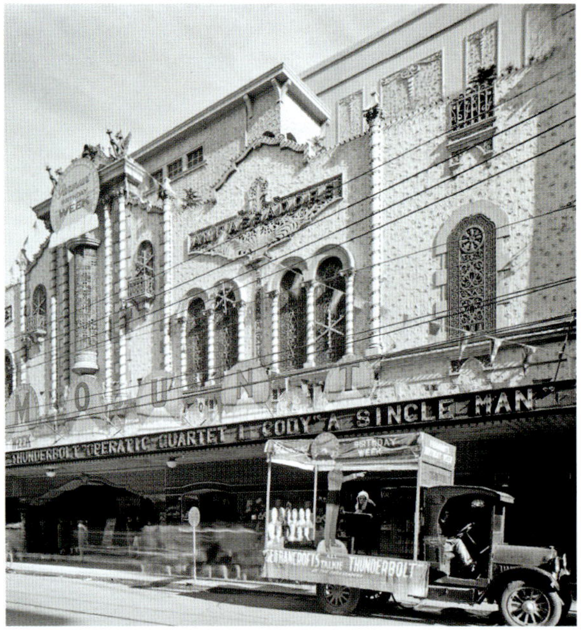

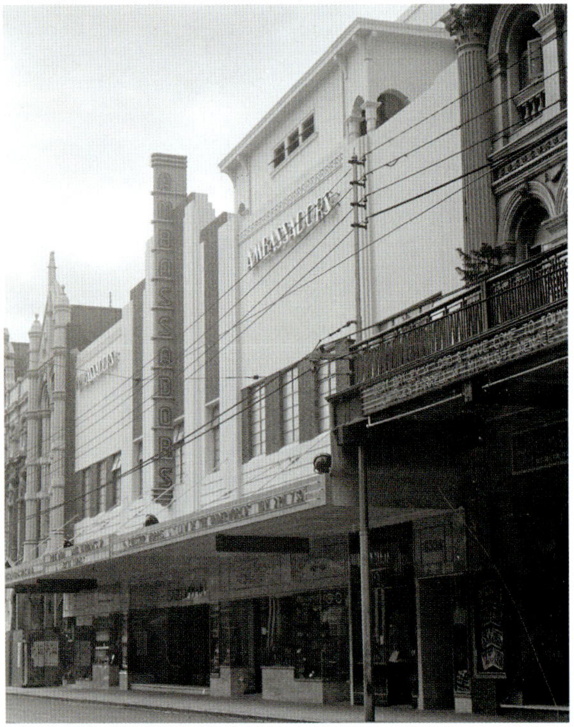

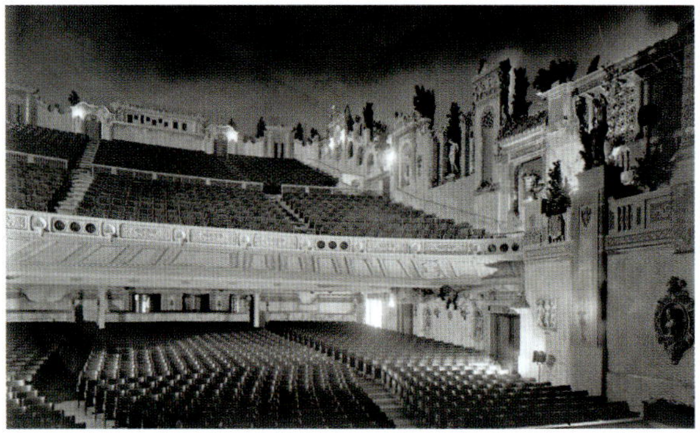

TOP The theatre and advertising truck celebrating Paramount Birthday Week in 1929. The incredible detail in the architecture of the building made it a memorable place to visit for every filmgoer.

ABOVE A view of the lavishly ornamented auditorium from the stage soon after the theatre opened in 1928.

LEFT The Art Deco revision to the façade, which considerably diluted its visual impact, as seen in the early 1950s.

RIGHT An evening audience leaves the theatre in 1932.

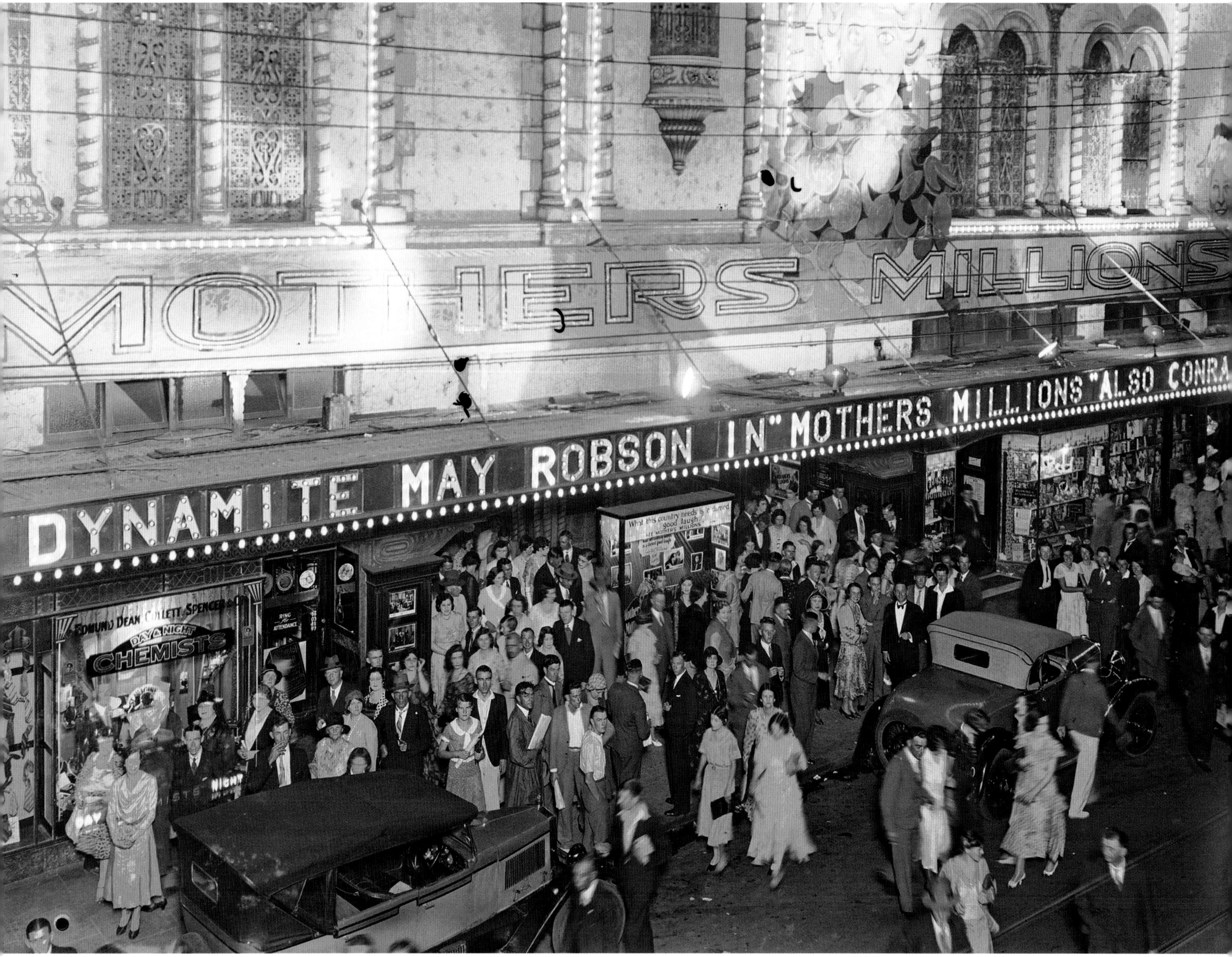
MOTHERS MILLIONS
DYNAMITE MAY ROBSON IN" MOTHERS MILLIONS" ALSO CONRA
EDMUND DEAN COLLETT SPENCER & CO
DAY & NIGHT
CHEMISTS
RING FOR ATTENDANCE

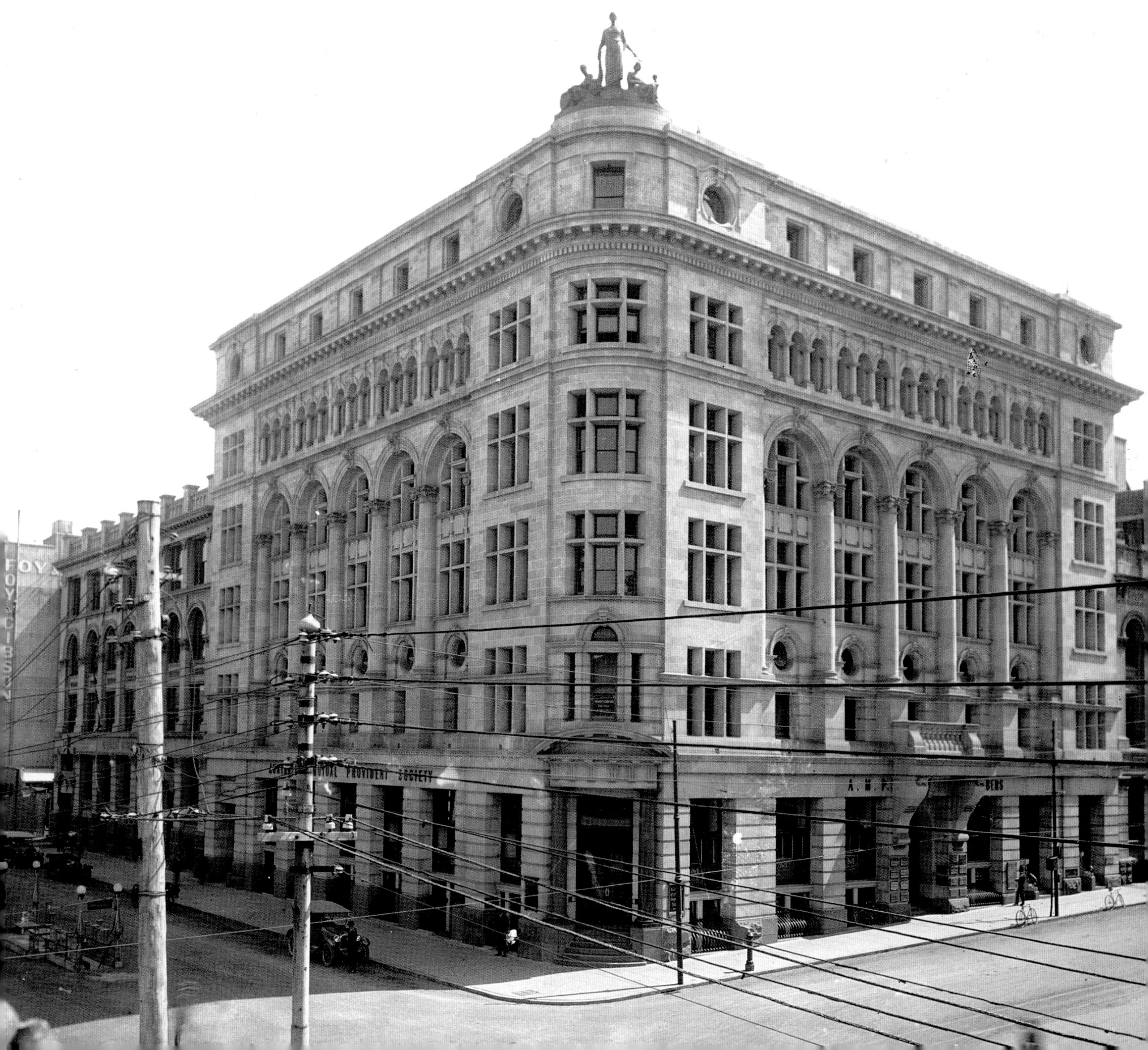
FOY &
PROVIDENT SOCIETY
A. M. P.
BERS

AMP BUILDING

DEMOLISHED 1972

The building whose loss is probably mourned more than any other by older residents of Perth is the AMP Building, which was situated on the north-west corner of the junction between St Georges Terrace and William Street.

The site was from the early 1850s known as Carr's Corner because it was the location of Julian Carr's shop, which, according to the sign over the door in an 1868 photograph, was styled as, "J.G.C. Carr, importer of wines, spirits, beer, drapery, ironmongery, and general merchandise."

Carr had arrived in Perth in 1848 and soon set up a general agency business which must have flourished, as by 1860 he had an estate valued at over £1,000. In addition to running his own business, Carr found time to be chairman of Perth City Council, a nominated member of the Legislative Council and a founder member of the Perth Building Society, which was inaugurated in 1862.

The site was acquired in 1910 by the Australian Mutual Provident Society with the intention of building a new headquarters on it. AMP Chambers was designed by the Perth firm of Oldham and Cox and built by Simon Alexander, a prolific building company of the early 20th century. The foundation stone was laid by the governor of Western Australia, Sir Edward Stone, in a ceremony on 8 November 1912.

This six-storey, plus basement, building was designed in what the local newspapers described as "a dignified adaptation of the Romanesque style" and clad in white Donnybrook stone, with an interior decorated with jarrah. The construction was not, however, without its problems. In 1913 there was friction between the clerk of works for the project and the stonemasons working on the building, who walked off site. The argument escalated and led to a very protracted libel case between the clerk of works and the architects.

Another incident was reported a year later when it was discovered that sulphuric acid had been deliberately poured over an area of sandstone on the second-floor exterior of the building. For a few days, the local papers were full of doom and gloom stories of how part of the building would need to be dismantled and blocks of stone replaced, but eventually a police investigation proved to be inconclusive as to the perpetrators of this wanton vandalism and the damage found to have been less destructive than had first been thought.

The top of the new building featured an iconic bronze statue, which became a landmark in the city. The 3.7 metre high statue of four figures, often called the "Amicus Group", was inspired by AMP's original seal and included a central figure symbolising Protection, flanked by a man, woman and child. When the statue was removed from the building in 1972, a piece of wood was found naming the four men who erected it in October 1914.

In 1972, when AMP announced plans to demolish the building and erect a modern skyscraper in its place, the National Trust refused to classify the building as being in need of protection. The trust administrator applauded the new development, stating that the open space in the forecourt of the new tower would make the road junction a much less gloomy place. While an unusual position for the National Trust to take, protection classification on its own was rarely a sufficient measure to prevent demolition.

Following the demolition of the AMP Building, the famous statue was saved and purchased by millionaire collector Lew Whiteman. After Whiteman's death the statue was sold to a private buyer and can now be seen on an island in Herdsman Lake.

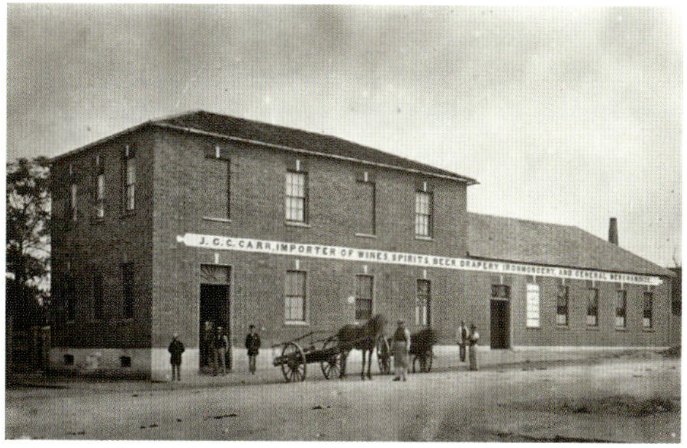

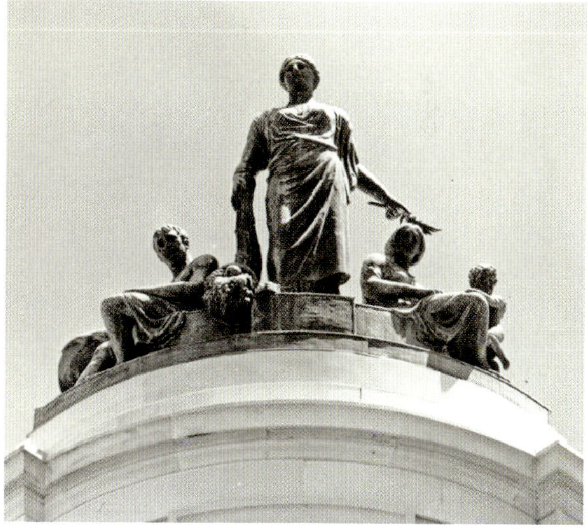

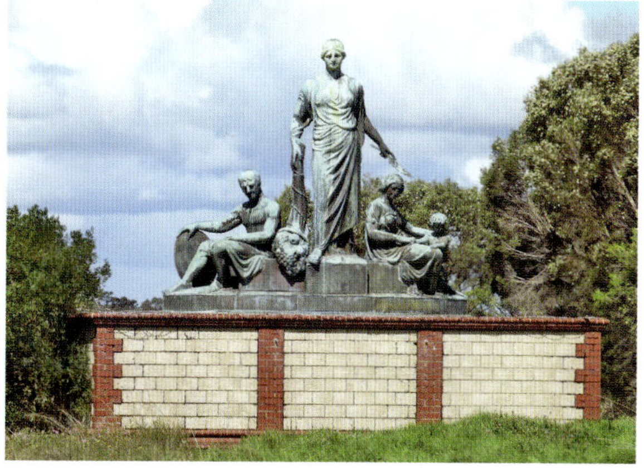

OPPOSITE The imposing lines of the AMP Building, which added considerable grandeur to the junction between William Street and St Georges Terrace.

TOP RIGHT Julian Carr's emporium, which occupied the site for many years, is seen here in 1868.

MIDDLE RIGHT The statue symbolising Protection. When removed, the names of the four men who erected it in 1914 were found inside the base.

BOTTOM RIGHT The statue in its present position beside Herdsman Lake.

ESPLANADE HOTEL

DEMOLISHED 1972

Situated close to the river and overlooking the Esplanade Reserve, the Esplanade Hotel certainly cornered the market for best location when it opened in 1898. One newspaper correspondent described it as "beautifully situated on the corner of Howard Street and Bazaar Terrace, overlooking the recreation grounds and the Swan River. The architects, Messrs. Cavanagh, Cavanagh, and Sedgefield have taken advantage of the site to place a very convenient and commodious hotel."

Built for two young mining entrepreneurs, Nathaniel Harper and James MacKenzie, the Esplanade was said to have been the most beautifully appointed in the colony. As there were four luxury hotels opened in Perth during 1898, this was high praise and it maintained its reputation for the next 50 years. The 41-room hotel was constructed of red brick in modern Renaissance style with broad verandas and was provided with every modern convenience. An extension to the east, which doubled the hotel's frontage, was added in 1910, built in materials matching the original.

Russian ballerina Anna Pavlova, who had toured Australia and New Zealand in 1926, stayed at the Esplanade Hotel. When she returned to Perth three years later to dance at His Majesty's Theatre, Pavlova chose to stay there once again. In so doing she unwittingly started a controversy that still rages. Who did invent the dessert, the "Pavlova"; was it the chef at the Esplanade Hotel, or one in Wellington, New Zealand? The Perth claim states the Esplanade Hotel's chef, Bert Sachse, created a meringue and cream cake, which the hotel owner tasted and declared to be "as light as Pavlova".

After World War II, the hotel continued to be not only the setting for Perth's high-society events, but also provided the accommodation for visiting prime ministers, ambassadors, musicians, dancers and actors.

In the late 1940s, Perth City Council introduced a bylaw that required the demolition of all post-supported verandas and balconies in the city centre. The owners of the Esplanade refused to comply. Using two prominent architects as witnesses, they argued that the veranda was one of the world's best-known and launched a Supreme Court action against the council in 1962. It is said that, late one night during the court hearing, a car veered off the Esplanade and hit one of the veranda posts. The damage was repaired before daybreak to ensure the council did not have grounds for enforcement.

According to the *Canberra Times*, during the hearing a City of Perth witness contended, "The main argument for the removal of the city verandas was the obstruction caused by posts on the footpaths. A secondary consideration was the undesirability of people sleeping over footpaths. The case was won by the hotelier!"

The hotel was sold to a developer in 1969 who planned to redevelop the site. Despite being listed by the National Trust and a public outcry, the hotel was demolished in 1972. Following demolition, the site remained undeveloped until the early 1980s when the 20-storey Griffin Building, now the BGC Centre, was constructed.

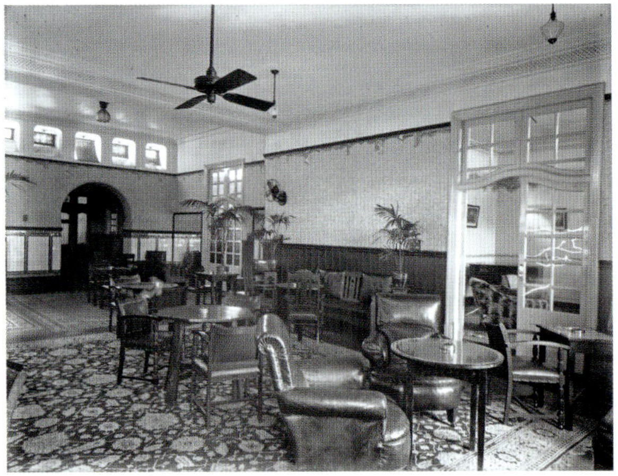

ABOVE The lounge in about 1935.

RIGHT The hotel in 1941. The sign on the balcony reads "Give and let live. Appeal Office 133 St Georges Terrace." This was the address for the Red Cross Women's Appeal Committee.

BELOW A photograph taken shortly before the hotel was demolished in 1972.

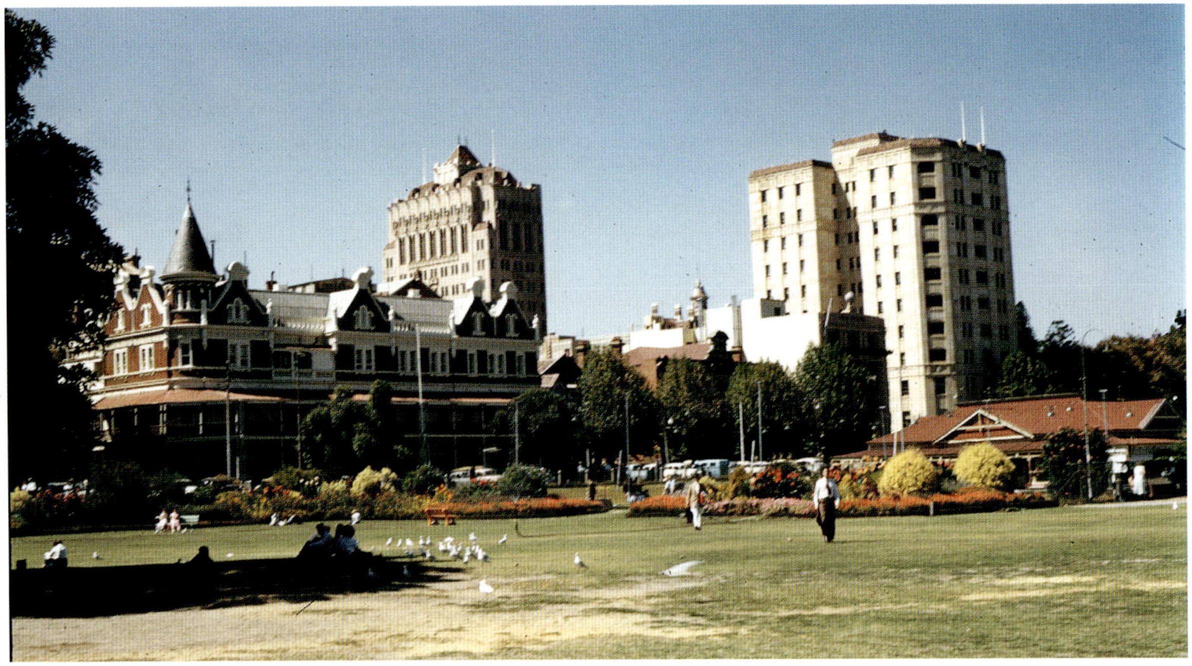

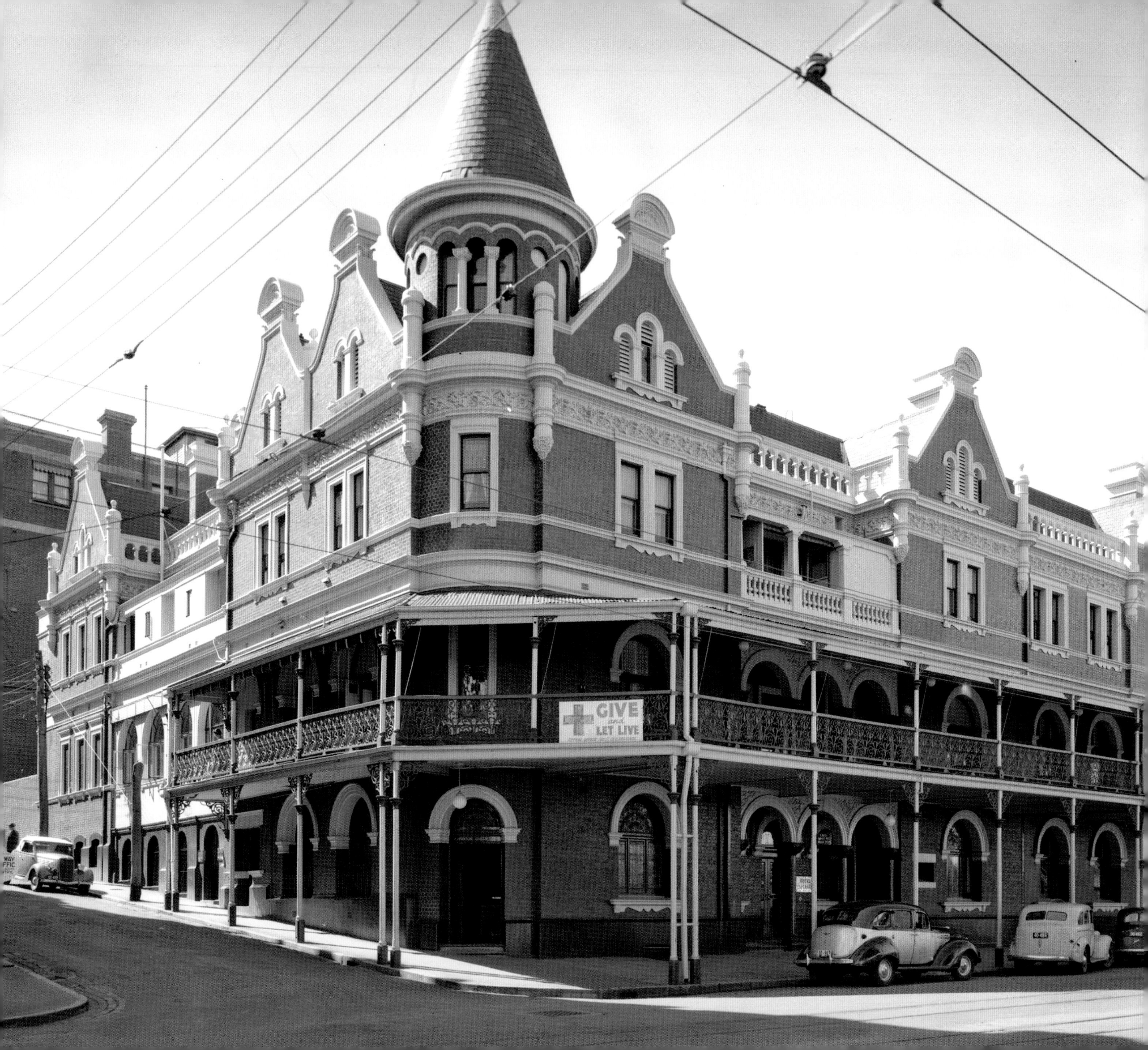
GIVE
and
LET LIVE

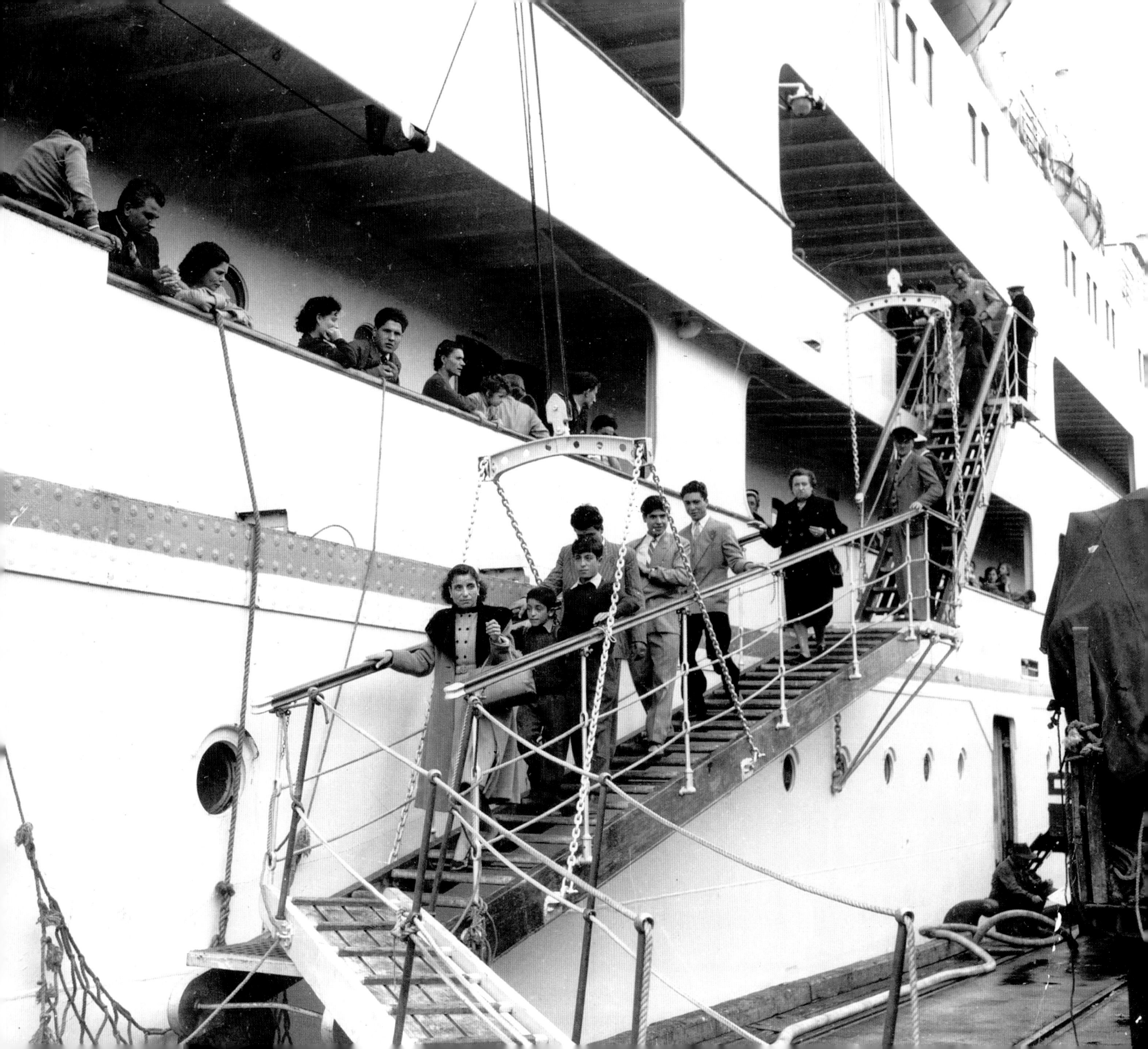

"TEN POUND POMS"

CEASED 1973

The first official migrants to settle Western Australia were those who came in 1829 to form the Swan River Colony. However, news of the difficulties the colony was experiencing with poor soils and lack of finance created little incentive for those considering migration. The colony grew very slowly in the first decade or so, not helped by a severe lack of labour to build infrastructure and carry out manual work on farms and elsewhere. To try and alleviate this problem, during 1847 the colonial government bought in contract labour from Britain and 51 indentured Chinese from Singapore.

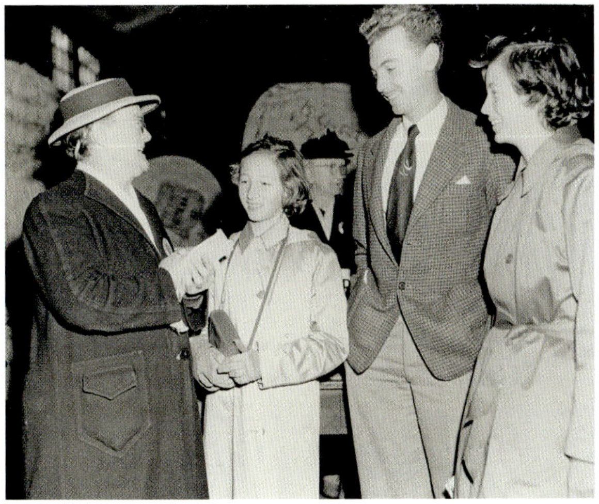

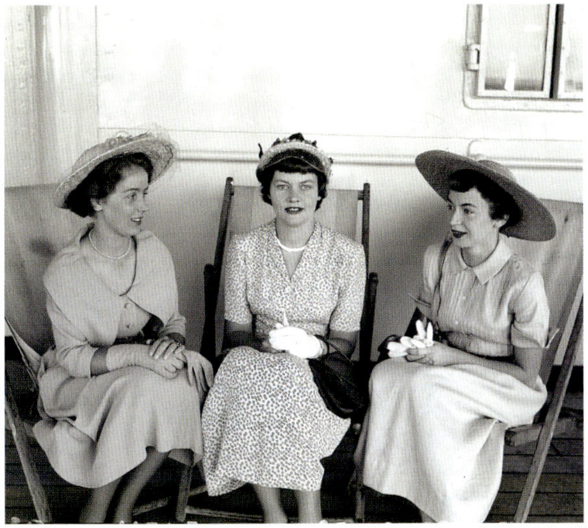

The first major growth spurt in the population occurred during the enforced immigration of convicts from 1850 to 1868. However, because of a stipulation by the colonial government that no female prisoners were to be transported to Western Australia, a serious imbalance in the gender of the population was caused, with males outnumbering females almost 2:1.

This problem was addressed by a recruitment drive targeting single women. Two forms of assisted passage were available to such women: nomination or selection. Nomination required a British friend or relative already living in the colony to sponsor a woman for emigration by providing a portion of the fare, with the remainder to be met by the government. Women not in that category were approved by the colonial authorities and were given free passage, funded by the British Government.

The discovery of gold resulted in a massive influx of people from around the world seeking their fortunes, of which nearly two thirds paid their own fare. At the time, the *West Australian* reported that: "In Perth and Fremantle everyone seems to be carrying tents, picks, shovels, and dishes, or otherwise preparing for the road." As a result the population of Western Australia rose from about 50,000 in 1891 to 184,000 in 1901.

Following World War I, assisted migration from the United Kingdom under the Group Settlement Scheme began. The aim was to help the British government alleviate unemployment by assisting some of its citizens to settle overseas. A similar assisted scheme operated in Western Australia from the early 1920s, engineered by Premier James Mitchell.

Over 6,000 people migrated to Western Australia under the scheme, which was funded jointly by the state, federal and UK governments. Unfortunately, this scheme was not a success as the land allocated was poor, the immigrants ill-equipped and many lacking in practical skills. This coupled with seemingly impossible loans to service, meant that many walked away from the scheme very early on.

After World War II the federal government created an Assisted Passage Migration Scheme as part of their "Populate or Perish" policy. Adult migrants, principally from Britain, were charged only £10 for their fare (hence the nickname "Ten Pound Poms"), while children travelled free. Migrants arriving under this scheme were required to remain in Australia for at least two years after arrival, or alternatively pay back the £10, plus fund the cost of the journey (at least £120) themselves.

Conditions for those who arrived were not comfortable and after customs clearance, those who did not have family to welcome them were taken to migrant camps, both in the metropolitan area and further afield. Many complained about the conditions. Around a million Britons took up the scheme during the 1950s and 60s, with around a quarter returning to their country of origin after the prescribed period.

There were various iterations of the scheme before it finally ceased in 1973.

LEFT Representatives of the Good Neighbour Council welcoming immigrants to Western Australia at Fremantle Harbour in August 1951.

BOTTOM LEFT Three physiotherapists arriving to "try their luck on the other side", travelling to Fremantle on the *Maloja* in 1950.

OPPOSITE New migrants disembarking in Fremantle in 1953.

QUEEN'S / HOYTS REGENT / METRO

DEMOLISHED 1973

On 6 September 1898, Sir John Forrest, the first Premier of Western Australia, and Sir George Shenton, President of the Legislative Council, laid the foundation stone of the Queen's Hall, which was part of a new building being developed by Wesley Church along William Street.

The opening was a grand affair, as the *West Australian* reported: "There was a very large audience, the body of the hall being filled, while the gallery was also well occupied. Those who attended the opening ceremony and who witnessed the interior of the building for the first time, were very favourably impressed."

Within months of opening, as a one-off event, a film was screened in the hall, which rapidly became one of Perth's premier performance venues and amongst many artists to appear there were Dame Nellie Melba and Clara Butt. In 1908 West's Pictures transferred their film shows from His Majesty's Theatre to the Queen's Hall, which became the venue for the first permanent film show in Western Australia. At the end of 1911 the lease was transferred from West's to Vic's Pictures. Vic's Pictures was a local company run by Victor Newton and Denise Dease, who also presented shows in Fremantle Town Hall. The company folded in 1918 and the hall was again used for concerts, meetings and other functions. Two years later, a fire consumed the Economic Stores on the opposite side of the road and a temporary department store was set up in the Queen's Hall, remaining there for about a year.

In 1927 the Queen's Hall was reconfigured by Melbourne architects, Bohringer, Taylor and Johnson, at the expense of the Methodist Church, for Hoyts Pictures Pty. Ltd. Hoyts was a cinema company formed in Melbourne in 1908, and the hall reopened in September 1927 as the Hoyts Regent Theatre.

The new theatre must have taken Perth by storm, ornamented with chandeliers and mirrors from Italy, an ornate proscenium arch and, a year later, a Wurlitzer theatre pipe organ from America. With a seating capacity of just over 1,400, Hoyts opened with the film *Three Bad Men* with George O'Brien and Olive Borden. Eighteen months later, in April 1929, the Regent screened its first talking picture, *The Red Dance*.

In 1938 the lease was acquired by MGM Theatres and the cinema was once again transformed, this time given the full Art Deco treatment by architects Baxter, Cox and Leighton. MGM opened the new Metro Theatre in September 1938 with *The Girl of the Golden West*. The theatre now seated 1,500 people and was the first in Perth to be air conditioned.

The Metro was taken over by Ace theatres in 1970, but by that time the writing was on the wall for many cinemas and the Metro closed its doors for the last time after a showing of *Gone With the Wind* in October 1973. The cinema was demolished in 1973 and replaced by Perth Building Society.

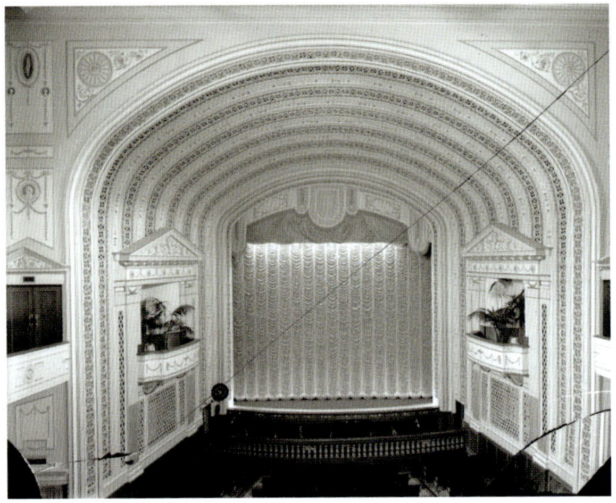

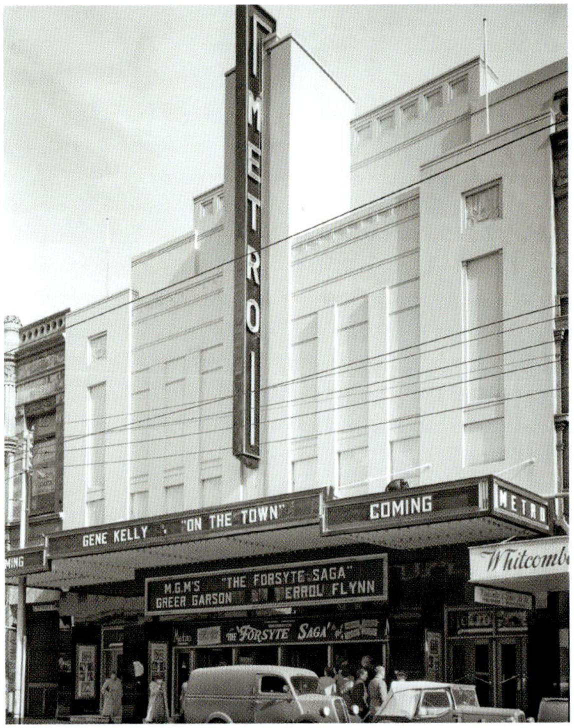

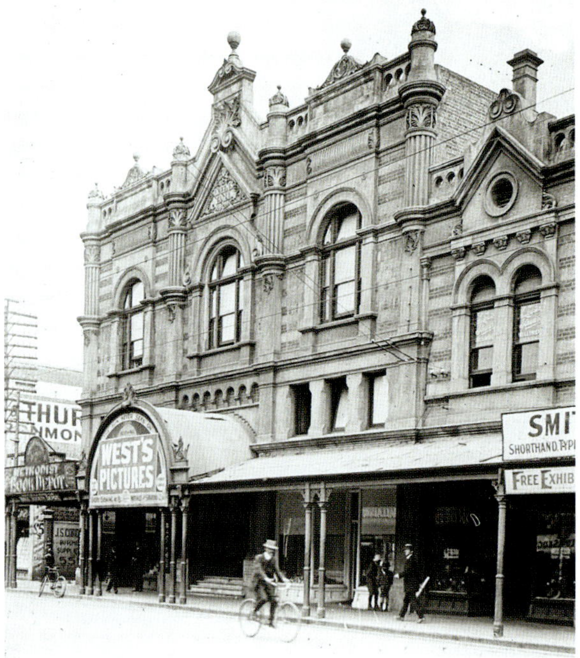

ABOVE The Queen's Hall in about 1910, when it was being used as a cinema by West's Pictures.

LEFT The remodelled Art Deco façade of the renamed Metro Cinema in 1950. The film advertised above the door is Greer Garson and Errol Flynn in MGM's *Forsyte Saga*.

FAR LEFT The plush interior of the considerably altered Queen's Hall, which Hoyts turned into the Regent Cinema at the time of its opening in September 1927.

RIGHT Hoyts Regent advertising the introduction of "talking pictures" (or the "talkies") in 1929.

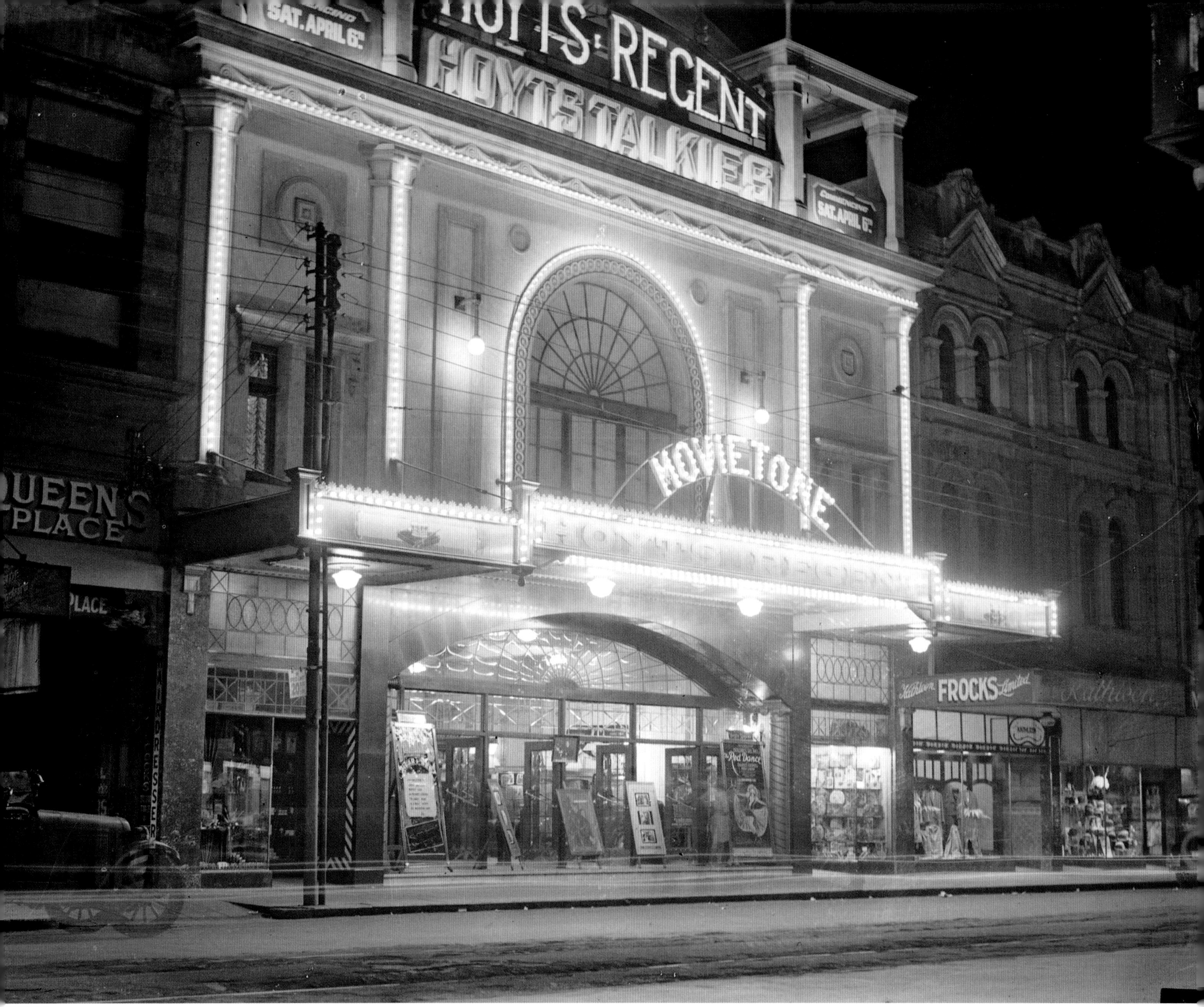
SAT. APRIL 6th
HOYTS REGENT
HOYTS TALKIES
SAT. APRIL 6th
MOVIETONE
QUEEN'S PLACE
PLACE
Kathleen FROCKS Limited

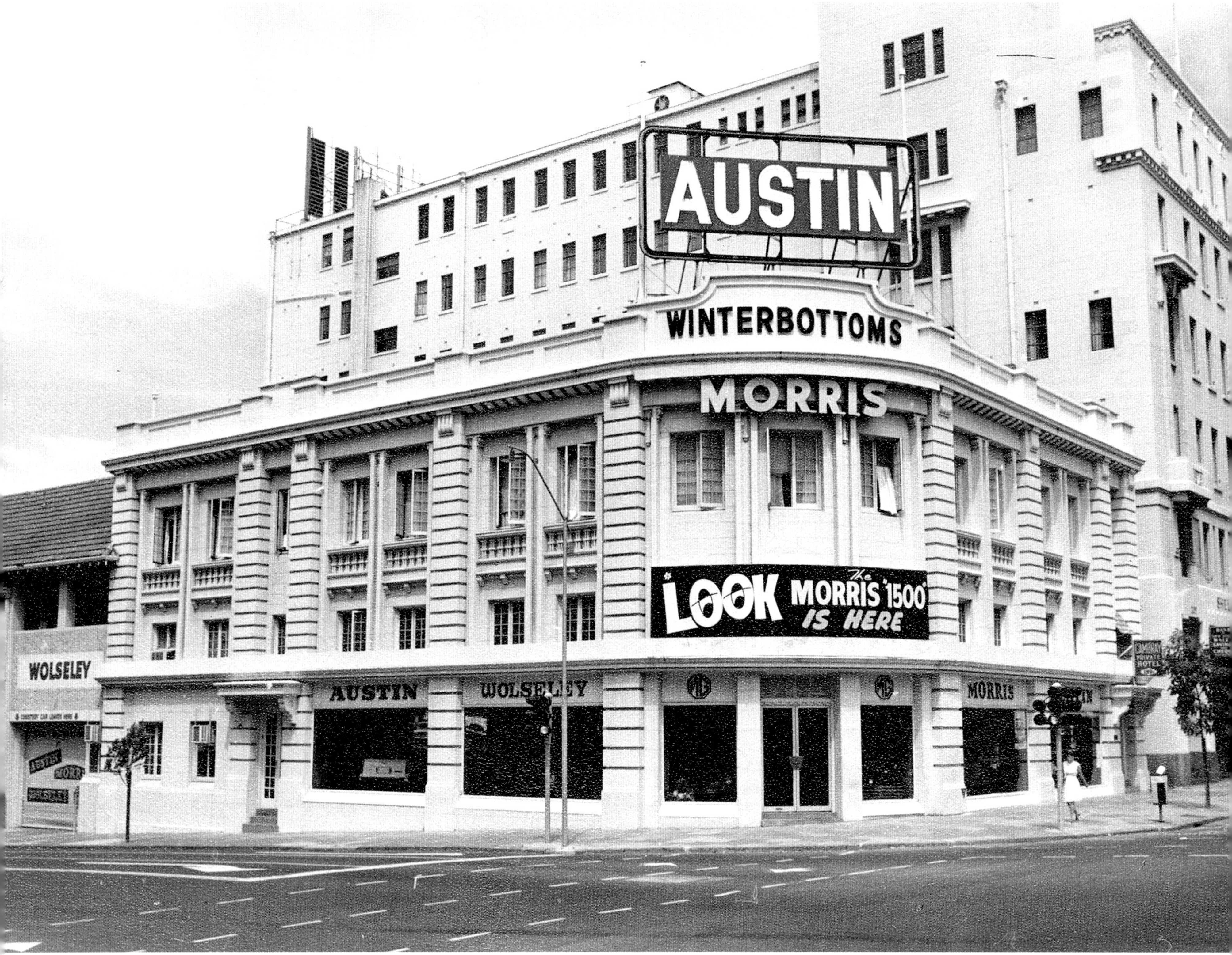
AUSTIN
WINTERBOTTOMS
MORRIS
LOOK The MORRIS '1500' IS HERE
WOLSELEY
AUSTIN
WOLSELEY
MORRIS

WINTERBOTTOM MOTOR COMPANY

DEMOLISHED 1976

W.J. (Jack) Winterbottom was born in South Australia and initially worked as a mechanic for the Lewis Cycle Company in Adelaide, where he made parts for that company's first motorcar. He moved to Western Australia in the early years of the 20th century, because he saw it as a place with many opportunities for an aspiring businessman, and opened his first garage in Perth in 1905.

Winterbottom, in partnership with a man named Adams, set up his garage and repair shop, Perth Motor House, just west of His Majesty's Theatre on Hay Street and imported the first Ford to Perth in 1906. In order to promote sales of the world's latest mode of transport, the firm, along with several other new dealerships in the town, organised hill-climbs and other motor sports to gain the public's interest.

The firm rapidly expanded, with the Winterbottom Motor Company being formed in 1915. A year later the company opened a motor car showroom at 367–371 Murray Street and, after becoming the Western Australia dealer for Dodge Brothers Cars, also opened a Dodge dealership on St Georges Terrace.

Following World War I the demand for motor transport grew rapidly in Perth, and by 1924 the company's turnover had increased to £334,000, as compared to just £21,000 in 1915. To accommodate their huge increase in business, the company paid £20,000 for a block of land on the corner of St Georges Terrace and Mill Street. In January 1924 the *West Australian* announced: "Cambray: a house of many associations in Western Australian history, is to vanish within a few days from the corner of St George's Terrace and Mill Street. In its place large premises dedicated to the activities of the Winterbottom Motor Co. Ltd., will be constructed at a cost of about £40,000. The contract has been secured by Mr. C.W. Arnott and work will be commenced immediately."

Cambray was a substantial house with fine views down to the river, the residence of Anthony O'Grady Lefroy, who arrived in Western Australia in 1843. Being well-educated, Lefroy soon entered the service of the government and became a very longstanding and effective civil servant in the Swan River Colony.

Opened in May 1925 by the Mayor of Perth, the new garage complex for the Winterbottom Company was said to be the largest in Australia and was designed by local architects, Oldham, Boas & Ednie-Brown as a multipurpose building. The building was in three sections going down the Mill Street hill, with two large car showrooms, workshops, spray paint shops and stores. Above the Mill Street section was a hostel, comprising 30 bedrooms, all with hot and cold water.

The upper floors of the St Georges Terrace section contained suites of offices for lease and became known as Cambray Chambers. The building was the first in Western Australia to be constructed with a suspended concrete floor slab, which used reinforced concrete for the upper floors. Excess building height was saved by eliminating steel beams and replacing them with "mushroom" columns, the broad tops of which merged into and supported the reinforced concrete floor slab above.

At the height of its success, Winterbottom Motor Company employed over 700 people. The company was eventually taken over and moved to other locations. What was claimed to be the largest garage premises in Australia was demolished by 1976 to make way for the 28-storey Governor Stirling Tower, which opened in 1978.

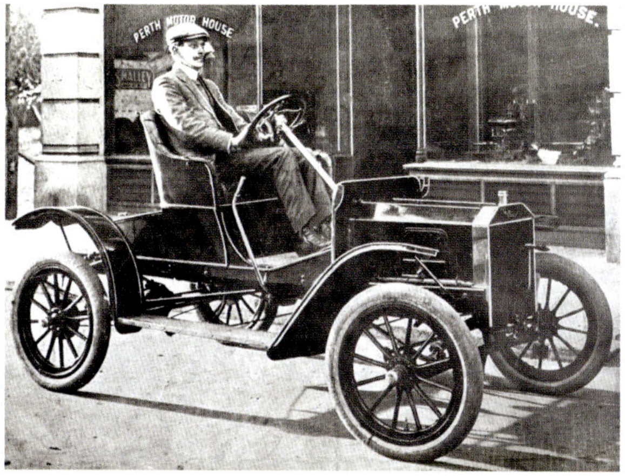

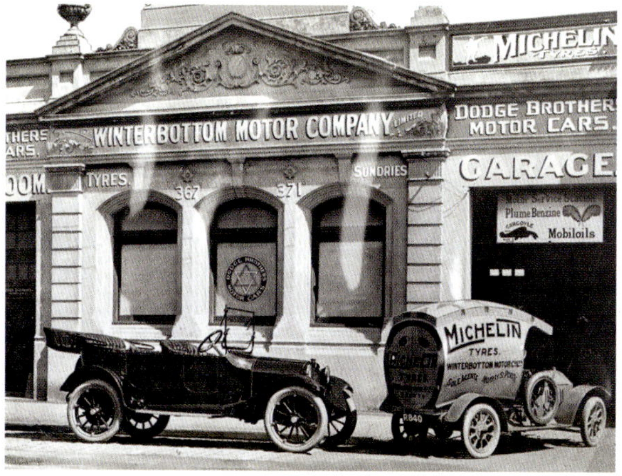

LEFT Vehicles parked outside the Winterbottom Motor Company building at 367–371 Murray Street in 1918. The vehicles are a Dodge tourer from about 1916 and a 1912 Mitchell van.

FAR LEFT "Jack" Winterbottom in the first Ford car in Western Australia.

OPPOSITE Winterbottom's in 1970. At the time it was an agent for British Leyland vehicles.

HIS MAJESTY'S THEATRE HOTEL

CLOSED 1977

One of Perth's most iconic historic buildings is His Majesty's Theatre, which was built for Perth businessman and politician Thomas Molloy and opened on Christmas Eve 1904.

Molloy entered the hotel trade by purchasing the interests of James Graves in various hotels around the city. He went on to build the Metropole Hotel on central Hay Street in 1894. To this he added, next door to the hotel, Perth's first custom-built theatre, the Royal Theatre, in 1897. Finding his hotels very profitable, he built His Majesty's Theatre and Hotel on the corner of King and Hay Streets in 1904. The total cost of the project was £46,000, which was an enormous sum for a development of that period.

The theatre and hotel were designed by William Wolf, who followed a design style that had become popular in Europe, whereby seating was laid out in a horseshoe, enabling the audience to be closer to the stage, improving sightlines and acoustics.

When first opened, the residential hotel was advertised as the most modern in the state. According to a long description in the *Western Mail* of Christmas Day 1904, it comprised "65 bedrooms, six bars, half a score of parlours or lounges, a large billiard-room in the basement, and a spacious dining-room, 53ft. x 41ft., on the first floor, besides an extensive kitchen with a large range, grill, and separate servery. There are also serveries, scullery, larders, pantries, storerooms, servants' bedrooms, etc. Hot and cold water is laid on throughout." To ensure fire safety, all of the hotel facilities were separated from the theatre by steel doors.

Molloy boasted that the hotel made good money and continued to be a popular venue throughout its life. After a number of different lessees, in 1952 the theatre was leased by the well-known theatrical Edgley family, who renamed the theatre Her Majesty's for a short period in the 1970s.

The hotel gained international publicity in 1962 when it introduced roller-skating barmaids. Two women, Nora Inwood and Brigetta Bruijneteijn, were recruited to carry drinks at high speed from the bar to the dining room, which was about 50 metres away. This novelty became very popular with customers. They claimed never to have spilt a drop during these journeys and were even featured in a British Pathé newsreel. Sadly the stunt only lasted for about nine months, and when the ladies left to go to more permanent jobs they were never replaced.

The building was nearly demolished in the early 1970s to widen Kings Street and make way for a larger and more modern theatre complex, but a vociferous public campaign saved His Majesty's. The theatre struggled on in a very rundown building until 1977, when the state government purchased it and closed it down for a major renovation project that took three years to complete.

The hotel section of the building was adapted to provide a headquarters for the resident West Australian Opera and West Australian Ballet, as well as facilities for touring companies. When the theatre was reopened in 1980, new bar and café facilities were provided, but the hotel and its roller-skating barmaids were gone for ever.

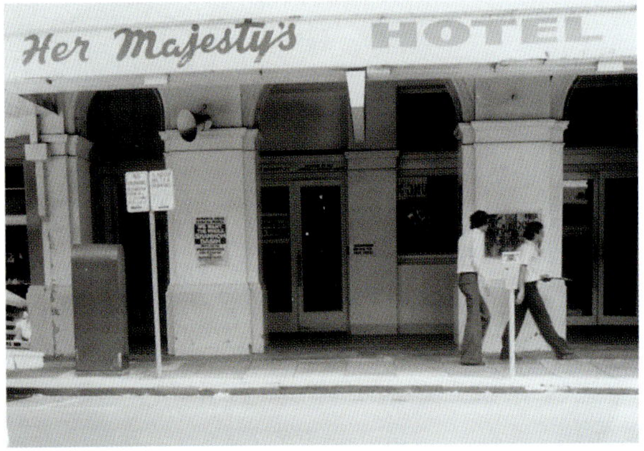

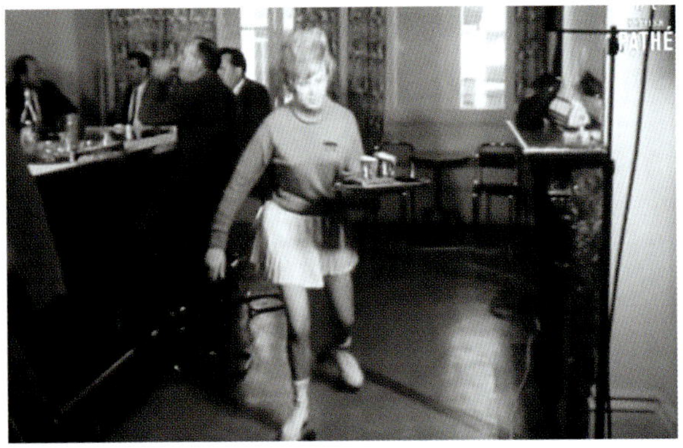

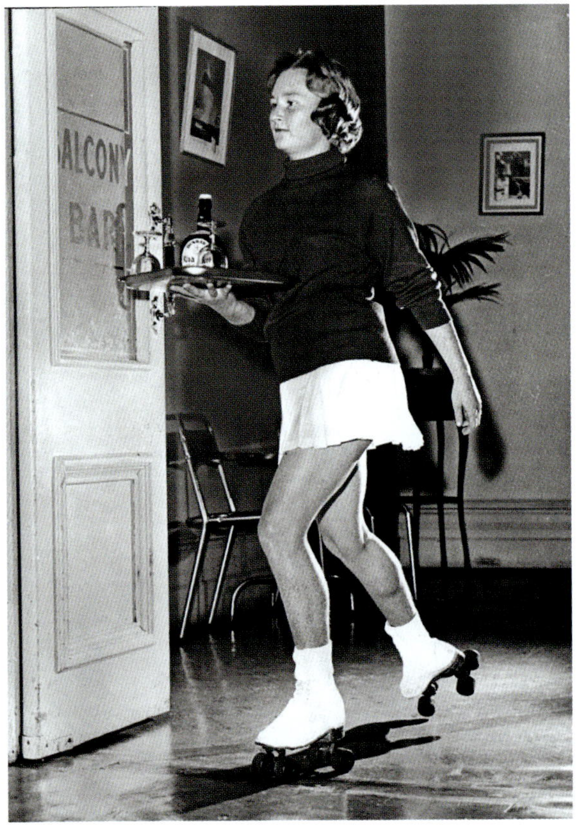

RIGHT His Majesty's Theatre and Hotel in 1926. The publicity banner is advertising a visit by British evangelist Rodney "Gypsy" Smith, so called because of his Romani background.

LEFT Nora Inwood does the skater's dash from the bar to the dining room in 1962, claiming never to have spilt a drop.

FAR LEFT TOP For a brief period in the early 1970s the theatre and hotel changed its name to Her Majesty's, but reverted to its original name when it reopened in 1980.

FAR LEFT BOTTOM Brigetta Bruijneteijn leaves the bar for yet another beer run down the corridor (1962).

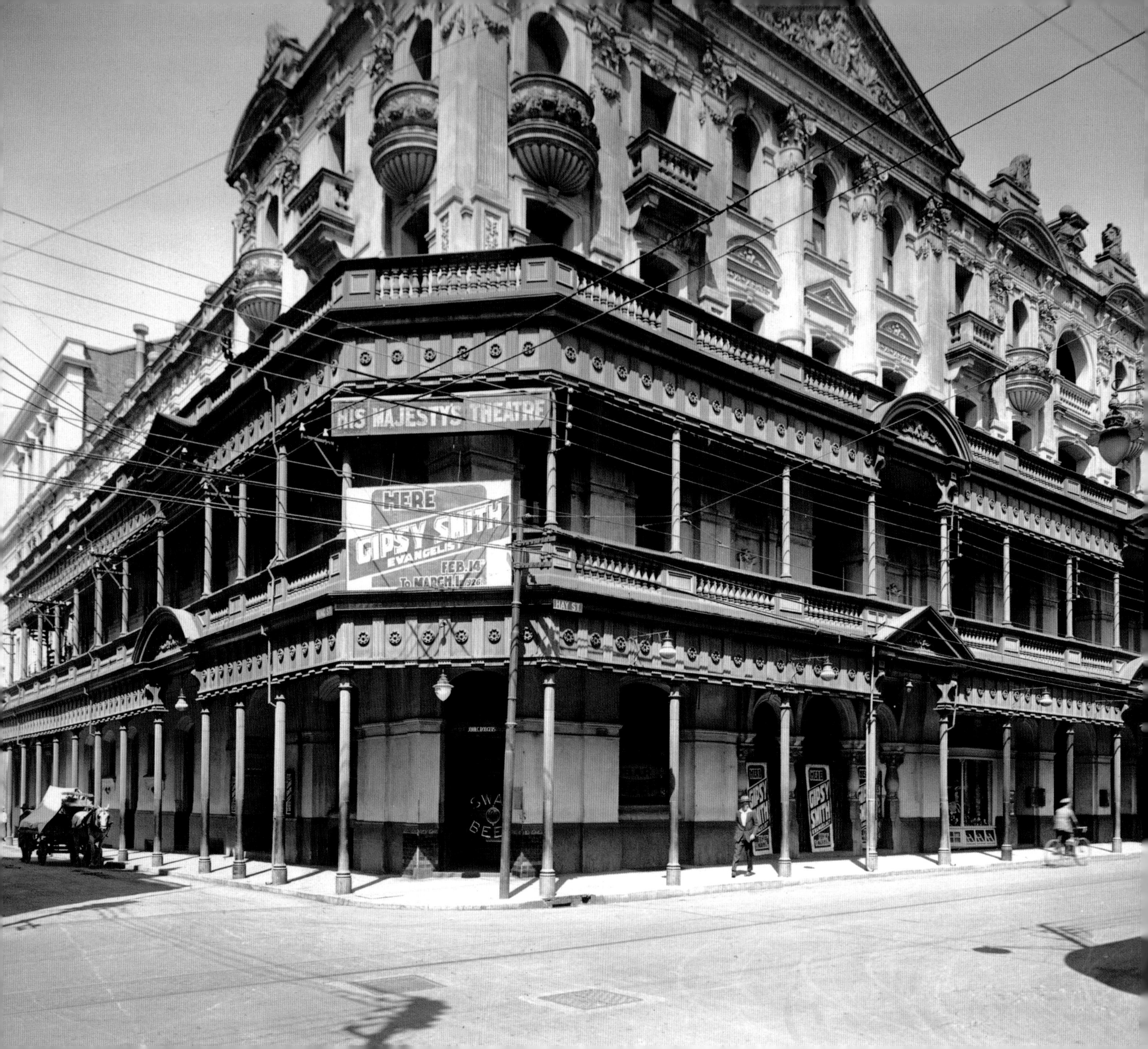
HIS MAJESTY'S THEATRE
HERE
GIPSY SMITH
EVANGELIST
FEB. 14th
To MARCH 1st 1926
HAY ST
JOHN C. RODGERS

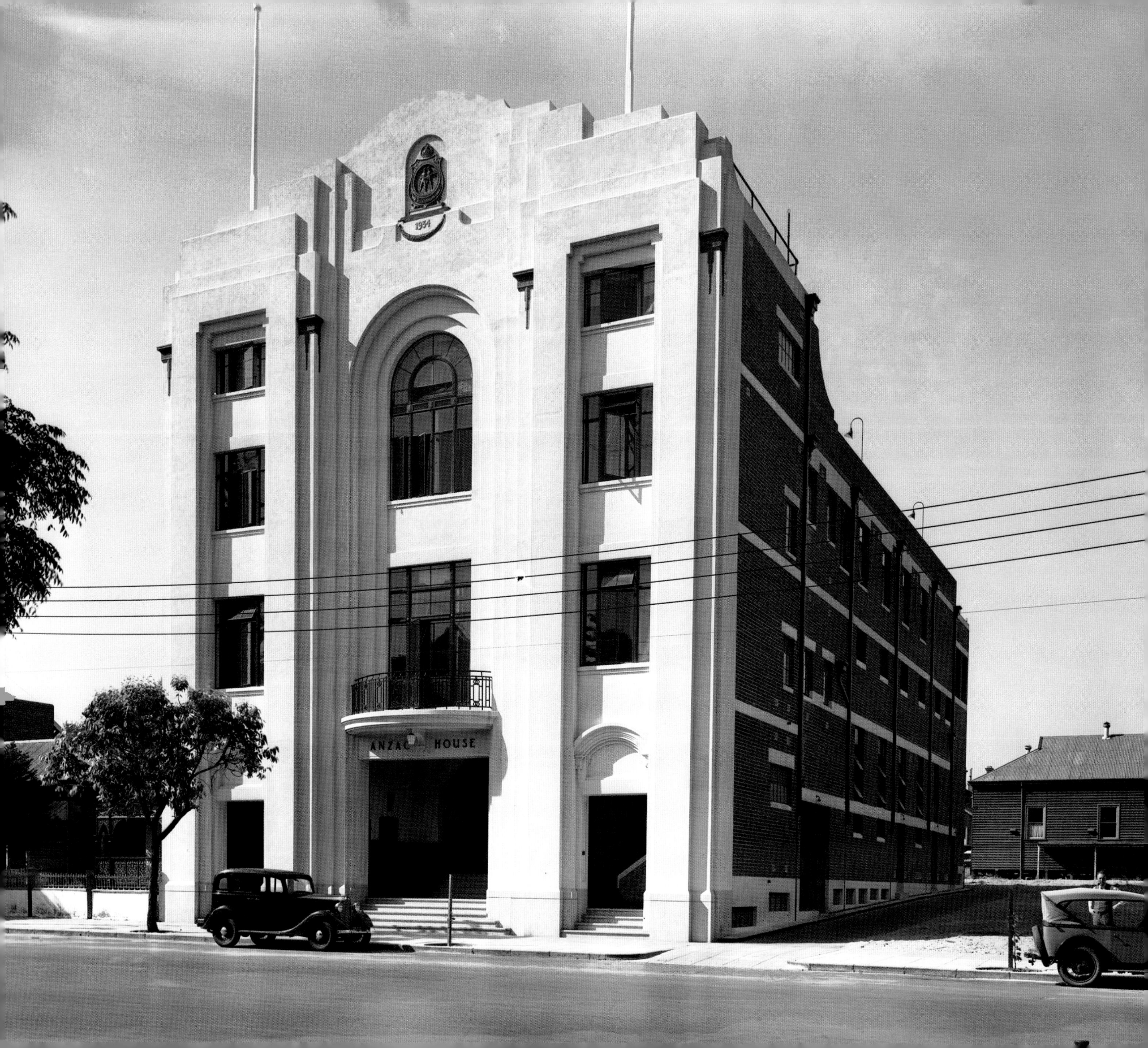
1934
ANZAC HOUSE

ANZAC HOUSE

DEMOLISHED 1978

The Returned and Services League of Australia was founded for the welfare of returned servicemen from World War I. In 1916 j10a conference recommended the formation of what was then called the Returned Sailors' and Soldiers' Imperial League of Australia, with all states having joined by the end of 1918 and the Australian Capital Territory forming a branch in 1927. The name of the organisation was eventually changed to the Returned Services League of Australia (RSL) in 1965.

In 1915 the Mayor of Perth suggested that a special home should be found for returned soldiers on a site that was "central, yet free from the turmoil of the city". A committee was set up to raise funds, but finding a site for the Soldiers' Institute, as it became named, proved to be controversial and it was eventually decided to adapt and alter the back of the old government building, on the site now occupied by Council House. The institute was opened by the Governor, Sir Harry Barron, on 20 October 1916.

Western Australia joined the Returned Sailors' and Soldiers' Imperial League in 1918 and the Institute building became the state's administrative headquarters. As the membership and activities grew, there became an urgent need for a much larger building. This was particularly felt during the first years of the Great Depression in the early 1930s, when many ex-servicemen found themselves out of work and on the breadline.

Land on the corner of Irwin Street and St Georges Terrace, where the University of Western Australia's "Tin Pan Alley" had stood just a few years before, was granted to the League and a fund-raising campaign to finance a new building was launched in 1933. The campaign included a "buy a brick" scheme, which was enthusiastically taken up by members, particularly in the country branches of the organisation, with many members proudly wearing the tin badge bearing an image of a brick they were given in return for their donation. However, with such financially constrained times, general fund-raising could not produce sufficient funds to finance the building, so permission was gained from the executive council to borrow up to £15,000 on the land on which the building would stand. The land had originally been granted on the understanding that "before any encumbrance could be placed upon the title: the permission of the Government must be obtained."

With an overdraft in place, the foundation stone for Anzac House, as it was to be named, was laid by the Governor of Western Australia, Sir James Mitchell, on 25 March 1934. The guests at the ceremony included three representatives of the Australian cricket team, who were about to board a ship in Fremantle on their way to a Test Series in England.

The new building was designed by Alfred R.B. Cox and included accommodation for a wide range of activities over its four floors, including a concert hall, meeting rooms, social areas, roof garden (where the RSL Band practices took place) and even a miniature rifle range. It also included an employment bureau for out-of-work "Diggers" and "Tommies". The building was opened in October 1934 by Prince George, Duke of Kent.

In 1976 the RSL transferred ownership of the land to the state government to enable a new magistrates' court to be built. In exchange for a peppercorn rent, the RSL retained the St Georges Terrace land on which they built a smaller headquarters. The old building was demolished in 1978 and the new Anzac House opened in 1981. This building was in turn found to be inadequate and was demolished in 2017 to be replaced by a 10-storey Anzac House.

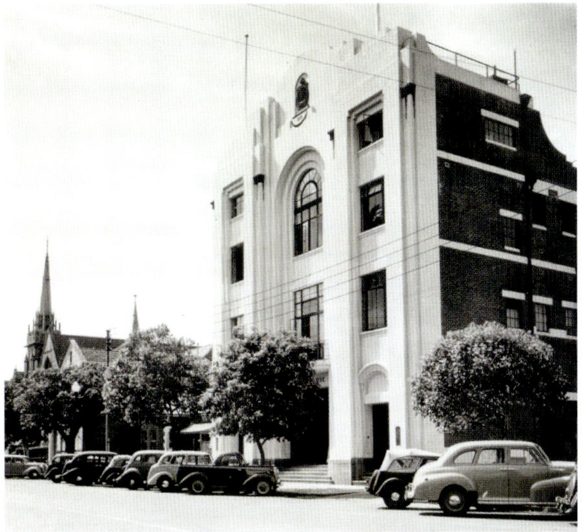

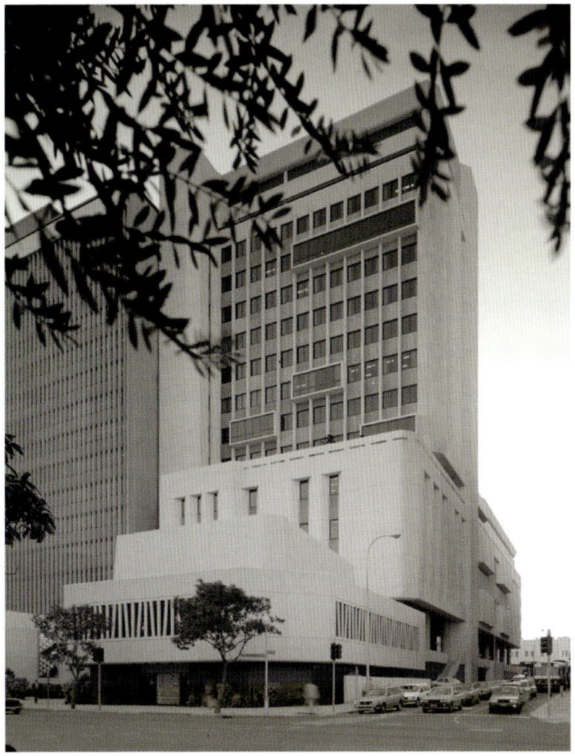

OPPOSITE The imposing Art Deco features of Anzac House in 1935, not long after it opened.

LEFT The new Anzac House, with Central Law Courts behind, in 1983.

FAR LEFT Cars parked on St Georges Terrace outside Anzac House in 1949.

EMANUEL CHAMBERS / PERPETUAL TRUSTEES BUILDING

DEMOLISHED 1979

Brothers Sydney and Isadore Emanuel were born in New South Wales and came to Western Australia when their father acquired large areas of land in the Kimberley, particularly around the Fitzroy River. By the 1890s, a partnership with Alexander Forrest enabled them to hold a monopoly over the live cattle trade between Derby and the Port of Fremantle.

In 1906 work began on Emanuel Chambers, a new building on the corner of Howard Street and St Georges Terrace, designed for the Emanuel brothers by Perth architect Charles Oldham. "In the Queen Anne style, with modernised treatment to suit the altered requirements", was how the *West Australian* described the building, which featured bricks specially made from a bluestone base supplied by the Coombe's Brickworks in Armadale, Victoria. These were formed into ornamental brickwork of a high quality with striking vertical cement mouldings. Construction was estimated to cost around £20,000, and the building was completed in February 1908. The newspapers described the building as a palatial and imposing structure on the streetscape of Perth, which, up until the first Gold Rush, had been built along the lines of a modest country town rather than a thriving city.

The design of this building gives a good idea of what was required for a well-designed office block at the beginning of the 20th century. The basement's innovative design meant that only half of the floor was below ground level, with windows just above ground level to maximise light. The ground, mezzanine and first floors were office accommodation, with the upper four floors set aside for luxurious residential apartments, making it one of the first mixed-use buildings in the city.

The *West Australian* of 15 February 1908 reported, "The upper four stories, which are occupied by Mr J.T. Glowery of the Palace Hotel ... represent a complete system of residential flats with an up-to-date restaurant, dining-room, and winter garden. The 17 suites of two and three living rooms, a bathroom, balconies, etc., complete, are all self-contained, distinct, and readily approached from large vestibules and corridors which form complete breaks to the various suite entrances."

The restaurant on the seventh floor had the latest in kitchen appliances and allowed diners to enjoy magnificent views over the city. At roof level there were servants' quarters, maintenance and storage areas, and a steam heating system, which heated the building during the winter months.

Emanuel Chambers was purchased by the investment and trustee company Perpetual Trustees in 1922 for £47,500 and soon became known as the Perpetual Trustees Building. A few years later Sydney Stott moved the Perth branch of his National Business College into the premises, after which it was often also referred to as Stott's Building. With his brother Edwin, Stott ran a number of companies, including one that imported some of the earliest typewriters into Australia.

By the late 1970s the building was in a poor state of repair. It was demolished in 1979 and replaced with an eight-storey building that opened in the early 1980s.

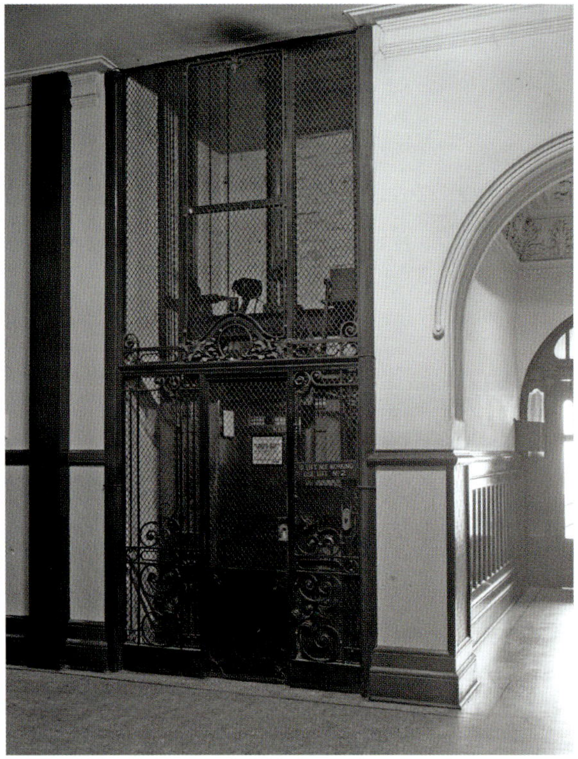

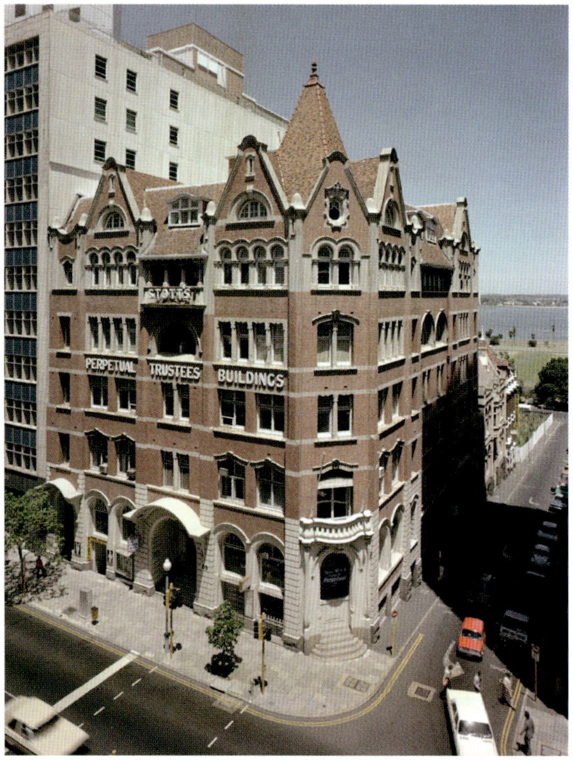

RIGHT Formerly known as Emanuel Chambers, it was taken over by Perpetual Trustees in 1922. A year later, Commonwealth Life Assurance and Stott's Business College had become tenants.

LEFT The building in 1979, shortly before it was demolished to make way for an eight-storey office block.

FAR LEFT The lift, as seen in 1961.

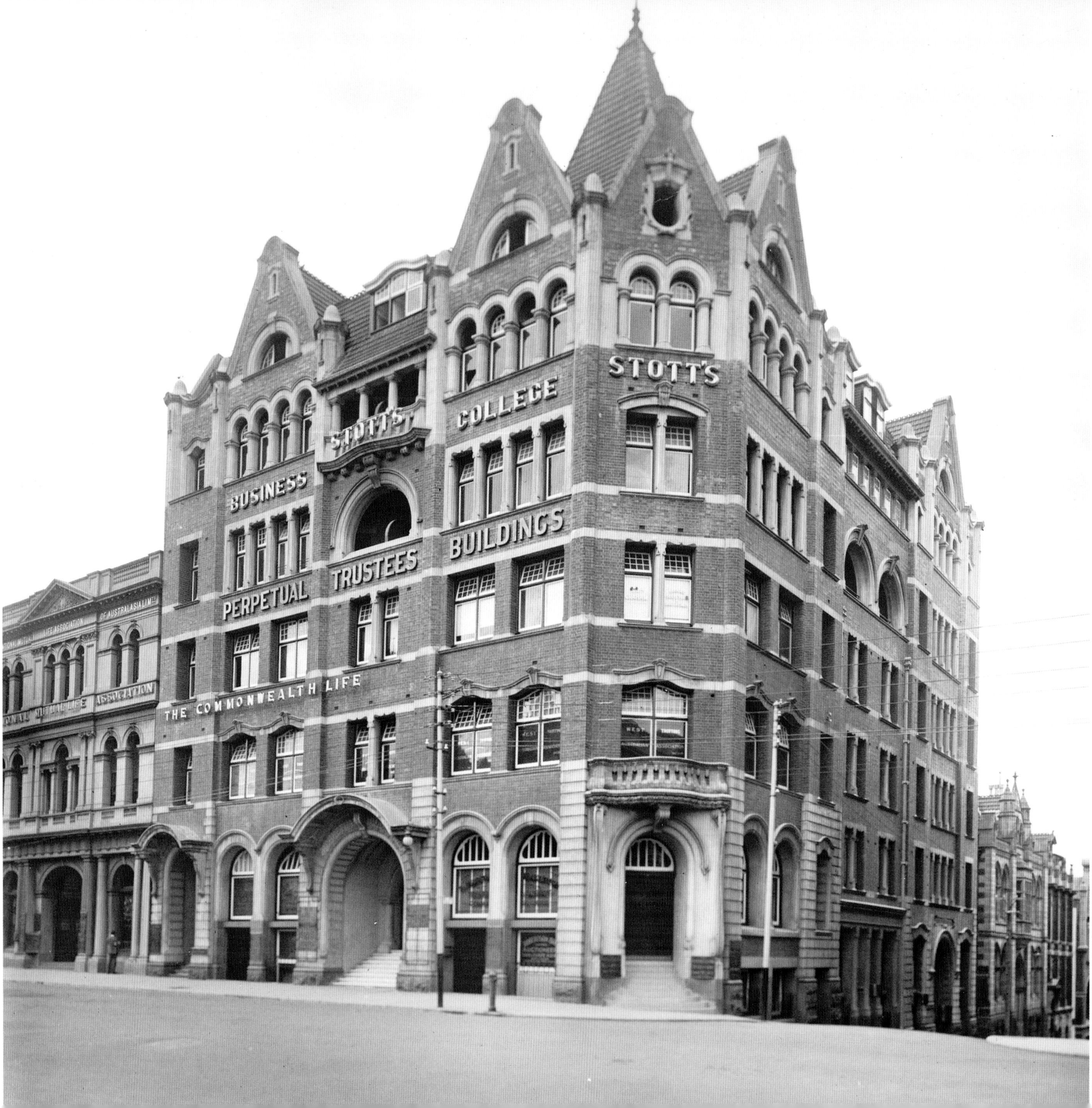
STOTT'S
COLLEGE
STOTT'S
BUSINESS
BUILDINGS
PERPETUAL
TRUSTEES
THE COMMONWEALTH LIFE
ASSOCIATION

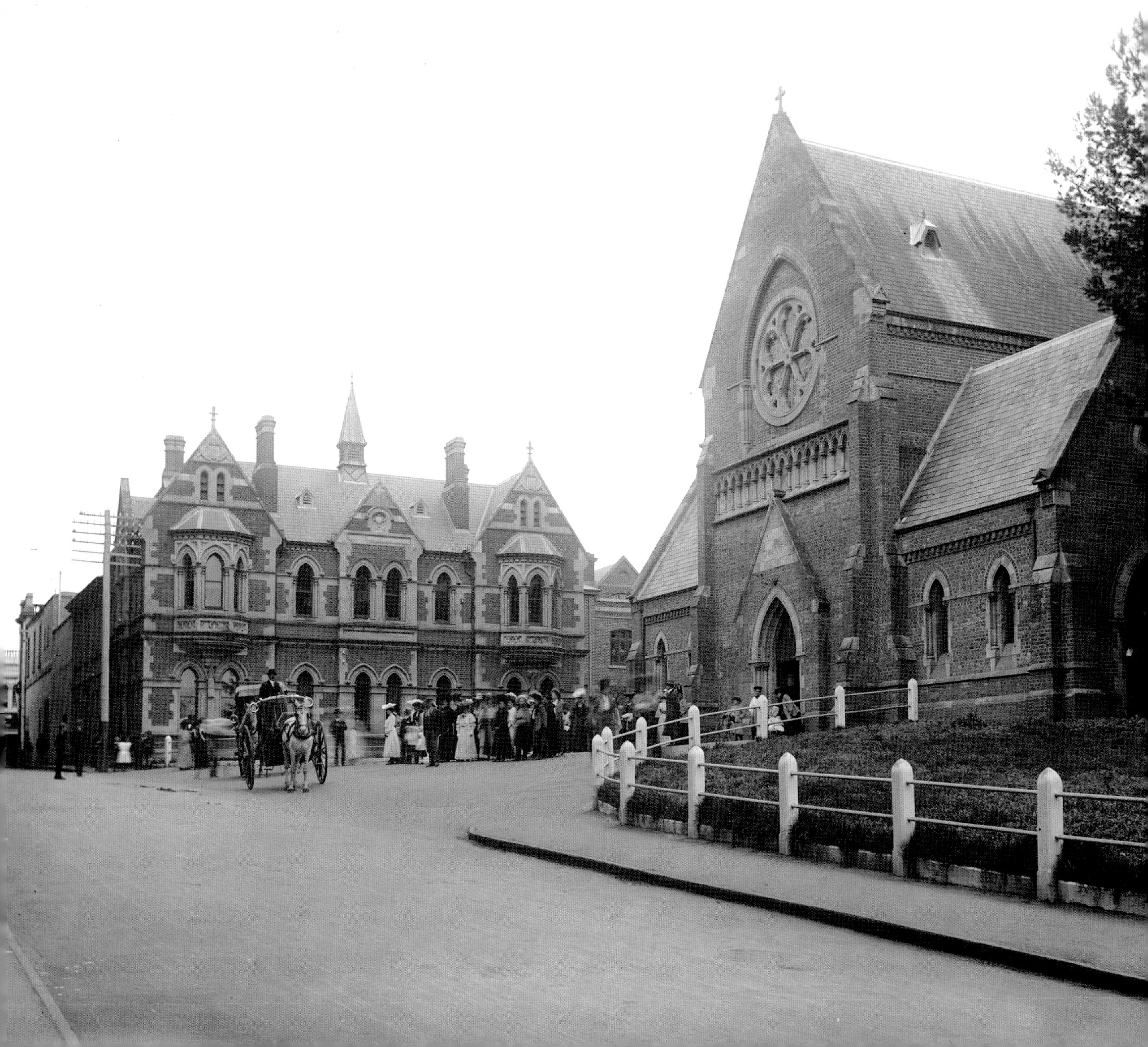

ST GEORGE'S CHAMBERS

DEMOLISHED 1979–1980

After the opening of the present St George's Cathedral, the old St George's Cathedral (1845–91) stood empty and forlorn until the state government approached the Diocese of Perth asking if they could purchase 30 feet of land, "facing St George's Terrace and Howick Street between the present Government offices and St George's Cathedral." They also wanted the materials from the demolition of the old cathedral and offered £1,500. This land was required to create Cathedral Avenue as a right of way.

On 12 August 1891 the *Inquirer* published notification that three tenders had been received for the demolition of the old St George's Cathedral: "Mr. James Doig requires £50 for doing the work, while Mr. David Gray offers to pay the Government £152 for the right to remove and retain the material, and Mr. J. Hurst offers £180 for the same privilege."

Hurst & Co. won the job and just after Christmas 1891 the *Inquirer* reported that they had discovered a bottle in the foundations of the old building: "The contents, comprising some papers and coins, appear to be in a fairly good state of preservation, judging from outside appearances. We understand it is the intention of Messrs. Hurst & Co. to hand the interesting memento, which has been buried for about fifty years, to Bishop Parry."

After demolition of the old cathedral, plans were made to develop an office building which would both be an administrative centre for the Diocese and a source of rental income. Eventually, St George's Chambers was the result.

This new office building was designed by J.J. Talbot Hobbs and constructed in 1897 at a cost of about £3,100. According to a report in the *West Australian* in July 1897, the building contained six ground floor offices, three first floor offices, a general office and a clerk's office, all with fireplaces and electric light, as well as a Bishop's room and library, which doubled up as a meeting room. The newspaper went on to explain that all of the offices, "except those to be used for church purposes, have been engaged by the Government for the use of the Agricultural Bank and Land Titles Department. The staircase will be of ornamental design, and of polished kauri, with jarrah treads. ... The structure has been designed in the Gothic style of the 13th century to harmonise with the cathedral."

St George's Chambers remained until 1979–1980 when it was demolished to make way for a new Law Chambers building, which opened in 1981.

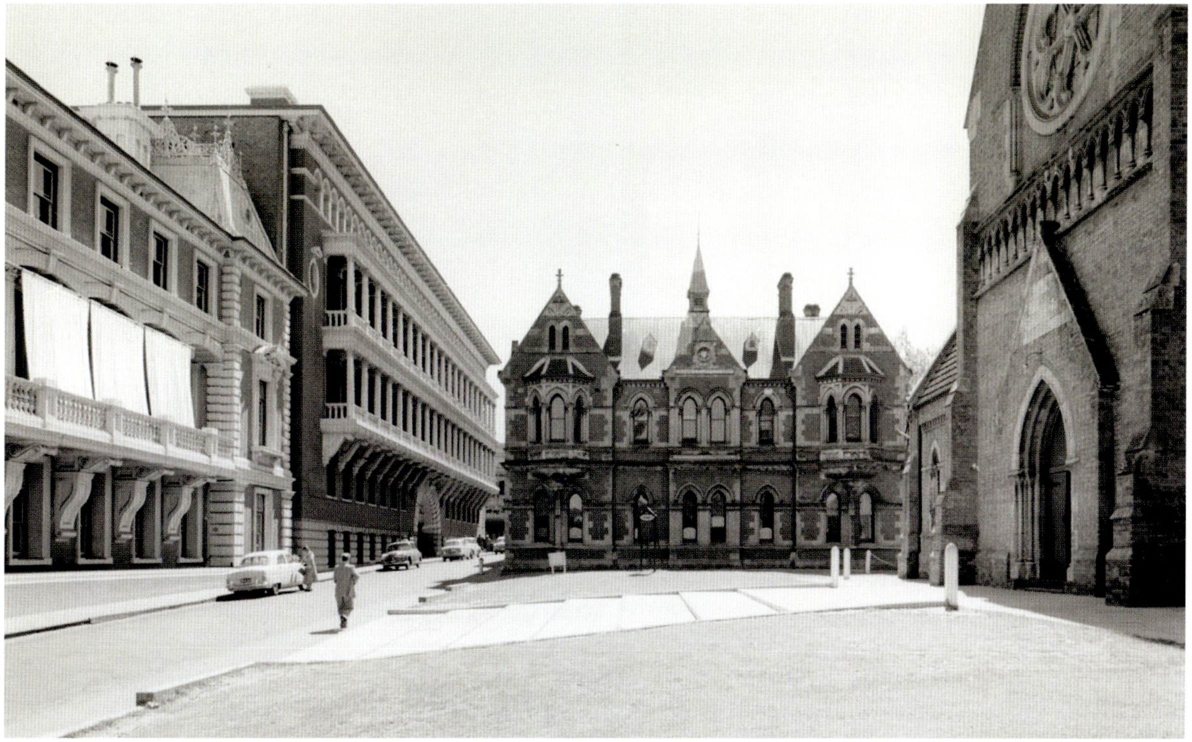

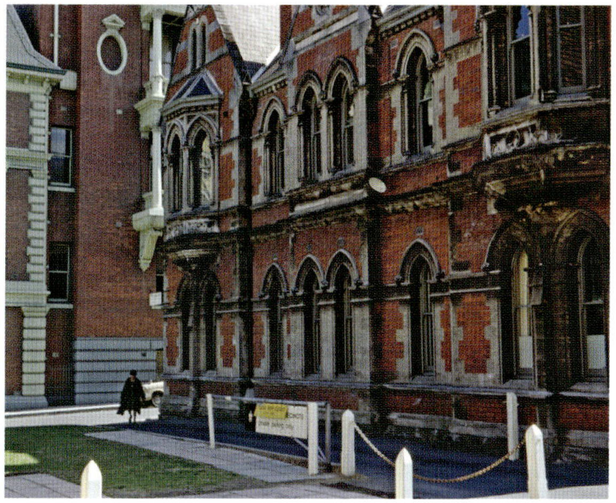

ABOVE St George's Chambers, with the Central Government Offices behind, in 1967.

LEFT St George's Chambers in 1958, with cars parked on Cathedral Avenue, outside the Central Government Offices. Note the large sun shades over some windows of that building.

OPPOSITE St George's Chambers in about 1905. A service has just taken place at the cathedral on the right.

CMLA BUILDING

DEMOLISHED 1980

After the Lombard Chambers building was acquired by the Colonial Mutual Life Assurance Society (CMLA), the old building was knocked down to make way for one of the buildings which would help to get Perth back to work after the Great Depression of the early 1930s.

During the period leading up to World War II, CMLA built offices in almost all Australian capital cities, using variations on a design supplied to the company by Jack Hennessy, of Hennessy & Hennessy. The first was erected in Brisbane in 1931 and was followed by similar CMLA buildings around the world

In September 1935 work commenced on deep foundations for what would become for many years the tallest office block in Perth. Once built to ground level, a foundation stone was laid by Sir James Mitchell, the first Australian-born governor of Western Australia, on 27 May 1936. Construction under the supervision of well-known Perth architect Reginald Summerhayes continued at a rapid pace, in part thanks to a new system of scaffolding supported by steel cables, which could be winched higher as the building grew.

During the building works, the *Daily News* carried a story about the two "billy boys" (tea boys), who, it was estimated, had carried some 3,000 gallons of tea around the site at "a daily average of 50 billies of tea, involving 22 gallons a day, for five days a week" over a six-month period.

The Art Deco building had some delightful architectural features, including carved figures representing the CMLA directors at the time the building was erected. The building cost half a million pounds and took just over a year to complete. It had provided work for 200 men at a time when jobs were still scarce and unemployment high.

The completed 11-storey building was the height of modernity and, until 1962, was the tallest office block in the city. The ground floor was occupied by an arcade of shops, with the CMLA offices above. The main areas of these offices were decorated with marble, plasterwork and bronze fittings. Further CMLA staff occupied the 10th storey, with other floors leased to various companies and organisations. All floors were accessed by two high-speed lifts. The building also boasted 250 power points, more than 300 fire alarms, 500 lighting points, and connections for internal and external telephones on every floor.

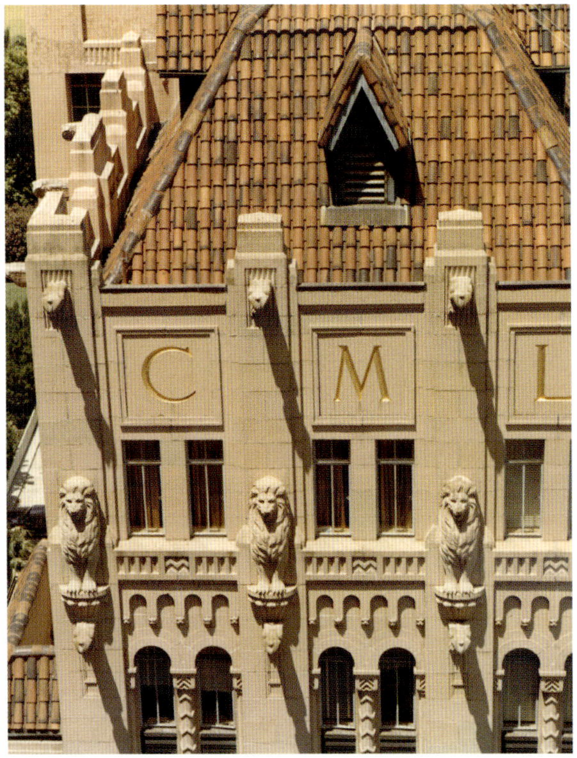

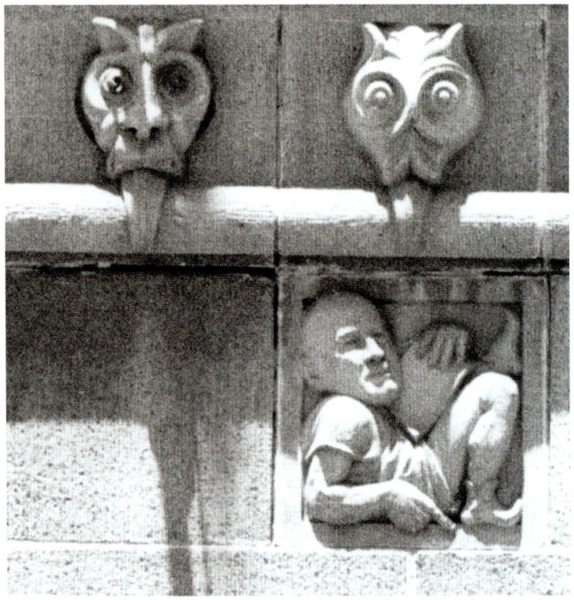

Part of the project was to widen the laneway that ran from St Georges Terrace to the Esplanade and there was a move by the CMLA to have the new road named Cecil Court after their Managing Director, Cecil Hearn. Strong opposition was put up by the Royal Western Australian Historical Society and the road was named Sherwood Court after Frederick Sherwood who had originally owned the land.

The building was officially opened by Sir James Mitchell on 26 October 1936. Just 44 years later it was demolished to make way for a new office block only one floor taller than its predecessor. By the late 1970s the CMLA Building was considered old-fashioned and not fit for service. Like Perth, Sydney has lost its CMLA Building, but examples of similar Hennessy buildings can still be seen in Adelaide, Brisbane and, on a smaller scale, in Hobart.

ABOVE AND LEFT Elaborate carvings, including likenesses of CMLA's directors, decorated the exterior.

RIGHT Probably one of the most elaborate Art Deco buildings ever constructed in Perth, as photographed four years before its demolition.

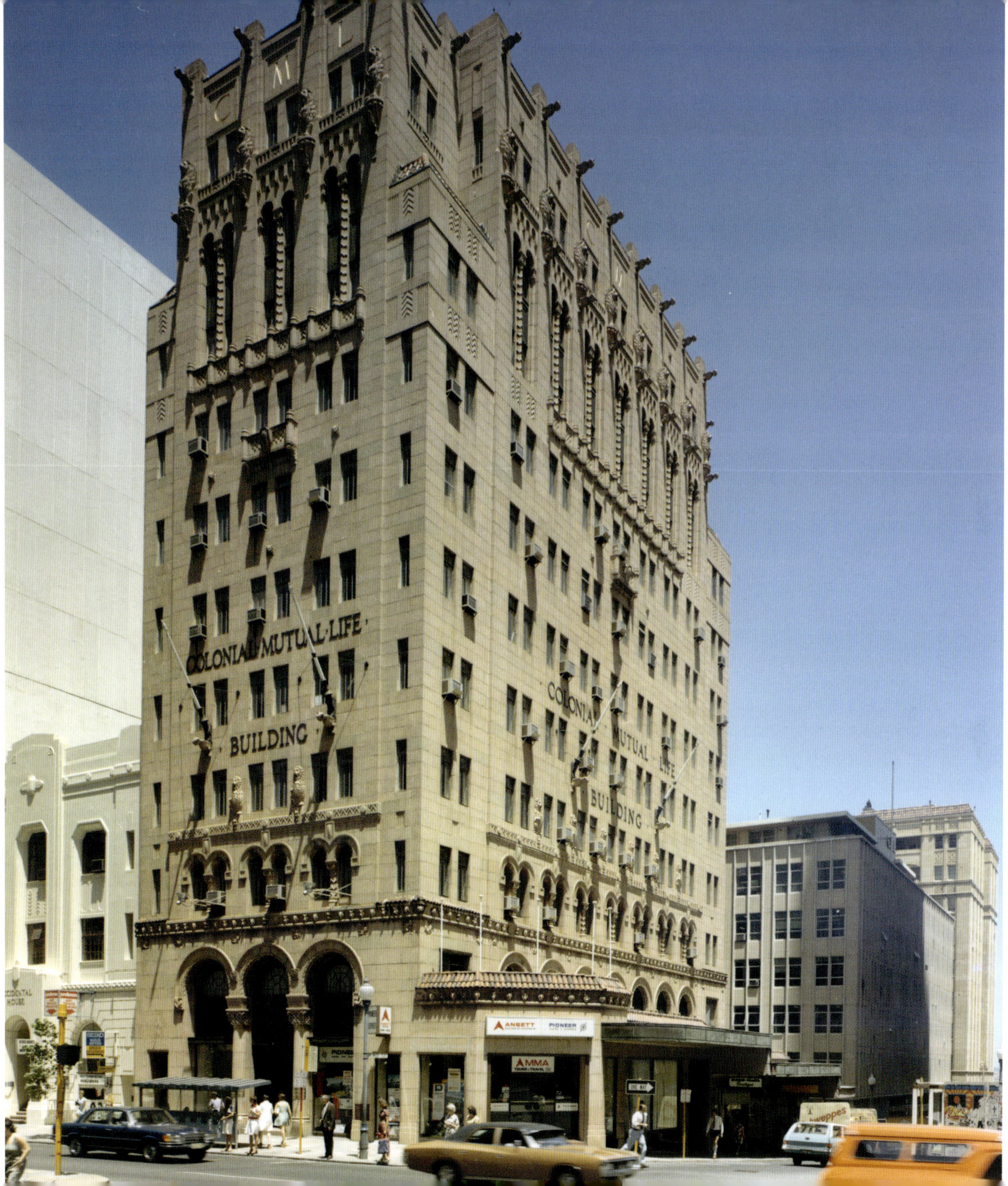
COLONIAL MUTUAL LIFE
BUILDING
COLONIAL MUTUAL LIFE
BUILDING
ANSETT
PIONEER
AMMA
ONE WAY

OLD STOCK EXCHANGE

DEMOLISHED 1980

Since the 1870s, an informal stock exchange had been run by the members of the Weld Club, but with the discovery of gold at Halls Creek and Southern Cross in the late 1880s, and the potential for more finds, it was felt a properly regulated stock market was necessary.

In August 1888 nine businessmen met in the United Serviced Hotel to discuss the possibility of creating a stock exchange in Perth. It was felt that the promotion of the purchase and sale of shares would help to stimulate share broking within the city and thus help the local economy. Rules were drawn up by a sub-committee and the Perth Stock Exchange opened for business on 1 October 1888.

The exchange experienced many teething problems and there was much dissatisfaction on the part of the customers, which eventually led to a rival exchange being created by a group of rebel brokers. The Stock Exchange of Perth opened for business on 22 July 1889 with 31 members. Business in the new exchange was so brisk that four months after opening the maximum number of members was raised to 42.

Later that year, a merger was suggested by the Stock Exchange of Perth but rejected by the older organisation. In February the following year the Perth Stock Exchange ceased trading and the *Western Mail* wrote, "There can be no question of the wisdom of this decision. There is not sufficient business to keep even one Exchange occupied, and the first of these in time was not formed on a sufficiently wide or popular basis."

The Stock Exchange of Perth initially operated out of Alexander Morrison's Auction Mart on St Georges Terrace, and then for a time out of Lombard House, but in 1895 acquired a property at 49 St Georges Terrace from the estate of Lionel Samson, on which they were to build a new exchange. A building committee was set up and decided to run an architectural competition for the design of the new Stock Exchange Building, with a prize of £15 for the winning design, with £10 and £5 for the runners up. The competition produced 16 designs, of which one was disqualified as not having met the specification set out in the competition rules. The winning entry was by Messrs. Drake and Whitwell of St Georges Terrace. A foundation stone was laid by Sir John Forrest in October 1896 and the construction work carried out by George Napier at a cost of around £8,000. Before the foundation stone could be laid, delicate site work had to be carried out to ensure the new footing did not undermine the neighbouring buildings.

The funding for the construction work was gained by forming a club, of which the existing members of the exchange were foundation associates. Membership was limited to 500 and was open to anyone provided they were "acceptable citizens in professional and commercial life". Originally called the Stock Exchange of Perth Club, it changed its name in 1901 to the Stock Exchange Club.

From early on the new building had a number of tenants in addition to the stock exchange. These included the Commonwealth Bank, to whom the building was sold in 1922 for £25,000. The stock exchange then moved into the Perpetual Trustees building before eventually moving to Exchange Plaza in 1990.

Along with the CMLA Building next door, the very fine Old Stock Exchange building had a date with a wrecking ball in 1980 to make way for Colonial House.

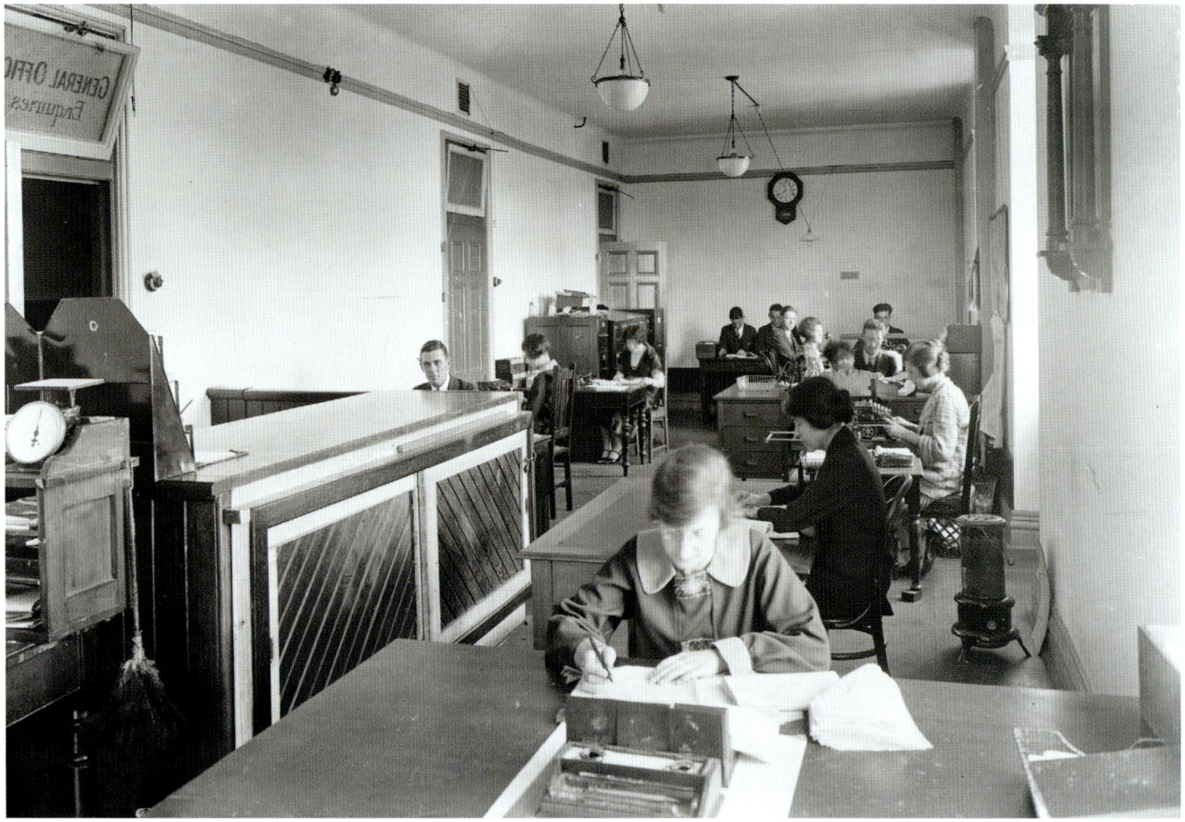

RIGHT A far cry from the cars that stockbrokers drive today, a bicycle is propped up against the curb outside the Perth Stock Exchange. The building also housed the Commonwealth Bank and other businesses.

LEFT A 1925 view of the General Office of the Commonwealth Bank in the old Stock Exchange building. The feather duster and paraffin heater lend the room a somewhat homely atmosphere.

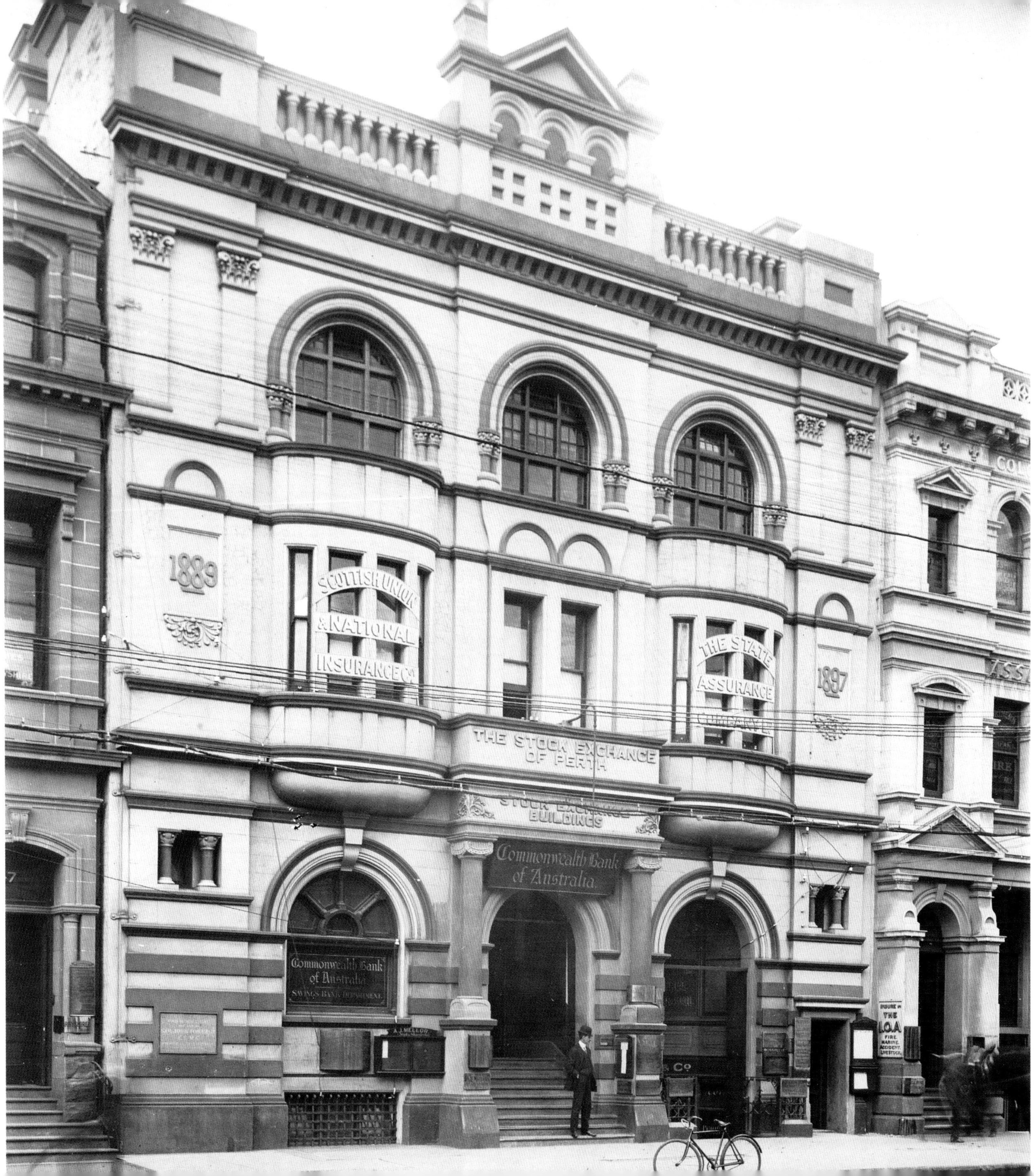
1889
SCOTTISH UNION & NATIONAL INSURANCE Co
THE STATE ASSURANCE
1897
THE STOCK EXCHANGE OF PERTH
BUILDINGS
Commonwealth Bank of Australia
Commonwealth Bank of Australia
THE L.O.A.

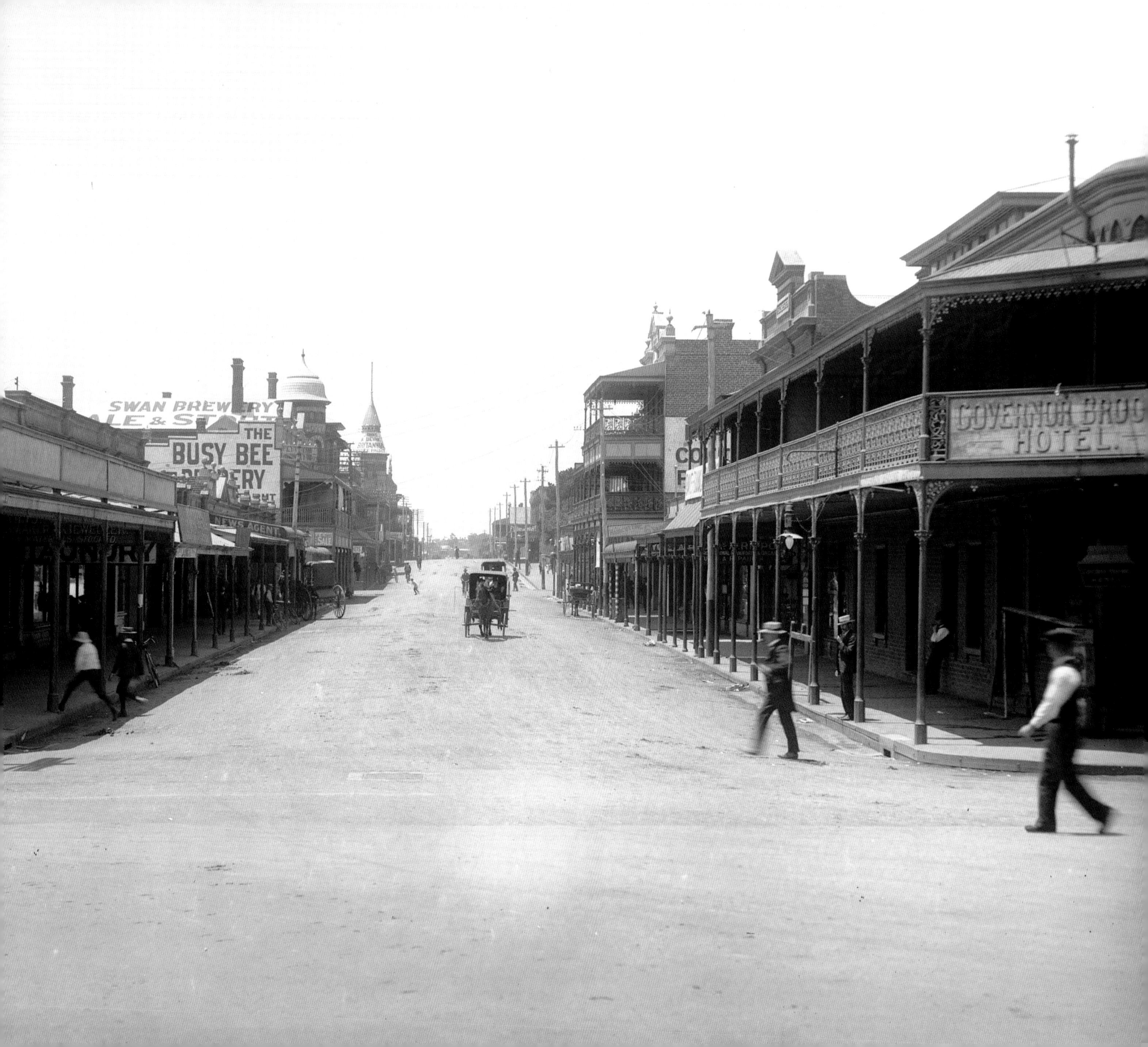
SWAN BREWERY
THE
BUSY BEE
NEWS AGENT
HOTEL.

GOVERNOR BROOME HOTEL

DEMOLISHED 1983

Situated on the north-east corner of Roe and William Streets, and very conveniently placed near the railway station, the Governor Broome Hotel seems to have led a troubled existence, with both minor and major incidents being regularly reported in the newspapers.

The earliest reference to the hotel was just before it opened in 1886. According to various newspaper reports, a debate took place during a justices' licensing hearing about the probity of having a hotel close to the girls' school in nearby James Street. A petition against the granting of a licence was submitted and during the proceedings the lawyer for the applicant pointed out one of those who had signed the petition was one of the magistrates for the hearing. The lawyer remarked, "I do not consider you are sitting there as a justice. You came here as a partisan and, therefore, I object to your sitting there at all." The magistrates retired to consider the case and came back to grant the requested licence.

The hotel, which one newspaper described as having "a peculiar style of architecture", must have opened soon after that hearing, but was back in trouble just a few months later when the owner of a neighbouring residence complained to the city council about a public urinal for the hotel that had been erected opposite his property. The city surveyor responded that it "appeared the place was kept perfectly clean, and that a screen had been erected in front of it", so the council decided they had no power to interfere in the matter.

About six months later, the *Daily News* ran the headline, "Atrocious Assault: Mr. J. Stuart Nearly Murdered in His Bed". An assailant had managed to gain entry to the hotel and attacked the landlord as he lay asleep in his bed, fracturing his skull and inflicting several nasty wounds. The supposed felon was later arrested, but after several court appearances was freed for lack of evidence, which was considered a diabolical outrage by the *Western Mail* leader writer.

In February the following year, one of the hotel's guests deliberately set fire to the bed in his room and was charged with attempted arson. Other minor crimes, mainly involving patrons of the hotel bars, were reported in the last 12 years of the 19th century.

In 1899 James Innes, who had become the licensee of the hotel, filed for bankruptcy, owing over £6,000. As a result of this, the licence was ascribed to George Fenner. Even as late as 1944 the Governor Broome made headlines when the then landlord Harry Ottwell sued a local estate agent over comments he had published about the service he had received at the hotel. The case was eventually withdrawn.

By the late 1970s the hotel had become a popular performance venue for early Perth punk bands, such as the Victims and the Nasties, who played there regularly.

Sadly, after a somewhat tempestuous history, the Governor Broome Hotel was demolished in 1983, with the State Theatre now standing on the site.

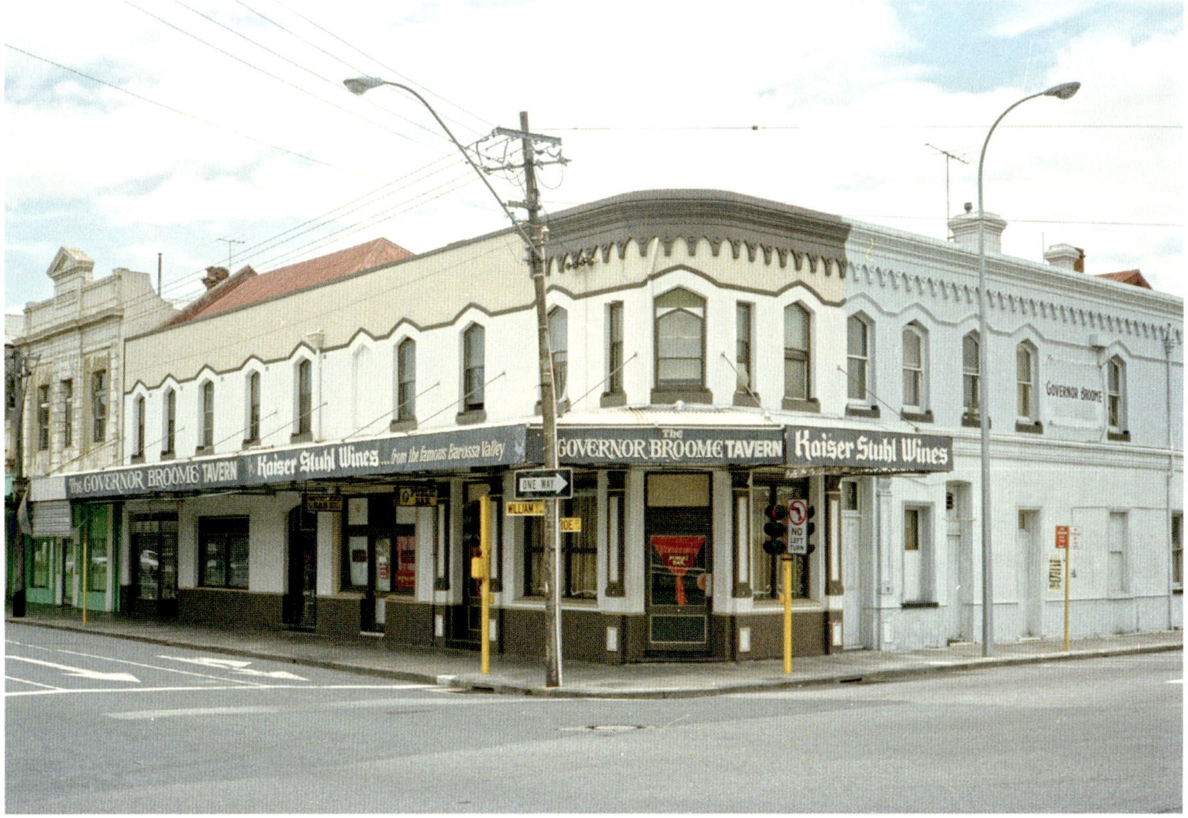

ABOVE The Governor Broome Hotel, the home of punk rock in Perth, minus its original balcony, just before it was demolished in 1983.

OPPOSITE The Governor Broome Hotel on the corner of William and Roe Streets in about 1905.

FOY & GIBSON

DEMOLISHED 1986

After an exploratory visit in 1895 to acquire a suitable building site, one of Australia's earliest department stores, Foy & Gibson, was able to announce that it was opening a store in Perth. After this it set up a temporary store in Murray Street and the following year moved to its permanent site.

Founded in Melbourne, the firm modelled itself on Le Bon Marché in Paris and other department stores around the world, selling a large range of goods, many of which were manufactured in-house, including clothing, furniture, hardware and food. It is interesting to note that the company chose Perth as the second city in which to start a shop, reflecting the newfound prosperity and opportunity the first Gold Rush offered entrepreneurial businessmen. Stores followed later in Brisbane and Adelaide.

The arrival of the store on Hay Street, which stretched to St Georges Terrace, was heralded by an item in the *Daily News* in September 1896: "The price paid for the ground is £10,000, and at a cost of £15,000 more Messrs. Foy and Gibson will erect a great arcade, with a frontage to each of these thoroughfares."

The plot the firm acquired gave the shop an opportunity to have entrances on Hay Street and St Georges Terrace. In order to get the emporium up and running as quickly as possible, a temporary timber and corrugated iron structure was prefabricated in the firm's Melbourne factory, and shipped round the coast to Albany, where it was loaded on to a train bound for Perth. The *Inquirer* suggested the new building was "a novelty in architecture and its method of construction and conveyance to this colony will no doubt come as a revelation to many people."

Having successfully opened in their temporary quarters, the Perth firm of architects Cavanagh and Cavanagh were commissioned to design a permanent building for the site. There was a stipulation, however, that construction of the new building should disrupt business in the temporary one as little as possible. The new building was to be four storeys high on Hay Street and, because of the slope of the land, five on St Georges Terrace.

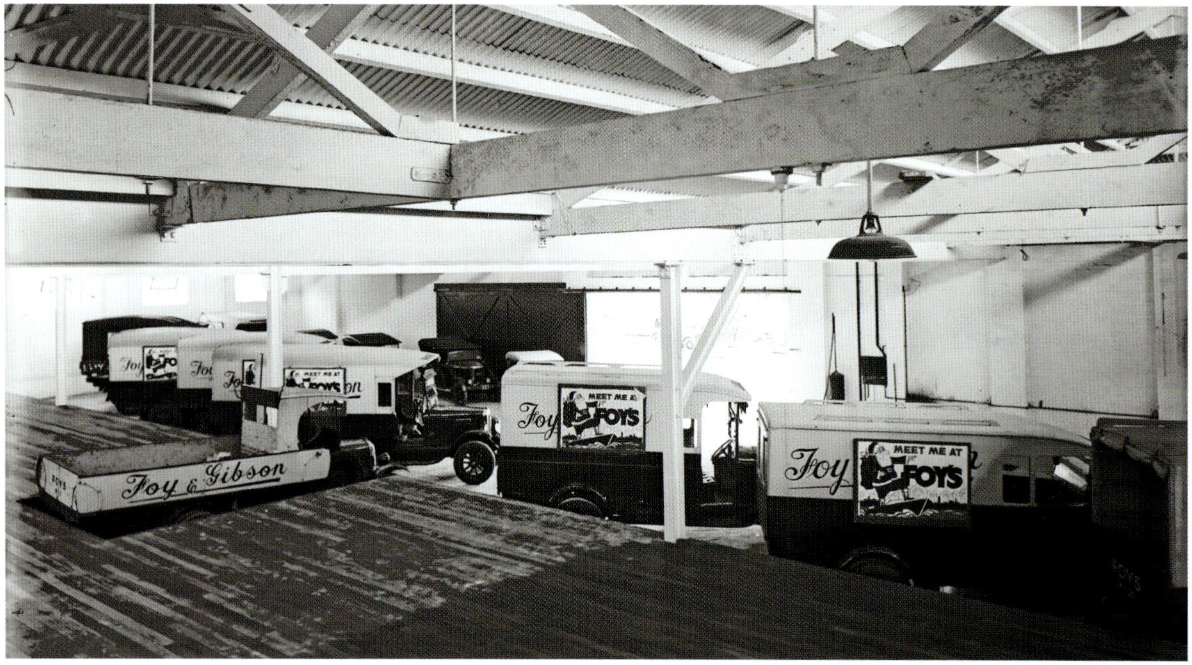

The first stage of the construction was to create a basement and two storeys, facing Hay Street and running back 300 feet towards St Georges Terrace. The design created an elegant building, with shopping areas illuminated by skylights along the roofs and electric lighting. The front veranda and super-structure was describes as "a very showy structure", with all the stone and ironwork having been shipped over from Melbourne. The extended building opened in 1902.

After World War II, Foy & Gibson claimed to be one of Australia's largest retailers, manufacturers and importers, expanding by buying up retail outlets in regional towns throughout the South-West. The Perth store became the first place in Australia where refrigerated display cabinets were installed to "completely protect food from germs and flies".

In 1955 the company was bought out by Cox Brothers, and in 1964 Foy & Gibson (WA) Ltd., including 10 stores throughout Western Australia, was sold to David Jones department stores. The fine Hay Street shop was demolished in 1986 to make way for Central Park, one of the tallest buildings in Perth.

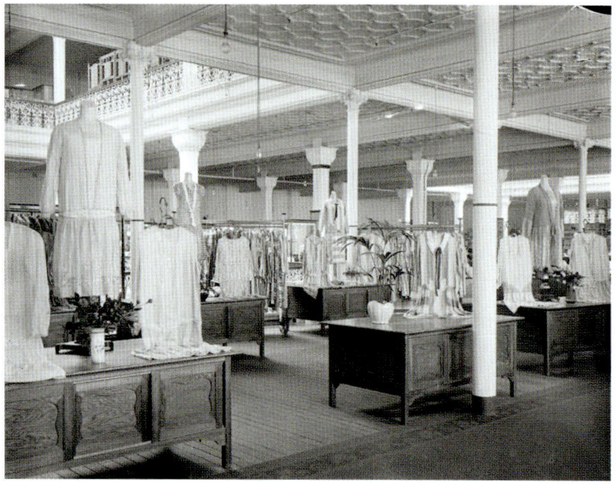

TOP The fleet of Foy & Gibson vehicles in the garage in 1934.

ABOVE A shop floor display of ladies' fashions in about 1930.

RIGHT Shoppers parked outside the Foy & Gibson's Hay Street store during the firm's Summer Fair in 1930.

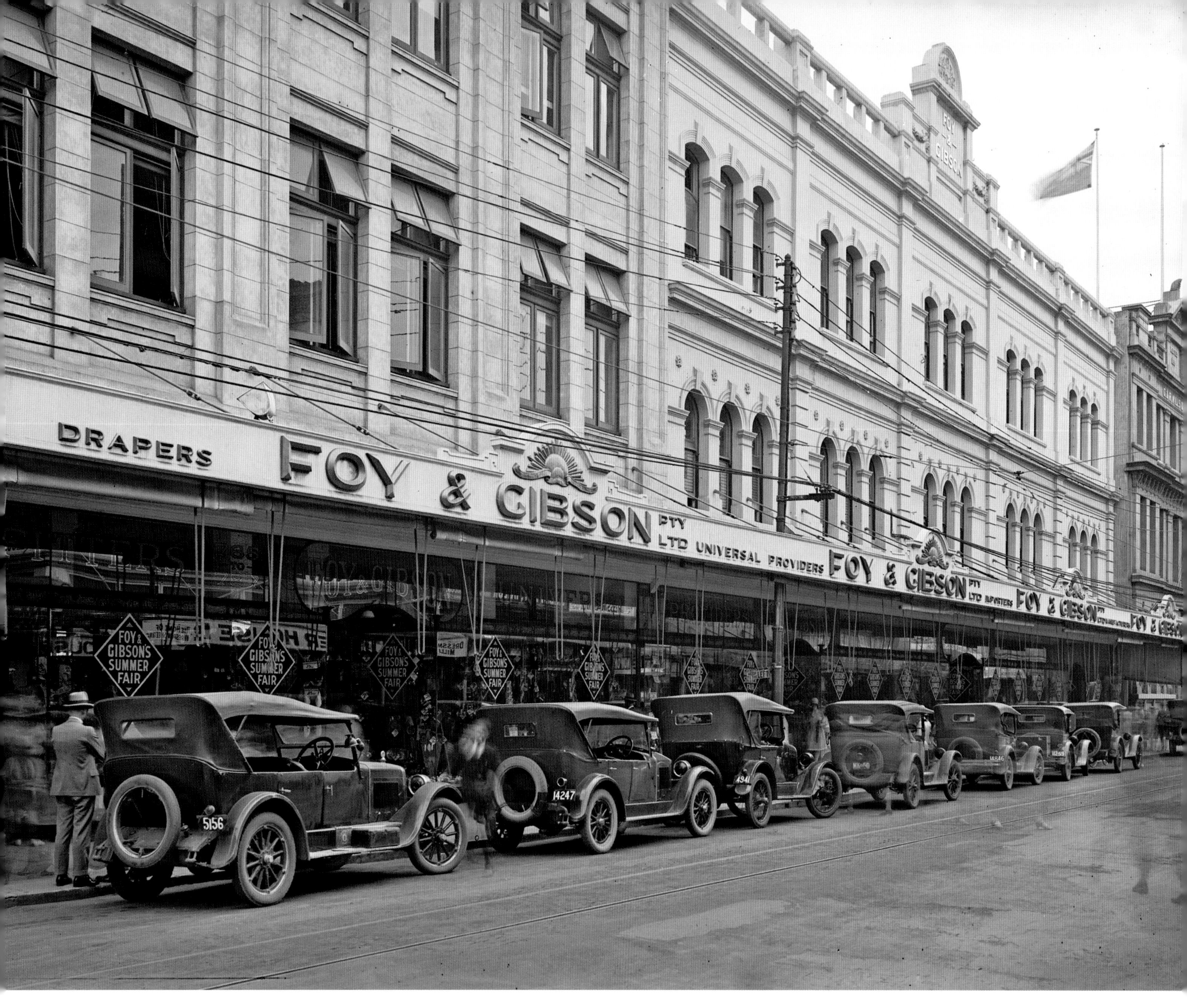
FOY & GIBSON
DRAPERS
FOY & GIBSON PTY LTD UNIVERSAL PROVIDERS
FOY & GIBSON
FOY & GIBSON'S SUMMER FAIR
5156
14247
4941

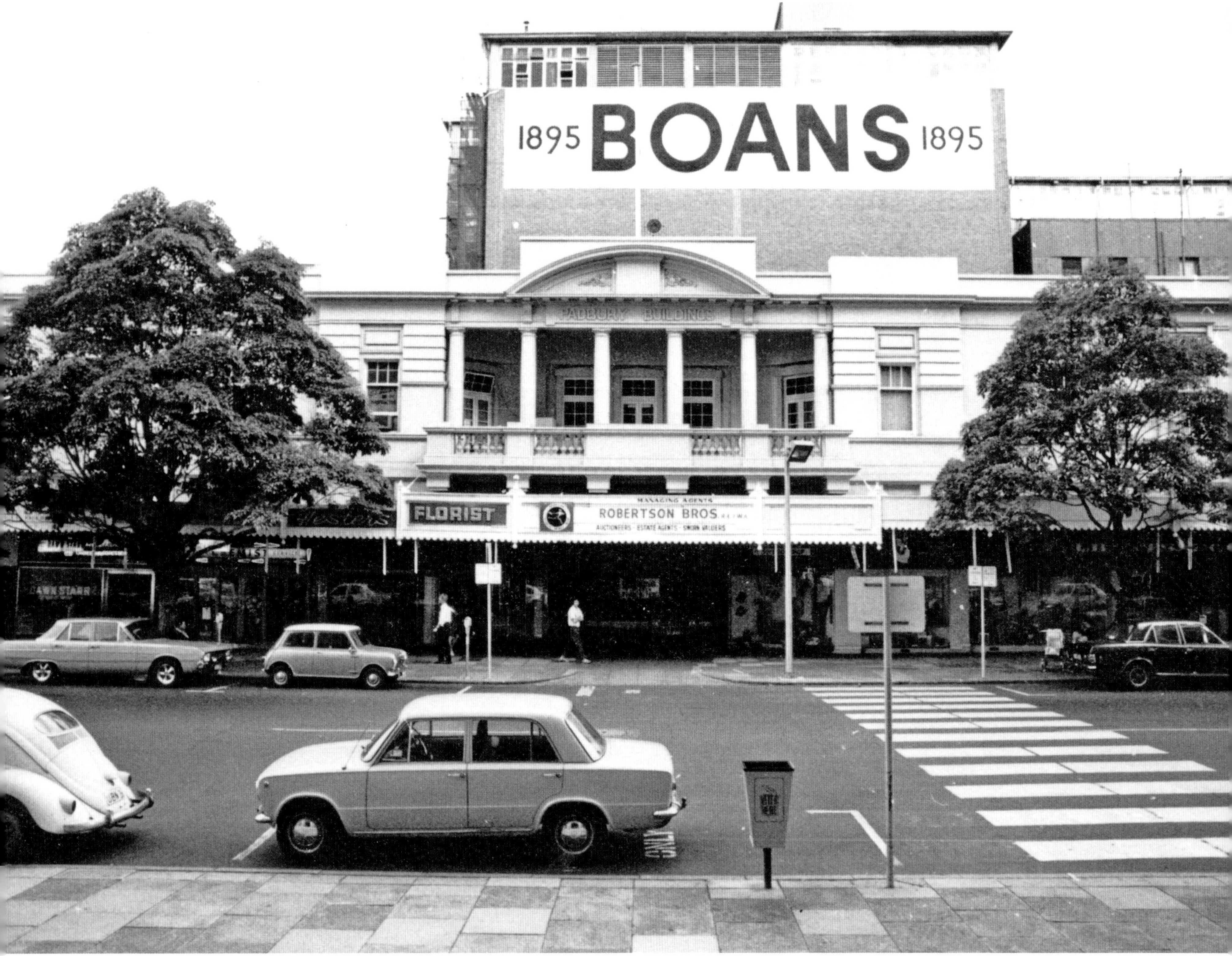
1895 BOANS 1895
PADBURY BUILDINGS
FLORIST
MANAGING AGENTS
ROBERTSON BROS
AUCTIONEERS · ESTATE AGENTS · SWORN VALUERS

PADBURY BUILDING

DEMOLISHED 1986

Land opposite the railway station, including Central Arcade, was acquired by the Commonwealth Government in 1911 to create a Commonwealth Government precinct, to which departments could move from the cramped Treasury Building. The proposal was for a new street through the site on which a General Post Office was to be built.

In order to improve the surroundings of the newly constructed GPO building, the Central Arcade was demolished in 1922 to make way for the new street, which was officially named Forrest Place in 1923. The land opposite the GPO building was leased to William Padbury with a 30-year term at an annual rental of £6,000. At the expiration of that term the land and improvements would revert to the Commonwealth Government. On this ground the Padbury Buildings (or Padbury Building as it was known) was constructed.

Original plans for the building were for a grand five-storey structure, but, thanks to a federal government policy decision, this had to be reduced to two, with the possibility of a basement, in the final design. News of the proposed basement seemed to cause some alarm, as the *West Australian* reported, "knowing the treacherous nature of the ground in this locality this will not be attempted. All of this ground, and where Boans Ltd. emporium, and the Perth railway station stand, was known a little more than 30 years ago as the 'Round Swamp', where the boys of the city were in the habit of fishing for 'Jilgies'."

The new Padbury Building was designed by Cox and Cox, who included a foundation capable of carrying a five-storey building should there have been a change of heart by the federal government. The building consisted of 24 shops on the ground floor and 40 offices on the first floor. By the end of 1925 all of the offices on the first floor had been let and only three shops at the Murray Street end, the last to be completed, remained to be filled, with all tenants holding a five-year lease.

During the construction, a tragic accident occurred when a crane collapsed whilst lifting a large load of crushed road metal destined for a mixer. The crane driver, who was trapped in the cabin of the crane for some time, suffered a fatal head injury.

One of the first organisations to lease one of the first floor units was the Metropolitan Branch Country Women's Association, who, through various fund-raising events, raised sufficient money to create rest rooms for country members visiting the city.

Over the years, a wide variety of companies and organisations used the Padbury Building as their base. These included well-known names such as Qantas and the Commonwealth Railways. The building was also home to the Naval Recruiting Office and the National Fitness Council who, during World War II, recruited lads between 14 and 18 with bicycles to act as emergency despatch riders.

In 1986 it was decided to turn Forrest Place into a pedestrian precinct. The Padbury Building and the adjacent Boans department store were demolished to make way for Forrest Chase Shopping Centre. A year later both buildings were gone and the new complex was officially opened by Queen Elizabeth II in 1988.

OPPOSITE Cars parked outside the Padbury Building on Forrest Place with Boans behind (1972).

BELOW The Padbury Building in 1928, with Boans behind. Businesses in the Padbury Building included Michelides Ltd., Tobacconists; Braham Bros., Dentists; Forrest Place Tea Rooms, owned by Albany Bell Ltd.; and Grose's Hats.

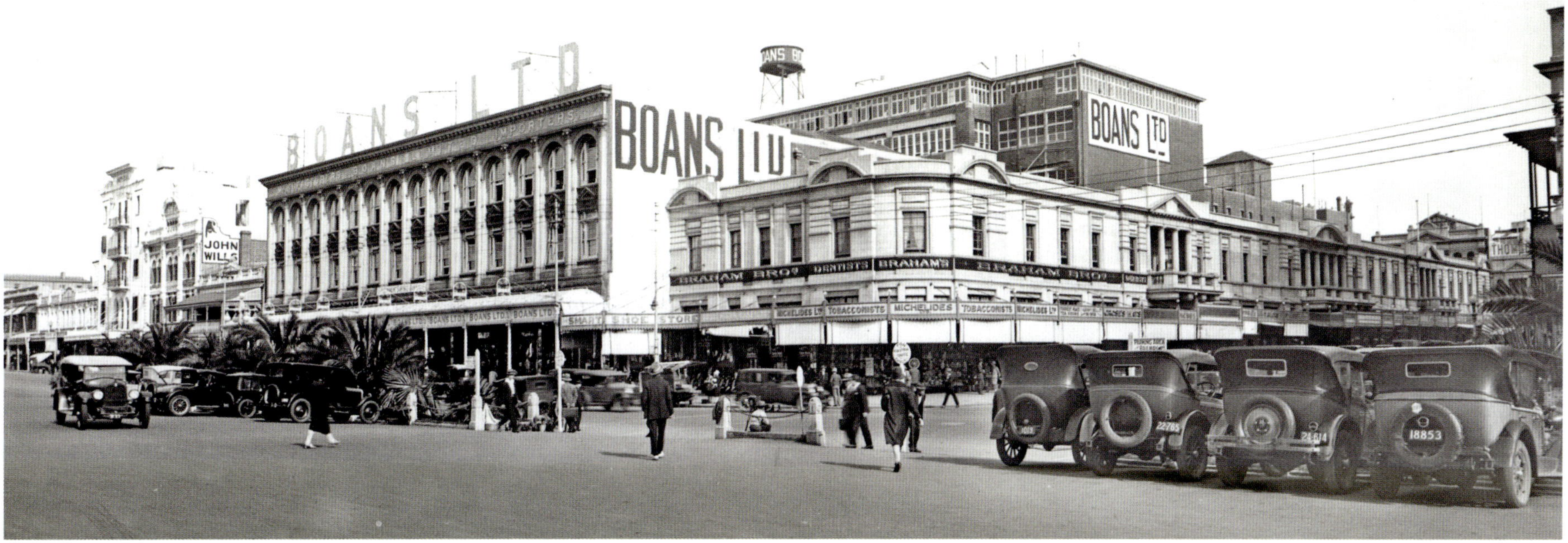

BOANS

DEMOLISHED 1987

Boans was probably the most iconic department store in Western Australia's retail history. It was founded in 1895 by Harry Boan and his brother Benjamin who both came to Perth from Broken Hill, where Harry and another brother, Ernest, had previously established a successful drapery shop known as Boan Bros. Ltd.

The brothers arrived in Perth in mid-1895 when Harry was 34, and purchased two prime quarter-acre blocks facing Wellington Street and the Perth railway station, which had been used as stabling for horses, at a price of £42 per foot of street frontage. The brothers borrowed £62,000 and within four months, despite acute labour shortages caused by the Gold Rush, built and stocked a single-storey emporium on the site, calling it Boan Bros.

The store's grand opening on Saturday 9 November 1895 was covered in the *West Australian*: "To those who have such recollections of the firm's operations at Broken Hill the novelty of the occasion may not be so great, but to the inexperienced in the firm's modus operandi it will probably prove of considerable interest. The facilities which the firm possesses for obtaining and concentrating large stocks is one strong point, and another is the rapid turnover in the essentially cash business – for it must be understood that Boan Brothers' is a cash business. Upon such a basis they claim to be able to sell much cheaper than other competitors."

The publicity worked and on the opening day there was such a crush of customers, both outside and in the store, that Boan Bros. were obliged to close shortly after opening. As a result, the *Inquirer* printed a statement for the company a few days later, "Messrs. Boan Bros, requested us to strain a point on their behalf and insert the advertisement, which appears on page 1 of to-day's issue, as an intimation they were compelled to close their establishment until Tuesday next owing to their being unable to compete with the great rush of customers."

The Boan brothers knew how to market their store and held many events such as promenade evenings to entice customers. An example of this is shown in a report by the *West Australian* in April 1896: "That there is a charm in Boan Brothers promenade evenings there is no denying. The spectacle the spacious Emporium of the firm presents on such occasions is irresistible. Long before the hour appointed for the admission of the public to the promenade last evening, a great concourse of both sexes waited round the entrance, in Wellington Street. When they were admitted the sight revealed to them was one which amply repaid them for their attendance. It was quickly seen that it was no vain boast on the part of the firm that they were going to make a show really unique in its way."

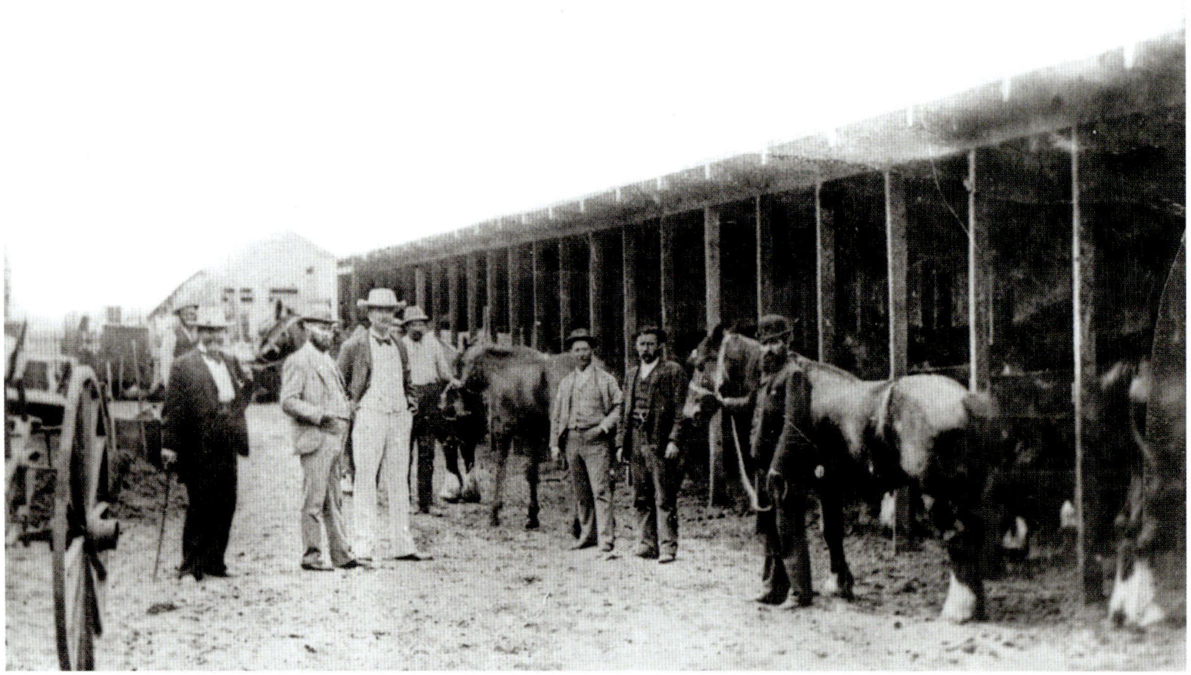

In 1901 Benjamin died and Harry assumed sole ownership. He purchased adjoining land which spanned the block between Wellington and Murray Streets, near Forrest Place, with a view to greatly increasing the size of his store. Following a fact-finding round-the-world trip in 1902 he visited well-known stores such as Selfridges in London and Macy's in the USA. As a result, he decided that it was time Perth had a thoroughly modern department store offering all the services other firms provided around the world. He employed the architectural firm of Hobbs, Smith and Forbes to design a large and imposing new three-storey store to replace his single-storey shop and turn the business into a world-class department store. The work was carried out in stages between 1905 and 1912.

The opening of the store in November 1912 was announced in the *Daily News* in the following terms: "Far and away the most important event in the world today, in the eyes of the average Perth housewife at any rate, is the opening of Boan Bros. new mammoth store. Motors are flying about in all directions loaded

ABOVE In 1895 Harry Boan bought these horse stables in Wellington Street as the site of his new store.

RIGHT Boan's original store decorated for Queen Victoria's Diamond Jubilee in 1897.

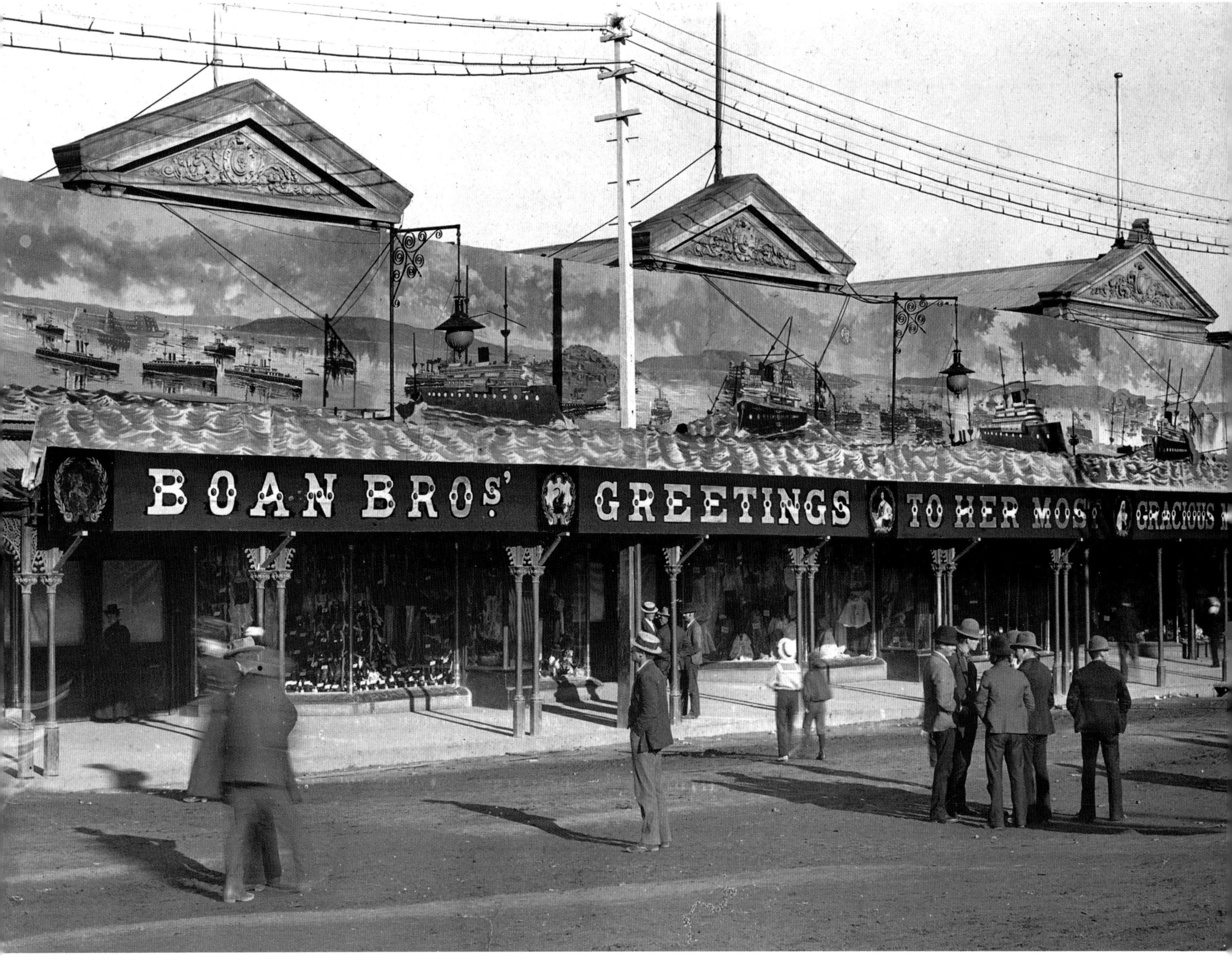
BOAN BROS'
GREETINGS
TO HER MOS
GRACIOUS

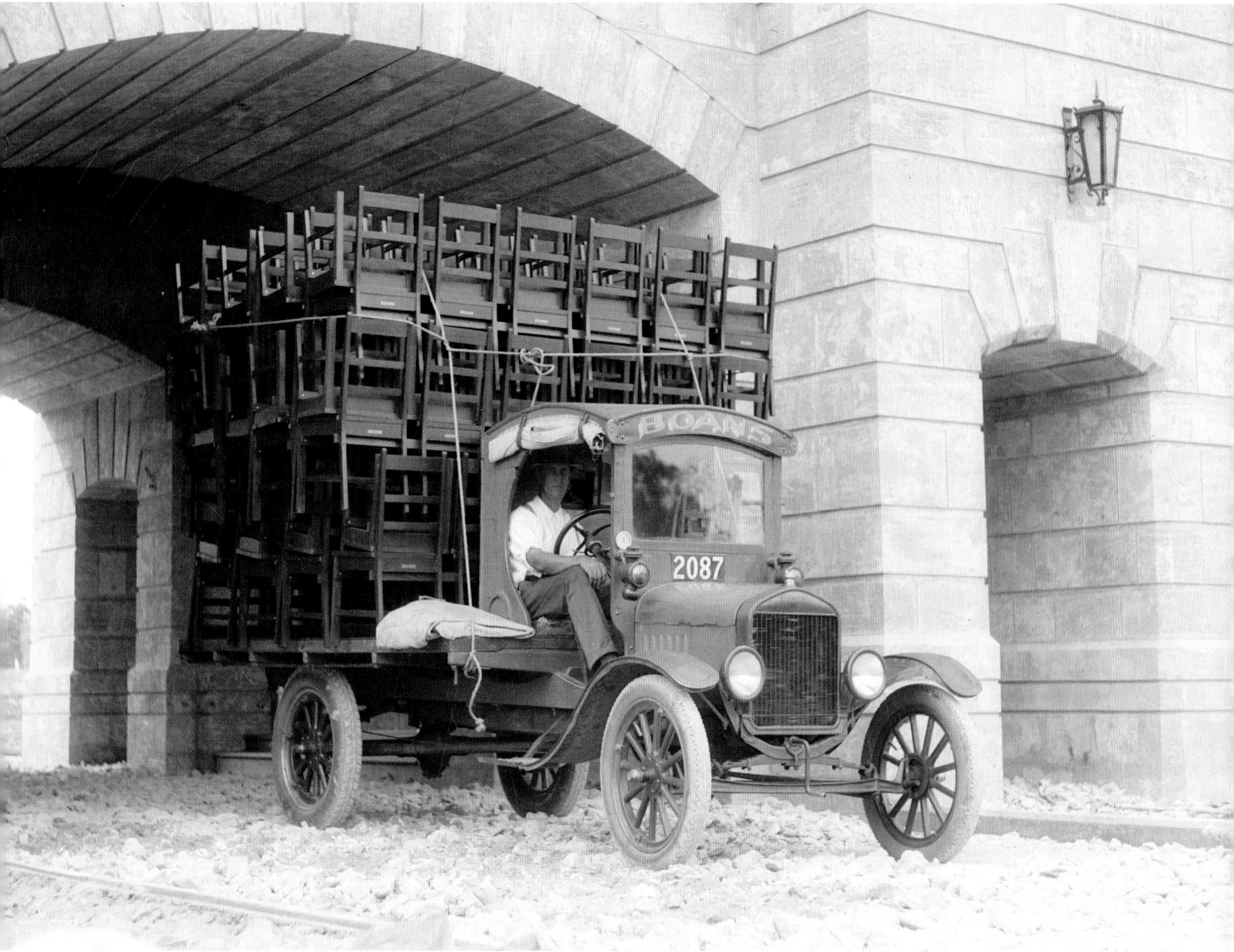
BOANS
2087

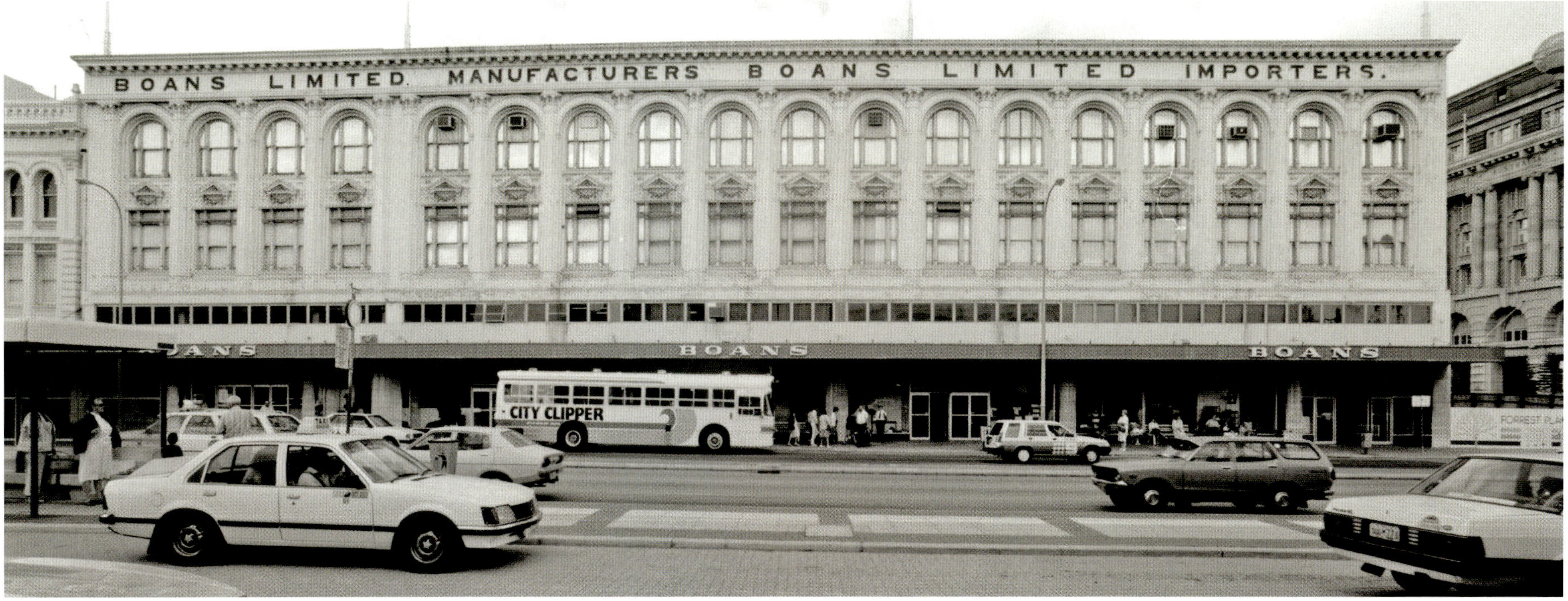

with happy women, whose eyes literally glow with the gladness of anticipation."

The new store was even more of a success than its predecessor and offered everything a shopper could desire, including an elegant tearoom and library. It is small wonder that their slogan became "Boans for Service".

In the same year, the business was restructured to become a limited company. Changing its name to Boans Ltd., it became the largest private employer in Western Australia. Like many other department stores, Boans had issued a mail order catalogue from the early 1900s, which continued into the 1950s. Each edition was heavily publicised and eagerly anticipated, being particularly useful for those living in isolated locations.

To have better control over its goods, Boans opened a furniture factory in East Perth in 1910 to service the shop. It produced bedroom furniture, mattresses, dining and kitchen furniture, cane-ware and upholstery. Following World War II, a bakery and butchers was added.

The firm realised from the outset that its staff was its greatest asset and was always at pains to ensure they were well looked after. During the Great Depression of the 1930s, Boans did not lay staff off as many firms did. Instead, it developed a roster whereby one-third

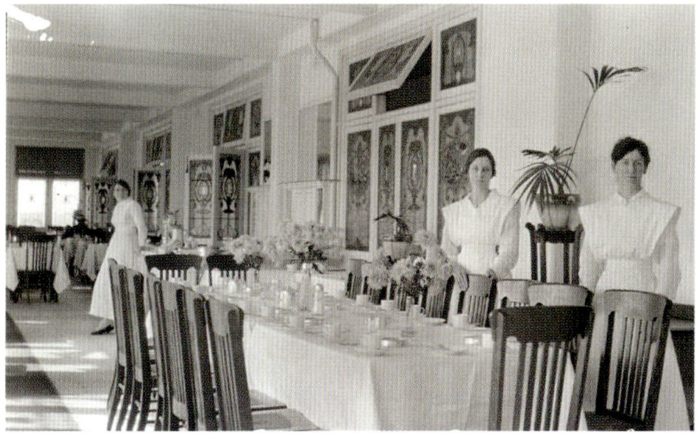

of the staff stood down each week on rotation, with a reduced wage packet. Knowing what the unpleasant alternative could be, the entire staff willingly accepted this scheme and remained in work throughout the Depression. Similarly, after World War II all staff that had been away at war were given their old jobs back on their return to civilian life.

In 1979 the store suffered a major fire and closed for some weeks. The store reopened, but in 1986 it was sold to Coles Myer Ltd., who demolished the neighbouring Padbury Building in 1986 and Boans the following year to make way for the new Forrest Chase Shopping Centre.

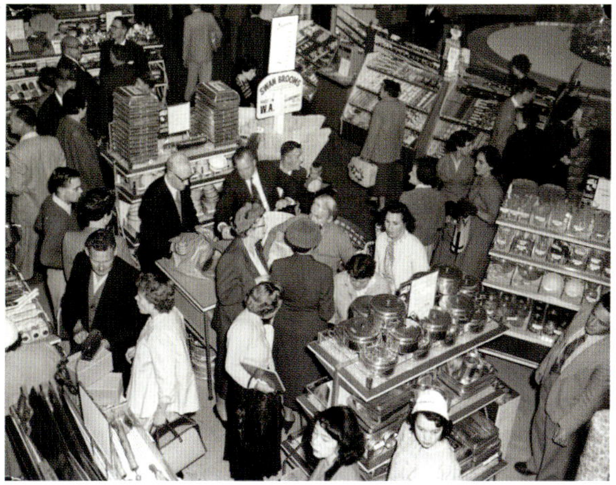

TOP The Wellington Street façade of Boans from the railway station forecourt, taken for the *West Australian* newspaper in the year before the building was demolished.

ABOVE LEFT The Boans Tea Rooms, just after World War I.

ABOVE Shoppers in the homeware department in the early 1950s. A sign advertises "Swan Brooms, made in WA".

OPPOSITE A Boans delivery truck heavily laden with a consignment of chairs ready for delivery.

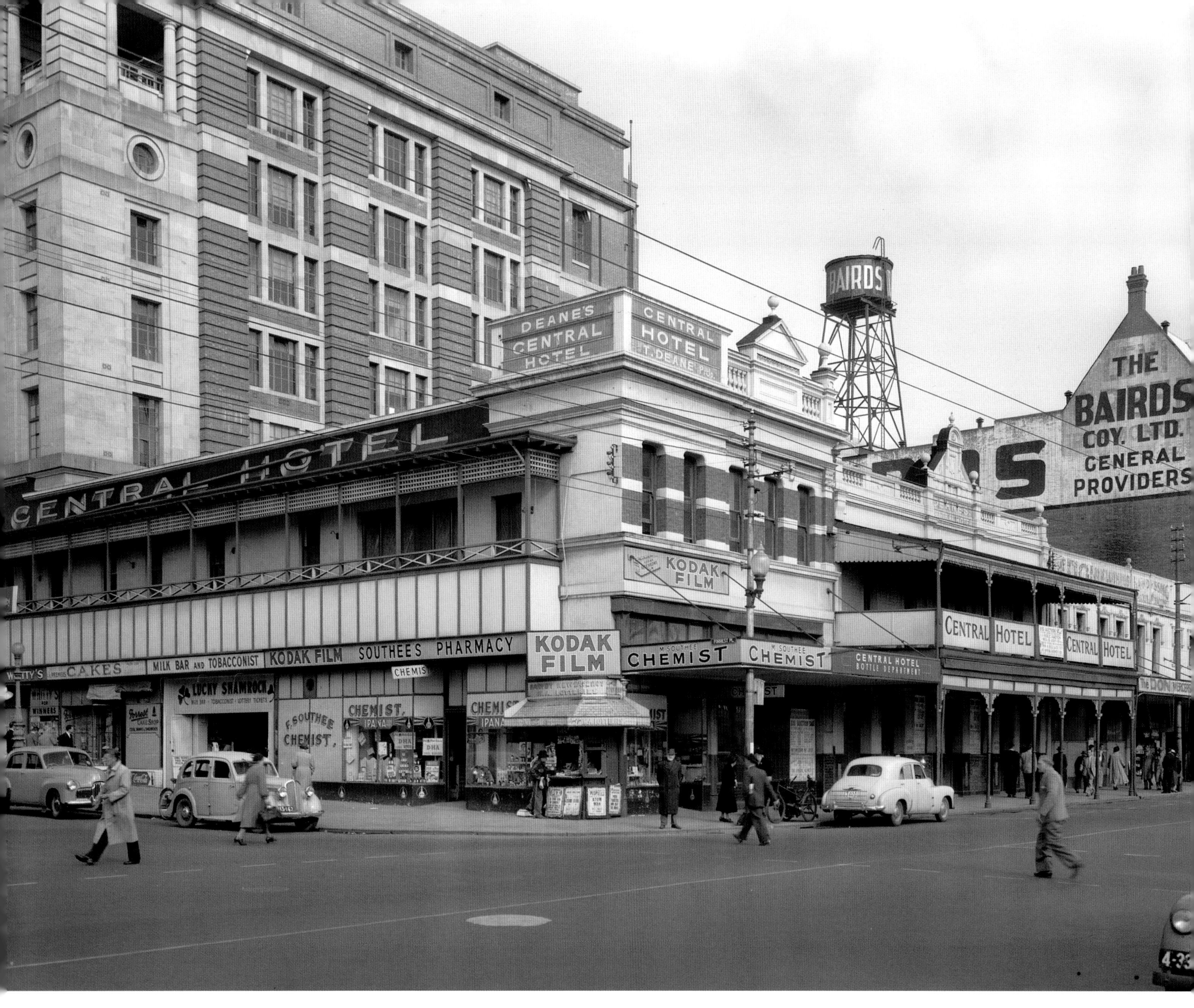
BAIRDS
DEANE'S
CENTRAL
HOTEL
CENTRAL
HOTEL
T. DEANE PTD.
THE
BAIRDS
COY. LTD.
GENERAL
PROVIDERS
CENTRAL HOTEL
KODAK
FILM
MILK BAR AND TOBACCONIST
KODAK FILM
SOUTHEE'S PHARMACY
CAKES
LUCKY SHAMROCK
F. SOUTHEE
CHEMIST.
CHEMIST.
IPANA
CHEMIST
CHEMIST
CENTRAL HOTEL
BOTTLE DEPARTMENT
CENTRAL
HOTEL
CENTRAL
HOTEL

CENTRAL HOTEL

DEMOLISHED 1989

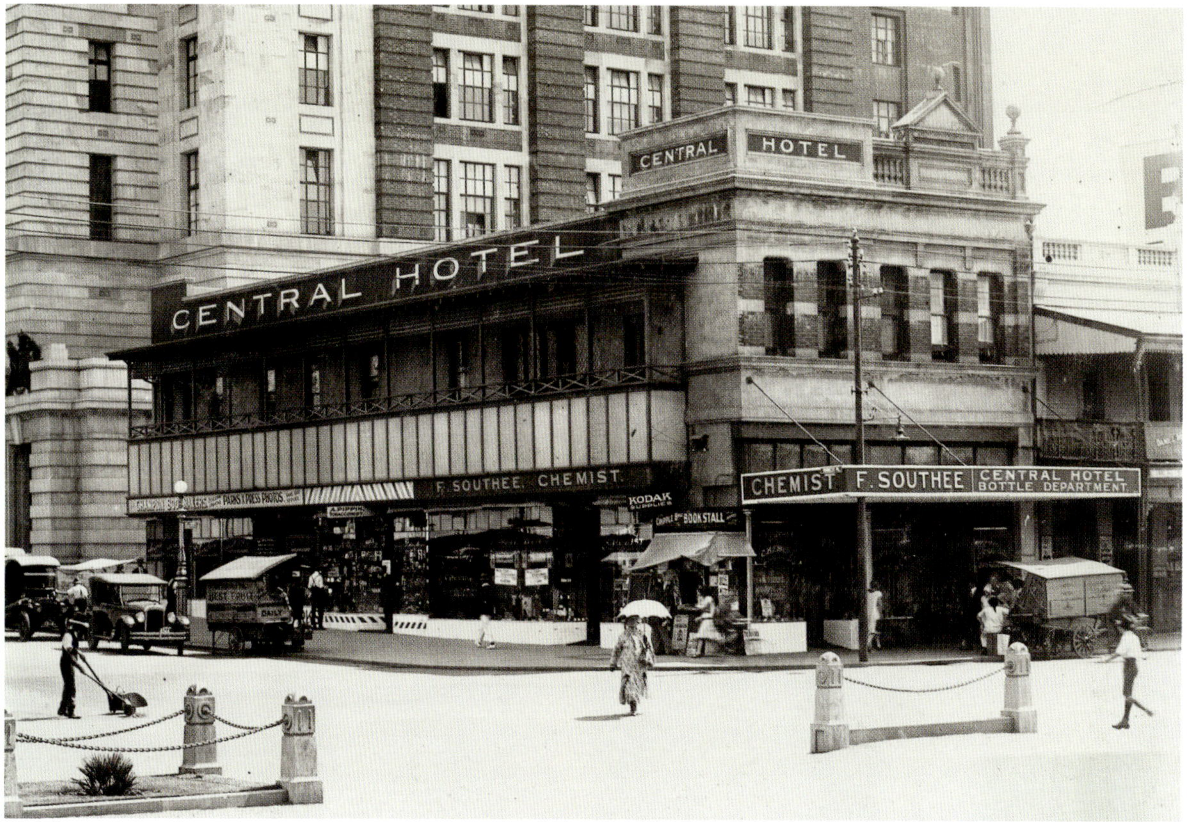

The Central Hotel started its life in the 1880s as the Miners' Arms Hotel. Throughout its history the hotel was continually in the news, usually for all the wrong reasons. During December 1898, for instance, not only did the landlord have his licence cancelled for "wilfully delaying the admission of the police to his hotel", but a daring robbery took place when a man calmly walked into the hotel, up to one of the bedrooms and stole money out of the trouser pocket of the occupant, whilst he was still wearing them. Six months later one of the guests committed suicide in the building.

By the beginning of the 20th century, the hotel was clearly considered to be a dive and was purchased by Daniel Mulcahy who, according to the *Sunday Times* of June 1901, transformed the building: "As evidence of how an eyesore can be changed into a beauty spot, one has only to pay a visit to the Central Hotel, Wellington Street, immediately opposite the railway station, where Mr. Mulcahy has effected a complete transformation." The report continued, "...on the eastern side of the public entrance is a large and beautifully fitted threepenny bar, at the back of which is the sitting room, while on the eastern-side is the saloon bar, a charmingly pretty place, artistically laid out. Immediately behind is the billiard saloon, a well ventilated and bright room, where a pleasant hour can be whiled away with the cue."

The report concluded that Mr Mulcahy intended to give the Central "his personal supervision at all times" in the hope that its associations with the Miners' Arms would be entirely eliminated.

The hotel was once again renovated in 1923 as part of the creation of Forrest Place, when the new GPO building next door was completed. Two years later Mulcahy died and the property was acquired by Thomas Deane. Yet more trouble was to ensue.

In 1928, a scuffle in the bar, when two men were refused service, resulted in one of the barmen dying two days later from injuries caused during the fracas. Several other minor incidents were reported during the ensuing years, until 1944 when the *Daily News* reported that the licensee, Thomas Deane, had been charged with attempting to influence a juror. Deane, along with another man, was convicted and had to forfeit the hotel licence, which was transferred to his sister, who a year later was fined for "not having had every door or other entrance by which admission could be gained to the bar room closed and locked at a time when the premises should not have been open for the sale of liquor."

Less controversial were some of the shops that occupied the ground floor of the building in Forrest Place, which included at various times, Dolly Varden, Millinery Specialist; J.L. McKinley, Watchmaker and Jeweller; Southee's Pharmacy; Lucky Shamrock Milk Bar and Tobacconist; and the Forrest Cake Shop.

The leases on the hotel expired in June 1953 and the building was converted into Commonwealth Government offices. It was demolished in 1989 to make way for Albert Facey House.

ABOVE The Central Hotel on the corner of Wellington Street and Forrest Place in about 1928. The hotel maintained a degree of notoriety throughout its life.

OPPOSITE The Central Hotel in 1953, with the Bairds Building and the GPO forming a backdrop.

CANTERBURY COURT

DEMOLISHED 1990

Shaftesbury Picture Gardens, as Canterbury Court was first known, was built on the site of a wood yard in Stirling Street. Also known as the Shaftesbury Theatre or Shaftesbury Picture Palace, it opened in March 1911. At that time, the main competitor to this venture was Melrose Gardens, but with a seating capacity of 3,000, as opposed to the Melrose's 2,000, and an aggressive pricing structure, the owners of the Shaftesbury were clearly determined to win the customers.

Seats were priced at 1s for front stalls, 6d for back stalls and 3d for the gallery. The pricing regime seems to have been quite flexible, however, and for the screening of a film of the famous Johnson-Jeffries prize fight in 1911, prices rose to 3s, 2s and 1s. The *West Australian* reported that "Prior to the commencement of the entertainment several scores of persons who had only paid for admission to the cheaper parts of the house found themselves without seating accommodation, and one of these suddenly scaled the barricades and occupied the 3s seats to the evident delight of the galleryites and some concern on the part of the management."

The programme was changed twice a week and usually consisted of a main feature film supported by vaudeville acts and musical items. Just before the outbreak of World War I, the theatre became primarily a vaudeville house during the week with a regular film programme on Sundays. Just before the end of the war, probably due to competition from other city-centre venues, film screenings stopped, with the theatre being completely given over to vaudeville acts. This continued until 1924 when the Shaftesbury closed and reopened the following year as the Luxor.

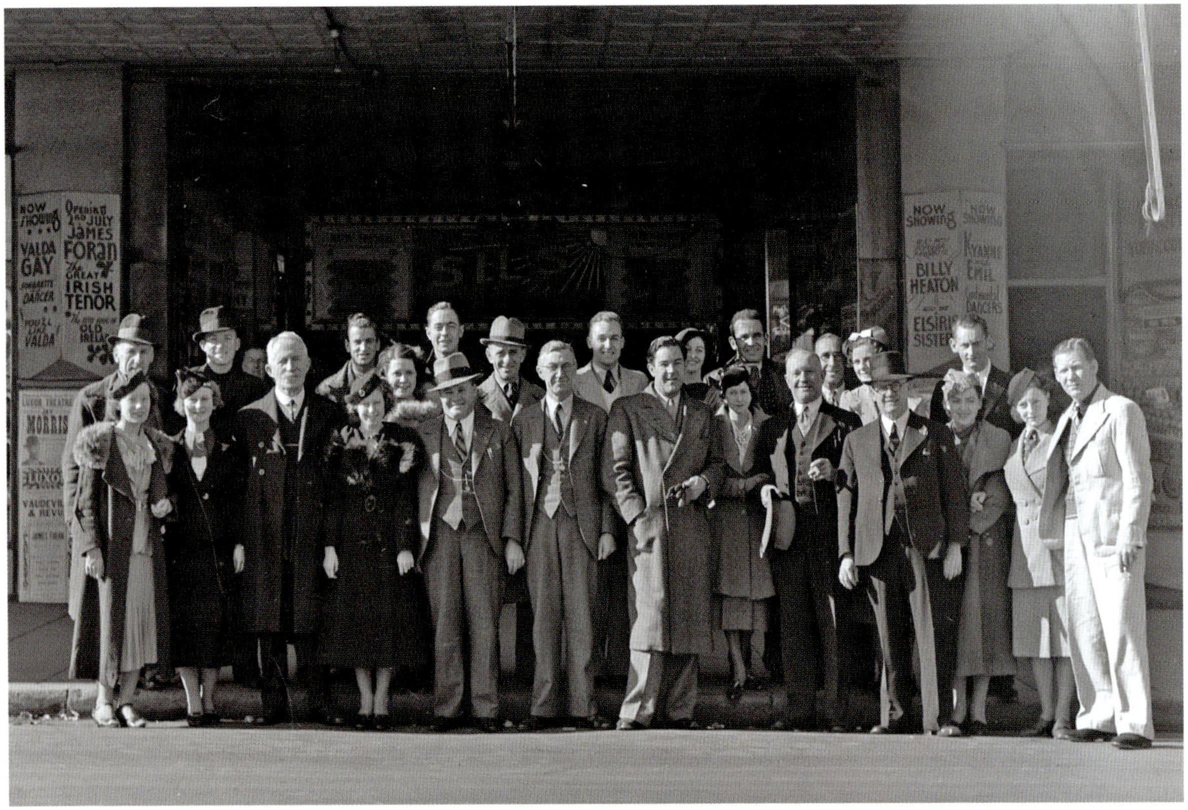

Styled as Perth's "Home of Vaudeville", the Luxor was very popular. Audiences enjoying the bizarre mix of acts offered by the theatre were blissfully unaware that health and safety was not paramount in the management's mind, with various council reports showing a heady cocktail of dangerous hazards lurking in the wings. Blocked fire exits, exposed wiring and rats' nests were just some of the problems besetting the theatre. Rats in the dressing rooms were such a problem that the lids on makeup boxes had to be locked each night for fear of the makeup being eaten.

From the mid-1930s to 40s, the venue was known as the Luxor Picture Theatre and screened popular films in an era when cinema-going was at an all-time high. Later in the 1940s it became known as the Tivoli Theatre and was once again staging variety shows. Late in 1949 the theatre was converted into Western Australia's first ice rink – quite a novelty for warm-weathered Perth.

Five years after this, the venue once again underwent conversion and a name change, becoming the Canterbury Court Ballroom, which was opened by Perth's Lord Mayor in September 1955. A multi-storey car park was added to the top of the building in 1969, but the dancing continued, with only a name change to the Canterbury Court Function Centre in the early 1980s, until the entire building, which had probably undergone more name changes than any other entertainment venue in Perth's history, was visited by the wrecking ball in 1990. It was replaced by a Myer Megamart, which in turn was replaced by a car park complex a few years later.

RIGHT Front entrance of Canterbury Court in 1956, with a Ford motorcar outside.

LEFT When this photograph was taken outside the Luxor Theatre in 1937, the Paulasto Bros. troupe were playing at the Luxor and it is thought the picture is of them.

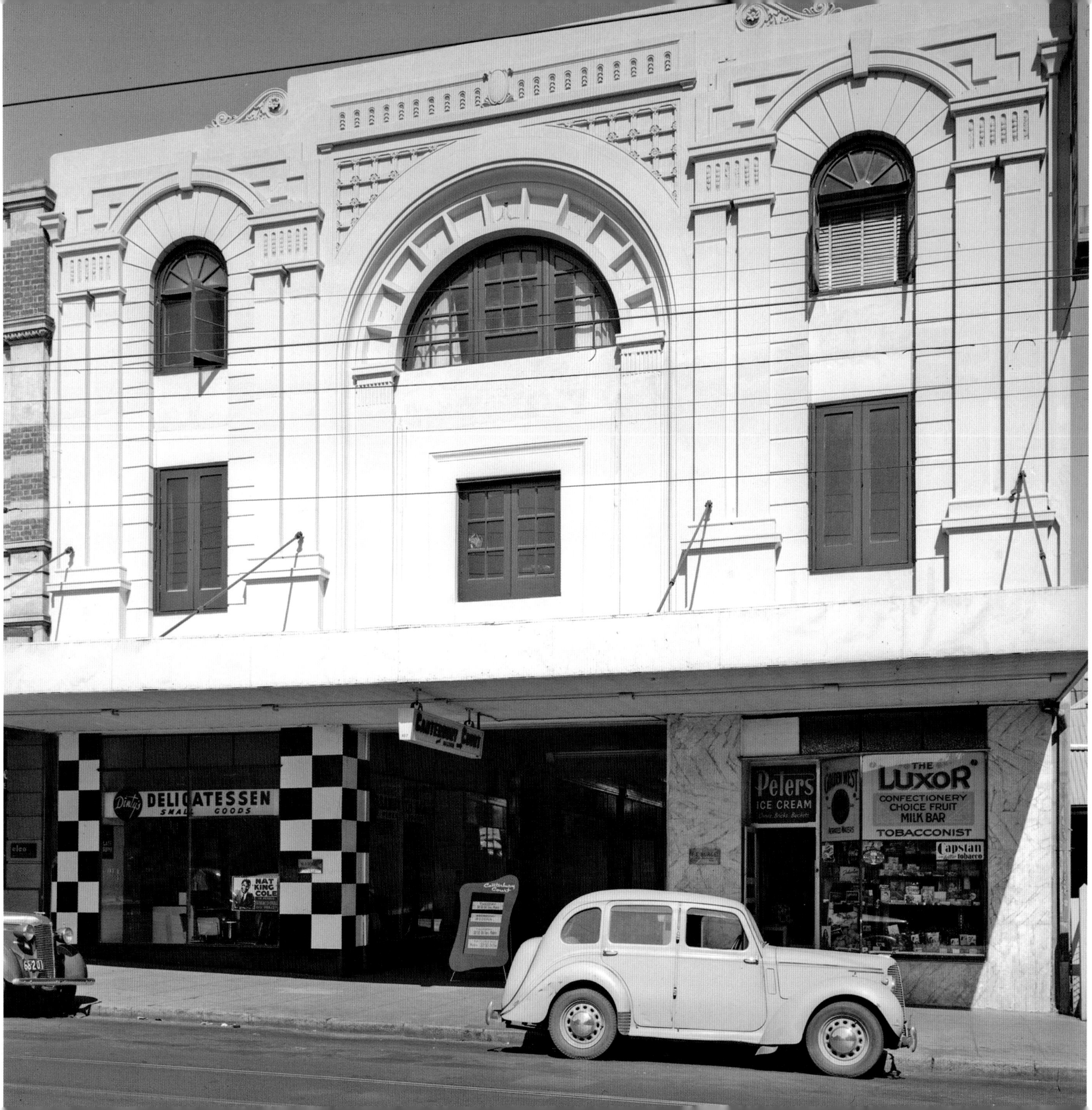
Dinty's
DELICATESSEN
SMALL GOODS
NAT KING COLE
Canterbury Court
Peters
ICE CREAM
THE
LUXOR
CONFECTIONERY
CHOICE FRUIT
MILK BAR
TOBACCONIST
Capstan
tobacco

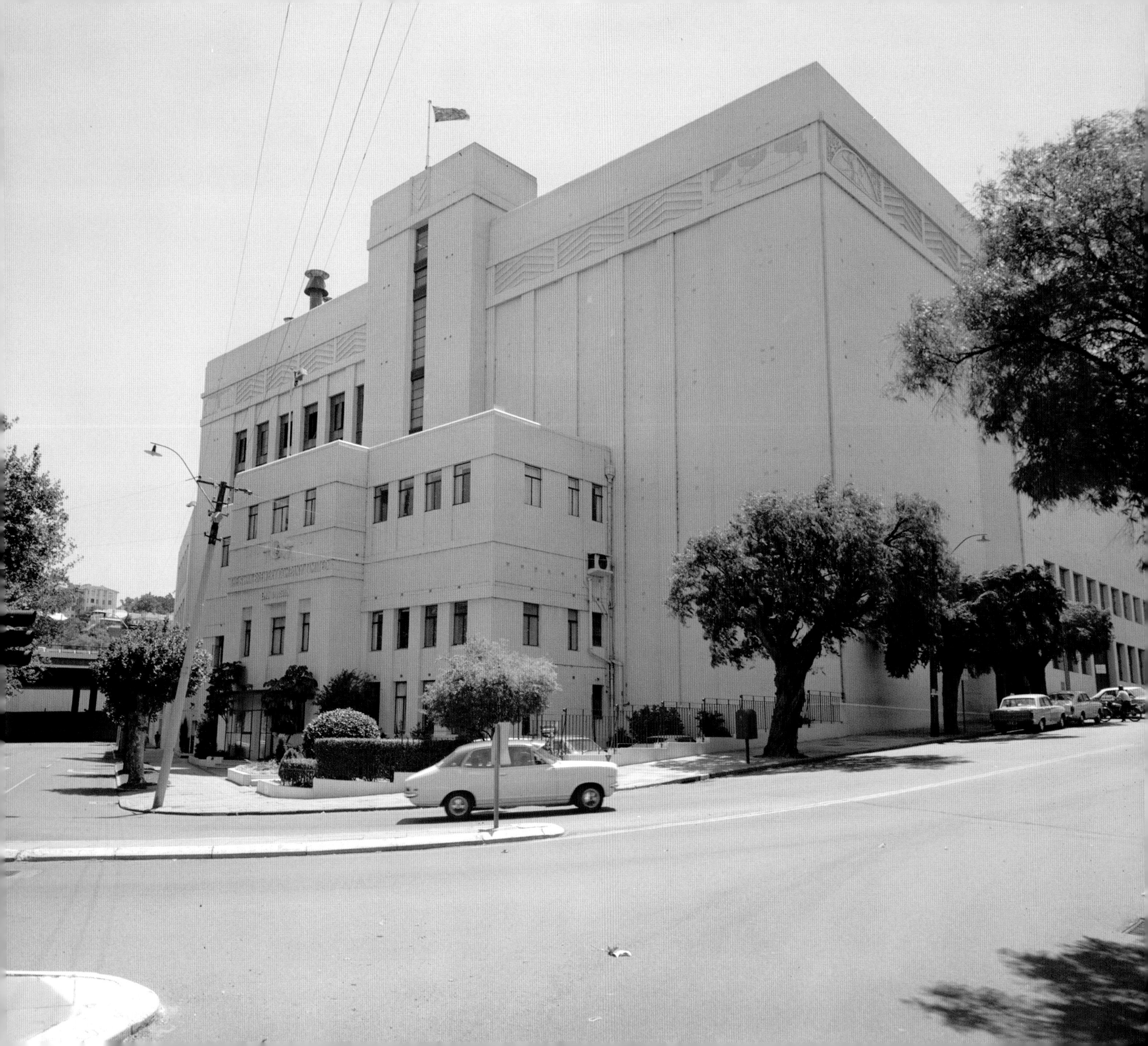

EMU BREWERY

DEMOLISHED 1991

The early Swan River Colony settlers would almost certainly have begun brewing beer for themselves as soon as raw materials became available, and possibly brought with them hops and barley with which to make a home brew. Very soon, however, those governing the fledgling colony realised that uncontrolled brewing and selling of alcohol of any kind could get out of hand and become a recipe for social disaster. They also realised that the introduction of a licensing system would be a good way of raising much needed revenue for the colony.

On 29 December 1829 notice was given that a licensing court would sit on New Year's Day to hear applications for licences for an inn and two alehouses in Fremantle, two inns and one alehouse in Perth and three alehouses in other locations. These establishments almost certainly brewed their own beer to supplement the very irregular shipments from the UK, often arriving in an undrinkable condition.

One of the early licensees was John Butler, who in 1830 was granted 250 acres of land on Freshwater Bay, where Peppermint Grove and Claremont are now situated. On this land he erected a house by the track from Perth to Fremantle and, to tide himself over until his crops could be harvested, Butler obtained a licence to establish a brewery and inn on his premises. Eventually, using barley grown on his farm, he made beer to sell at the Bush Inn, which did a roaring trade with locals and passing river traffic.

A young Scotsman by the name of James Stokes arrived in Western Australia in 1834 and saw the opportunity for a brewery, so he acquired land on Spring Street with a good natural water supply and by 1837 had opened the colony's first major brewery. Although officially named the Albion Brewery, it was known locally as Stokes' Brewery.

In November 1848 Stokes opened a new brewery called the Stanley Brewery on the site of the Albion Brewery and sold what he described as a "nutritious body ale superior to any imported", costing £4 per hogshead. The Stanley Brewery's most popular ale was sold under the "Emu" trademark. To inform drinkers of its place of origin, the company was renamed the Emu Co-operative Brewery Ltd. in 1908. This lasted until 1927, when its competitor, the Swan Brewery, acquired the Emu Brewery and continued to operate it as a separate business from its own operations.

In 1936 the old Spring Street buildings were demolished for a new brewery complex designed by Oldham, Boas & Ednie-Brown in the Art Deco style. To top off this new building, Perth sculptor Edward Kohler crafted a decorative bas-relief border for the front and sides of the main building, each panel depicting a different brewing stage.

Emu Brewery continued brewing on the site until the late 1970s, when operations moved to a new brewery in Canning Vale. The old buildings remained empty for many years, until they were demolished in 1991. The site was left empty until the commencement of work to create Capital Square began in 2016.

OPPOSITE The Emu Brewery in 1977 in a photograph that clearly shows the decorative bas-relief border crafted by Edward Kohler around the top of the building.

BELOW LEFT The semi-automated bottle washing plant in 1952.

BELOW FAR LEFT An aerial view of the brewery in 1968 taken from the roof of the Barracks Arch.

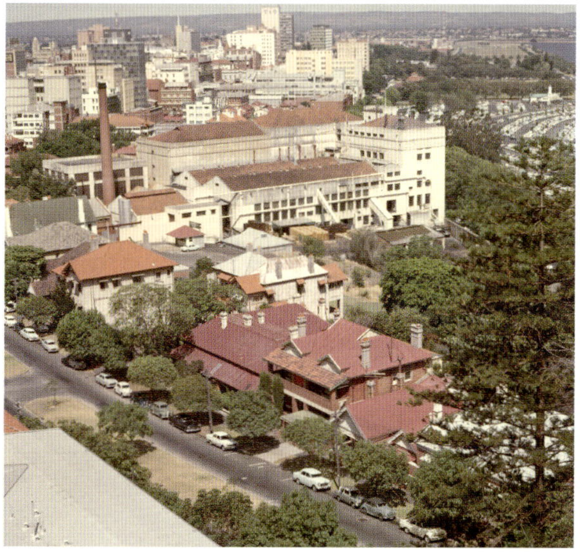

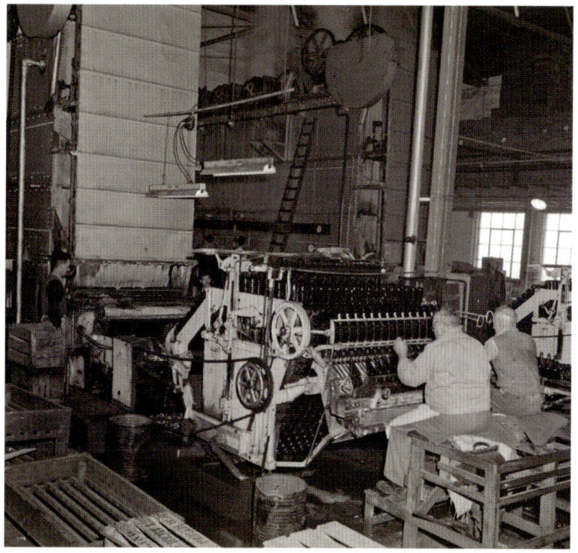

JOHN OLDHAM

John Oldham was born in Perth in 1907, where his father, John Oldham Senior, was a well-known local architect, who had designed a number of buildings in Fremantle including the Fremantle Markets. From 1924, John Oldham Junior served an architectural apprenticeship to the firm Oldham, Boas and Ednie-Brown which had bought his father's business five years before. Four years later he joined the staff of Rodney Allsop Oldham, where he worked on designs for the University of Western Australia, after which he spent a year studying architecture at the University of Melbourne. On his return to Perth he capitalised on his graphic skills to set up the Poster Studio with Harold Krantz. During the Depression, this business, producing lino-cut poster prints, kept him financially afloat. In the latter part of his career Oldham worked as a designer and landscape architect for federal and state government projects, particularly a master plan for Kings Park and the Swan River foreshores, which included the Emu Brewery. He died in 1999.

MITCHELL'S BUILDING

DEMOLISHED 2005

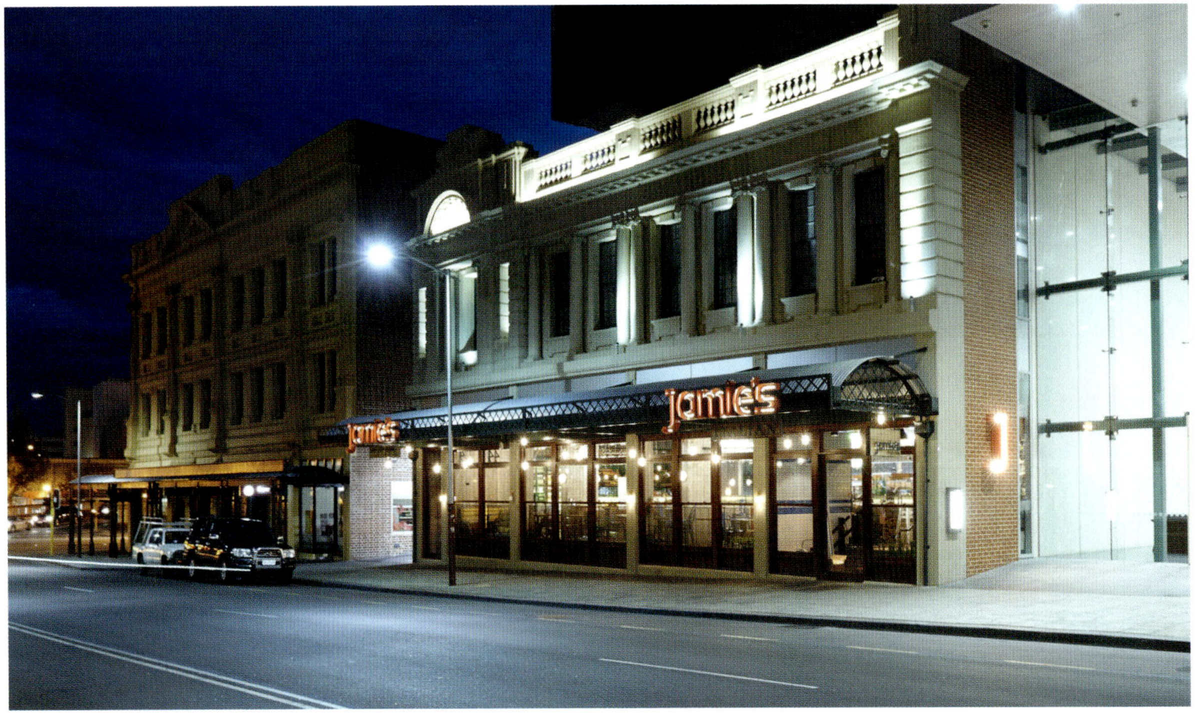

Joseph Mitchell was born on 10 June 1829, just days after the arrival the first British settlers, and was the first European baby born in the Swan River Colony. In 1878 Mitchell inherited land that had been granted in 1837 to his father, John Mitchell, a bugler in the 63rd Regiment of Foot.

In March 1880 Joseph Mitchell took out a mortgage of £150 with the Perth Benefit Building Investment & Loan Society, possibly to construct a building on the land he'd inherited. By 1884 the City of Perth Rate Book shows that the land was occupied by six cottages, two cottages with adjoining shops, and a residence and grounds occupied by Joseph Mitchell and his wife Harriet.

Joseph died in 1886 and the property was inherited by his widow. Records show that by the early 1900s, various shops had been constructed along the William Street section of Harriet's property and the occupants of these shops included a boot manufacturer, picture frame maker, hairdresser and fruiterer. By 1910 these shops were in a bad state as this review in the *Sunday Times* shows: "Passing the new Wellington Buildings on the east side, we come to seven one-storeyed shops, starting with a tea shop and finishing up at a boot emporium. These places, which are owned by Mrs Harriet Mitchell, should be wiped out of existence. It is a wonder to everyone that they have been allowed to stand so long."

Clearly this hit home, as in 1912 Harriet commissioned the architect L. Bowser Cumpston to design an elaborate two-storey façade with stucco detailing and a parapet. The new building was to comprise four shops with yards and a main entrance lobby at ground floor level, plus four offices on each side of a central corridor at first floor level.

Some of the tenants of the previous shops moved into the new building, while additional businesses included a wine saloon; a music teacher; the offices of the bulding's architect, L. Bowser Cumpston; and Clelan & Co., who regularly posted advertisements for unusual items such as a "Vacuo-Vascular Massage Machine".

After World War II, retail and commercial tenancies in the area of William and Wellington Streets declined as a result of a marked growth in the number of suburban shopping centres, plus the creation of a car-free retail area in Murray and Hay Streets. A proposal to convert the first floor of Mitchell's Building into a boarding house was shelved and the building was almost entirely demolished in 2005 as part of the 140 William Street redevelopment.

The elaborate façade of the Mitchell's Building, however, had been removed and held in storage during the construction of the 140 William Street office tower. The façade was eventually returned and attached to the front of the new building, but not quite in its original location. Today a Jamie Oliver restaurant operates from behind the 1912 façade.

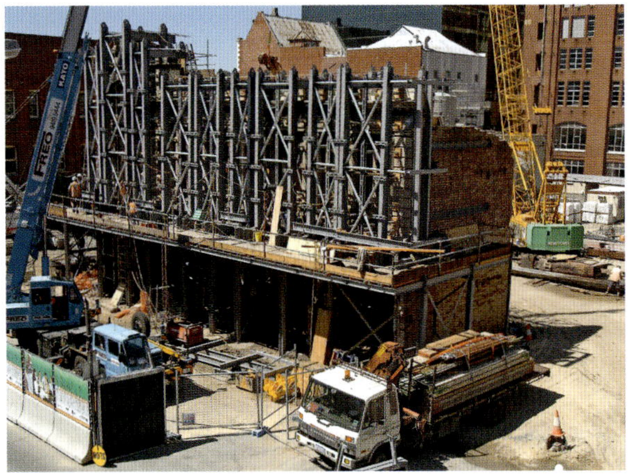

TOP The building's façade in its new position above a Jamie's restaurant.

ABOVE Preparations to remove the façade of the Mitchell's Building during construction of Perth Underground Station in 2005.

RIGHT The elegant classical lines of the building in 1982.

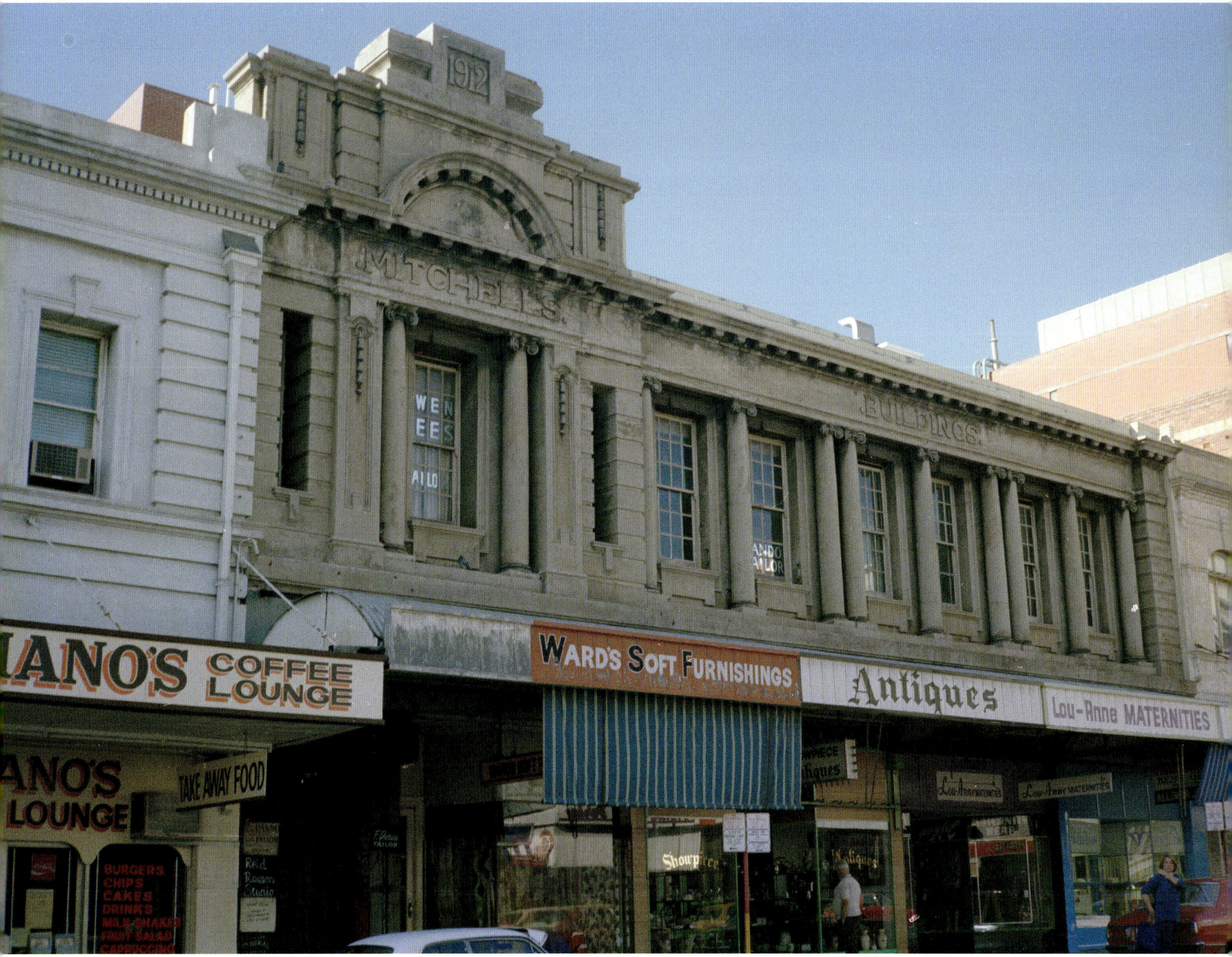
1912
MITCHELL'S
BUILDINGS
ANO'S COFFEE LOUNGE
WARD'S SOFT FURNISHINGS
Antiques
Lou-Anne MATERNITIES
TAKE AWAY FOOD
BURGERS
CHIPS
CAKES
DRINKS

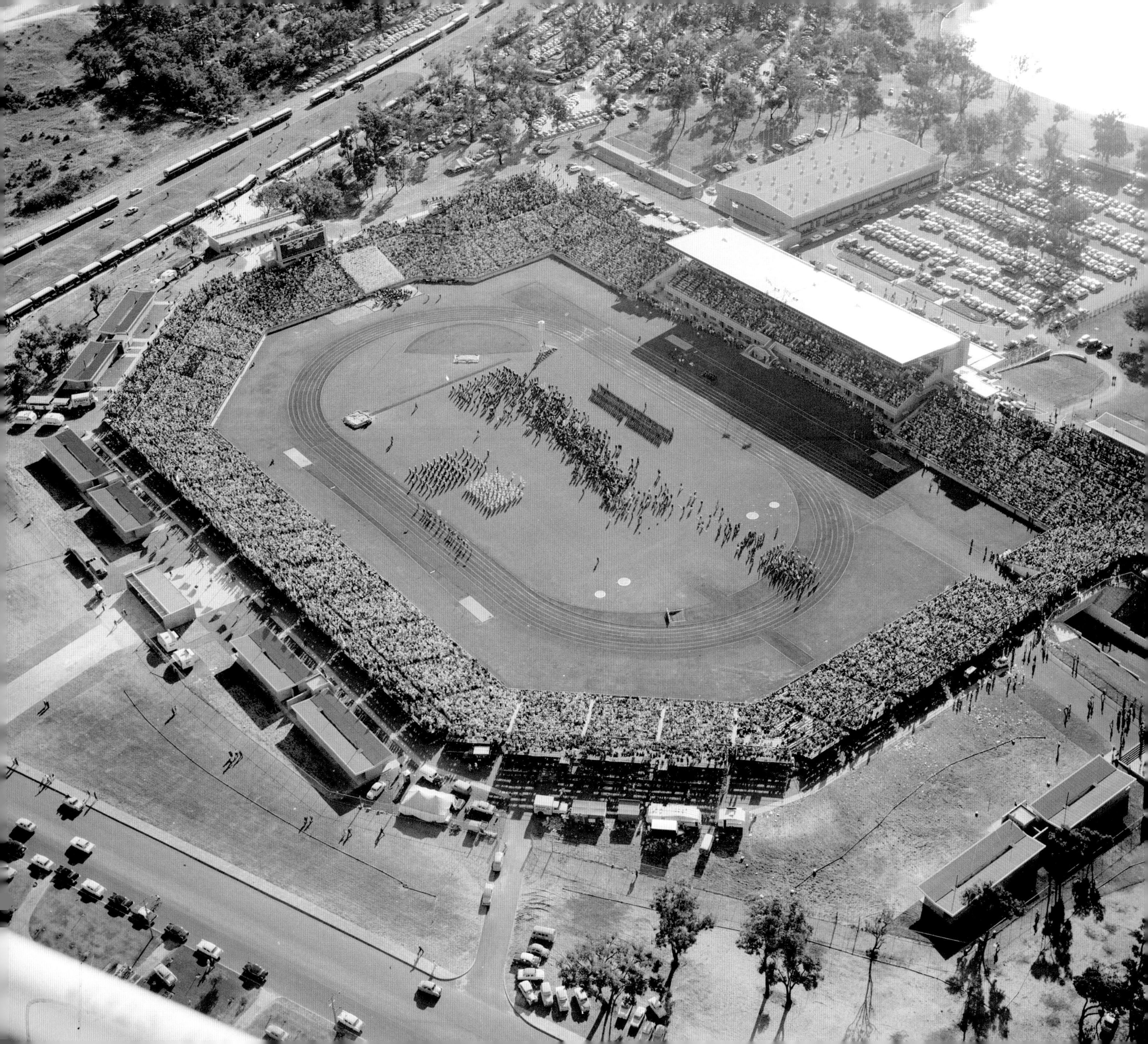

PERRY LAKES STADIUM

DEMOLISHED 2010

In 1956 the Lord Mayor of Perth, Sir Harry Howard, and the town clerk, William Green, made a determined and successful bid to hold the 1962 Empire and Commonwealth Games in Perth. It was felt that hosting these games would put Perth firmly on the Commonwealth map and also encourage a sense of civic pride amongst the city's residents.

At the time, Perth had no major sporting facilities and so Green, an architect and engineer by profession, took on the job not only of designing the Perry Lakes Stadium, Beatty Park Aquatic Centre and a dedicated residential village for athletes and officials, but also co-ordinating and supervising the works programme to create state-of-the-art sporting venues.

Like all the buildings developed for the Empire and Commonwealth Games, the stadium and scoreboard were built in a Modernist style and were fine examples of advances in construction techniques developed after World War II. The stadium had a cantilevered canopy to provide spectators with shade.

The scoreboard, with its incandescent lights, was the talk of the games and a forerunner of the digital scoreboards we know today. No longer did a person have to flip over number cards or write figures on a large chalkboard. Messages, results and scores could be easily and clearly displayed for all to see. The structure housing this 1960s technological wonder was a substantial three-storey brick building, which also featured storerooms, toilets and even a public post office. A viewing room at the very top of the building was reserved for distinguished Empire Games guests and offered unparalleled views of the sporting activities.

To accommodate the visiting athletes and officials, a village was built on land at City Beach provided by the Perth City Council. Although athletes' villages are now commonplace, the 1962 games were the first to provide such a facility. Design competitions were held for the layout of the games village and house designs. The eventual village consisted of two areas containing 150 houses, grouped around a central spine, incorporating areas of natural vegetation and temporary facilities.

During the games, the village accommodated more than 12,000 athletes. Men and women were housed separately and within each area athletes were assigned houses according to country of origin. With no telephones on the site, Boy Scouts and Girl Guides were provided every day to run messages.

The opening ceremony for the games took place in the presence of HRH Prince Philip in scorching 40° C heat, on the hottest November day in Perth for over 20 years. More than 300 people in the crowd of 53,000 were treated for heat-related illnesses.

Following the games, the stadium was used for everything from soccer matches to Rolling Stones concerts. The stadium was eventually superseded by the nearby Perth Superdrome (now HBF Stadium), built in 1986 to help the pursuit of excellence in a wide range of sporting activities.

By the early 2000s the building had become dilapidated and with other more modern stadiums around the city, plans were approved in 2008 for demolition. By 2012 the site was clear of everything except the famous scoreboard. While the stadium has been replaced by a modern residential development, the scoreboard is still there and now serves as a lounge and gym for residents – a reminder of Perth's debut on the world athletics stage.

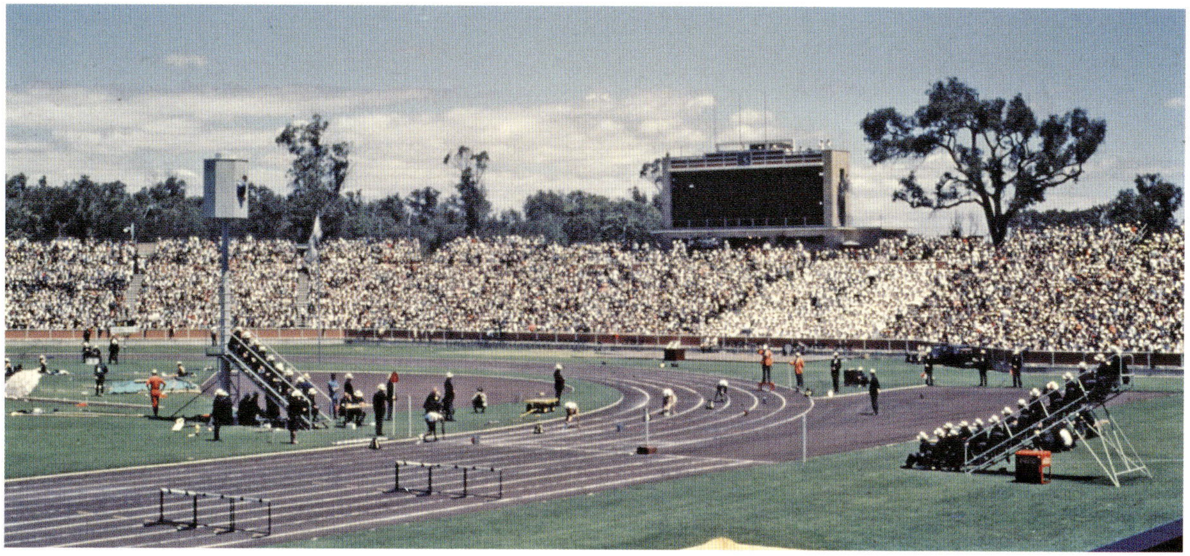

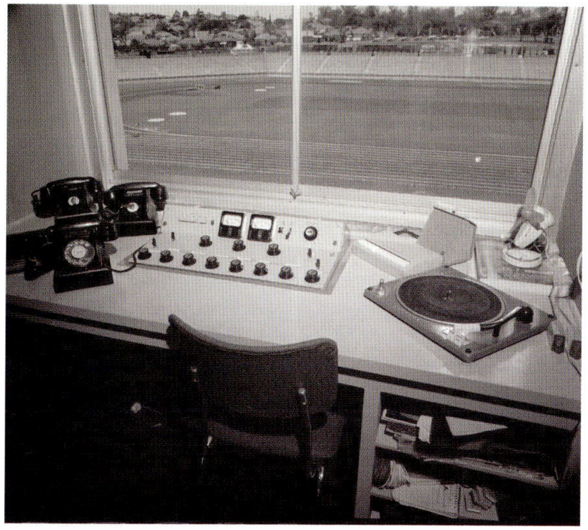

TOP Under starters orders for a hurdles heat at the British Empire and Commonwealth Games, Perry Lakes, November 1962.

ABOVE The interior of the commentary box for the games.

OPPOSITE A spectacular aerial view of Perry Lakes Stadium, taken by a photographer from the *West Australian* during the opening ceremony of the British Empire and Commonwealth Games in 1962.

PERTH ENTERTAINMENT CENTRE

DEMOLISHED 2011

Anyone in Perth who went to see David Bowie, AC/DC or Abba during the 1970s or 80s will remember the Perth Entertainment Centre.

Following World War II there was a significant increase in the population of Perth, and by the 1970s there was a need for larger and better facilities in which to present culture and the arts. During this period, new buildings were provided for the State Art Gallery and State Library and the Western Australian Museum gained a large extension to its building.

For the performing arts, there was a dire need for a venue capable of accommodating the large audiences needed to make it financially viable to bring overseas shows to Perth. His Majesty's Theatre only sat about 2,000 people and the slightly larger Capitol Theatre had infamously bad acoustics. To fill this gap, the Perth Entertainment Centre was built on land between the railway line and Wellington Street in West Perth.

The brainchild of Brian Treasure of television station TVW-7 and theatrical entrepreneur Michael Edgley, this building was developed primarily to enable the two companies to mount large stage and television shows in a custom-built venue. The venue was designed by architects Hobbs, Winning and Leighton and was forecast to cost $5 million, but its construction coincided with a period of industrial action in the building industry. Numerous disruptions, including strike action, were all timed to coincide with key building operations such as concrete pours. These actions led to a huge cost blow-out, with the final bill being around $8.3 million.

The 8,000-seat complex was immediately listed in the *Guinness Book of World Records* as the largest purpose-built theatre containing a proscenium arch in the world. At the time of its opening, it was also the largest covered auditorium in Australia. In addition to the theatre, the building contained two cinemas, a restaurant and a tavern.

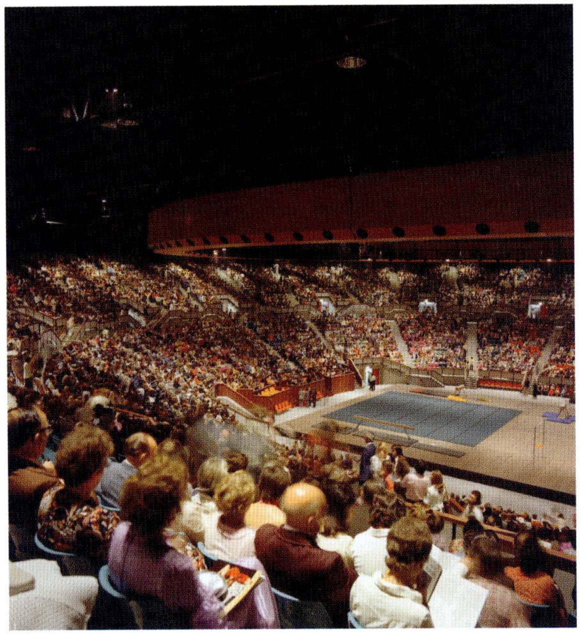

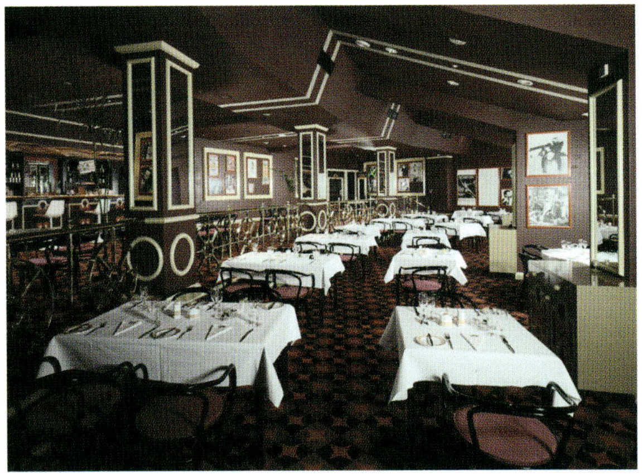

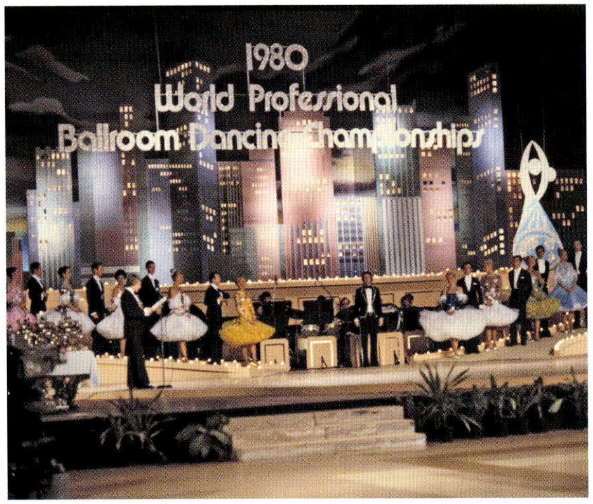

Opening on 27 December 1974 with the Australian debut of the second *Disney On Parade* show, the complex was named the Channel 7 Edgley Entertainment Centre. About a year later, the proprietors approached state and federal governments for financial assistance and the state government acquired the building, renaming it the Perth Entertainment Centre.

From its opening until 2002 the Entertainment Centre played host to a large range of events, including musicals, circuses, Rolling Stones concerts and, in July 1979, a Miss Universe contest, which caused an unintentional spectacle just after the international television coverage had concluded. A timber catwalk, carrying eight contestants and two journalists, collapsed throwing them to the floor. Thankfully, those involved sustained only minor injuries.

From 1990 until its closure, the centre was also home to Perth Wildcats basketball team. Following closure, the Western Australia Government unveiled plans for a new arena to be built next to the old centre and the Perth Arena was opened in November 2012.

Making an ever increasing loss for its owners, Perth Entertainment Centre finally closed its doors in 2002. After laying empty for almost 10 years, the disused building was demolished in December 2011 to make way for the Perth City Link, which reconnected the city centre to Northbridge by means of sinking the railway line.

RIGHT The entrance of the Perth Entertainment Centre in 1974, at the time known as the Channel 7 Edgley Entertainment Centre. A sign over the doors reads "Disney on Parade".

ABOVE LEFT The dining room in 1975.

LEFT The World Ballroom Dancing Championships of 1980.

FAR LEFT The inaugural event, a gymnastics competition, in December 1974.

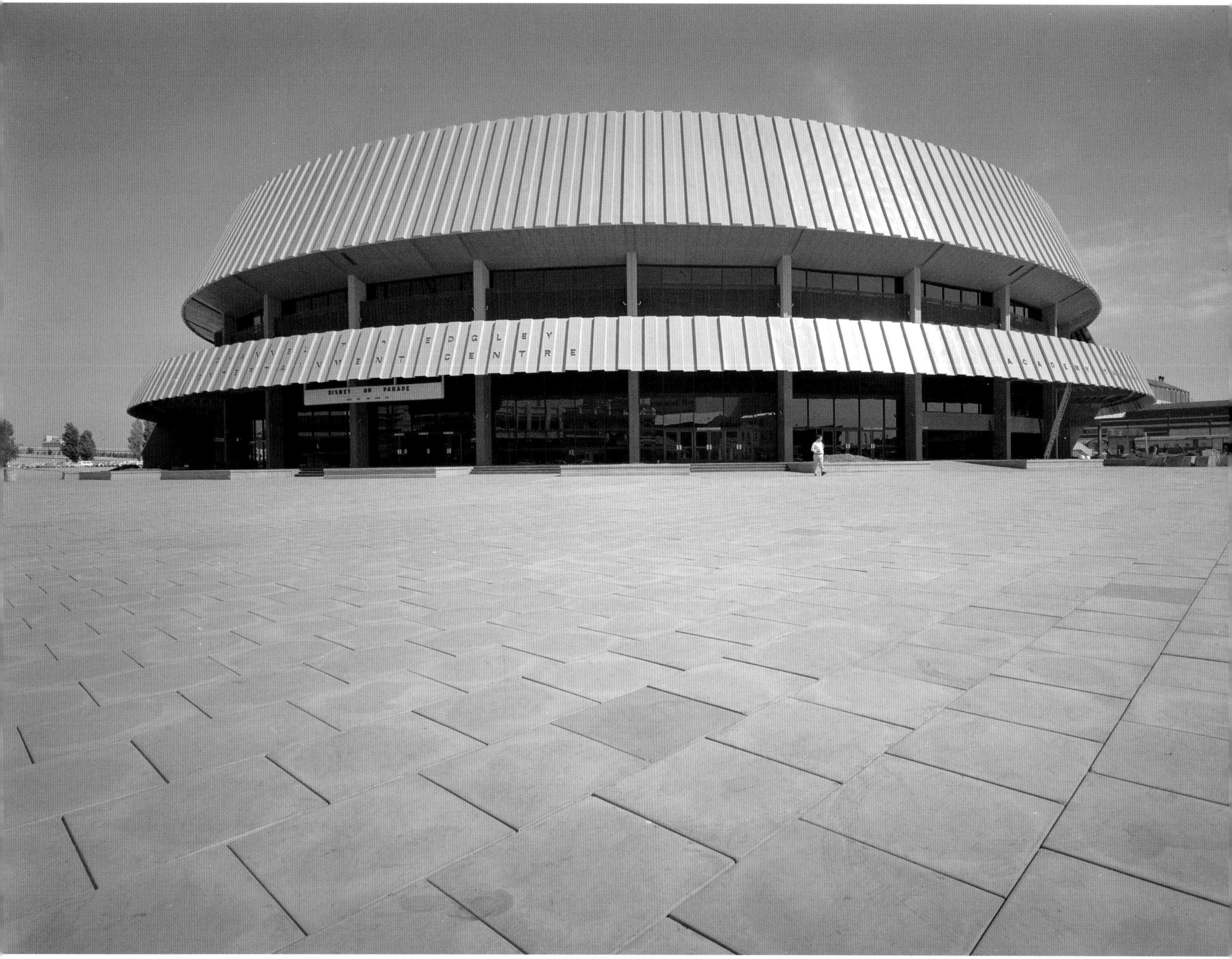
DISNEY ON PARADE

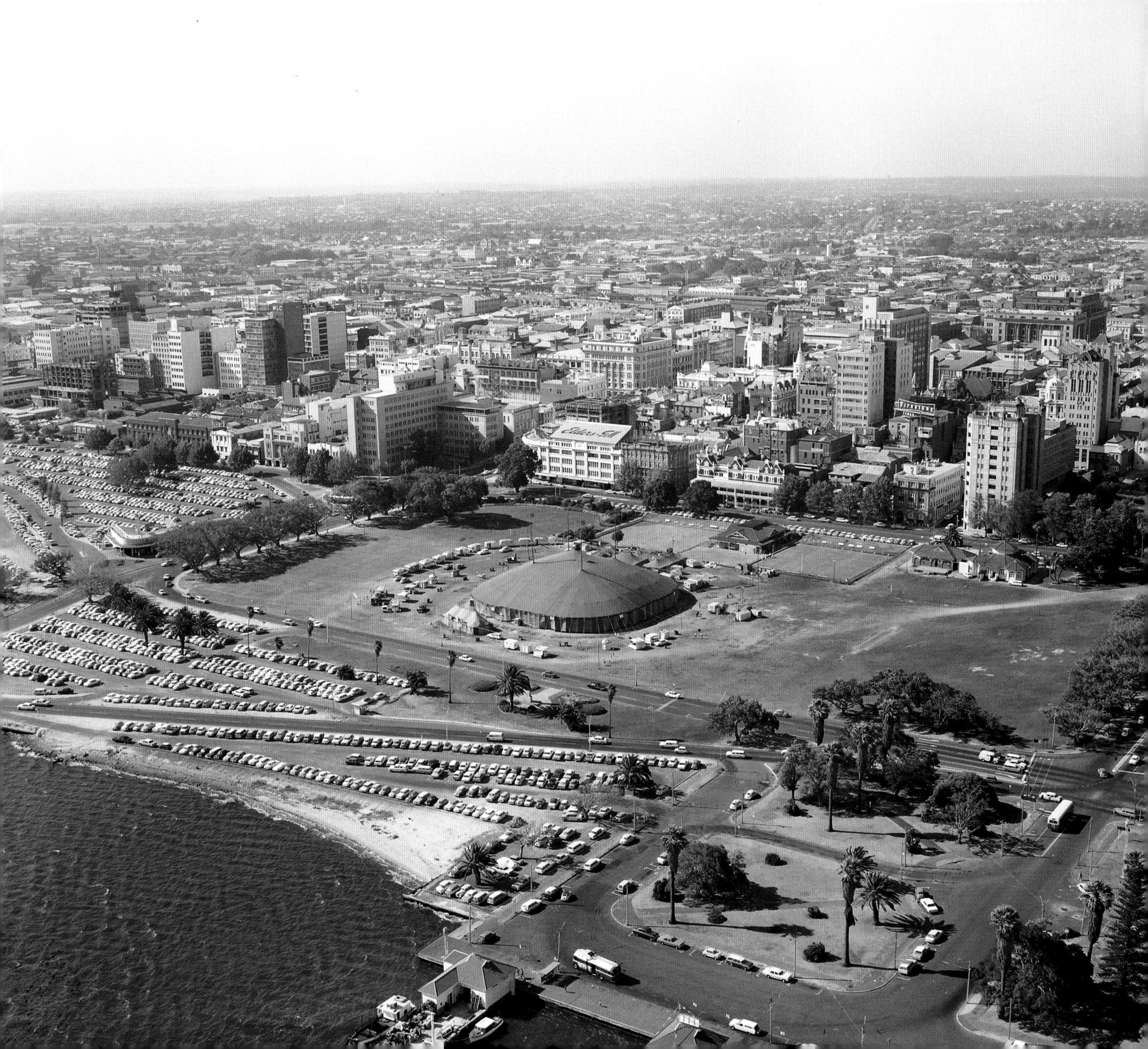

ESPLANADE RESERVE

REDEVELOPED 2012

The Esplanade Reserve was part of a major land reclamation project carried out along the foreshore in the 1870s and 80s. At this time it was felt necessary to create more public parks and gardens in the city to improve its citizens' quality of life.

In the early days of settlement, a large area of the river foreshore, extending from Barrack Street to Point Fraser, near Heirisson Island, was set aside for the purposes of parkland and government buildings. Although by the mid-1830s much of it was subdivided for residential purposes, leaving only the area between Barrack Street and Lord Street (now Victoria Avenue) as public space.

As Perth grew, recreational use of the foreshore and river increased and in 1862, believing it ought to encourage "moral amusements and manly sports", the Perth City Council agreed to the use of part of Bazaar Street, west of William Street jetty (now Mounts Bay Road), as a practice wicket for the city's cricket club. To further meet the need for recreational facilities, the council opened discussions with the Colonial Secretary about the possibility of reclaiming foreshore between the Barrack and William Street jetties to create a recreation ground.

Reclamation work began in 1873 by dumping dredging silt and shell from the river, but work was spasmodic and did not really begin in earnest until the early 1880s, when a project to level St Georges Terrace generated large amounts of fill readily on hand. The partially reclaimed land, known as the New Recreation Ground, was handed over to the Perth City Council by deed of grant "for the free recreation and enjoyment of the people forever" in March 1880.

At first the new ground was very unpopular because of problems with a drain from Sherwood Street, which had previously emptied into the river and now deposited its contents over the new ground, making it swampy, unhealthy and producing a very unpleasant odour. Even though the council was extremely short of funds at the time they spent £1,000 closing the drain by filling it with sand carted from the foot of Mount Eliza.

The park officially became known as the Esplanade Recreation Ground in 1885 and soon became the venue for gatherings, displays, exhibitions, rallies and sporting functions. The first major event held there was the Perth Exhibition, which lasted for six weeks at the end of 1881 and housed displays of overseas products. To accommodate the exhibition, a large timber and iron building was constructed by prison labour. The first permanent structures built on the site were a pavilion and grandstand in 1885, with the Metropolitan Cricket Club occupying pavilion rooms with lockers and showers.

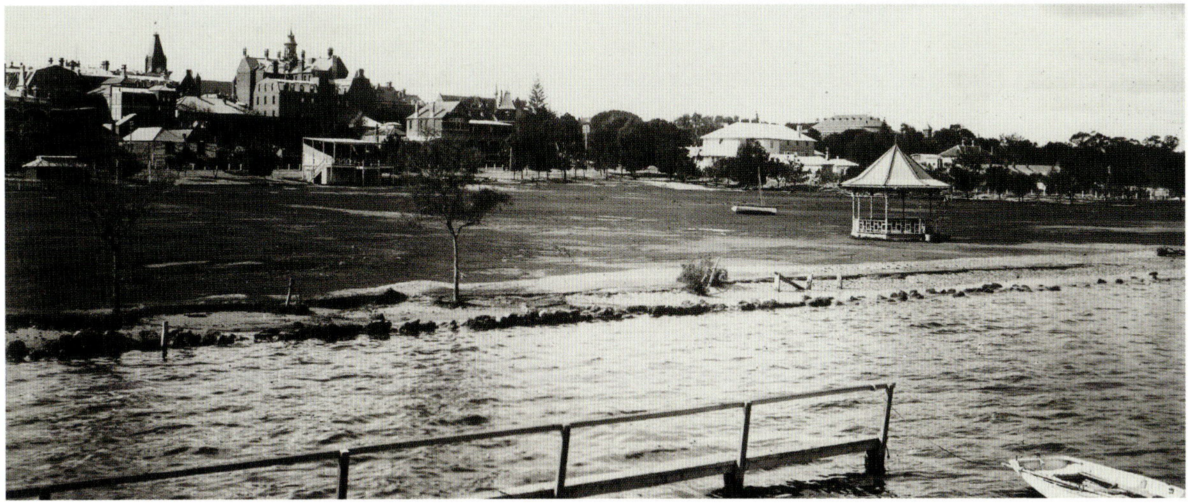

Recreational use of the area increased considerably with the establishment of tennis courts, cricket pitches and bowling greens. It also at this time became the venue for public celebrations such as that for the granting of responsible government to Western Australia, which was proclaimed on the Esplanade Reserve in 1890 and witnessed by 6,000 people.

The early plantings of avenues of Moreton Bay Figs and Canary Island palms were carried out in 1898. Further works to improve the reserve continued into the 1920s and in 1928 the old grandstand was demolished to make way for a refreshment kiosk, public conveniences and changing rooms.

In more recent times, the reserve was heavily used as a sports practice ground and was a much favoured venue for events such as circuses, rock and classical concerts, exhibitions and pageants.

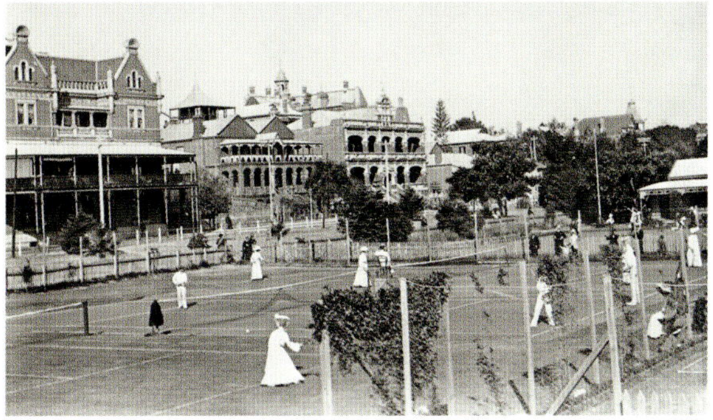

In 2011 the state government announced the creation of Elizabeth Quay, with the somewhat ironic intention of reconnecting the city with its river. To make way for the new waterside amenities, the Esplanade Reserve was partially redeveloped, with its southern half dug out and returned to the Swan River.

TOP The Esplanade Reserve in 1890, with the river lapping at its southern edge.

ABOVE Tennis being played at the Wanda Tennis Club on the reserve in 1907.

OPPOSITE Taken during a visit of the Great Moscow Circus in January 1968. A number of buildings mentioned in this book, including the Esplanade Hotel, AMP and CMLA buildings, can be seen here.

MICHELIDES TOBACCO FACTORY

DEMOLISHED 2014

From tobacco factory, to ice cream manufacturers, then a menswear shop, followed by a controversial demolition. This is the history of a former well-known landmark on Roe Street in Northbridge: the Michelides Tobacco Factory.

Tobacconist Peter Michelides, a Greek immigrant, arrived in Perth in 1904 at the age of 26. He soon set up his first cigarette shop and sent for his younger brother, Michael, only 12 at the time, to join him. According to a short biography published in the *Sunday Times* four years after his arrival, Peter had been "rapidly earning a good name for himself amongst lovers of good cigarettes by supplying the very finest qualities of Turkish, Egyptian and Virginian tobaccos at prices which bring his products within the reach of all."

Prudently importing small quantities at a time, keeping him supplied for no more than a fortnight, Michelides was selling tobacco at the peak of its condition, before it had time to get musty or to lose its aroma. All his tobacco was cut by hand and it was claimed this was the only cigarette factory in Western Australia where customers could have their cigarettes made while they waited. The tobacco laws in the early 20th century prevented manufacturers selling their products through their own retail outlets, but the Michelides brothers got around this rule by having the factory in Peter's name and the shop in Michael's.

Over time, the brothers acquired several adjoining plots around the junction of Roe and Lake Streets, and in 1912 opened their own tobacco and cigarette factory with an office next door.

Ten years later the factory was extended and modernised, and on 5 October 1922 Premier James Mitchell announced it was a privilege to open the new cigarette factory. He switched on a machine that could make 24,000 cigarettes an hour. To man the new factory, newspaper advertisements sought both male and female workers, but women were preferred because it was felt that their fingers were more suitable for delicately stripping the tobacco leaves for "Westralia's favourite smoke", the "perfect 'Golden West' cigarette".

The following winter, the *Sunday Times* reported that Golden West cigarettes were "in everybody's mouth. This is undoubtedly due to their freshness, unique flavour, and excellent smoking qualities."

As the business grew, new brands of cigarettes (Mena, Golden Blend and Golden Wattle), plus Bona Rosa cigars, were added to the range. Having previously imported tobacco leaf, in the early 1930s Michelides started their own tobacco plantations, thus ensuring their products were both manufactured and grown locally.

In 1933 architects Oldham, Boas & Ednie-Brown designed a new two-storey extension to the factory for the manufacture of Rizla cigarette papers. The company now employed 200 in the factory and offices, with a further 100 in the Pemberton and Manjimup tobacco plantations.

Through the 1950s and 60s imported filter-tipped cigarettes gained in popularity and the factory ceased manufacture early in 1960. Later that year the factory was sold to Peters, which expanded their adjacent ice cream factory into the old tobacco factory. In the late 1980s the building was leased to a menswear chain.

After the closure of the menswear shop, the building was left unoccupied and, amidst considerable controversy over the building's heritage value, the Michelides Tobacco Factory was demolished in 2014, leaving a brownfield site which, at the time of writing, is still undeveloped.

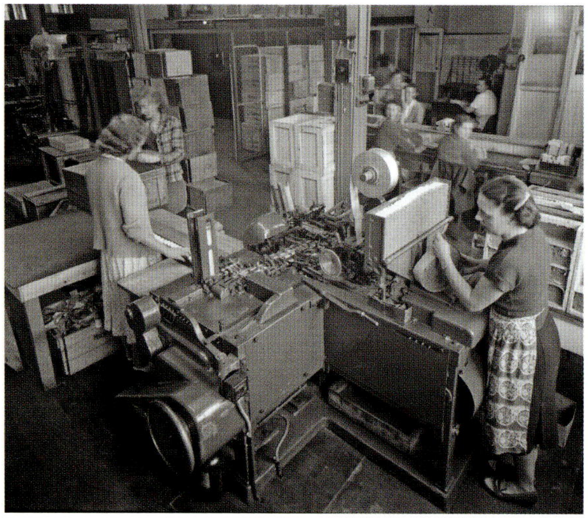

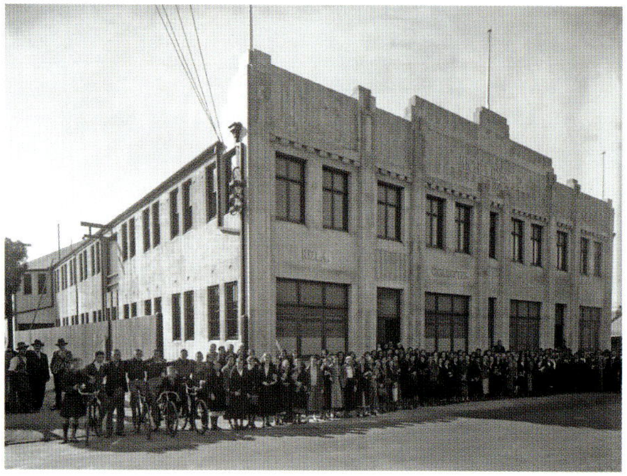

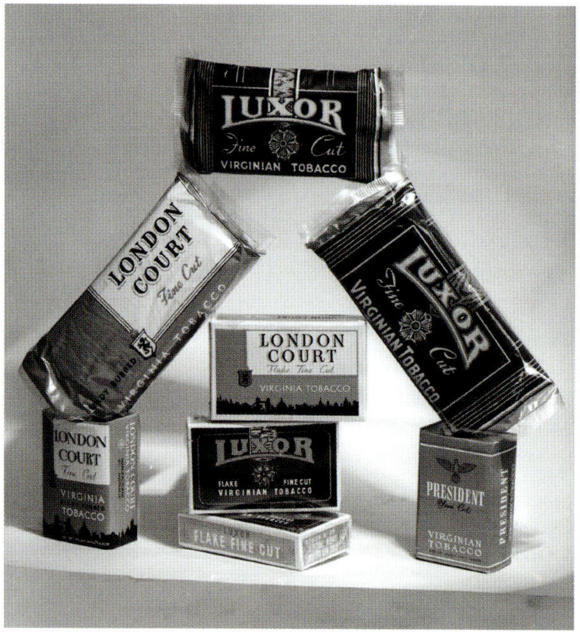

TOP Staff outside the newly-built two-storey extension in June 1934.

ABOVE A 1951 Michelides tobacco product display – brands long-gone from the shops.

LEFT A cigarette paper machine in 1951.

RIGHT The Michelides factory in about 1940. Probably the best known of the company's products was the Golden West brand of tobacco and cigarettes.

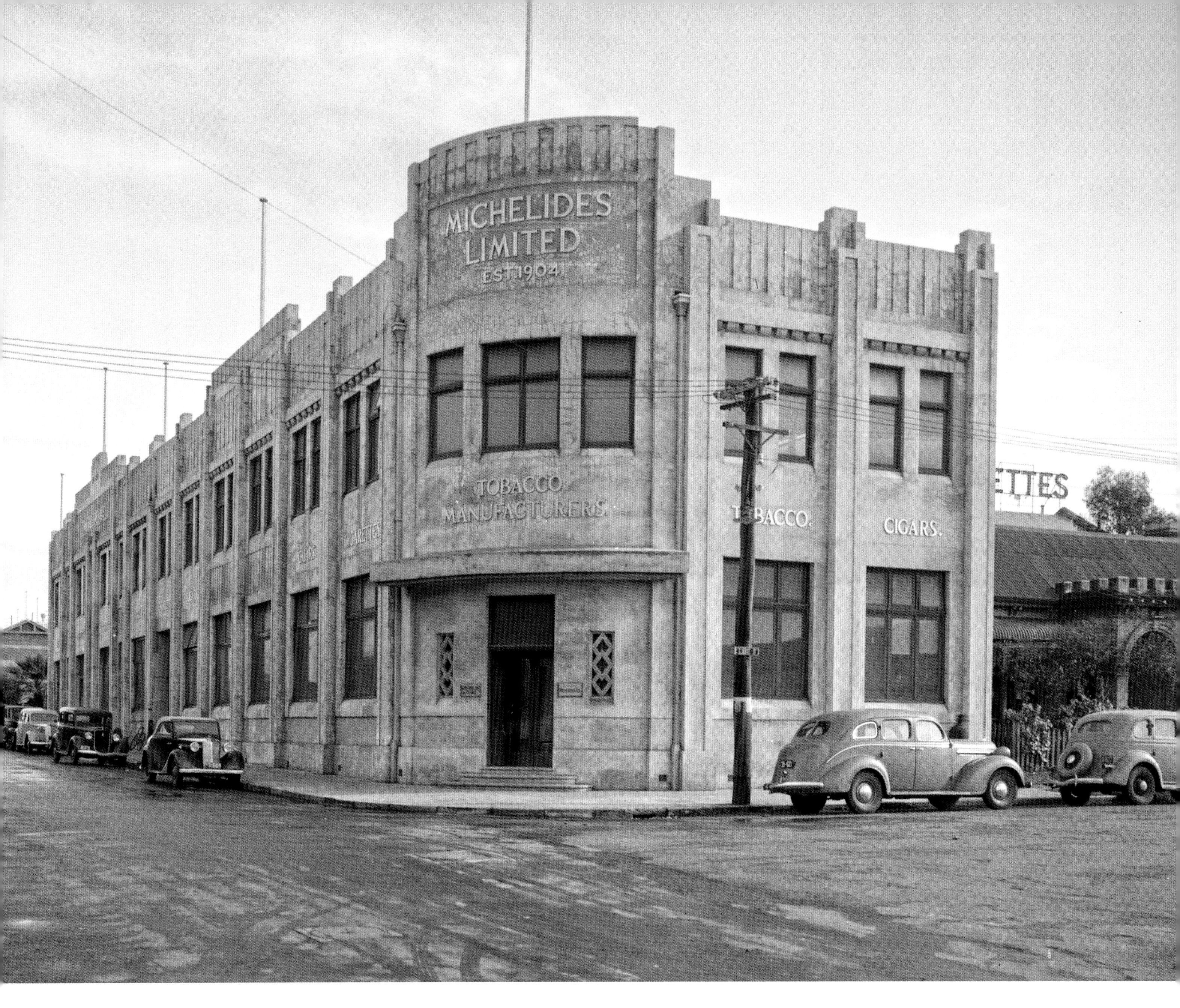
MICHELIDES
LIMITED
EST.1904
TOBACCO
MANUFACTURERS.
TOBACCO.
CIGARS.
CIGARETTES
ETTES

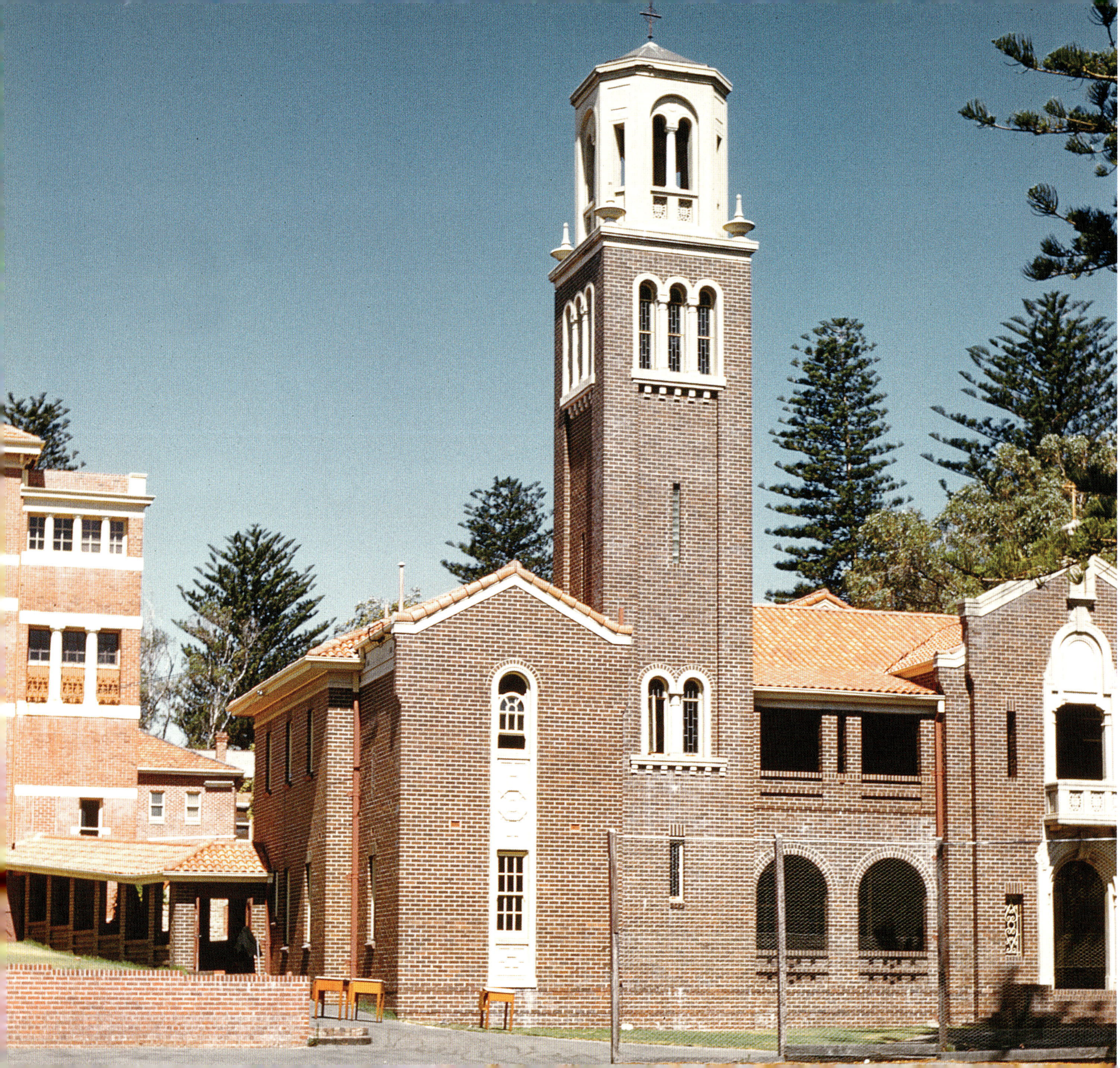

LORETO BELL TOWER

DEMOLISHED 2017

In 1894 businessman James Grave built the Osborne Hotel on a cliff-top in Claremont. Said to have been one of Perth's finest hotels, it was surrounded by two acres of gardens and offered fine views of both the ocean and river. In 1898 the hotel was sold to William Dalgety Moore, as Grave had found himself to be "financially embarrassed".

Around this time the Catholic Institute of the Blessed Virgin Mary (also known as the Loreto Sisters) arrived in Western Australia and opened a school on Adelaide Terrace. Loreto is a popular place of pilgrimage on the Adriatic coast of Italy, where a small house was venerated as the home of Mary of Nazareth and the site of the annunciation. This name became associated with the order because their first house in Ireland was so named to associate the place with the piety of the holy family of Nazareth.

In 1901 the Sisters bought Osborne Hotel from Moore and converted it into a new boarding school and convent. From then on, the convent was officially known as Loreto Osborne, Claremont. Boarders from the Adelaide Terrace school became the first pupils, whilst day pupils stayed at the Adelaide Terrace branch, which eventually closed in 1937.

By the 1930s the school had grown in size and needed additional accommodation, as this item in the *Sunday Times* of 9 January 1938 explains: "Right now a complete building scheme is being undertaken to meet demands. This provides for a chapel, accommodation for 30 sisters, a classroom block, a domestic science section, science room, art room, kindergarten, library, nuns' refectory, lunch and cloakrooms, laundry and kitchen block. The buildings will be constructed about a central court which will be laid out in a formal manner with an open space set aside as a small amphitheatre for open air classes."

The designs for the project, which was to be built on Bindaring Parade, were prepared by Reginald Summerhayes, who was born in Claremont in 1897 and followed in his father's footsteps to become an architect.

The *West Australian* reported the opening of the additions on 6 December 1938: "The ceremony, which was performed by His Grace the Archbishop of Perth (Dr R. Prendiville), consisted of the dedication of an attractive new chapel, which was blessed on Saturday, and the blessing of a large administrative block. The cost of the additions was stated to be about £13,000."

In 1963 the old hotel building was demolished to make way for a new building and Loreto Claremont amalgamated with St Louis College in 1977 to become John XXIII College, which moved to its present site in Mount Claremont nine years later. As a result, the convent buildings on Bindaring Parade were demolished in 1990 to make way for residential housing. Only the bell tower section of the 1938 building additions was saved. It was carefully dismantled and rebuilt on the corner of Francis and William Streets in Northbridge, using some of the original bricks. This work was overseen by Reginald Summerhayes's son Geoffrey.

In 2017 the tower, which was considered to have lost its heritage value when moved from Claremont, was demolished to make way for the redevelopment of the Australian Tax Office building.

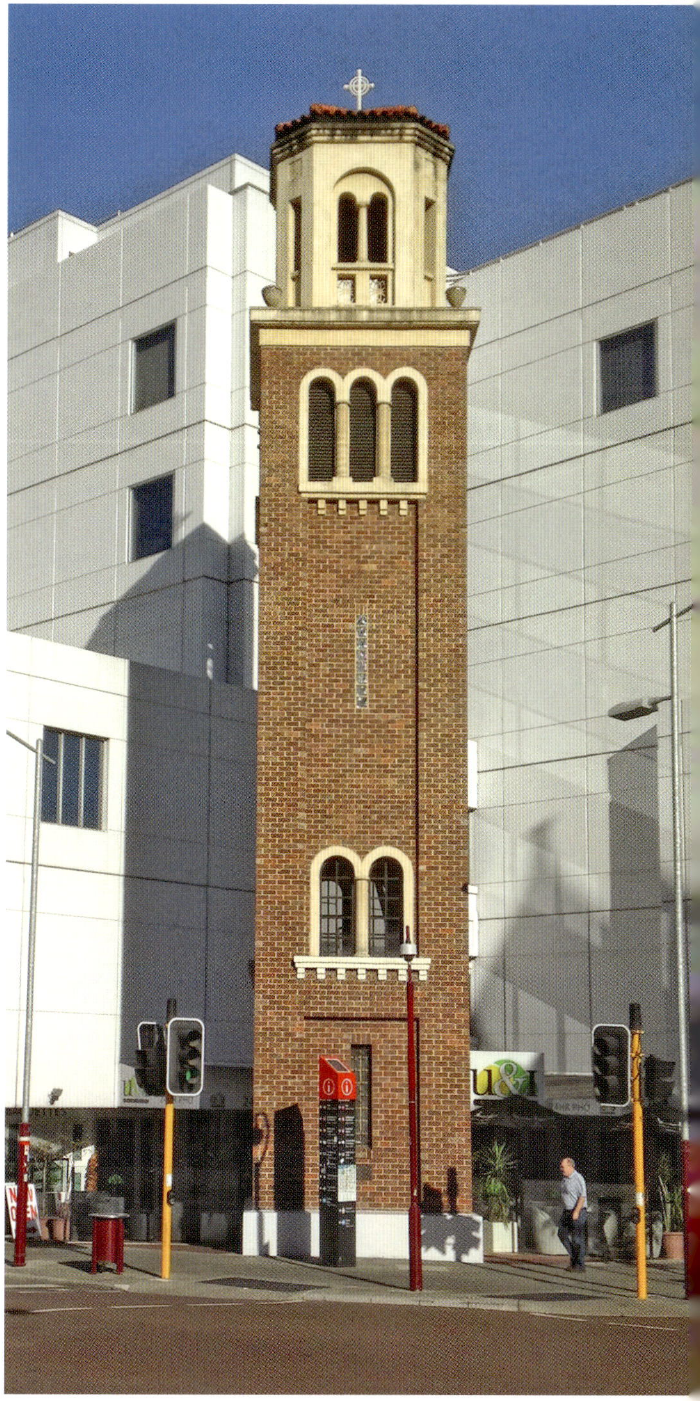

OPPOSITE The chapel and tower of Loreto Convent, Claremont in 1961.

RIGHT The tower as rebuilt on the corner of William and Francis Streets, Northbridge, in 2014.

LANGLEY PARK AERODROME

AIRSTRIP CLOSED 2017

Western Australia can claim to be the true birthplace of civil aviation in Australia, for it was here that the country's first significant flight took place in 1911. The state also had the earliest and largest civil aviation network in Australia at the time, which was initially based in what is now called Langley Park.

The driving force for the aviation network was Major Norman Brearley, who arrived in Perth in mid-1919 with two small British training aeroplanes in which he gave public displays and joy rides using the WACA ground as his aerodrome. Brearley later said that despite a very small margin to spare at the WACA ground, "I landed and took off several times without accident and only one take off did I actually pluck the electric light wires that then encircled the ground over the trotting track." None of this can have been helped by the atrocious weather and torrential rain during these demonstrations.

Brearley was convinced that air flight had commercial applications and was determined to prove it. He managed to persuade the MP for Kimberley, Michael Durack, of the advantages. By 1921 Durack had invited Brearley to build a hangar at the bottom of his garden, on the corner of Victoria Avenue and Adelaide Terrace, and use a newly reclaimed reserve as his base. The area Brearley used for the air strip was about 300 by 200 metres, between Victoria Avenue and Hill Street. This became the base for his aviation business for the next three years.

The first mention of this reserve – which was reclaimed from the marshy shallows of the Swan River and later named Langley Park – was in 1912, when an area was allocated for a sewerage pumping station. The reserve was officially gazetted late in 1920, but it was still a somewhat marshy and unplanted area.

Brearley petitioned the Commonwealth Government for an air mail service between Fremantle and Broome. As a result, Australia's first subsidised air service was established in Western Australia. Initially a route from Geraldton to Derby was chosen, the argument being that Geraldton was already linked with Perth by rail.

Of the two tenders submitted for the service, Brearley won the contract and formed Western Australian Airways to operate it. The service had a tragic start in December 1921 when a plane crashed near the Murchison River, killing the pilot and his mechanic. After this unfortunate accident, the service got fully underway in 1922, 10 months before Qantas started operations.

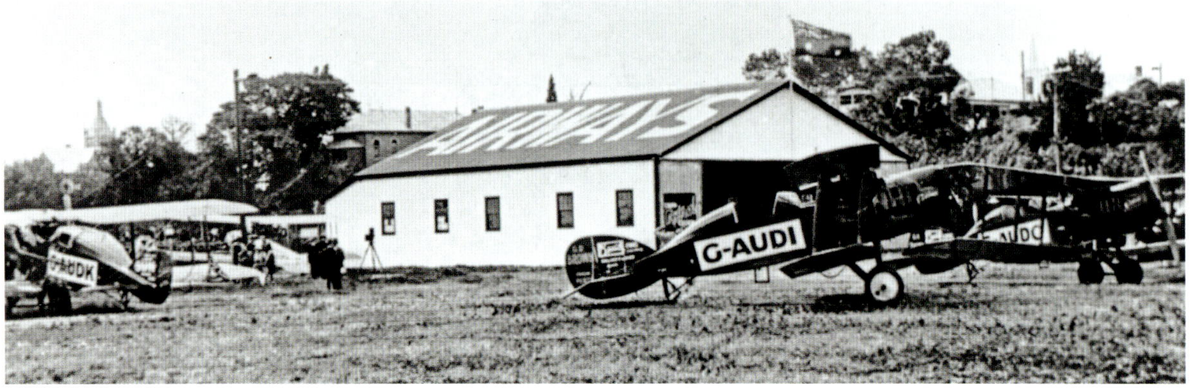

ABOVE The Western Australian Airways aircraft on Langley Park in late 1922. The tower of Christian Brothers' College can be seen in the background.

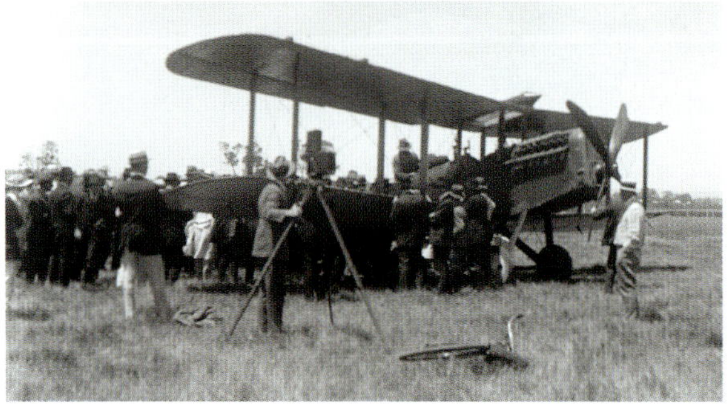

RIGHT The first aeroplane to land in Western Australia from the Eastern States on Belmont Racecourse at 1 p.m., 2 December 1920. The racecourse served as Perth's first regular landing area before Langley Park was established.

Eventually, in 1924, the service was extended to Perth, but by then it had been found that Langley Park was not a suitable location for a permanent airport due to the high water table and close proximity of buildings. Consequently, a move was made to a site in Maylands, which became Perth's first permanent aerodrome.

Langley Park continued to be a registered landing strip, serving as the landing place for RAAF Caribou aircraft when transporting accident victims to Perth. It has also been the venue for Sport Aircraft Association of Australia fly-ins and the base for Red Bull Air Races, which was attended in 2008 by 250,000 people. However, in 2017, the advent of Elizabeth Quay and its high-rise buildings led to the Civil Aviation Safety Authority to withdraw the airstrip certification and almost 100 years of flying came to an end.

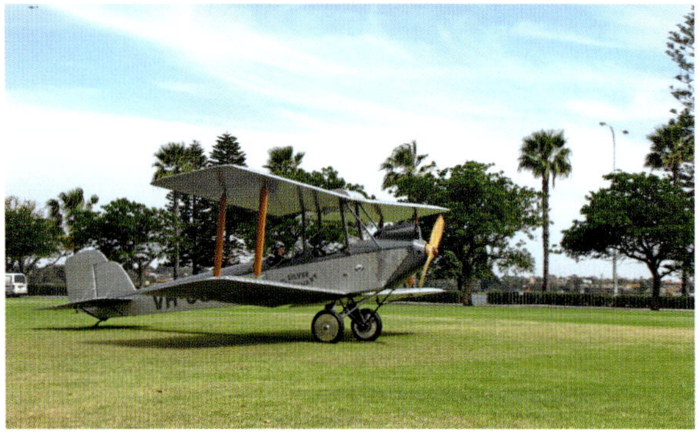

ABOVE A Silver Centenary biplane taking part in a Sport Aircraft Association of Australia fly-in at Langley Park in October 2011.

RIGHT Left to right in this photograph from 4 December 1921 are Charles Kingsford Smith, Robert Fawcett, Norman Brearley, Len Taplin and Val Abbott. They were preparing to take planes from Langley Park to Geraldton for the inaugural flight to Derby. Robert Fawcett's plane lost speed and crashed, killing the pilot and his mechanic.

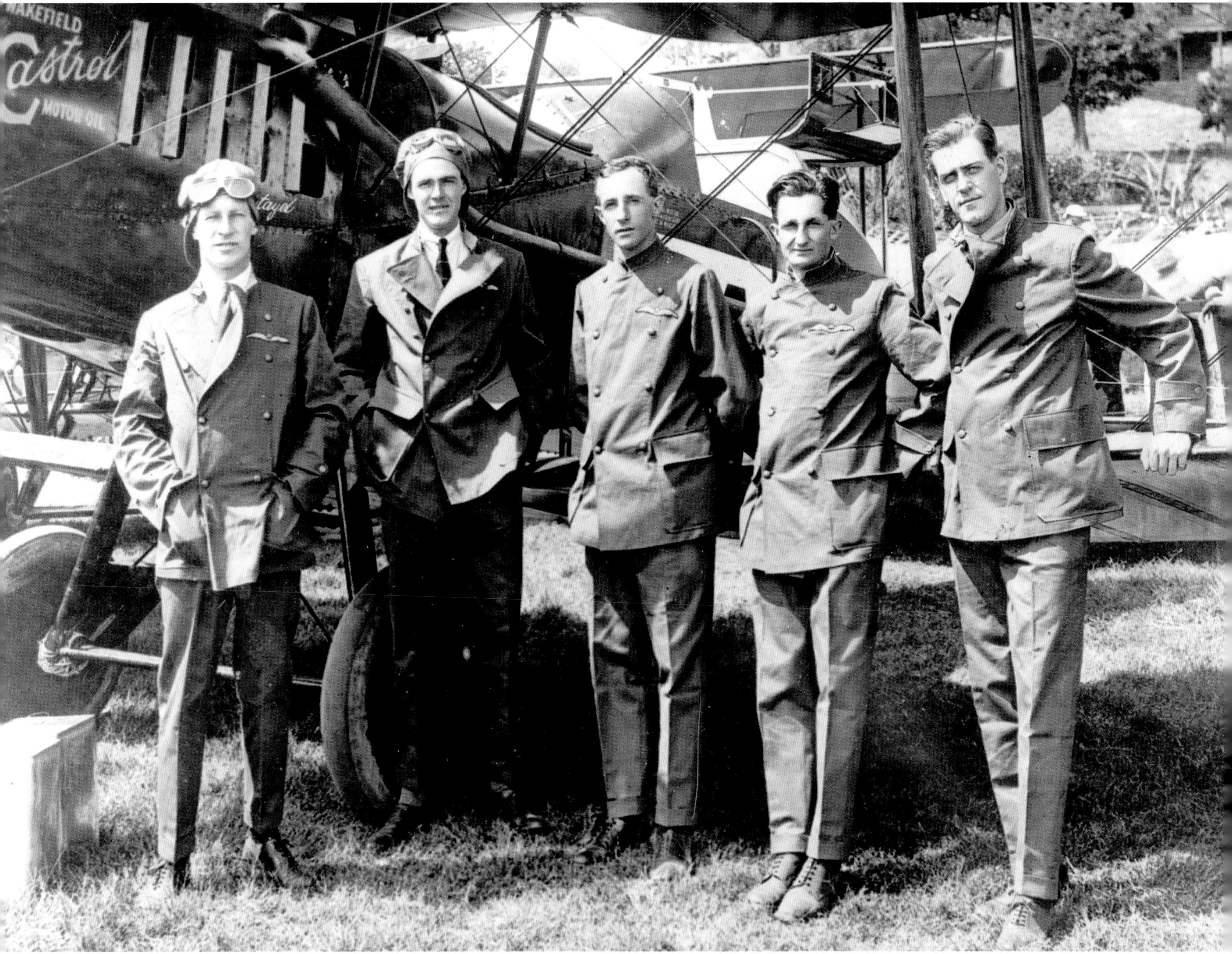
WAKEFIELD
Castrol

INDEX

OTHER AVAILABLE TITLES

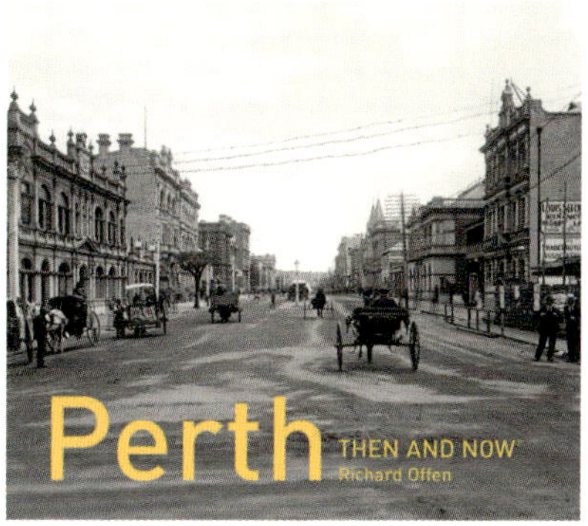

ISBN 9781911595601

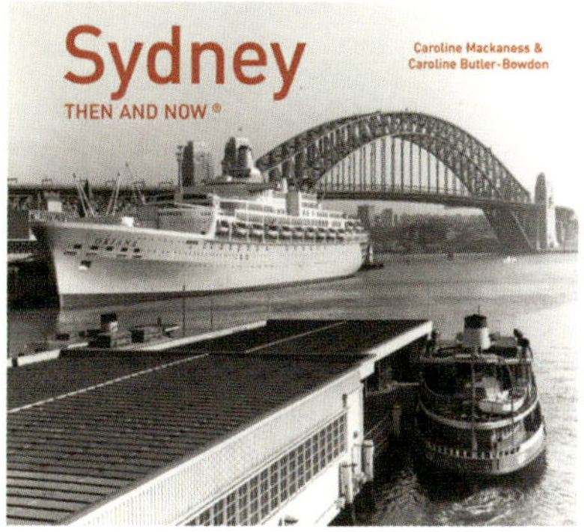

ISBN 9781909815322

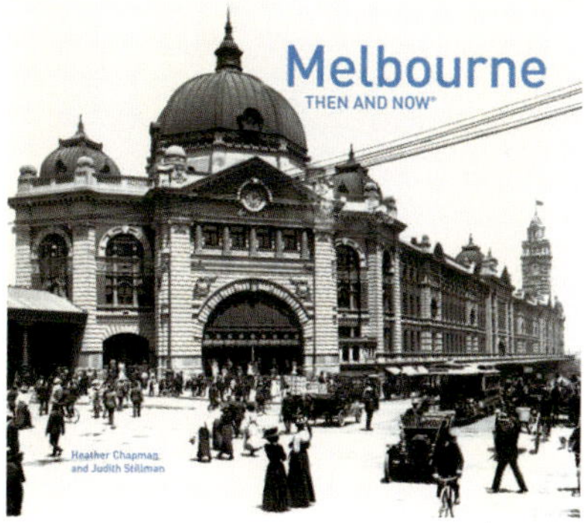

ISBN 9781909815315

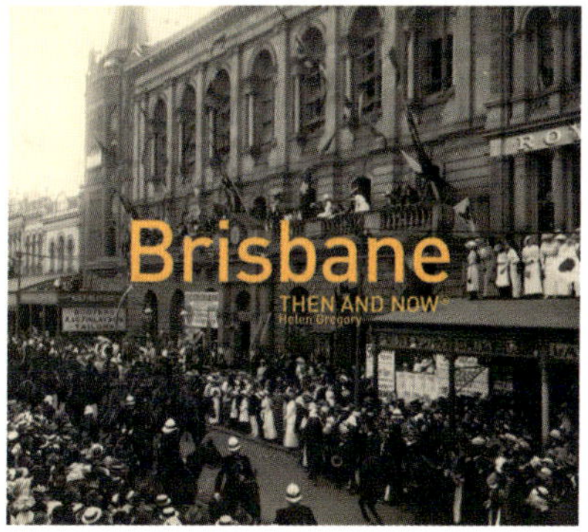

ISBN 9781910496732

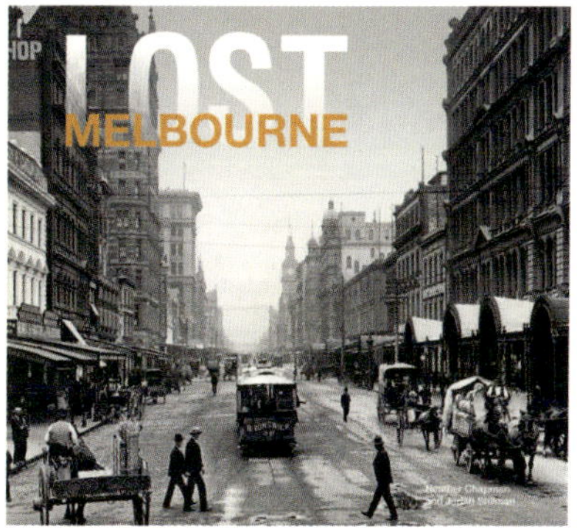

ISBN 9781910496749

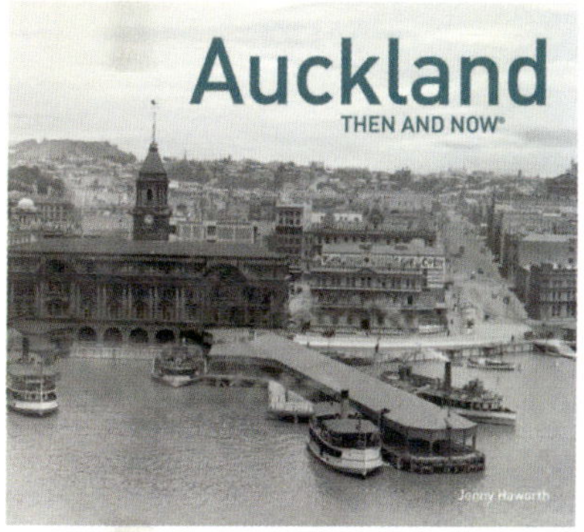

ISBN 9781910904794

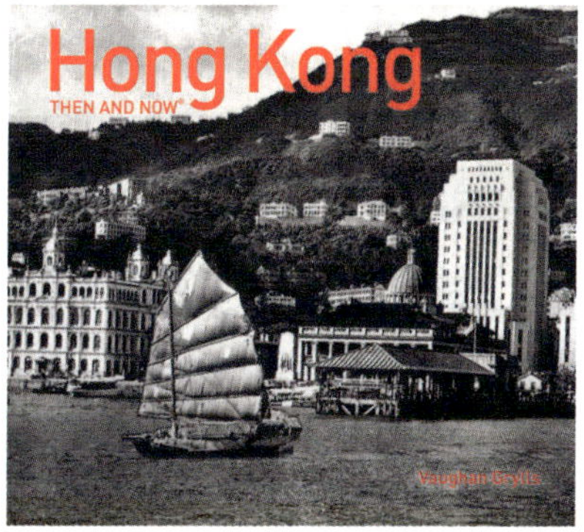

ISBN 9781910904084

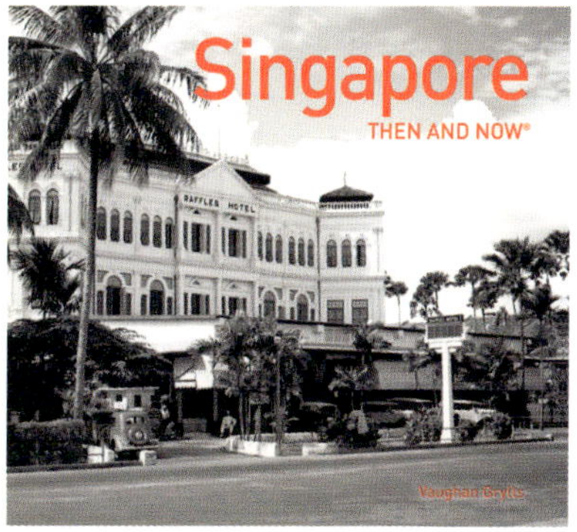

ISBN 9781910904091

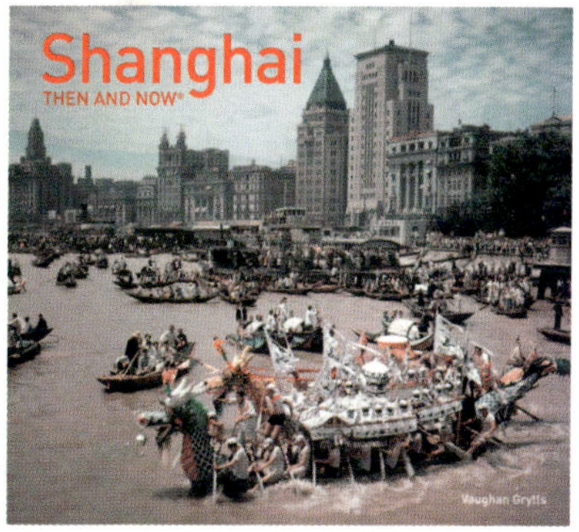

ISBN 9781911216926